AVOIDING THE HEADACHES OF ACCOUNTING FOR THE PUBLIC SECTOR

Written by: Stephen Allen, Matthew Guntrip and Jackie Ross

Published by:

Allen Accountancy
1 Pollard Hatch
Greygoose Park
Harlow
Essex
CM19 4LA

First published 1988 by the Accounting Tuition Centre

Second Edition   1989 published by Allen Accountancy

Third Edition   1993 published by Allen Accountancy

The text was printed by Da Costa Print and Finishing Company

ISBN 0 9515361 4 1

Contents

This book is a replacement for "Accounting for the Public Sector into the 1990's". The name has changes and two new authors have contributed to the text.

The two new authors are Matthew Guntrip and Jackie Ross. Both Matt and Jackie are CIPFA qualified accountants, who are both very keen to promote training, and are actively involved in training. Stephen Allen wishes to thank both Matt and Jackie for their contributions which have been provided wholeheartedly with great enthusiasm.

Matthew Guntrip has prepared the Central Government Section of the book, and his contribution has been invaluable, drawing on his experiences of working for the National Audit Office, and more recently the Public Records Office.

Jackie Ross works for the NHS Special London Childrens Hospital at Great Ormond Street, and has prepared the National Health Service Section. Jackie has provided an excellent section which demonstrates in a practical way the requirements of NHS accounting.

The Private Sector and Local Authority Sections of the book have been written by Stephen Allen. In these sections alone the changes that have taken place since 1988 are quite staggering, and as usual the changes are evolutionary and continue as the book goes to print.

The authors are confident that the book represents the highest quality work available, and provides students with the means to be able to learn and test themselves in probably the most difficult subject on the CIPFA professional year 1 course. The book will also be very useful for final year AAT students.

In writing the book we have consumed a great deal of time and effort, and the London Guildhall University (Stephen Allen's employers) have supported and encouraged the preparation of the book.

In particular, thanks are recorded to Jill Jarvis and Debbie Rees for their assistance. The cover is drawn by Sarah Allen. The cover is intended to show that Stephen Allen has had a few headaches writing the book which can be avoided by readers.

The book will retail at £21.50. The book is available direct from Allen Accountancy and if ordering please add £3.50 for postage and packaging.

Allen Accountancy
1 Pollard Hatch
Harlow
Essex CM19 4LA

Introduction to Avoiding the Headaches of

Accounting for the Public Sector

Introduction

This book is the third edition in a series of books aimed especially at the first year of the CIPFA professional examinations and the final year of the AAT qualification. In writing the introduction it is useful to think back to the previous two editions, and an interesting trend emerges which at present seems unstoppable. This trend is towards a much closer convergence of Private and Public Sector accounting.

The first edition was concerned solely with the Public Sector which at that point was distinctive in the extreme from private sector accounting. The second edition included three chapters of eighteen on commercial accounting while in this third edition private sector accounting takes up a greater proportion of the book but is still in the minority. But maybe more importantly the similarities between public and private sector accounting are obvious.

This makes one wonder what the fourth edition will look like. It is possible to see a similar convergence of accounting theory and practice taking place on an international basis, and at some point in the future I can imagine a core of accounting concepts which are applied in slightly different detailed standards world wide.

Structure of This Book

Private Sector

The book begins by considering the legal framework and basic concepts and principles of accounting for companies.

A major element of this is dedicated to the work of the Financial Reporting Council.

Having examined the standard setting and regulation process. The most recent work of the Financial Reporting Council will be considered.

Specific issues are then dealt with and these include discussion on the topic of current cost accounting, and the practicalities of dealing with finance leases. Cash flow statements are considered, and the pronouncements of the Financial Reporting Standard 3 are considered in detail.

It is intended that students should be able to build up a feeling for the aims and objectives of accounting methods, and grasp the theory behind the practical application of these methods.

The final element of the Private Sector section deals specifically with accounting for companies, and concentrates on the external financial reporting requirements.

Local Authority Accounting

The local authority section of this book is made up of six chapters.

The whole of these six chapters are influenced by the radical changes that have been agreed for capital accounting. Chapter 8 is the first of the local government chapters and sets out the requirements for external reporting. The statutory and non-statutory rules which are termed as proper accounting practice are considered, and the requirements for annual reports are included. The CIPFA statement on Financial Reporting is also discussed.

Chapter 9 considers the new requirements to provide capital charges in the form of an asset rent. This difficult subject is explained in detail and exercises are provided.

Chapter 10 sets out the accounting requirements for revenue. The standard classification is discussed, and different revenue accounts demonstrated including consortia accountings. The Repairs and Renewals fund is demonstrated and all exercises are based on the new system of capital accounting.

Chapter 11 considers the central theme of accounting for support services, CCT of white collar services and the accounting needs of trading services. This chapter provides the latest view on costs that should be charged to business units and other costs.

Chapter 12 looks at the problems associated with preparing the consolidated cash flow statement which will be required under the SORP on local government accounting to be published in September 1993. Once again, the problems of the new capital accounting regime are explained and examples provided.

Finally chapter 13 looks at the central issues of financing local government including the Revenue Support Grant, the Council Tax, National Non-Domestic Rates, and the accounting requirement of the Collection Fund.

Central Government Accounting

The Central Government Section provides a thorough background into the financing of Central Government, the composition of Government expenditure, the management of public expenditure. The subject of Public expenditure, the estimate process, the cash limit system and monitoring and reporting to parliament are all featured.

Reforms to Central Government are considered and changes in the structure of Central Government and the development of agencies are featured.

Central Government Accounts are prepared and extensive examples and examination questions provided. The accounts provided are as follows:

- Government Department/Appropriation Accounts
- Off Vote Agency Accounts
- On Vote Accounts

The principles are examined in exercises and fully worked examples while 7 examination questions are provided for self study.

National Health Service Section

There are three chapters provided on the Accounting for the National Health Service. The first chapter introduces the topic by looking at the changes the NHS has undergone since its establishment in 1948. The structure of the current NHS is outlined and the financing of the service considered.

Capital charges in the NHS are dealt with in detail and the contracting arrangements are set out. The accounting requirements are demonstrated by exercises and fully worked examples.

Finally examination questions are provided. The exercises provide accounting for directly managed units. National Health Service Trust Hospitals as well as looking at performance measurement in terms of unit costs and ratios. Trust fund and memorandum trading accounts are also shown.

Conclusion

This book provides a wealth of knowledge which is targetted at teaching the topics to the reader through fully worked examples. Examination questions are provided for self testing and an answer book will be available for lecturers and students.

All three authors hope that the book provides a practical asset for students. In fact the book will only be successful if students believe it to be top quality because CIPFA will be producing their own open learning material.

CHAPTER 1

The Legal Framework and Work of the Financial Reporting Council

Introduction

The purpose of this chapter is to provide information on the provision of accounting standards in the accounting process, considering the development of the standard setting process and influences on the standard requirements. The chapter covers the following main issues:

* The objectives of accounting standards and their development under the auspices of the Consultative Council of Accounting Bodies (CCAB)

* Identify problems associated with the CCAB standard setting process;

* Consider the terms of reference of the review undertaken by Dearing and the revised framework for producing standards:

* Provide information on the roles of the component parts of the Financial Reporting Council, which is the new standard setting body as follows:

    + Accounting Standards Board (ASB);

    + Urgent Issues Task Force (UITF);

    + Financial Reporting and Review Panel;

* Consider the challenge facing the Financial Reporting Council

* Provide information on the progress and work undertaken by the Financial Reporting Council

* Explain the influences on financial reporting of the International Accounting Standards Committee, the Stock Exchange and Statement of Recommended Practice (SORP's)

Outline of Regulations

Accounting students should be aware in general terms of the need to ensure that entities produce accounting statements that fairly reflect the financial position of the entity.

However, the requirements to comply with recognised accounting principles depend on the organisation that is producing the financial statements.

For the sole trader it is obviously in the interests of the trader to prepare accounting information which fairly reflects the activity of the period in question. However in practice accounting information is likely to be extracted from the traders books by an accountant for submission to the Inland Revenue. The accountant in performing this task will comply with rules established by the Inland Revenue. The sole trader may also wish to use the accounts to assist in raising loans, but will not be unduly worried about publication of the accounts, and in fact it is very unlikely that the trader will keep more than one personal copy. Regulations regarding sole traders are therefore limited to the requirements of the tax office.

Company Accounting

Regulations regarding company accounting is a completely different subject. Here Directors manage the day to day affairs of the organisation and report to shareholders on the performance of the company.

Strict requirements can be found in legislation, a series of Companies Acts culminating in the Companies Acts 1985 and 1989 provide a tight legal framework.

This strict legal framework includes specific powers to enforce accounting standards which are produced under the Auspices of the Financial Reporting Council.

Development of the Legal Framework

It is interesting to consider the evolution of the legal framework, and the following provides a very brief history.

Landmarks along the route of developing regulations include

Companies Act 1929

This Act introduced the requirement for public companies to file a profit and loss account, but gave very little advice on the preparation and content of the account.

Companies Act 1945

This Act introduced more detailed requirements for inclusion in the profit and loss account and balance sheets produced. In addition the requirement to produce group accounts were established for the first time.

Companies Act 1985

This Act places a requirements on companies to produce accounting statements for the profit and loss account and balance sheet in a standard format. These formats are reproduced in the company accounting section of this book. The 1985 Act consolidated all previous company legislation into a single Act.

Companies Act 1989

One of the major requirements included in this Act was an amendment to the Companies Act 1985, which grants power to enforce rectification of accounts if they do not comply with the accounting standard required by the Financial Reporting Council.

The Statutory requirements therefore have become much more intense and detailed. Furthermore the ability to force rectification of accounts to ensure that accounting requirements are complied with effectively gives much greater strength to the accounting standards. It is important that the historical process of developing accounting standards is acknowledged.

History of the Development of Accounting Standards

Prior to the recent developments of the Financial Reporting Council in 1989, accounting Standards were developed by consensus by the accounting professions through the Consultative Council of Accounting Bodies (CCAB).

Formation of the Consultative Council of Accounting Bodies

Work in developing detailed requirements for accounting has been carried out by the accounting profession, and in 1974 the Consultative Council of Accounting Bodies (CCAB) was formed in an attempt to ensure a consistent approach to accounting statements by all members of the accounting profession.

The CCAB is made up of representatives from all the major accounting institutions.

Preparation of Statements of Standard Accounting Practice (SSAPs)

These statements were approved by the CCAB and carried the consent therefore of all the accounting professions, however, these statements were the product of a great deal of work over a considerable length of time. This was to ensure users as well as practitioners and others were consulted on the proposals to standardise an approach to an aspect of accounting. The Accounting Standards Committee (ASC) carried out the work on behalf of the CCAB, but for a standard to be issued all members of the CCAB had to agree to the proposal.

Background Needs for SSAPs

Before the 1970s, a great deal of subjective application of accounting principles was possible because no clear guidelines existed. This did mean a lack of comparability between companies, including problems of comparing one year with another within the same company.

Objectives of SSAPs

The major objectives of SSAPs are as follows:

a)   to narrow the variety of different accounting practices and improve accountability and comparability;

b)   to ensure any changes of accounting bases would be disclosed if material, and therefore comparability would be improved;

c)   to provide a consultational framework for wide consensus on developing accounting standards;

d)   to ensure best practice is employed wherever possible;

e)   to standardise presentation of information and improve understanding.

To summarise the objectives the standards should provide generally accepted accounting rules and principles, which enable comparisons to be made by users of the accounting statements, and consideration of the organisations financial position.

Review of the SSAP Process

Need for Review Identified

The CCAB recognised that the process of setting standards need to be reviewed, the system had come up against much criticism, including from the chairman of the Accounting Standards Committee who recommended a massive increase in the financial support given to the process to permit the appointment of additional technical staff, in order that more basic research could be carried out by the Accounting Standards Committee.

Appointment of the Dearing Committee

Undoubtedly problems cannot always be solved by increasing the funding provided, and it is normally wise to consider the whole process to ensure solutions are produced which will result in long term lasting and robust answers to the problems.

In July 1987 the CCAB president announced that the review would be carried out by the committee under the chairmanship of Sir Ronald Dearing former chairman of the Post Office.

Composition of the Dearing Committee

Each of the CCAB bodies were represented on the committee, the chair of the Accounting Standards Committee, senior people from the City and Industry, while a representative of the Department of Trade and Industry (Companies Division) attended as an observer.

Terms of Reference - Dearing Committee

The committees terms of reference were:

1   To review the development of the standard setting process, including the role of the International Accounting Standards Committee.

2   To have regard to the purpose of accounting standards in the future in the light of changes in financial markets, the approach to financial statements and report preparers, and the attitude of the government and the public towards the regulation of the corporate sector.

3   To consider:

* the most appropriate form which accounting standards should take;

* the status of standard regarding company law;

* procedures for compliance and enforcement of standards;

* the need for consultation with regard to the production of standards;

* funding the cost of the standard setting process;

* to consider the composition and power of the body responsible for the standard setting process.

4   To report during 1988 to the CCAB, and make recommendations.

Problem Perceived with the (CCAB) Standard Setting Process

Compliance Problems

Many commentators believed that the difficulties of achieving compliance, (for example with regard to the arguments related to current cost accounting, which resulted in the withdrawal of the mandatory status of the standard) need to be resolved. This current cost accounting example proved that the system of enforcement by the true and fair view requirement was inadequate, and legislation enforcing standards should be aimed for. One of the factors the case of SSAP 16, current cost accounting was that compliance fell below acceptable level of large companies, and no longer assisted towards the True and Fair View Statement.

Lack of Precision

Standards are not always precise with regard to the detail in which the provisions of the statement should be applied, and this leads to a variety of ways in which the standard can be interpreted, and can significantly effect the published account of the organisation.

Delays in Producing Statements

Partly due to the lack of finance for the accounting standards Committee, the need to get a consensus of approval and the reliance on voluntary effort has led to delays in the preparation of standards, and a definite inability to respond to issues which require rapid action, or could be classified as emergency issues.

Too Much Reliance Is Placed On The Accounting Professions

Accountants obviously need to be very much involved in the preparation of standards, but if directors have no pressures to comply with the SSAPs, it is argued that the accounting profession is placed in an impossible position, and many have suggested that company directors are selective in the choice of their auditors, and search for flexible auditors.

Standards Often Involve Compromise

The method of setting standards and the need for consensus and consultation lead inevitably to compromise, and this unfortunately can result in standards not meeting clearly their objectives.

Establishing A New Framework for Accounting Standards

The result of the Dearing Committee review has been to establish a completely new framework for the preparation and regulation of accounting standards.

The new system operates through three major companies limited by guarantee as follows:

* Financial Reporting Council (FC)

* Accounting Standards Board (ASB) plus the Urgent Issues Task Force (UITF)

* Financial Reporting Review Panel (FRRP)

These changes were introduced when the then Secretary of State for Trade and Industry invited Sir Ron Dearing to chair the Financial Reporting Council and bring the new arrangement into being. At the same time the Government introduced related provisions into Company Law through the Companies Act 1989.

A significant company law change already mention was the power for the compulsory revision of accounts, where the courts are satisfied that the original accounts do not show a true and fair view, or do not comply with the Companies Act 1985, where revision is required revised accounts can be required to be sent to all those who received the original accounts, and it may also be required that the Directors who were party to the approval of the defective accounts should personally bear the costs.

The legislation also allows for voluntary revision of accounts, and therefore it would only be in extreme cases that court action would be required. Much of the legal provisions for rectification were inserted into the 1985 Companies Act Section 245 (a) - 245 (c) by sections of the Companies Act 1989.

The three major companies set up to regulate the accounting standards are not Government controlled, but rather part of the private sector process of self regulation. Financing of the new arrangements is largely obtained as follows:

Approximate percentage of funds provided to the Financial Reporting Council Companies

	%
Government Bodies	33 1/3rd
CCAB	33 1/3rd
London Stock Exchange }	
and Banking/Investment sector}	33 1/3rd
	100

The annual budget of the financial reporting council companies is around £2 million, and a legal costs fund stood at £2 million as well at the 31 March 1992.

The Annual Report and Financial Statements of the Financial Reporting Council are available free of charge from their Holborn Hall headquarters in London.

The Financial Reporting Council

The Financial Reporting Council Limited (FRC) is constituted as a company limited by guarantee. The company's constitution provides for a Council whose function is to determine the general policy of the company.

The Chairman and the three Deputy Chairmen of the Council (who also act in the same capacity as directors of the company) are appointed by the Secretary of State for Trade and Industry and the Governor of the Bank of England acting jointly.

Normally, under the company's constitution, the board of directors can be expected to include a representative from the Consultative Committee of Accountancy Bodies or accountancy generally, a representative from the London Stock Exchange Council or the City generally, and a representative from the governing body of the Confederation of British Industry or industry and commerce generally. The present chairman is Sir Ron Dearing CB.

The Chairman of the Accounting Standards Board and the Chairman of the Financial Reporting Review Panel are members of the Council ex officio, and the Government and the Bank of England each have the right to nominate one member. The remaining members and observers are appointed by the Chairman and Deputy Chairmen. The membership is designed to include wide and balanced representation at the most senior level of preparers, auditors and users of accounts and of others interested in them.

The remit of the Council is to provide support to the operational bodies, the Accounting Standards Board and the Financial Reporting Review Panel, and to encourage good financial reporting

generally. At its first meeting, in May 1990, the Council
codified this role as being

1   to promote good financial reporting, and in the context from
     time to time make public reports on reporting standards. In
     that role it would from time to time make representations to
     Government on the current working of legislation and on any
     desirable development of it;

2   to provide guidance to the Accounting Standards Board on
     work programmes and on broad policy issues;

3   to verify that the new arrangements are conducted with
     efficiency and economy and that they are adequately funded.

The Council's constitution provides for it to publish an annual
report reviewing the state of financial reporting and making
known the views of the Council on accounting standards practice.
The first such report was published in November 1991, and the
second in December 1992.

The Council, through its chairman was one of the three initiators
and sponsors of the Committee on the Financial Aspects of
Corporate Governance (the Cadbury Committee) and four members of
the Council are members of the Committee.

The Council normally meets twice a year.

The Accounting Standards Board

Like the FRC, the Accounting Standards Board Limited (ASB) is a
company limited by guarantee, and is formally a subsidiary of the
FRC which acts at its sole director. The company contains an
Accounting Standards Board whose role is to make, amend and
withdraw accounting standards. The Board took over this role
from the former Accounting Standards Committee on 1 August 1990.
By the Accounting Standards (Prescribed Body) Regulations - SI
1990/ 1667 - the Secretary of State for Trade and Industry
prescribed the Accounting Standards Board for the purposes of
section 256 (1) of the Companies Act 1985 with the effect that
statements of standard accounting practice issued by the Board
are "accounting standards" for the purposes of the accounting
requirements of that Act. Unlike the former Accounting Standards
Committee, the Accounting Standards Board is autonomous it needs
neither outside approval for its actions, nor approval from the
company's director. It is however the practice of the Board to
consult widely on all it proposals.
Membership of the Board is limited to a maximum of ten; at
present there are nine members, of whom two are full time and
seven part time.

Appointments to the Board are made by an Appointments Committee
which comprises the FRC Chairman and Deputy Chairmen together
with three members of the Council.

A majority of six out of the present nine Board members (seven if
there were ten Board members) is required under its constitution
for any decision to adopt, revise or withdraw an accounting
standard.

At its first meeting the Board agreed to adopt the 22 extant Statements of Standard Accounting Practice (SSAPs) issued by the former Accounting Standards Committee or its predecessor. Adoption by the Board gives the SSAP's the status of "Accounting Standards" within the terms of part VII of the Companies Act 1985. The Board will review these SSAPs individually as appropriate opportunities arise during the course of its work.

The Board has indicated that its general aim in the making of accounting standards is to centre them as far as possible on principles rather than by the prescription of highly detailed rules. One of the Board's current tasks therefore, on which work is well advanced, is the development of a Statement of Principles as a framework within which consistent accounting standards can be formulated.

As indicated above, the Board's policy is to consult widely on all its proposals which are issued in a variety of forms. For some the proposal is first issued informally in Discussion Draft or Discussion Paper form. For all new proposals there is a formal Exposure Draft stage, the comments received on which are normally placed on the public record.

Urgent Issues Task Force

An Urgent Issues Task Force (UITF) has been established as a sub committee of the Accounting Standards Board. Its main role is to assist the Board in areas where an accounting standard or Companies Act provision exists, but where unsatisfactory or conflicting interpretations have developed or seem likely to develop. In addition the Board may from time to time seek the UITF's view on significant developments in accounting and financial reporting in areas where no legal provision or accounting standard at present exists. The UTIF operates in a broadly similar way to its USA and Canadian counterparts by seeking to reach a consensus on the issue under consideration. There are 15 voting members, of whom 11 constitute a quorum. The requirement for the achievement of a consensus is that not more than two of the voting members present at the meeting dissent. Unless the consensus thus established conflicts with the law, accounting standards, or the Board's policy or plans, the Board would expect it to be regarded as accepted practice in the area in question, and intention is that it should be considered to be part of the corpus of practices forming the basis for what determines a true and fair view. Thus the expectation is that companies will conform to it, if necessary by changing previously adopted accounting policies.

The urgent nature of the matters tackled by the UITF necessarily means that it is not possible for it to follow an extended consultation and use process procedure. The Board has therefore taken special measures to publicise the matters on the UITFs agenda, and UITF Information Sheets are now circulated to some 3,000 people, including the finance directors of all listed companies.

Accounting Standards and the Public Sector

The prescription of accounting requirements for the public sector in the United Kingdom is a matter for the Government. Where public sector bodies prepare annual reports and accounts on commercial lines, the Government's requirements may or may not refer specifically either to accounting standards or to the need for the financial statements concerned to give a true and fair view. However, it can be expected that the Government's requirements in such cases will normally accord with the principles underlying the Boards pronouncements accept where in the particular circumstances of the public sector bodies concerned the Government considers others to be more appropriate.

The Accounting Standards Board has established a Public Sector Liaison Committee. It is chaired by Graham Stacy, an ASB Board Member.

The Financial Reporting Review Panel

The Financial Reporting Review Panel Limited (FRRP) is constituted as company limited by guarantee and is formally a subsidiary of the FRC which acts as its sole director. The company contains a Review Panel which is autonomous in carrying out its functions; it needs neither outside approval for its actions nor approval from the company's director.

The role of the Panel is to examine departures from the accounting requirements of the Companies Act 1985 and if necessary to seek an order from the court to remedy them. Its authority stems from The Companies (Defective Accounts) (Authorised Person) Order 1991 - SI 1991/13 - made by the Secretary of State for Trade and Industry which, from 1 February 1991, authorised the Panel for the purposes of section 245B of the Companies Act 1985 (which was inserted into that Act by the Companies Act 1989). By agreement with the Department of Trade and Industry the normal ambit of the Panel is public and large private companies, the Department dealing with all other cases. The companies within the Panel's ambit are thus.

*   public limited companies (PLCs) (except PLCs that are subsidiaries in a small or medium - sized group);

*   companies within a group headed by a PLC;

*   any company not qualifying as small or medium sized as defined by section 247 of the Companies Act 1985.

*   any company within a group that does not qualify as small or medium - sized as defined by section 249 of the Act.

For these categories the Panel is concerned with accounts for financial years beginning on or after 23 December 1989.

As part of the financial arrangements for the new bodies the panel has available to it a legal costs fund of £2m maintained on a rolling basis to cover the cost of litigation.

The Panel's main concern is with an examination of material departures from accounting standards with a view to considering whether the accounts in question nevertheless meet the statutory requirement to give a true and fair view while such a departure does not necessarily mean that a company's accounts fail the true and fair test it will raise that question; and a Companies Act 1989 amendment to the Companies Act 1985 requires large companies to disclose in their accounts any such departures together with the reasons for them, thus enabling them to be readily identified and considered.

The Panel does not scrutinise on a routine basis all company accounts falling within its ambit. Instead it acts on matters drawn to its attention, either directly or indirectly.

In considering an individual case the Panel normally operates by means of a Group of five or more members drawn from the overall Panel membership constituted to deal with it. That Group is responsible for carrying out the functions of the Panel for that case; there is no collective involvement by the other Panel members.

Groups normally aim to discharge their tasks by seeking voluntary agreement with the directors of a company on any necessary revisions to the accounts in question. (The Companies Act 1989 made possible the voluntary revision of accounts as well as their revision by court order). But if that approach fails and the Panel believes that revisions to the accounts are necessary it will seek a declaration from the court that the annual accounts of the company concerned do not comply with the requirements of the Companies Act 1985, and for an order requiring the directors of the company to prepare revised accounts. If the court grants such an order it may also require the directors to meet the costs of the proceedings and of revising the accounts.

Where accounts are revised at the instance of the Panel, either voluntarily or by order of the court, but the company's auditor had not qualified his audit report on the defective accounts the Panel will draw this fact to the attention of the auditor's professional body.

Appointments to the Panel are made by an Appointments Committee which comprises the FRC Chairman and Deputy Chairmen together with three members of the Council. There is no upper limit to membership.

The Challenge Faced by the Financial Reporting Council

The new framework for providing and enforcing 'accounting standards' is undoubtedly a clear positive step in the right direction. The financial reporting council and its companies represent a funded and establish process, which should be able to produce clear standards, respond reasonably rapidly to urgent issues and enforce compliance.

However, the task of regulation should not be underestimated, and the inadequacies in the present standards not overlooked.

Consider Some Events in the Recent Past

Coloroll is an example of how a Company can rise and fall with such rapidity that one can only be staggered by the facts. The company entered the financial market in mid 1985 with sales of less than £40 million, however growth was dramatic with sales exceeding £550 million at their peak. The companies share price virtually trebled in two years rising to just under 390p, but dealing was suspended in the shares when the share price fell to

under 10p and the receivers appointed in 1990. Many investors
were misguided by the accounts of the company over this period.

Polly Peck will be remembered by many for the high profile
chairman Asil Nadir. But it should also be remembered for its
amazing fall from favour within the month of September 1990 the
company released half year results which were nearly double the
first half year of 1989, with shareholders funds at just below £1
billion. In the third week of September 1990 shares were
suspended, and one month later the receivers appointed.

Maxwell rated by many as the Mother of all collapses doesn't
even have to have the facts relaid for the average person to
identify a major empire collapsing in a very short time, with
associated worries about the stewardship and financial accounting
employed.

Each of these examples demonstrates that companies can rise and
fall from great heights. But they also leave the question of how
could it happen? what were investors told? Why were the problems
not recognised in the accounting statements? The problems of each
company would need to be discussed in detail, but their is
undoubtedly some explanation required of why the financial
reporting requirements were able to mask the underlying weakness
of such companies.

Creative Accounting and The Blob Index

It is not unusual for large companies to embark upon accounting
policies and practices which have been permitable under the
Standard Statement of Accounting Practice (SSAP), but have
resulted in misleading financial statements. Many of the
creative devices used concentrated on grey areas in SSAP's.
Others not being addressed by SSAP's but not considered to be
illegal.

Terry Smith is the author of a book which highlights the use of
such creative techniques. The book is "Accounting for Growth".
Stripping the camouflage from company accounts. This book
includes an analysis of the top 200 quoted UK Companies, and
provides a blob index.

The analysis is simple and unscientific. The index lists twelve
different creative accounting devices, and simply provides a blob
if the device is used by the company. Some companies employed
eight of the devices. Terry Smith claims that the share
performance of companies using many devices correlates to poor
share price performance and in some cases shares being suspended.

However, the most important statistic in my view regarding the
financial accounting regulation of these companies is that only 15
of the 200 companies apply none of the creative accounting
devices and therefore score nil on the blob index.

The challenge for the financial reporting council (FRC) and it
companies is to tighten the financial framework of standards, and
to this end the FRC is pursuing the issue of new statements, and
the rectification of accounts where necessary for non compliance.
It should be remembered that the creative accountancy techniques
employed by the top companies do not necessarily break the true

and fair view convention, and the redefining of standards is
necessary to improve financial reporting.

Work of the Financial Reporting Council

The Financial Reporting Council publish annual reviews of their
work. These reviews are entitled "The State of Financial
Reporting". The most recent review available at the time of
writing this book was November 1992.

The Financial reporting council has devoted a good deal of
resources towards the production of the "Statements of
Principles". This work is being undertaken by the Accounting
Standards Board (ASB). These statement of principles are
chapters which are aimed at providing the underlying concepts
which the ASB wish to pursue, and to that end will provide a
reference point for the consistent development of standards. The
statements of principles will not in themselves become accounting
standards.

Statements of Principles

The statements of principle will eventually cover the following:
*   The objectives of financial statements
*   The qualitative characteristics of financial information
*   Presentation of financial information
*   Elements of financial statements
*   The recognition of items in financial statements
*   The valuation of assets and liabilities
*   Boundaries of the reporting entity

At the time of writing three chapters had reached the Exposure
Draft stage, two chapters were at the discussion draft stage, and
the remaining two had not been released.

Amending and Creating Accounting Standards

It was previously establish in this text, that the 22 accounting
standards in existence when the ASB took over the role of the old
Accounting Standards Committee were adopted by the ASB. These
were as follows:

ASB Adopted Standards

SSAP Number	Title	Amendments
1	Accounting for Associate Companies	
2	Disclosure of accounting policies	
3	Earnings per share	in FRS 3
4	Accounting for government grants	
5	Accounting for valued added tax	
6	Extraordinary items and prior year adjustments	removed by FRS3
8	The treatment of taxation under the imputation system	
9	Stocks and long term contracts	
10	Statements of source and application of funds	replaced by FRS1
12	Accounting for depreciation	
13	Accounting for research and development	

14	Group accounts	replaced by FRS2
15	Accounting for deferred tax	amended by FRC
17	Accounting for post balance sheet events	
18	Accounting for contingencies	
19	Accounting for investment properties	
20	Foreign Currency transactions	
21	Accounting for leases and hire purchase contracts	
22	Accounting for goodwill	
23	Accounting for acquisitions and mergers	
24	Accounting for pension costs	
25	Segmental reporting	

Financial Reporting Council Exposure Drafts (FREDs)

Financial Reporting Standards (FRS's) can be issued without having been the subject of an Exposure Draft. However it is common for an exposure draft to be issued first. The following FRED's have been issued.

No	Title	Date of Issue
FRED 1	The Structure of Financial Statements reporting of financial performance	December 1991
	Superseded by FRS3	
FRED 2	Amendment to SSAP 15 - Accounting for deferred tax	November 1992
	(Superseded by amendment to deferred tax SSAP) SSAP 15 reissued.	
FRED 3	Accounting for Capital Instruments	December 1992

NB   The full text of FRED's can be obtained from Accountancy
       Books telephone 0908 668833 extension 3227

These FREDs address major issues and the first two have already been acted upon. FRED 1 becoming FRS3 and representing a fundamental change to the presentation of information on the face of the profit and loss account.

FRED 3 is also likely to result in fundmantal changes and addresses some of the creative accounting problems raised by Terry Smith

Accounting Standards Board Plans to Publish discussion or exposure drafts for new standards

In the 1992 annual review the following topics were listed.

* Off Balance Sheet Finance

* Capital Instruments

* Mergers and Acquisitions

* Acquisition Accounting

* Goodwill

* Related Party Transactions

* Valuation of Assets

Financial Reporting Standards

New financial reporting standards are issued where a fundamental change to an old standard, or a completely new standard is proposed. However, if an old SSAP is only amended as with SSAP 15 it can be re-issued.

No	Title	Date
FRS1	Cash Flow Statements	September 1991
FRS2	Accounting for Subsidiary Undertakings	July 1992
FRS3	Reporting Financial Performance	October 1992
Amendment to SSAP 15	Accounting for deferred tax	December 1992

NB   The full text of FRS's can be obtained from Accountancy Books.

FRS 1 Cash Flow Statements

This statement replaced SSAP 10, and provides a much clearer presentation of cash movements for a financial year although it is important to see the notes supporting the statements. This topic is extensively covered in a subsequent chapter.

FRS 2 Accounting for Subsidiary Undertakings

This addresses important issues of accounting but is not dealt with in this text because it is beyond the scope of the book. This standard replaces SSAP 14.

FRS 3 Reporting Financial Performance

This standard is very important and is covered extensively in the company accounting chapter. It has a primary function of requiring the P & L account to provide information about ongoing activities separated from discontinuing activities.

The FRS 3 statement also makes significant and important changes to the earnings per share requirement, and removes the provisions of SSAP 6 extraordinary items and prior year adjustments.

Urgent Issues Task Force (UITF)

The urgent issues task force is often involved in the preliminary work which eventually finds its place in a new standard. But it is also important to note that the UITF can provide instructions which are binding on financial statement, carrying the full weight of the FRC, for an interim period while a FRS is being prepared. An example of this was when the UITF Abstract 2 was issued as follows:

Title   Restructuring Costs

Date   31 October 1991

The Issue

1   The Task Force acknowledge that uncertainty exists
        regarding the interpretation of the definitions of
        extraordinary and exceptional items in SSAP 6. In
        particular, the treatment of restructuring and
        reorganisation (hereafter referred to as restructuring)
        costs in the profit and loss account has been a source of
        varying and selective interpretations. Until such time as
        SSAP 6 is replaced by another accounting standard, for the
        avoidance of doubts and to prevent a perceived drift towards
        the inclusion of more and more items as extraordinary, the
        Task Force issues the following consensus with regard to
        restructuring costs.

UITF Consensus

2   The Task Force concluded that where the cost of restructing
        or reorganising business activities needs to be disclosed
        by virtue of its size of incidence, it should be dealt with
        as an exceptional item, not an extraordinary item, unless it
        stems directly from a separate extraordinary event or
        transaction.

3   SSAP 6 defines extraordinary items as 'material items which
        derive from events or transactions that fall outside the
        ordinary activities of the company and which are therefore
        expected not to recur frequently or regularly'. Restructing
        costs, even if they relate to a fundamental restructuring of
        a business, are usually part of the ordinary activities of a
        company and should normally be treated as charges in
        arriving at the profit or loss on ordinary activities,
        disclosed, if material, as exceptional items. Where a
        company presents restructuring costs as extraordinary items,
        the onus of proof rests with the company to demonstrate that
        such treatment is appropriate; in these circumstances the
        financial statements should include a full description both
        of the nature of the separate event or transaction that it
        considers to be extraordinary and of the nature of the
        related restructuring costs.

4   In order to ensure consistency of treatment, comparative
        figures for preceding years should be restated where
        applicable.

Date from which effective

5   The accounting treatment required by this consensus should
        be adopted in financial statements relating to accounting
        periods ending on or after 23rd November 1991.

FRS 3 issued in October 1992 deals with the subject of extraordinary items in details and confirms the approach specifically required by the UITF which had by that time been in operation for a year.

The work of the urgent issues Task Force is therefore very worth considering as it is likely to be the preliminary work towards establishing a position on accounting issues which may find there way into future FRS's. The following is a list of the work of the urgent issues Task Force.

No	Title	Date
UITF Abstract 1	Backdated Supplemental interest on Convertible Bonds	July 1991
UITF Abstract 2	Disclosure of Restructuring Costs	October 1991
UITF Abstract 3	Treatment of goodwill on disposal of a Business	December 1991
UITF Abstract 4	Presentation of long term debtors in current accounts	July 1992
UITF Abstract 5	Transfer from Current Assets to fixed assets	July 1992
UITF Abstract 6	Accounting for Post Retirement benefits other than pensions	November 1992
UITF Abstract 7	Disclosure of the use of the true and fair view override in company accounts.	17 December 1992

The Financial Reporting Review Panel (FRRP)

During 1992 the FRRP issued press notices on their findings in respect of company accounts investigated.

The FRRP remit is as follows:

> The remit of the Financial Reporting Review Panel is to examine the annual accounts of public and large private companies to see whether they comply with the requirements of the Companies Act 1985. Within this framework a main focus is on material departures from accounting standards where such a departure results in the accounts in question not giving a true and fair view as required by the Act.

> The Panel's responsibilities do not extend to summary financial statements or the directors' report, which are dealt with by DTI. Nor does the Panel cover Interim Statements.

> Where a company's accounts are defective the Panel will wherever possible endeavour to secure their revision by voluntary means, but if this approach fails will make an application to the course under section 245B of the Companies Act 1985 for an order compelling the revision. To

date no court applications have been made.

The Panel does not itself monitor or actively initiate scrutinies of company accounts for possible defects, but acts on matters drawn to its attention, either directly or indirectly.

Although only ten press releases were issued a total of 78 cases had been referred by late November 1992. These referrals were from the following sources.

Qualified Audit Reports	25
Individuals or Corporate Bodies	30
Press Comments	23
	78

Of these cases 28 were not pursued beyond an initial investigation in 31 cases action was concluded of which ten required press notices, and the remaining 19 were still under consideration.

The following is an example of a press release:

PRESS NOTICE

FINDINGS OF THE FINANCIAL REPORTING REVIEW PANEL IN RESPECT OF THE ACCOUNTS OF

S.E.P INDUSTRIAL PLC FOR THE YEAR ENDED 30 SEPTEMBER 1991

The Financial Reporting Review Panel has considered the Report and Accounts of S.E.P Industrial Holdings plc for the year ended 30 September 1991.

The Review Panel raised two matters with the directors of the company: (i) the treatment as a prior year item of an amount in respect of stock provisions and (ii) the non depreciation of freehold properties contrary to Statement of Standards Accounting Practice (SSAP) 12. The report of the auditors was qualified in respect of the second matter.

The Review Panel is satisfied with the explanation provided by the directors in respect of the prior year item. As regards the non depreciation of freehold properties the directors have accepted that their departure from the requirements of SSAP 12 was not justified, and they have given the Panel an assurance that in future accounts the company's freehold properties will be depreciated in accordance with SSAP 12. In the light of this assurance the Panel has concluded that no further action should be taken on the Accounts of the company for the year ended 30 September 1991.

Progress made by the Financial Reporting Council

Undoubtedly the Financial Reporting Council and its associated companies have a great challenge in front of them. However the foundations of being able to meet that challenge are being laid slowly, but relentlessly.

The focus of the Accounting Standards Board work is being aimed at many aspects of accounting which require tighter control, and many of these areas are those identified by Terry Smith and his blob index.

It is of course extremely difficult to regulate companies financial reporting and accounting, but the task is now being met head on.

It is also worth considering the enhancement rectification of accounts provides to the external auditor. A qualification should result in the FRRP considering the matter and many result in action against the Directors. Also the auditors need to be aware that if the FRRP decide to investigate a company which has not carried a qualification, the investigation could lead to the auditor being reported to the professional body concerned.

Other Influences on the Accounting Statement

In addition to the work of the FRC. It is important to note the influence of International Accounting Standards and of Statements of Recommended Practice developed by industry groups under the auspices of the FRC. These contributing factors are now considered in turn.

International Accounting Standards

A study of the Financial Reporting Council's work and the previous Accounting Standards Board, reveals the immense amount of work involved in producing, reviewing and replacing standards.

Many Nations undertakes a similar amount of work. For example The America equivalent is known as the Financial Accounting Standards Board (FASB) and interestingly enough America also has a Public Sector Standards body known as Government Accounting Standards Board (GASB).

In 1973 the International Accounting Standards Committee (IASC) was set up to work for the improvement and harmonisation of financial reporting. The IASC has prepared International Accounting Standards through an International due process that involves

* The World Wide Accountancy Profession
* The Preparers and users of Financial Statements
* National Standard Setting bodies

The IASC stated objectives are to:

a) Formulate and publish in the public interest accounting standards to be observed in the presentation of financial statements and to promote their World Wide acceptance and observance,

b)   Work generally for the improvement and harmonisation of
        regulations, accounting standards and procedures relating to
        the presentation of financial statements,

The Use and Application of International Accounting Standards

International Accounting Standards have done a great deal to both
improve and harmonise financial reporting around the world.

The standards are used:

a)   as national requirements, often after a national due process;

b)   as the basis for all or some national requirements;

c)   as an international benchmark for those countries which
        develop their own standards;

d)   by regulatory authorities for domestic and foreign companies;

e)   by companies themselves;

Growing Importance of International Standards

The globalisation of business, investment and capital markets
together with advances in technology have created pressures for
common, high quality standards for financial reporting. The
pressures for changes have come from users and prepares of
financial statements as well as securities regulators and stock
exchanges.

National standard setting bodies are also increasingly
recognising the need for common high quality standards.

The International Accounting Standards Committee has developed
and issued 31 international standards. The UK among other major
countries conform to the substantial majority of international
standards. While Norway and Sweden and many countries in
Eastern and Central Europe are using international standards as
the basis for new national requirements.

Much of the IASC standards conform to the Europeans directives as
a result, the majority of businesses in the Europeans community
are able to present financial statements that conform with both
Europeans directives and international accounting standards.

The following is a list of International Accounting Standards

IAS 1   Disclosure of Accounting Policies
IAS 2   Valuation and Presentation of Inventories
           in the context of the Historical Cost System
IAS 3   Consolidated Financial Statements
IAS 4   Depreciation Accounting
IAS 5   Information to be Disclosed in Financial Statements
IAS 7   Statement of changes in Financial position

IAS 8	Unusual and prior period items and changes in Accounting Policies
IAS 9	Accounting for Research and Development Activities
IAS 10	Contingencies and Events Occurring After the Balance Sheet Date
IAS 11	Accounting for Construction Contracts
IAS 12	Accounting for Taxes on Income
IAS 13	Presentation of Current Assets and Current Liabilities
IAS 14	Reporting Financial Information by Segment
IAS 15	Information Reflecting the Effects of Changing Prices
IAS 16	Accounting for Property Plant and Equipment
IAS 17	Accounting for Leases
IAS 18	Revenue Recognition
IAS 19	Accounting for Retirement Benefits in the Financial Statements of Employers
IAS 20	Accounting for Government Grants and Disclosure of Government Assistance
IAS 21	Accounting for the Effects of Charges in Foreign Exchange Rates
IAS 22	Accounting for Business Combinations
IAS 23	Capitalisation of Borrowing Costs
IAS 24	Related Party Disclosure
IAS 25	Accounting for Investments
IAS 26	Accounting and Reporting by Retirement Benefit Plans
IAS 27	Consolidated Financial Statements and Accounting for Investments in Subsidiaries
IAS 28	Accounting for Investments in Associated
IAS 29	Financial Reporting in Hyper Inflationary Economics
IAS 30	Disclosure in the Financial Statements of Banks and similar Financial Institution
IAS 31	Reporting of interests in Joint Ventures

Revised International Accounting Standards (effective 1994)

IAS 7	Cash Flow Statements

Proposed New Standard

E40	Financial Instruments

Proposed Revised International Accounting Standards

E37	Research and Development Activities
E38	Inventories
E39	Capitalisation of Borrowing Costs
E41	Revenue Recognition
E42	Construction Contracts
E43	Property Plant and Equipment
E44	The Effects of Changes in Foreign Exchange Rates
E45	Business Combinations
E46	Extraordinary items, fundamental errors and changes in Accounting Policies
E47	Retirement Benefits Costs

Financial Reporting Council Working Towards Harmonisation

The Accounting Standards Board's formal input into international harmonisation process takes place at present at three levels;

> * assisting in the briefing sessions for the UK board representatives on the board of the IASC.

> * attending the twice yearly meetings of the EC Accounting Advisory Forum, as well as forum working groups;

> * participating in the meetings of national standard setting bodies which may well develop into an annual event.

In each FRED and FRS issued compliance with International Accounting Standards is considered and an explanation provided. For example the following is extracted from FRS 3.

> "The requirements of the FRS are consistent with International Standard 5 'information to be disclosed in financial statements', and International Accounting Standard 8. ' Unusual and prior period items and changes in Accounting Policies. The FRS is also consistent with the exposure draft of proposed revised International Accounting Standards - 'Extraordinary items, fundamental errors and changes in Accounting Policies' issued by the IASC in July 1992".

The Accounting Standards Board Targets for International Harmonisation

i)   To be aware of the main lines of divergence in accounting standards and their causes.

       The divergence often stem from legal, fiscal, and regulatory constraints, and the fundamental difference of approach on whether statements should give a true and fair view or merely be in accordance with accounting standards.

ii)   In researching projects to follow as far as possible the relevant international accounting standard, and to consider the work of other standard setters, including their reasons for adopting or rejecting certain solutions.

       A recent example where the International Accounting Standard was followed despite the need for a significant change of practice in the UK was the requirement of FRS 3 to calculate the gain or loss on sale of a revalued asset against the carrying amount rather than Historic Cost.

iii)   To be prepared to offer its own experience and insights as input to international debates.

iv)   To work with others to improve the structures for international harmonisation.

Conclusion

It can be seen that the work of the International Standards Committee, as a direct effect on countries that use the (IASC) standards for national standards, but also has a significant impact on other national standard setting bodies. The UK's own ASB is very keen, as has demonstrated by the four principle targets of harmonisation listed in this section of this book, on harmonising its pronouncements with those of the IASC.

Stock Exchange Requirements

Companies which require their shares to be traded on the Stock Exchange are subject to the Stock Exchange rules contained in the yellow book. These rules have no standing in law but companies who do not comply will not be listed on the Exchange. These rules are over and above the company accounting rules embodied in the companies act.

When companies issue their prospectus as part of raising new capital it is normal for profit forecasts to be made. These profit forecasts are not specified under the companies acts but the yellow book section 3 states:

> 'Where a profit forecast appears in any listing particulars, the principal assumptions, including commercial assumptions, upon which the directors have based their profit forecast, must be stated. The accounting policies and calculations for the forecast must be examined and reported on by the reporting accountants and their report must be sent out. The issuing house, or in the absence of an issuing house, the sponsoring member firm must report in addition whether or not they have satisfied themselves that the forecast has been stated by the directors after due and careful enquiry, and such report must be sent out.'

A profit forecast is also required in circulars issued to shareholders in connection with a takeover bid or merger proposal. The duties of reporting accountants to satisfy themselves as to the 'honesty' and 'accuracy' of such profit forecasts are governed by the City code on mergers and takeovers.

Published Accounts

The Yellow Book (section 5) makes the following requirements with respect to the published accounts of listed companies:
a)   Companies must issue their annual report and accounts within six months of the end of the accounting period to which they relate.

b)   Companies must prepare a half yearly or interim report which must be either:

  i)   sent to holders of securities in the company (ie shareholders and loan stock holders); or

  ii)   inserted as a paid advertisement in two leading daily newspapers not later than four months after the end of the period to which it relates.

c)   The figures in the interim report, in table form, must state
     at least the following:

     i)   net turnover;

     ii)   profit or loss before taxation and extraordinary
              items;

     iii)   taxation on profits (United Kingdom taxation and,
              if material, overseas and share of associated
              companies to be shown separately);

     iv)   minority interests;

     v)   profit or loss attributable to shareholders,
              before extraordinary items;

     vi)   extraordinary items (net of taxation);

     vii)   profit or loss attributable to shareholders;

     viii)   rates of dividend(s) paid and proposed and amount
              absorbed thereby;

     ix)   earnings per share expressed as pence per share
              (computed on the figures shown for profits after
              taxation as defined in FRS 3); and

     x)   comparative figures in respect of (i) to (ix)
              inclusive for the corresponding previous period.

The explanatory statement in the half yearly report must include
any significant information enabling investors to make an
informed assessment of the trend of the group's activities and
profit or loss together with an indication of any special factor
which has influenced those activities and the profit or loss
during the period in question, and enable a comparison to be made
with the corresponding period of the preceding financial year.

d)   The annual report and accounts should contain or be
     accompanied by the following information:

     i)   a statement by the directors explaining the reasons
              for any significant deviation from SSAPs in the
              published accounts;

     ii)   an explanation of the variances between the
              trading results in the published accounts and the
              expected results in any profit forecast published
              by the company;

     iii)   a 'segment' analysis of overseas results according
              to geographical area. This geographical analysis
              should report turnover and contribution to profit
              from operations carried on outside the UK;

     iv)   the principal country in which each subsidiary
              operates;

v)   the following information about each company in
      which the group holds 20% or more of the equity.

      1) the principal country of operation;
      2) the issued share capital and loan capital of
          the company;
      3) the percentage of each class of loan capital
          in which the reporting company has a direct or
          indirect interest;

vi)   a statement of outstanding bank loans, overdrafts
      and other borrowings at the end of the financial
      year, showing the amounts repayable:

      1) in one year or less, or on demand;
      2) between one and two years;
      3) between two and five years;
      4) in five years or more;

vii) a statement of the amount of interest capitalised
      by the company (or group) during the financial
      year;

viii) a statement showing the interests of each director
      in the share capital, as at the end of the
      financial year;

ix)   a statement showing the interest of any other
      person, other than a director in a substantial
      part of the share capital of the company, and the
      amount of interest (as at a date not more than one
      month prior to the date of the notice of the
      meeting);

x)   a statement showing whether or not (as far as the
      directors are aware) the company is a close
      company for taxation purposes;

xi)   information about any substantial contract during
      or at the end of the year, in which a director of
      the company had or has a material interest (or a
      statement that there has been no such contract);

xii) particulars of any arrangement whereby a director
      has waived any emoluments;

xiii) particulars of any arrangements whereby a
      shareholder has waived (or agreed to waive) any
      dividends;

xiv) information about any substantial contract between
      the company, or one of its subsidiaries by a
      corporate substantial shareholder;

xvi) particulars of any shareholders' authority for the
      purchase by the company of its own shares existing
      at the end of the year and the names of the
      sellers;

xvii)   details of any issue of securities where the equity
          element is not offered to the existing equity
          holders in proportion to their holdings;

xviii)   short biographical notes on each independent non-
          executive director;

xix)   where a company issues summary financial
          statements as permitted by the Companies Acts,
          earnings per share should be disclosed in addition
          to the required contents.

Statement of Recommended Practice (SORPS)

A SORP is significantly different from SSAP's and FRS's. This is
due to the fact that they do not carry any weight in determining
that the accounts show a true and fair view. Neither would the
FRRP be concerned if SORPs were not adhered to in the preparation
of financial statements.

The reason for this is that SORPs are intended to encourage best
practice but are on subjects which are not of universal interest
to all companies or not considered of vital importance in
determine a true and fair view.

The concept of a SORP was born in the early 1980's when the then
Standard Setting Body undertook a review of the whole process.
This review established that there were some aspects of
accounting which did not warrant a full SSAP, but none the less
standard advice of best practice could make a useful
contribution.

Two main ways of developing SORPs emerged from the review.

          - SORPs set by the Standard Setting Body

          - SORPs set by Industry Groups (Franked SORPs)

SORPs set by the Standard Setting Body

The old Accounting Standards Committee produced two SORPs. The
first was related to the presentation of Pension Fund Accounts.
The SORP deals mainly with the format required. More important
fundamental issues on accounting for pension costs are included
in the SSAP No 24 on the subject.

The second SORP produced by the old Accounting Standards Board
was related to accounting for charities. This SORP again
provided accounting formats which not only complied with the
charity commissioners requirements, but also produced useful
information for the reader of the accounts. The SORP on
charities is a good example of advice that could not override
SSAP's or the law. Large charities which were also companies
would not be able to comply with the SORP because the Companies
Act Financial Statements and the True and Fair View requirement
took precedence over the SORP.

These SORPs have not been adopted by the new Accounting Standards Board (ASB) because they do not have the same statutory implications of accounting standards. However, the ASB have stated that SORPs do have a useful role to play in good financial reporting. The ASB continue to encourage the development of the industry SORPs, and review SORPs produced and issue a statement as to whether the SORPs have been developed in accordance with the ASB's Code of Practice on producing SORPs and state that they do not conflict with accounting practice. This process is referred to as "negative assurance".

SORPs Set by Industry

Many industry SORPs have been developed but of particular interest in this respect is the work of CIPFA on Public Sector Accounting.

The CIPFA accounting practice rules developed for application in the public sector are considered to be best accounting practice for the industry (public sector). The two most important SORPs in this respect are:

> * The application of SSAPs to local authority accounts in England and Wales

> * Local authority accounting. The Code of Practice on local authority accounting for Great Britain.

Both these SORPS have been revised and feature in later sections of this book. Interestingly the SORPs developed by CIPFA have much more statutory support than normal SORPs developed by industry. The reason for this is the fact that these SORPs are considered to be proper practices. Local authority accounts must be prepared using proper practices and these are enforced by the Audit Commission. The statutory provision related to proper accounting practice can be found in the Local Government and Housing Act 1989. The new ASB have recognised the following bodies for the purposes of developing SORPs:

> * Association of British Insurers

> * Charity Commission (to carry out a review of SORP 2 on accounting by charities)

> * National Federation of Housing Associations in conjunction with the Scottish and Welsh Federations of Housing

> * Committee of Vice Chancellors and Principals

> * Joint Committee of the Chartered Institute of Public Finance and Accountancy (CIPFA) and Local Authority (Scotland) Accounts Advisory Committee (LASAAC)

During 1992 the following SORPs were issued:

* Off balance sheet instruments and other commitments
and contingent liabilities.

British Bankers Association / Irish Bankers Federation

* Advances - British Bankers Association / Irish
Bankers Federation

In summary SORPs are currently prepared by industry groups,
including the CIPFA for the Public Sector. SORPs developed by
industry groups are not of the same importance as SSAP's or
FRS's. However in the public sector they do represent proper
practices, and are therefore very important and considered by the
Audit Commission when the external audit is being undertaken.
SORPs generally represent best practice but are not enforced by
the framework of the Financial Reporting Council and Financial
Reporting Review Panel.

Conclusion

This chapter has attempted to consider in broad terms the
regulation of Companies, with particular regard to the Standards
of accounting required. It has dealt with UK regulation,
influences of International activity in providing standards, as
well as the use of SORPs to assist best practice, and the
requirements of the Stock Exchange.

CHAPTER 2
Accounting for Inflation

Introduction

The Importance of Studying Inflation Accounting

A study of accounting techniques available for dealing with
inflation is an important aspect of considering the concepts on
which accounting is based. It also enables further consideration
of why the Financial Reporting Council was deemed to be an
appropriate development from the self regulated standards of the
Consultative Council of Accounting Bodies (CCAB).

For students studying CIPFA courses the topic takes on much more
significant, because current cost accounting is employed in many
fields of the public sector. At present the public sector
organisations using current cost accounting techniques are as
follows:

> Nationalised Industries
> Government Trading Funds and some Executive Agencies
> The National Health Service
> Local Government Services subjected to Compulsory
> Competitive tendering

These topics are to be studied at the CIPFA P2 level. However,
CIPFA are also making proposals for the application of a form of
current cost accounting to non trading local government services,
and the technique is also applied to NHS directly managed units,
and these topics are within the CIPFA P1 syllabus.

This chapter therefore considers the weaknesses inherent in
historic cost accounting in the Private Sector. An explanation
of, and examples demonstrating the dangers of relying solely on
historic cost accounting. The development and demise of SSAP 16,
and the weakness in the old accounting standards enforcement.
Examples of the application of SSAP 16 are provided, but
consideration of the uses of inflation accounting in non trading
local government services and directly managed units are left to
later chapters.

Short Comings of Historic Cost Accounting

The shortcomings of Historic Cost Accounting are well documented
in many accounting texts, and the issue can be dealt with in a
number of different ways. The prominence of the topic in
debating circles is also heavily affected by the prevailing rate
of inflation in the economy. At the time of writing price
inflation is reported to be 1.7% and property values have
declined over the past few years of recession. At present
therefore the urgency of dealing with the problem is not intense.

There are two major weaknesses of Historic Cost Accounting.

i)   Fixed asset and stock balance sheet carrying values, and the rate of depreciation

ii) Calculation of profit: based on historic cost, which may endanger operational capacity.

Fixed Asset Balance Sheet Carrying Values

When the historic costs are used to record the asset values on the balance sheet the cost convention is being applied. The cost convention this has the advantage of being an undisputable value which can be proved to the prime records.

If any other value is placed on the asset in the balance sheet it can be subjected to debate, as to whether the value is true and fair. The value may be based on replacement cost, valuation or some other indexation measure.

The problems with using historic costs are that the balance sheet does not reflect the real value of the asset, and very often the net worth of the business is understated. This in itself in the extreme can lead to a take over and breaking up of the assets to realise the gain on real values of the assets not recorded in the accounts.

Furthermore the depreciation provision on the assets is based on the carrying value of the asset. For example if an asset cost £20,000 and is being fully depreciated over four years with no residual value, the annual depreciation will be £5,000. At the end of the four years accumulated depreciation provided and withdrawn from profit would amount to £20,000. However, the asset could easily cost £25,000 to replace. This leaves a gap of £5,000. It would be possible to devise a method of revaluing the asset year by year and depreciating on the bases of the revalued sum to narrow or remove the £5,000 gap. This is dealt with later in this chapter when SSAP 16 is discussed in detail.

Calculation of Profit, based on Historic Cost, which may endanger operational capacity

Historic cost accounting can endanger the continued operation of a business in inflationary times. This can be proved by a very simple example which assumes for simplicity that all historic profit calculated is distributed and no external finance is available. Both of these assumptions may not be true, but it enables the example to prove the point.

Example Mr C Aravan

Mr C Aravan is a retired lecturer who starts up a business on the 1 April 1993. The business plan is simply to buy and sell caravans. To make the example clear assume their are no expenses involved in purchasing or selling other than the cost of caravans themselves.
*   Mr C Aravan invests £50,000 in cash. On the 1 April 1993 ten caravans are purchased for resale @ £5,000 each

*   During the year Mr Aravan sells 6 caravans the selling price of each being £6,500

* Mr Aravan withdraws all the historic profit made from the business on 31/3/94

* The replacement cost of caravans @ 1.4.94 has increased to £6,000 each.

We can use these facts to

a) calculate the historic profit
b) consider the cash position and ability to replensih stocks.

a) Calculation of Mr Aravan's profit for the financial year ending 31/3/94.

	£	£
Sales (6x £6,500)		39,000
Purchases (10,£5,000)	50,000	
Less closing stock		
(4 x £5,000)	20,000	
Cost of goods sold		30,000
Profit		9,000

This simple calculation of profit reveals profit of £9,000. However, if we consider the cash position, and Mr Aravan's ability after withdrawing profit to replace the six caravan's sold, and therefore continue operating at the same activity level the following results can be found.

Mr Aravan's Cash Position

	£	
1/4/93 Cash Invested	50,000	(+)
1/4/93 Purchase of Caravans	50,000	(−)
during year sales	39,000	(+)
31/3/94 Cash Withdrawal	9,000	(−)
Cash balance 31/3/94	30,000	

The replacement of Caravan's sold is now considered. Unfortunately the replacement price is higher due to inflation. Only five Caravans can be purchased with the available cash, i.e £6,000 x 5 Caravans = £30,000. The result being that if more cash is not injected or loans raised Mr Aravan will start the new financial year with only nine caravans as follows:

	No.
Caravans not sold in 1993/94	4
Replacement caravans	5
1/4/94 Total Stock	9

Operational Decline

If this situation were to continue year on year the number of caravans stocked would fall, and this may affect the business, adversely fewer caravans lead to less choice and assuming 10 caravans stocked was ideal, customers may gradually drift away from purchasing from Mr Aravan. The operational capacity has not been sustained.

Solution for Mr Aravan

The solution is simple when calculating profit an adjustment needs to be made to ensure adequate funds are held in the business to preserve operational capacity. This could be achieved my Mr Aravan withdrawing £3,000 rather than the historic profit calculated at £9,000. Practical accounting methods have been developed to achieve this on a reasonably accurate basis. One such example is to calculate a realised holding gain, and another in accordance with SSAP 16 is to calculate a cost of sales adjustment (COSA).

The method employed in SSAP 16 will be fully explained later in this section, and examples provided.

Consideration of Profit / Gain

This simple example has enabled the problems of maintaining operational capacity to be considered clearly. However, it can be taken a little further to consider what figure should profit be or how much gain can Mr Aravan lay claim to over the year.

The accounting profit based on historic costs has been established at £9,000 but the following analysis of gain should be considered.

Table of

Mr Aravans Gains 1993/94

	£
Current Operating Profit	3,000
Realised Holding Gain	6,000
Equals Accounting Profit	9,000
Unrealised holding gain (4x£1,000)	4,000
Total Gain	13,000

Current operating profit of £3,000 is the level of profit Mr Aravan should withdraw to ensure that the operational capacity of the business will not be adversely effected.

Realised holding gain is the amount that has been realised as a gain under historic cost accounting, but is being held rather than distributed to ensure that operational capacity will remain at the same level.

Accounting profit is based on the historic cost convention of accounting for profit.

Unrealised holding gain. The unrealised holding gain is

argueably a gain related to the increase in the replacement cost of the four caravans held in stock at the end of trading, which had cost £5,000 each and now cost £6,000 each. This unrealised holding gain cannot be taken/withdrawn because it has not been realised. However, if Mr Aravan had decided to stop trading and sell off old stock at replacement cost, which is far less than normal selling price, then Mr Aravans real gain over the year would possibly be the full sum of £13,000 described as a total gain in the above table.

Conclusion on Operating Capacity and Assessment of Gains

The example provided of Mr Aravan is undoubtedly over simplified, and calculated very simply to provide an understanding of the issues involved. It is now necessary to consider the more complex approach taken in SSAP 16.

History of Inflation Accounting

The accounting standard SSAP 16 was by far the most contentious standard produced by the Consultative Council of Accounting Bodies (CCAB). The first standard on this subject dates back to 1973 and was SSAP 7 Current Purchasing Power, which was heavily criticised, and the Sandilands Report in 1975 started the long process of creating a new standard which eventually after two exposure drafts was finally promulgated in 1980 and was known as Current Cost Accounts SSAP 16. The standard survived until June 1985 in the private sector, when it became non mandatory on members. In 1988 it was completely withdrawn.

Failure of the standard, in part at least, is due to the effect adjusting the Profit and Loss account has on the profits of the business/entity. Profits are reduced to withhold funds within the business to ensure that the current level of activity can be sustained.

The new Financial Reporting Council are considering the problems of inflation accounting. Inflation accounting was dropped for many reasons, but one important one which has been overcome by the change in regulating accounting standards is the enforcement process.

Under the old self regulation CCAB system, standards were only capable of being enforced if they contributed to a true and fair view certificate. If a particular standard falls generally into dis-use it is very difficult if not impossible to suggest that the true and view is effected. Only if the vast majority of accounting statements are produced on current cost principles, and the minority disregarding the principle would qualification be possible.

The CCAB recognised the non use of SSAP 16 and were forced to withdraw its mandatory status. At the time it was hoped that SSAP 16 would be quickly replaced in the private sector, but it was not to be the case. Under the new Financial Reporting Council enforcement could have been pursued if appropriate by the FRRP.

This section seeks to re-explain the mechanics of Current Cost

Accounting, and in subsequent sections of the book the application of Current Cost Accounting in the public sector will be explored, with comments on the applicability of the technique in the public sector. These comments will be specifically related to non trading function of local authorities, and directly managed units and purchasing functions of District Health Authorities.

SSAP 16 - Current Cost Accounting

Under SSAP 16 the following accounting adjustments are necessary to convert historic accounts to current cost.

> COST OF SALES ADJUSTMENT (COSA)
> MONETARY WORKING CAPITAL ADJUSTMENT (MWCA)
> DEPRECIATION ADJUSTMENT
> - CURRENT AND BACKLOG
> REVALUATION ADJUSTMENT
> GEARING ADJUSTMENT
> OPTIONAL STOCK REVALUATION

The requirements above could be met by providing full current cost accounts, or by producing historic cost accounts with supplementary statements of current cost.

Current Cost Accounting Rationale

When inflation is predominant in the economy there is a possibility that if profits are calculated on an historic cost and distributed, no account would be taken of the increased working capital requirement, or the need to provide higher provisions for the depreciation of assets, whose replacement cost would have risen along with the rate of inflation.

The result of such a situation if not adjusted for by Current Cost Accounting could be a reduced capacity to continue trading, not enough working capital, and a lack of funds to replace obsolete assets resulting in inefficient production / output.

Cost of Sales Adjustment (COSA)

The following exhibit trading account can be used to demonstrate the need to adjust for increased cost of sales due to the inflationary effect on stock prices.

Example

Trading A/C for the year ending 31.3.93

	£	£	£
Sales			136,000
Opening Stock	14,000		
Purchase	82,000	96,000	
Les Closing Stock		23,000	73,000
Bal c/d gross profit			63,000
Stock index @ 1.4.92		122	
Stock index @ 31.3.93		158	

From the example it is clear that the purchase price for stock has increased due to the change in the stock price index. It is also clear that the stock holding at the 31.3.93 is £23,000 while the holding of stock at 1.4.92 was only £14,000 showing an increase of £9,000. In order to adjust the accounts to withhold from profit distribution an amount to continue the activity of the business it is necessary to estimate how much of the increased stock holding of £9,000 is related to inflation and how much is related to higher quantity of stocks being held; Current Cost Accounting only adjust for inflationary factors.

Method of estimating the cost of sales adjustment

1) Convert the opening and closing values of stock to a mid year price base, both figures will therefore be adjusted to the same price base, and any difference will be quantity (increase stock holding).

2) From the total variance of stock holding, in this case £9,000, deduct the amount due to quantity which has been calculated in accordance with (1) above. This will give the amount to be adjusted, known as the cost of sales adjustment.

3) Adjust the accounts as follows:

	DR	CR
	£	£
Profit and Loss A/C	****	
Current Cost Reserve A/C		*****

The effect of this adjustment is to ensure profit required for working capital is not distributed, but is held in the non-distributable capital reserve called the current cost reserve.

Calculation as per the figures given in the example trading a/c

Mid year price base = opening price index	122
plus closing index	158
Total	280
÷ 2	
= Ave. mid year price base	140

Adjustment of figures to same price base:

```
opening stock    = £14,000   x (mid year) 140 = £16,066
opening price base     122

closing stock    = £23,000   x (mid year) 140 - £20,380
closing price base     158

                                              £
      THEREFORE CHANGE IN QUANTITY   =    20,380
                                         -16,066
                                          4,314

      THEREFORE CHANGE DUE TO INFLATION =
             total change in stock        9,000
             LESS change due to quantity  4,314
      = Cost of sales adjustment          4,686  COSA
```

```
ACCOUNTING ENTRIES              DR        CR
                                £         £
   P & L a/c                    4,686
      Current Cost Reserve a/c            4,686
```

being the withholding of COSA from profit distribution to allow
for the increased cash requirement due to inflation.

Monetary Working Capital Adjustment (MWCA)

Exactly the same rationale is used to justify this adjustment, the
difference being that MWCA is concerned with basically debtors
less creditors. Although a similar calculation is carried out
here the index used will be the retail price index rather than
the stock purchase index, being a more suited index to the task
in hand.

Demonstration of the calculation for (MWCA)

```
DATA              OPENING BALANCE SHEET   CLOSING BALANCE SHEET
                          £                       £
Trade Debtors          60,000                  78,000
Trade Creditors        35,000                  38,000
   Net Total           25,000                  40,000
```

NB   Increase in MWC = £15,000

Retail Price Index (RPI)   160   200

```
1)   Adjust to same price base.

     opening MWC £25,000   x (mid year) 180 = £28,125
     opening RPI    160

     closing MWC £40,000   x (mid year) 180 = £36,000
     closing RPI    200

     CHANGE DUE TO QUANTITY = £36,000 - £28,125 = £7,875 Quantity
     CHANGE DUE TO INFLATION= £15,000 -  £7,875 = £7,125 MWCA
```

```
     Account Entries              DR        CR
                                  £         £
   P & L a/c                      7,125
      Current Cost Reserve a/c              7,125
```

being the adjustment required by SSAP 16 for MWCA withholding profit from distribution to ensure adequate cash remains in the business to provide the working capital requirement.

Depreciation Adjustments

Current cost accounting requires further provisions of depreciation to be made to ensure that assets can be replaced when planned. The following is a simple example which should enable students to grasp the concepts.

Example

A self employed coach driver buys his coach for £45,000. The coach will only be of use to the driver for three years. The realisable value of the coach at the end of the three years will be £15,000, and we will assume the residual value figure will not be affected by inflation for clarity of explanation purposes.

If the coach driver provides depreciation on an historic cost basis, and inflation increases the replacement cost of the coach at the end of the three years to £60,000 there will obviously be a shortfall of funds to replace the coach, and the following example shows how Current Cost Accounting alleviates this.

Historic cost accounting over the three year would change annual depreciation as follows:

NB   Annual historic depreciation = £45,000 - £15,000 = $\frac{£30,000}{3 \text{ years}}$

$$= £10,000 \text{ per annum}$$

Historic cost balance sheet at the end of year 3

	Cost £	Dep £	Net £
Fixed Assets - Coach	45,000	30,000	15,000
Current Assets - Cash in theory			
(withheld depreciation)			30,000
			45,000
			======
Financed by - Capital			45,000

Problems for replacing the Coach

		£
Cash available for the replacement		30,000
Cash realised on the sale		15,000
Total Cash	=	45,000

		£
Therefore cash required		60,000
LESS available		45,000
Shortfall	=	15,000

How Does Current Cost Accounting Alleviate this Problem?

The first thing to note about Current Cost Accounting is that it requires the assets to be stated in the balance sheet at replacement cost, and this figure would be revised annually. Therefore we can assume that the replacement cost of the coach was as follows:

	Replacement Cost
	£
Year 1	48,000
Year 2	54,000
Year 3	60,000

The revised replacement cost needs to be recorded within the accounts and this is achieved as follows:

	DR	CR
Fixed Asset a/c	*****	
Current Cost Reserve a/c		*****

being the adjustment required to the fixed asset a/c to show full replacement cost of the asset, showing the credit entry in the non-distributary current cost reserve.

Depreciation Adjustment

Under the rules of SSAP 16 the maximum chargeable to the current year's Profit and Loss account is limited to:

$$\frac{\text{Replacement cost-residual value}}{\text{Estimated life}} = \text{Maximum chargeable to P \& L}$$

The maximum calculated would include the element made for the historic depreciation. The following figures demonstrate this in respect to the example of the coach driver.

Year 1

    Replacement cost at the end of year 1 = £48,000
    Residual value   = £15,000
    Estimated life   = 3 years

THEREFORE:
    £48,000 - £15,000 = $\frac{£33,000}{3\text{ years}}$ = £11,000 - £10,000 historic
                                                   -   £1,000 adjustment

Year 2

    Replacement cost at the end of year 2 = £54,000
THEREFORE:
    £54,000 - £15,000 = $\frac{£39,000}{3\text{ years}}$ = £13,000 - £10,000 historic
                                                   £3,000 adjustment

The shortcomings of the depreciation adjustment can be seen in Year 2 as follows:

	£
Current replacement cost	54,000
LESS residual value	15,000
Total	39,000

We should have provided depreciation to date of £26,000 calculated by taking the
£39,000 ÷ 3 estimated life x 2 years expired = £26,000
However depreciation to date provided equals:

YEAR 1 £11,000 + YEAR 2 £13,000 = £24,000

It can be seen that there is a shortfall of depreciation of £2,000 and under the rules of SSAP 16 no further charge can be made to the P & L a/c. We need to adjust the accounts to show the full amount which should have been provided to ensure the written down value in the balance sheet is not overstated. The following entry is therefore made and is known as BACKLOG depreciation.

	DR	CR
Current Cost Reserve	£2,000	
Depreciation a/c		£2,000

NB   This entry does not fulfil the requirements to withhold from profit the necessary sum to ensure replacement of the asset, but ensures the balance sheet is correct.

Year 3

£60,000 - £15,000 = $\underline{£45,000}$ = £15,000 - £10,000 historic
                      3 years   £5,000 adjustment

Shortfall in depreciation provision = backlog
Therefore total depreciation which should have been provided = £45,000 however, only the following has been provided:

Year 1 £11,000 + Year 2 £15,000 including backlog + Year 3 £15,000 = £41,000

THEREFORE BACKLOG DEPRECIATION = £45,000 - £41,000 = £4,000

The Following Table Summarises the Depreciation more clearly

Year	Historic Depreciation £	CCA Adjustment For Depreciation £	Backlog £	Total £
1	10,000	1,000	–	11,000
2	10,000	3,000	2,000	15,000
3	10,000	5,000	4,000	19,000
	30,000	9,000	6,000	45,000

Where does this leave the coach driver?

Current Cost Balance Sheet as at the end of Year 3

	Replacement Cost £	Depreciation £	Net £
Fixed assets - coach	60,000	45,000	15,000
Cash (withheld depreciation)			39,000*
Total			54,000
Financed By:			
Capital	45,000		
Current cost reserve	9,000		
			54,000

Cash available to replace coach

	£	£
Replacement cost		60,000
LESS		
Cash at bank(in theory)	39,000	
Realised on sale	15,000	54,000
Cash shortfall		6,000 = BACKLOG DEPRECIATION

Current Cost Reserve Account

	£		£
Backlog dep.	6,000	revalue	
		year 1	3,000
		year 2	6,000
balance c/d	9,000	year 3	6,000
	15,000		15,000

The shortfall is of course due to backlog depreciation i.e not with holding cash from the profit distribution. In the view of accounting this is obviously a weakness in the SSAP. However, students must be aware that Accounting Standards were in fact based on consensus under the CCAB, and this in turn is due to there previously being no statutory requirement to comply with the SSAPs. This issue was discussed in much greater detail in chapter 1 which dealt with accounting standards.

Cash Position

Students should appreciate that this example dealing with the Coach Driver is a very simplified demonstration of the concept, and the Cash Position at the end of the three year period would probably bear no relationship to the £39,000 set aside by the charging of depreciation to the Profit and Loss Account. This is due to other movement in working capital, such as increasing debtors etc. which may be increasing and soaking up the cash undistributed to shareholders.

Gearing Adjustment

All the current cost adjustment which have had the effect of reducing profits by retaining amounts in the non-distributable

capital reserve have reduced profits available to the
shareholders. Another way of looking at this issue is to say
that the effect of these adjustments has been to ensure that
extra capital requirements are made available from the current
shareholders' equity. Problems arise where the gearing of
the business is such that as well as shareholders' equity,
finance is provided by loans to the business.

If a part of the finance of the business is long-term loan, then
it is argued that the shareholders should only be required to
meet a proportion of the extra capital required to continue the
business. This will ensure that the balance of finance is not
distorted, presuming that more loan finance will be sought for a
proportion of the new capital requirement. The following example
is a simplified demonstration of the gearing adjustment, which,
in effect, reduces the charges made to the P & L a/c by Current
Cost Accounting, in direct proportion to the capital structure of
the business.

Example of the Gearing Adjustment

<u>NB</u> These figure provided are not related to earlier used figures.

FACTS: the total CCA adjustments to the P&L a/c this year =£10,000
      the business is financed as follows:

Shareholders' Equity   £80,000
Long Term Loans   £20,000

SIMPLIFIED FORMULA

= <u>Long Term Loans</u> x CCA Adjustments to P & L a/c
   Total Capital

= <u>£20,000</u> x £10,000 = <u>£2,000 gearing adjustments</u>
  £100,000

	DR	CR
Current Cost Reserve a/c	£2,000	
Profit & Loss a/c		£2,000

being the reduction of entries made for CCA accounting related to
the gearing of the business.

Therefore the shareholders' profit will not be reduced by the
full £10,000 but only by £8,000.

The actual gearing formula is slightly more complex as follows:

FORMULA =
   <u>Long Term Liabilities - Cash</u> **or** <u>Long Term Liability - Cash</u>
   Shareholders' Equity plus   Net assets - Cash
   Long Term Liabilities - Cash

ADDITIONALLY, THE AVERAGE FOR THE YEAR IS REQUIRED THEREFORE
WE NEED TO TAKE THE OPENING POSITION AND THE CLOSING
POSITION ON GEARING AND ÷ BY TWO. ALTHOUGH THIS FORMULA IS
SLIGHTLY MORE COMPLEX THE CONCEPT IS THE SAME AS THE SIMPLE

EXAMPLE.

Optional Adjustment for Stock Valuation

This adjustment is only required when material, and is an optional adjustment which can be applied to the balance sheet to ensure the balance sheet shows the replacement cost of stock at the end of the financial period, rather than the cost which may be substantially different.

Two factors are crucial in determining this adjustment: First, the age of the stock and secondly the rate of inflation since the stock was purchased.

Example of Stock Valuation Adjustment

Historic cost as per balance sheet @ 31.3.92   £500,000

Average age of stock = 2 months

Stock price index @ 1.2.92 = 108 @ 31.3.92 = 112

THEREFORE

Current replacement cost = $\frac{£500,000}{108}$ x 112 = £518,519

Accounting entries required to show replacement cost
= £518,519 - £500,000 = £18,519

| | DR | CR |
	£	£
Stock a/c	18,519	
Current Cost Reserve a/c		18,519

being the stock adjustment required to show stock at full replacement cost.

<u>NB</u>   This entry would be reversed in the new year being only for balance sheet purposes.

This adjustment is not often required in exam questions.

This chapter is now completed with the following question and answer which students would be advised to consider carefully before attempting the exam questions at the end of the section.

EXERCISE 2.1

FULL EXAMPLE CCA - PERFECT LTD

Current Cost Balance Sheet as at 31.3.90 and 31.3.91

	1990		1991	
	£	£	£	£
Fixed Assets				
Land		50,000		70,000
Building/Plant (replacement cost)	230,000		280,000	
Less Depreciation	69,000	161,000	?	?
Current Assets				
Stock	30,000		45,000	
Debtors	50,000		75,000	
Cash	5,000		9,000	
	85,000		129,000	
Current Liabilities				
Creditors	24,000		26,000	
		61,000		103,000
Net Assets		272,000		?
Less Debentures		40,000		60,000
		232,000		?
		=======		========
Share Holders Equity				
Ordinary Shares @ £1		100,000		110,000
P&L a/c		35,000		?
Current cost reserve		97,000		?
		232,000		?
		=======		========

Trading Profit and Loss Account for the year ending 31.3.91

	£	£
Gross Profit		450,000
Less Expenses:		
Depreciation (historic)	15,000	
Other Expenses	438,000	453,000
Net Loss		3,000
		=======

Notes

1 The following information is available:

	Stock Index	RP1 Index
1/4/90	150	180
31/3/91	190	210

2 The building and plant have an estimated replacement cost at 31/3/91 of £280,000. However the building is prefabricated and only has a ten year life. The policy of the company is to depreciate over ten years, assuming no residual value for either plant or buildings. All these assets have been depreciated for three full years as at 31/3/90.

3 The company accounts clerk has discovered that the value of stock stated in the closing balance sheet at historic cost is £4,500 below current replacement cost and an optional stock adjustment is required.

4 The increase in Land value is a result of a revaluation and it is company policy to make adjustment for this in the current cost reserve account rather than in a separate revaluation reserve.

YOU ARE REQUIRED TO:

Prepare a Current Cost Profit and Loss Account for the year ending 31/3/91, along with a Current Cost Balance Sheet as at 31/3/91. You should adopt the practices employed in SSAP 16.

Tutorial Example 2.1 CCA - Perfect Ltd

Interpretation of Notes to the Question

Note 1   This note give the indices with which you are
                required to calculate the cost of sales
                adjustment, and the Monetary Working Capital
                adjustment.

Note 2   This note signifies that the assets in the balance
                sheet for building and plant are all being
                depreciated over ten years, and were all
                acquired at the same time. The note enables
                the Current Cost Depreciation and Backlog to be
                calculated.

Note 3   Unusually this question requires a stock
                adjustment and this will be achieved by Dr
                Stock A/C, and CR Current Cost Reserve A/C
                with £4,500

Note 4   Self explanatory

Proceed to Answer the Question as follows:

1st Step calculate CCA adjustments

2nd Step prepare closing net assets figure

3rd Step calculate gearing adjustment

4th Step prepare trading P&L a/c

5th Step prepare balance sheet

Step 1 Calculate CCA adjustments

COSA $\frac{£30,000}{150}$ x 170* = £34,000 $\frac{£45,000}{190}$ x 170 = £40,263

<u>Mid Year Index</u>   Quantity Variance = £40,263
   Opening 150   - £34,000
   Closing <u>190</u>   Q   6,263
        340   =======

        ÷ 2   Inflation
x mid year= 170*   £
              (45,000)   Total Variance   15,000
              (-30,000)   Less Quantity   £6,263
                    COSA   8,737
                               ======

Required

    DR P&L a/c

      CR Current Cost Reserve a/c

<u>MWCA</u>   1/4/90   31/3/91
          £   £

Debtors   50,000   75,000 $\frac{26,000}{180}$ x 195   = £28,167

Less
Creditors   <u>24,000</u>   <u>26,000</u>
        26,000   49,000
        ======   ======
                          $\frac{49,000}{210}$ x 195   = £45,500

<u>Mid Year RPI</u> =   Quantity Variance = 17,333
                                            =======

Opening   180
                                         £
Closing   <u>210</u>   Inflation Variance =
          390   Total Variance   23,000
        ÷ 2   (49-26) Less Quantity <u>17,333</u>

mid year =   195   MWCA   £5,667
                                         =====

Depreciation Adjustment - Building and Plant

Replacement Cost   = Total which can be charged to P&L a/c
Estimated life

$$\frac{£280,000}{10} = £28,000$$

This can be split £15,000 Historic (see P&L a/c)

£13,000 Current adjustment
_____
£28,000
_____

This charge for depreciation represents the fourth years provision on a straight line basis. Therefore the accumulated depreciation A/C should amount to

4 years x £28,000 =   £112,000

However the depreciation a/c at present would reflect the following

	£
Opening Accumulated depreciation from balance sheet	69,000
Plus maximum to P&L a/c	28,000
	97,000
(112-91) ∴Backlog must equal	15,000
	£112,000
	=======

Step 2 Prepare the closing net asset figure. This can be prepared in such a format that will enable its use for the Closing Balance Sheet.

Perfect Ltd Balance Sheet as at 31.3.91

Fixed Assets	£	£
Land		70,000
Buildings and Plant	280,000	
Less Depreciation	112,000	168,000
		238,000

Current Assets

Stock (45,000+£4,500)	49,500	
Debtors	75,000	
Cash	9,000	
	133,500	
Less		
Current Liabilities	26,000	107,500
Net Assets		£345,500

Calculation of Gearing Adjustment

Formula = Averaged $\dfrac{\text{Long Term Loans - Cash}}{\text{Net Assets - Cash}}$

Opening			Closing		
Long Term			Long Term		
Loans - Cash	=	X	-Loans Cash	=	Y

$$\frac{\text{Long Term Loans - Cash}}{\text{Net Assets - Cash}} = X \quad\Bigg|\quad \frac{\text{Long Term -Loans Cash}}{\text{Net Assets - Cash}} = Y$$

$$\frac{X + Y}{2} \times 100 \;=\; \text{Gearing percentage}$$

$$\therefore X = \frac{£40,000 - £5,000}{£272,000 - £5,000} = .1311 \quad \therefore Y = \frac{£60,000 - £9,000}{£345,000 - £9,000} = .1472$$

$$\frac{.1311 + .1472}{2} \times 100 = 13.92\%$$

		£
Therefore Gearing Adjustment =	COSA	8,737
	MWCA	5,667
	Depreciation	13,000
		27,404
	X 13.92%	
	=	£3815

DR Current Cost Reserve a/c

CR P&L a/c

Step 4 Prepare Trading Account

Perfect Ltd Trading Profit and Loss Account for the year ending 31/3/91

	£	£
Gross Profit		450,000
Depreciation Historic	15,000	
Other Expenses	438,000	453,000
Historic		3,000
Net / Loss		
CCA Adjustments		
COSA	8,737	
MWCA	5,667	
Depreciation	13,000	

	27,404	
Less Gearing	(3,815)	23,589
Current Cost Loss		26,589

Bal b/fwd		35,000

Bal c/d		8,411
		=====

Step 5 Prepare Balance Sheet

Start From Net Asset Position

	£	£
Net Assets		345,500
Less Debentures		60,000
		285,500
		=======

Share Holder Equity		
Ordinary Shares £1	110,000	
P&L a/c	8,411	
Current Cost Reserve A/c	167,089	285,500
		=======

Current Cost Reserve

	£		£
Backlog	15,000	Balance b/fwd	96,000
		Revaluation	
Bal C/d	167,089	- Land	20,000
		- Buildings & P	50,000
		- Stock	4,500
		COSA 8737	
		MWCA 5667	
		Gearing (3815)	10,589
	182,089		182,089
	=======		=======

Examination Question 2.1

Historic Bungay Blackdog Ltd Profit and Loss Account for the Year Ending 31 March 1993

	£	£
Sales		340,000
Opening Stock	30,000	
Purchases	204,000	
Less Closing Stock	54,000	
		180,000
		160,000
Expenses	12,000	
Depreciation	40,000	
		52,000
Net Profit		108,000
		=======

Current Bungay Blackdog Ltd Cost Balance Sheet as at 31 March 1993

			£
Fixed Assets at cost (note 1)			600,000
Less Depreciation			80,000
			520,000
Current Assets (note 2)			
Stock		54,000	
Debtors		88,000	
Bank		22,000	
		164,000	
Current Liabilities			
Trade Creditors		42,000	
			122,000
Net Assets			642,000
Less Debentures			80,000
Total			562,000
			=======
Share Capital			200,000
Revenue Reserves			162,000
Current Cost Reserve			200,000
			562,000
			=======

Notes

1   Fixed Assets are being depreciated over 10 years with a nil
     residual value.

     Replacement cost 31 March 1993 £710,000

2   Current assets 1 April 1992

	£
Stock	30,000
Debtors	62,000
Bank	4,000
	96,000
Less Trade Creditors	44,000
	52,000

3   Stock Index   1 April 1992   120
                              31 March 1993   160

     RPI   1 April 1992   180
                              31 March 1993   200

4   Debentures have remained unchanged over the year 1992/93.

REQUIRED

CCA accounts having regard to all relevant adjustments under SSAP
16 including the adjustment needed for backlog depreciation.
Show workings.

Reserve Limited

Historic Cost Balance Sheets as at 31.3.92 and 31.3.93

	1992		1993	
	£	£	£	£
Fixed Assets (Cost)	200,000		200,000	
less depreciation	90,000		100,000	
		110,000		100,000
Current Assets				
Stock	10,000		15,000	
Debtors	60,000		78,000	
Cash	10,000		10,000	
	80,000		103,000	
Current Liabilities				
Creditors	35,000		38,000	
		45,000		65,000
Net Assets		155,000		165,000
Less debentures		30,000		30,000
		125,000		135,000
		=======		=======
Financed By:				
Shares Auth	100,000		100,000	
& Issued @ £1				
P & L a/c	25,000		35,000	
Current Cost Reserve		125,000		135,000
				=======

Question continued on the next page

Trading Profit and Loss Account for Year Ending 31.3.93

	£	£	£
Sales			950,000
Opening Stock	10,000		
Plus Purchases	700,000		
		710,000	
LESS Closing Stock		15,000	695,000
Gross Profit			255,000
Expenses	235,000		
Depreciation	10,000		245,000
Net Profit c/d			10,000
Profit b/fwd			25,000
Balance			35,000

Additional Information

	RPI INDEX	Stock INDEX
1.4.92	160	140
31.3.93	200	160

Replacement Cost of Asset
     @ 31.3.93 = £280,000
The asset is 10 years old at the 31.3.93. Assume a straight line policy with no residual value.

NB This is the first year that Reserve Ltd have adopted current cost accounts in accordance with SSAP16. It will not be possible therefore to work out the gearing adjustment on the average net assets. Historic and current cost balance sheets can not be mixed. Therefore calculate the gearing adjustment on final adjusted current cost values.

Required

Prepare a current cost profit and loss account for the year ending 31 March 1993, and a current cost balance sheet as at that date.

CHAPTER 3

Accounting for Leases by Lessees

Introduction

At this stage of a students study it is likely that the accounting requirements of financing through loans is well understood. However, a significant leasing market exists which can be an alternative method of obtaining finance.

The accounting treatment of this topic is governed by SSAP 21 which in fact covers a broader area than this chapter. SSAP 21 also considers hire purchase contracts, and accounting for leases by lessors.

Leasing

The reasons for covering in detail accounting for leases by lessees is that it is a very important means of financing. Leasing is used extensively and creatively in both the public and private sector. The SSAP 21 basically requires the accounting for leases which are purely of a financing nature to be treated in a similar fashion to the accounting treatment of loan finance. However, if the leasing arrangement is an operational lease, then it is more akin to a rental and can be treated completely differently from a finance lease, like an normal expense.

Distinction between Finance Lease and Operational Lease

In reality it is sometimes very difficult to distinguish these two types of leases. However, the following examples will help to set out the basic concepts. Once these have been established the specific detail and more accurate interpretation of SSAP 21 will be considered. This section will consider the subject in the following order:

> * Finance Leases
> * Operational Leases

Finance Lease - Characteristics

A finance lease is an arrangement which enables a lessee to receive an asset from a lessor. The asset in substance belongs to the lessee for a non cancellable contract period. This initial period is known as the primary period.

The lessee receives the asset, and will have uninterrupted use of the asset during the primary period. The lessee will take on the risks of the asset, being responsible for maintenance, safe keeping and insurance.

This type of lease arrangement in substance passes all risks and rewards associated with the asset to the lessee. Ownership in the legal form however rests with the lessor.

Payment is made for the asset typically quarterly, and over the primary period virtually the whole purchase price plus finance charges will be paid by the lessee to the lessor.

At the end of the primary period the lease may continue into a secondary period at a peppercorn rental charge. It maybe that eventually the asset will be sold by the lessee acting as the agent of the lessor, and it maybe arranged that the lions share of the sale proceeds are paid to the lessee for acting as agent in respect of the sale.

The detailed description given here is a crystal clear example of a finance lease. It could be argued that the only difference between this arrangement and a loan agreement is the legal documentation. In both cases finance has been obtained, but by different arrangements.

SSAP 21 Definition of a Finance Lease

Characteristics of the finance lease provided give a crystal clear example of a finance lease. In the SSAP a more specific rule is provided. The standard states that in addition to the characteristics previously explained lease payments including any initial payments, should amount to substantially all (normally 90% or more) of the present value of the Fair Value of the asset.

Finance houses dealing in leasing have taken this quite literally and when marketing leases may classify a lease as an operational lease if the asset when returned to the lessor is worth 10% or more of the fair value. This practice has been questioned by the new standard setting body because it ignores all other factors related to characteristics. It is therefore possible in the long term that this interpretation of the standard may be changed, but at present the rule remains.

The Accounting Treatment of Finance Leases

Simplistically the Accounting requirement is as follows:

*   The Asset must be shown in the balance sheet of the lessee as a tangible asset. Assets held under finance lease are not owned by the lessee, but should generally be integrated with owned fixed assets on the balance sheet. The notes to the accounts should contain details of assets held under finance lease by class. Or alternatively information can be given in the fixed asset note supporting the accounts.

*   The asset value shown in the lessees balance sheet would be in most cases the estimated outright purchase amount (known as the fair value), although more specific advice will follow on this point.

*   A student may wonder how the double entry for the creation of the asset will be effected. The answer is that as well as the creation of an asset amount, a equal sum needs to be introduced on the liability side of the balance sheet for future "obligations under a finance lease".

*   The obligation under finance lease represents the liability to pay the amount over the primary period of the lease. The liability should be split into the

following categories.

Creditors: Amounts falling due within one year
Creditors: Amounts falling due after more than one
year

An Example of the double entry might be as follows: a lease is entered into which involves the leasing of an asset with a fair value of £12,680 of the rental £4,000 to be paid in year 1, £1265 is related to finance charges and £2732 is related to the repayment of the obligation. If the balance sheet was drawn up on the 1st day of the leasing agreement the entries would be as follows:

Step 1

	DR £	CR £
Fixed Assets	12,680	
Obligation under Finance Lease		12,680

being the introduction of the asset and the obligation to repay the fair value.

Step 2

The obligation under finance lease would be divided between current year and longer term liabilities as follows:

Presentation of obligation under finance lease in balance sheet

	£
* Creditors falling due within one year	2,732
* Creditors falling due after more than one year	9,948
Total obligation under finance lease	12,680

Step 3

When the rental of £4,000 is paid £1,268 (the finance charge) will be charged directly to profit and loss account. While the obligation repayment will remove the creditor liability in the balance sheet.

What are the detailed requirements of SSAP 21 in respect of the fair value of the asset?

SSAP 21 provides a specific method of calculating the sum of fair value to be included in the balance sheet. The terms used are as follows:
"A leasee should, strictly record a finance lease at the present value of the minimum lease payments".

For the benefit of completeness if the fair value (outright purchase price) were not known, which is exceedingly unlikely the present value calculation would be as follows:

The minimum lease payments per year are £2500

The primary (non cancellable) period of the lease is 5 years

A typical rate of interest charged on such leases is 11% for this example.

Present Value Calculation

Year	Discount factor	Payment £	Present value £
0	1.000	2,500	2,500
1	0.901	2,500	2,252
2	0.812	2,500	2,030
3	0.731	2,500	1,828
4	0.659	2,500	1,647
		12,500	10,257

This process confirms that the equivalent of the outright purchase price of fair value is £10,257. Finance costs are £2,243. If this agreement had been structured in such a way that the lessor paid less than 90% of the fair value on a present value calculation, and then returned the asset to the lessor the lease would have been categorised as an operational lease.

What accounting is required to depreciate the asset created?

Assets in the balance sheet must be depreciated on the basis of their carrying value, and in accordance with the companies policy for assets of that class.

For example if the asset is held under a finance lease with a primary period of 4 years. The depreciation would pay no regard to the lease period, but would be more concerned with the company policy. This might be as follows: plant will be depreciated on a straight line basis over 7 years assuming a nil residual value.

In applying the company depreciation policy to the asset leased, we need to establish that the asset may be held for 7 years. This will mean retaining the lease for a secondary period of 3 years. Obviously the asset must be intended to be of use for the 7 years.

How are the rentals paid to the leasing company accounted for?

The lessee will pay the lessor a rental for the finance lease. The rental will be made up of an element related to the financing cost and an element related to the original cost of the asset, known as the repayment of obligation. The important point to note is that the finance element of the rental is charged to the P&L a/c as an expense. While the repayment of obligation element is used to remove the outstanding obligation on the balance sheet.

If for example a lessee enters an agreement to lease an asset over four years at a quarterly rental of £2,000, and that had the asset been purchased outright instead of being leased its cost would have been £25,360. We can calculate the total finance being paid as follows:

Total rentals paid equal £2,000 x 4 quarter x 4 years = £32,000

Therefore the breakdown of the rental between repayment of
finance element and the repayment of original cost / finance
obligation can be shown as follows:

	£
Fair value outright purchase	25,360
Finance element	6,640
	32,000

Therefore the picture is clear over the four year primary period.
The problem now to resolve is how much of the quarterly rental
can be considered to be finance element as opposed to repayment
obligation.

To answer this question we need to consider SSAP 21, which
advises that the straight line method is not appropriate where
material amounts are involved.

This would mean that the following pattern of repayment would not
normally be acceptable, because it represents a straight line
method.

Straight Line Method − not acceptable

Years	Finance Element	Finance Obligation	Total Rentals Paid
	£	£	£
1	1,660	6,340	8,000
2	1,660	6,340	8,000
3	1,660	6,340	8,000
4	1,660	6,340	8,000
	6,840	25,360	32,000

The reason that the straight line approach is not approved is due
to the fact that, where finance charges are involved the finance
element is going to bigger in the earlier years where the
greatest amount of principal is outstanding. The SSAP 21
therefore states that the finance charge should be allocated to
the profit and loss account based on a constant periodic rate of
return.

The following two methods are acceptable in allocating finance
costs to the profit and loss account both being in line with the
constant periodic rate of return.

- Actuarial Method

- Sum of Digits Method

Example of Actuarial Method

*   The finance lease rentals are £2,000 per quarter

*   The fair value / outright purchase price would be £25,360.

*   The primary period of the lease is four years.

The lessor has calculated the finance element of the rental on the basis of an interest rate of 10% on the balance of the asset outstanding on the first day of each year. The following table shows the calculation.

1 Years	2 Balance B/fwd £	3 Finance Charge £	4 Rental Repayment £	(3+4) Total Rental £	(2-4) Balance C/fwd £
1	25,360	2,536	5,464	8,000	19,896
2	19,896	1,989	6,011	8,000	13,885
3	13,885	1,389	6,612	8,000	7,277
4	7,277	727	7,273	8,000	-
		6,640	25,360	32,000	

This table shows that of the total rental payments each year, the finance charge column 3 is greatest in the earlier years. This is consistent with the constant periodic rate of return.

Example of the Sum of Digits Method

The sum of digits is an arbitrary method of allocating finance charges to the profit and loss account which can simulate the constant periodic rate of return. Students may well come across this method being called the rule of 78 calculation.

To calculate the sum of digits on a yearly basis the years are listed and added up, i.e years 1 + 2 + 3+ 4 = 10. The finance charge is then apportioned in year 1 by taking the last year in the series 4 divided by the sum of years 10. Therefore the year one apportionment is 4/10ths.

If we apply this process to our example the results can then be seen.

*   The finance lease rentals are £2,000 per quarter

*   The fair value / outright purchase price would be £25,360

*   The primary period of the lease is four years

Years	Sum of Digits Factor	Finance Charge £	Repayment Obligation £	Total Rental £
1	4/10	2,656	5,344	8,000
2	3/10	1,992	6,008	8,000
3	2/10	1,328	6,672	8,000
4	1/10	664	7,336	8,000
		6,640	25,360	32,000

NB   The sum of digit factor is multiplied by the total finance charge 4/10 x £6,640 = £2656

It is therefore possible to compare the three examples of apportioning the finance charge to the P&L a/c as follows:

Three Methods of
Allocating of Finance Charges to Profit and Loss Account

Year	Straight line £	Actuarial £	Sum of digits £
1	1,660	2,556	2,656
2	1,660	1,989	1,992
3	1,660	1,388	1,328
4	1,660	727	664
	6,640	6,640	6,640

The above table demonstrates that while the straight line method clearly does not allocate finance charges fairly over the four years. The other methods produce a profile of finance charges that are very similar.

Lessees may therefore employ the actuarial or sum of digit methods in computing the amount of rental payments which should be classified as finance expense, as opposed to the repayment of the obligation.

A Step by Step Summary of the Process of Accounting for Finance Leases

Step 1   Initially bring into account the fair value of the asset by capitalising the amount in the balance sheet.

Step 2   Counter balance the entry in the fixed assets by creating liability provisions for the obligation under finance lease.

Step 3   The obligation under finance lease should be split into current liability and longer term liability.

Step 4   Provide depreciation in accordance with the normal policy of the company for that class of asset, providing the asset will be in use for the life used.

Step 5   When notified of the rental to be paid.

    a)   Calculate the finance element on the basis of the sum of digits or actuarial method. Charge the sum to the P&L account.

    b)   The amount included in the rental related to the repayment of obligations under finance lease should be removed from the balance sheet liabilities.

Step 6   When closing off the balance sheet take care to ensure future obligations under finance lease are split between current and longer term liabilities.

Exercise 3.1
Fully Worked Example - SPAM Ltd Finance Lease Facts

A lessor leases to a lessee an asset on a non cancellable contract. The primary period of the agreement is four years. The following additional information is available.

* The annual rental will be £4,000

* The lessee intends to use the asset for 12 years. Depreciation should be straight line.

* A nominal sum will be payable in the secondary period of the lease.

* The asset could have been purchased outright for £12,680.

* The rate of finance implicit in the lease is 10% on the opening liability.

Tutorial Note

When accounting for leases the significance of a secondary period (ie years 5-12 in this example) is that it demonstrate the asset can be held for 12 years. We ignore the nominal payments.

Establish the Fair Value as follows:

	£
Total rentals over primary period	
4 x £4,000	16,000
Less Fair Value	12,680
Finance Charges	3,320

	DR £	CR £
Fixed Assets	12,680	
Obligations under finance lease		12,680*

This being the capitalisation of the finance lease. *This obligation is still to be split between current and longer term.

Calculate the Repayment Profile

Year	Balance Obligations B/fwd	Finance Charge	Repayment of Obligation	Total Rental	Balance of Obligations C/fwd
	£	£	£	£	£
1	12,680	1,268	2,732	4,000	9,948
2	9,948	995	3,005	4,000	6,943
3	6,943	694	3,306	4,000	3,637
4	3,637	363	3,637	4,000	-
		3,320	12,680		

- 63 -

The finance charge is based on the instructions in the example of 10% of the brought forward obligation. The repayment of obligation figure is calculated by deducting the finance charge from the rental, and the balance of obligation carried forward is the difference between the opening obligation less the obligation repaid.

Obligation Under Finance Lease Current / Non Current

To split the obligation between current liability and non current, at the end of year 1 for example the total liability c/fwd is £9,948 of this year 2 repayment of obligation will be £3,005. Therefore the split for balance sheet purposes can be stated as follows:

End of Year 1 Balance Sheet Extract

	£
Current lability	3,005
Non current liability more than one year	6,943
	9,948

Calculation of Depreciation

Depreciation can be calculated over the life of the asset i.e 12 years. There is no residual value stated, and depreciation is require by the question to be calculated on a straight line basis.

Therefore annual depreciation = $\frac{£12,680}{12 \text{ years}}$ = £1,057 per annum

Extracts from the Final Accounts over the four year primary period

It is possible for illustrative purposes to show the extracts of the finance lease entries as follows:

Extract Profit and Loss Account Four Years

Years	1	2	3	4
	£	£	£	£
Finance Charges	1,268	995	694	363
Depreciation Provision	1,507	1,057	1,057	1,057
Total	2,325	2,052	1,751	1,420

This extract shows that the sum total of finance charge and depreciation fall on the profit and loss account. Obviously in year 5 the depreciation will continue where as the primary lease payment will cease.

Extract Balance Sheet Fixed Assets for Four Years

	Years			
	1	2	3	4
	£	£	£	£
Fixed Assets held under fiance less	12,680	12,680	12,680	12,680
Less Accumulated depreciation	1,057	2,114	3,171	4,228
Written down value	11,623	10,466	9,509	8,452

The fixed asset extract shows the written down value of the asset based on the depreciation policy adopted.

Extract of Balance Sheet for obligations under finance leases for the four years

	each of Years			
	1	2	3	4
	£	£	£	£
Creditors falling due within one year	3,005	3,306	3,637	-
Creditors falling due after one year	6,943	3,637	-	-
Total	9,948	6,943	3,637	nil

This extract shows the outstanding obligations split between the two headings required.

It should be noted that the balance sheet of fair value for fixed asset purposes, and the repayment of lease obligation is only likely to be the same on the original introduction of the asset. From then on the obligations are removed by repayments over the primary period while the depreciation is writing down the asset at a different speed.

Comparism of Accounting for Finance Leases with Accounting for Loans

The intention of the SSAP 21 is to provide an accounting framework which enables the presentation of financial statement to be unaffected by the method of financing assets.

If loan finance is used, rather than a finance lease, the treatment is very similar - consider the following:

* The asset appears in the balance sheet at cost. The finance lease uses fair value which is a proxy for cost.

* The loan liability appears in the balance sheet.

* The asset is depreciated

* **Repayment of the interest on loans are charged to P&L**

account while principal is accounted for by reducing the loan outstanding liability on the balance sheet.

* The loan liability should be split between short and long term on the balance sheet.

it can therefore be concluded that the treatment is very similar. The major difference being the timing of cash movements, and the legal form or the arrangement.

Finance leases are treated in the accounts as if the asset is owned by the lessee acknowledging the importance in accounting of substance over form.

Operating Lease

An operating lease is treated completely differently to a finance agreement covered by an operating lease.

The characteristics of an operating lease would be as follows:

* The lessee has the asset for a shorter period of time.

* The lessee is not necessarily responsible for the upkeep of the asset.

* If the asset breaks down it would be the lessor who would suffer the loss, the lessee should demand an immediate replacement.

* The lessor would normally insure the asset.

* The lessor should be interested in the value and condition of the asset, because the lessor is likely to re-lease the asset or sell it at the end of the lease period.

To provide some examples of crystal clear operating leases consider the following.

Example 1 Equipment Operational Lease

The company have decided to undertake some research work for six months, and have brought a top employee over from their American operation. The company leases some equipment for six months. The payment for the lease of the equipment represents one fifth of the equipment value. At the end of the lease period all equipment is returned to the lessor.

Example 2 Vehicle Operational Lease

A visiting dignitary needs the use of a vehicle for a year. The company arrange a lease from its marketing budget. Here again the vehicle will be returned at the end of the year. The vehicle will be maintained by the lessor. Any mechanical problems will require the lessor to provide a replacement vehicle.

These two examples provide a clear distinction between operational leases and finance lease. However, remember that in practice the distinction is much less tangible. The rule has not been operated based on the characteristics, but tends to be

interpreted very much on the basis of the 90% payment of present
value method.

Why Should Organisations Wish to Creatively Count Finance Leases as Operational Leases?

The answer to this is that if a operational lease is provided,
the balance sheet does not have to carry the asset. This results
in the obligations to finance future lease payments not to be
reported on the face of the balance sheet.

Where obligations are not reported as liabilities the gearing
ratio can appear more favourable to the company. Investors may
be cautious of companies with high gearing ratios.

In the public sector controls over capital spending have been
avoidable in the past by classifying assets leased as operational
rather than finance leases.

The Accounting Treatment of Operational Leases

Operational leases are not recorded in the balance sheet as
assets, and obligations are not shown in the balance sheet.

Rentals are charged in totality to the profit and loss account.
In effect the payments are treated as simple expenses.

Disclosure Requirements for Leases - Companies Act

Paragraph 53 (b) of schedule 8 to the Companies Act 1948 requires
disclosure of the amount if material, charged to revenue in
respect of sums payable in respect of the hire of plant and
machinery.
To comply with this requirement it is necessary to disclose the
amounts charged to revenue for operating leases and finance
leases. Finance leases would require both finance charges and
depreciation to be disclosed.

Disclosure of Commitments Under Operating Leases

In the case of operating leases, the SSAP requires a lessee to
disclose, in addition to the amount charged in the year, the
yearly amount of repayments to which he is committed at the year
end. (the annual commitment). This will not necessarily be the
same as the amount paid in the year, because it will take account
of leases to commence, and leases expiring.

Exercise 3.2
Fully worked finance lease example using the sum of digits method

Ham Ltd lease a machine as follows:

* Primary period four years (non cancellable)
* Asset life eight years
* Residual value nil, depreciation method straight line
* Annual rental agreed £3,425
* Outright purchase price £10,000

You Are Required To

1) Calculate the repayment of obligations and finance charges over the four years on the sum of digits methods

2) Show extracts from the profit and loss account, and balance sheet for the four year period.

Tutorial Answer

Calculation of the rental split between finance and repayment of obligation elements

Annual rental x primary period   =   Total Rentals
£3425   x 4 years   =   £13,700

Calculation of finance element

	£
Total rentals	13,700
less fair value	10,000
Total finance element	3,700

Apportionment of Finance Costs based on sum of digits

Take the sum of digits and work out the proportions for each year. Then apply the proportions to the overall finance cost of £3.700 as follows:

Years	Total Finance cost £	sum of digits	apportionment of finance £
1		4/10	1,480
2		3/10	1,110
3		2/10	740
4		1/10	370
	3,700		3,700

NB   Year 1 is calculated by taking 4/10ths of £3,700.

Compute the Repayment of Obligation for Each Year

This is achieved by deducting the finance charge from the annual rental payment.

Years	Total Rental £	Finance Charge £	Repayment Obligation £
1	3,425	1,480	1,945
2	3,425	1,110	2,315
3	3,425	740	2,685
4	3,425	370	3,055
	13,700	3,700	10,000

The calculations for part 1 of the question are therefore complete.

Part 2

Extract from the Profit and Loss Account - Ham Ltd

Years

	1 £	2 £	3 £	4 £
*Depreciation	1,250	1,250	1,250	1,250
Finance Charge	1,480	1,110	740	370
Total	2,730	2,360	1,990	1,620

Depreciation has been calculated over eight years, assuming a nil residual value, and straight line policy as follows:

$$\text{Cost} = \frac{£10,000}{8} = \text{Depreciation annual amount of } £1,250$$

Extract from Balance Sheet Fixed Assets - Ham Ltd

Years

	1	2	3	4
	£	£	£	£
Fixed Assets held under finance lease	10,000	10,000	10,000	10,000
Less accumulated depreciation	1,250	2,500	3,750	5,000
Written down value	8,750	7,500	6,250	5,000

Extract from the Balance Sheet Obligation held under Finance Lease - Ham Ltd

End of Years

	1	2	3	4
	£	£	£	£
Creditors less than one year	2,315	2,685	3,055	-
Creditors more than one year	5,740	3,055	-	-
Total	8,055	5,740	3,055	nil

NB End of year 1. These figures are calculated by taking the fair value £10,000 and deducting year 1 repayment of £1,945. This equals a total obligation of £8,055 at the year end. It is then necessary to show the very next years repayment of obligation as a current liability and the remainder as longer term.

Examination Question 3.1

The following information relates to the BIGFOOT Company. This company needs to adjust their accounts for the following items in accordance with standard practice.

Finance Leases

This year a Finance lease was entered into as follows:

- Non cancellable agreement, with a five year primary period and an unspecified secondary period.

- The outright purchase of the asset would have resulted in a capital cost of £145,000.

- Rentals will be paid quarterly and each quarter will be £8,000.

- The company believe the asset will last for a maximum 7 years, at which stage it might be possible to realise £12,000 from the asset sale.

The company have decided to depreciate the asset on a straight line basis but will calculate the repayment of lease obligations on rentals on the sum of digits method.

You are required to:

1   Calculate the repayment of obligations and finance charges over five years on the sum of digits method

2   Show the original accounting entries for the finance lease before any rentals are paid.

3   Show extracts from the Profit and Loss Account and Balance Sheet over the five year period.

Examination Question 3.2

The following information relates to the Really Hopeful Company. This company needs to adjust their accounts for the following items in accordance with standard practice.

Financial Leases

This year a finance lease was entered into as follows:

non - cancellable agreement, with a five year primary period and an unspecified secondary period.

the outright purchase of the asset would have resulted in a capital cost of £345,000;

rentals will be paid quarterly and each quarter will be £22,000;

the company believe the asset will last for a maximum seven years, at which stage it might be possible to realise £30,000 from the asset sale;

the company have decided to depreciate the asset on a straight line basis but will calculate the repayment of lease obligations on rentals on the sum of digits method.

Required

You should:

a)   Calculate the depreciation on the asset and show an abstract of the balance sheet over the primary period;

b)   Prepare a schedule which identifies the split of rental payments on a yearly basis between operating expenses and repayment obligation;

c)   by way of a balance sheet extract over the primary period show the gradual repayment of lease obligation, and the split between current and non-current obligation;

d)   Prepare a statement which will show the charges to Profit and Loss Account over the primary period;

e)   Explain the method of presentation and rationale behind the required treatment of finance leases, and contrast with the requirement regarding operational leases, and loan finance:

f)   Explain the reason for finance lease account adjustments being related to the primary period.

g)   Consider the entries had a loan been raised rather than a lease negotiated. The loan would have annual EIP of £69,000 and carry an interest coupon of 9.17874% computed on the opening outstanding loan balances. Which would you recommend the loan or the lease.

CHAPTER 4

Cash Flow Statement
Financial Reporting Standard 1

Introduction

The Statements of Accounting, which provide shareholders and proprietors with the vital accounting information required to evaluate performance are, of course, the profit and loss account and the balance sheet. However, these statements do not provide information related to the movement of cash. Furthermore it can often be cash flow problems that lead to the demise of a business rather than profitability.

Source and Application of Funds Statement

The important of reporting cash movements has long been recognised, and SSAP 10 issued in 1975 required all business enterprises with a turnover of £25,000 or more per annum to provide a source and Application of Funds Statement as part of their audited accounts.

In the standard SSAP 10 no prescribed statement existed although it was necessary to show the following items separately where material:

    (i)   dividends paid;

    (ii)   acquisitions and disposals of fixed and other non current assets;

  (iii)   issues and redemption of shares and loans;

  (iv)   increase and decrease in working capital, sub divided into its components and movements in net liquid funds.

SSAP 10 survived until the Financial Reporting Council introduced the new cash flow statement which came into force for periods ending on or after 23 March 1992, although it could have been used earlier if a business wished.

The techniques involved in producing a Cash Flow Statement are much the same as those applied in preparing a Source and Application of Funds Statement, but the presentation requirement is considerably different.

The main criticisms of SSAP 10 were that it did not provide a standard format and this led to many different approaches to the presentation. It did not concentrate directly on cash movements but required book adjustments and movements in working capital to be analysed. Many believed the statement could be confusing to the user of accounting information.

The Issue of Finance Reporting Standard 1

The Accounting Standards Board issued its first Financial Reporting Standard on Cash Flow Statements. Although it is derived from ED 54, the exposure draft issued in the last year of the old Accounting Standards Committee, the Financial Reporting

Standard is substantial different in approach; whereas a cash flow statement under ED54 could have been described as a re-formatted statement of source and application of funds, a purer cash flow statement is now required, from which non-cash transactions are completely excluded.

FRS 1 supersedes SSAP 10 - Statements of source and application of funds. It became mandatory for accounting periods ending on or after 23 March 1992. Full comparative figures are required.

FRS1 requires a cash flow statement to be presented as one of the primary financial statements by all enterprises whose accounts are intended to show a true and fair view. However, there are substantial exemptions, which mean that many companies will not have to present such a statement. The following are exempt:

Small companies entitled to the accounts filing exemptions set out in Ss.246 and 247 of the Companies Act (or equivalent Northern Irish legislation). Broadly, these are companies which satisfy two of the following test:

- turnover not more than £2 million;

- balance sheet total not more than £975,000;

- not more than fifty employees.

However, PLCs, banks, insurance companies and companies authorised under the Financial Services Act do not qualify for the exemption, nor do members of a group which contains any of these types of company (unless they qualify because they are wholly owned subsidiaries - see below).

Other small enterprises i.e those which are not companies but otherwise meet the above tests.

Wholly owned subsidiaries of EC parents which publish consolidated accounts in English under the Seventh Directive and these consolidated accounts include a cash flow statement which substantially complies with FRS 1.

Building Societies which are required by law to produce a statement of source and application of funds.

Mutual life insurance companies. Other insurance companies are not exempt, but should include the cash flows of their long term business only to the extent that the cash flows are those of the company itself, rather than of the long term funds.

Since FRS 1 could be applied early, it follows that enterprises which meet any of these exemptions could immediately dispense with a SSAP 10 funds statement if they wish to. However, it should be remembered that the exemption for wholly owned subsidiaries can only be taken if the parent has produced a cash flow statement under FRS 1 for the relevant period. This is one reason why it may be advantageous for the parent to adopt the statement early.
The standard requires that the statement should list all the inflows and outflows of cash (and cash equivalent) classified under the following headings:

Operating activities;

Returns on investments and servicing of finance;

Taxation;

Investing activities;

Financing.

Guidance is given on what falls into each of these categories. Cash flows relating to exceptional or extraordinary items should also generally be shown under the above headings, with sufficient disclosure in the notes to explain their effect.

Cash is defined as cash in hand together with cash on deposit with banks and other financial institutions which is repayable on demand.

Cash equivalents are defined as short term, highly liquid investments which are readily convertible into known amounts of cash without notice and which were within three months of maturity when acquired, less advances from banks repayable within three months from the date when the advance was made/ Note cash and cash equivalents may be denominated in sterling or in foreign currencies.

As stated above, non-cash transactions, such as acquisitions for shares or the conversion into equity of convertible loan stock will not appear in the cash flow statement. However, the standard calls for footnote disclosure of major non-cash transactions. Often, such disclosures will already be made elsewhere in the accounts and an additional note may not be required, although a suitable cross reference may have to be made.

Cash Flow Statements (FRS 1)

A Cash Flow Statement is required to show where cash has been generated and how cash has been used during the accounting period. The statement in summary form is prepared to ensure the focus of attention is always on cash movements and shows the final figure in the statement as increase or decrease in cash and cash equivalents.

Logical Presentation

The statement (FRS 1) starts with a figure described as

Heading 1 - Net Cash Flow from Operating Activities

This figure is related to the trading operation of the business for the year. However, the figure used is an adjusted profit for the year figure, the adjustments being to convert the profit figure to a cash figure.

Why is Profit not the Same as Cash Movement?

The reasons why profit is not the same as cash should be obvious to students. The profit is calculated on the basis of the following:

- matching concept;

- include book entries.

Matching Concept

Profit is calculated to take account of amounts receivable and payable. The profit and loss account is therefore not a payments and receipts account. For example, if we take sales, the amount included in the P&L account for sales will be the sales made during the period. However, all sales would not have been made for cash. It would follow therefore to find the cash generated by sales in the year regard would need to be had to the indebtedness of customers as follows:

Sales Example

ABC Plc made £400,000 of sales during 1991/92, however, debtors for sales on 1 April 1991 were £35,000 and on the 31 March 1992 were £50,000.

It can now be seen that cash received would not be £400,000 as follows:

	£
Debtors @ 1/4/91	35,000
Plus sales during 1991/92	400,000
	435,000
Less	
Debtors @ 31/3/92	50,000
Cash received	385,000

Therefore, for the purposes of cash flow we would be interested in the figure of £385,000,while in the P&L account the figure of £400,000 would be required.

It would also be necessary to adjust profit for the change in creditors and stock to convert the figure for profit to cash and this can be demonstrated as follows:

Accrued Expenses and Creditors

ABC PLc were due to pay their instalments of business rates during 1991/92. However, due to delay in making the final two instalments, only eight were paid. One instalment from 1990/91 was paid during 1991/92. Each instalment due in 1991/92 was for £1,500. The instalment paid in 1991/92 for 1990/91 was £1,200.

Compare the amount recorded in P&L account with the cash movement.
Solution

The amount which needs to be included in the P&L account is the sum due in 1991/92. This is simple to calculate being 10 x £1,500 = £15,000.

The cash paid in 1991/92 can be found as follows:

```
                                              £
Accrued expenses @ 1/4/91
(1x £1,200)                                1,200
Plus amount payable in 1991/92            15,000
                                          16,200


Less
Accrued expenses @ 31/3/92
(2x £1,500)                                3,000
                                          _____
                    Cash paid             13,200
                                          =======
```

This example applies equally to other payments including the
purchases of the business.

Stock Movements

Finally an integral part of the matching concept is that the
commodities used up in the accounting period must be recorded as
expenses, but any stocks which are available to benefit the
company in a future period should not be regarded as an expense.
In this way only costs related to the business activity of the
year are accounted for and matched in the year.

Example - Stocks Held

ABC Plc had stocks at 1 April 1991 of £25,000. while at the end
of the year 31 March 1992 stocks were £50,000. Purchases were
£200,000 and were all paid for in cash.

How much would be charged to the profit and loss account and to
what degree would this differ to cash movements.

Solution

The P&L account would be required to record the cost of goods
sold as follows:

```
                                    £
    Opening Stock               25,000
    Plus Purchases             200,000
                               _____
                               225,000
    Less
    Closing stock               50,000
                               _____
    Cost of goods sold         175,000
                               ========
```

However, the cash movement would have been far greater. This is
due to the fact that the cost of goods sold only records
purchases made and used, the increase in stock has been deducted
off of the purchases to match the cost of good sold to sales
made.

It therefore follows that the cash movement will be the
following:
                                    £

Closing stock	50,000	
Less		
Opening stock	25,000	

	25,000	
Plus cost of goods sold	175,000	

Cash payments	200,000	

These examples comparing profit and loss figures to cash movement figures demonstrate that the adjustments necessary to the profit figures to find the cash movements are related to the changes in the following:

- increase or decrease in debtors;

- increase or decrease in creditors / accruals;

- increase or decrease in stocks.

The second problem associated with using profit as cash figure is that book entries find their way into the profit and loss account, even though they do not involve the movement of funds. Consider the following two aspects:

purchase of fixed assets;

sale of fixed assets.

Purchase of Fixed Assets

When fixed assets are purchased the profit and loss account does not record the expenditure. The reason for this is that it would be unfair to burden the profit for the current year with all the costs of purchasing an asset which may last many years (say ten years). The matching concept requires profit to be effected by an assessment of the wearing out of the asset during that accounting period. This of course is depreciation. Let us now use an example to demonstrate the cash movement when fixed assets are purchased as opposed to the effect on profit.

Example - Purchase of Fixed Asset

ABC Plc purchases a production machine for £50,000 on 1 April 1991 and have agreed a policy of depreciation over ten years, assuming no residual value. The depreciation is to be provided on a straight line basis.

Solution

The cash movement is clear it must be £50,000. However this will not be included in the profit calculation. We must therefore ensure that the payments associated with the purchase of fixed assets are recorded in the cash flow statement and this will be done in a section known as 'INVESTING ACTIVITIES' to which we will refer to later in this section.

The profit and loss account would have been effected by a charge for depreciation as follows:

$$\frac{£50,000}{10 \text{ years}} = £5,000$$

	Dr £	Cr £
P&L A/C Depreciation	5,000	
Accumulated Depreciation A/C		5,000

being the journal to provide a charge for the wearing out of the asset in the year 1991/92, against the profit for the year.

NB   This is not a real cash movement, it simply involves a book entry.

It is therefore necessary when taking a profit figure for the year to remove any non-cash movements like depreciation.

Example - Sale of Fixed Asset

A fixed asset was sold on 1 April 1991 for £60,000. This asset had originally been purchased for £70,000 and accumulated depreciation to the date of sale was £25,000.

Solution

The cash figure required in the cash flow statement is of course the amount received in proceeds from the sale £60,000.

However, this receipt would never be recorded in the P&L account just as the purchase of fixed assets would never be recorded in P&L account.

The £60,000 will appear in the 'INVESTING ACTIVITIES' section of the cash flow statement.

Our problem now is to determine what adjustments are required to the figure produced as profit for 1991/92/

Sales of fixed assets are accounted for in the profit and loss account by recording any profit or loss resulting from the disposal. The entries made to establish profit or loss would be as follows:

-    transfer the cost of the asset disposed of to the disposal account;

-    transfer depreciation provided to date on the asset to the disposal account;

-    record the cash proceeds in the disposal account;

-    any remaining balance on the disposal account represents a profit or loss on the sale of the asset.

In our example, the following would be our disposal account for 1991/92.

Disposal Account

	£		£
Fixed Asset Cost	70,000	Accumulated Depreciation	25,000
		CASH PROCEEDS	60,000
			85,000
			=======

It can be seen that the missing figure is £15,000 which represents the profit on sale of fixed asset. This would be journalled to the profit and loss account as follows:

	Dr £	Cr £
Disposal account	15,000	
Profit and loss account		15,000

being the profit on disposal and closure of the asset disposal account.

NB   The entry to the profit and loss account is not a real cash movement. We must therefore remove any entry made to the profit and loss account for profit or losses on sale of fixed assets _if_ we are trying to find the cash movement from trading, which we are for the purposes of the cash flow statement.

Students will undoubtedly come across other entries which do not involve the movement of funds, such as the issue of bonus shares and other movement in reserves. The principle must be followed always when adjusting the profit and loss account to reflect real cash flow operations remove book entries.

Summary - Net Cash From Operating Activities

In the financial reporting standard on cash flow statements, the first figure that must appear is the net cash flow from operating activities. This figure is after adjusting for the following.

Fig 1 - Operating Profit Note

	£000
Operating Profit	6,000
ADJUSTMENTS	
- Depreciation	900
- Loss on sale of fixed assets	10
- Increase in stock	(200)
- Increase in debtors	(100)
- Increase in creditors	300
NET CASH INFLOWS FROM OPERATING ACTIVITY	6,910

The figure £6,910,000 is the only figure which should appear on the face of the cash flow statement if the student is preparing an indirect method of cash flow statements. Fig 1. is a note on operating profit and must be given by way of a note to the accounts.

Direct Method of Showing Cash Flow from Operating

An alternative to stating one figure in the cash flow statement is the direct method of stating cash flow from operating. The direct method shows payments and receipts such as:

> cash received from customers;
>
> cash paid to suppliers;
>
> cash paid to employees etc.

If the direct method is used by a business they must still show in the notes to the accounts the information set out in Fig 1. which reconciles the net cash flow to the profit for the year.

Heading 2 - Net Cash Flow from Returns on Investments and Servicing of Finance

Within this heading the following items would appear:

> Interest Received
> Interest Paid
> Dividend Paid

Care would need to be taken when preparing this item from information which is available in a general question. For example, you must take amounts paid and received not the figures for amounts payable and receivable.

An example using dividends would be as follows:

Dividends Paid

Dividends are appropriated from annual profits, but they may not be paid out to shareholders during the year. An item for dividend proposed may appear in the closing balance sheet of the business at its year end. These dividends will soon be paid but not until the next accounting year is under way.

It is therefore likely that cash paid in a year say 1991/92 might be the final dividend proposed for 1990/91 and the interim dividends for 1991/92.

The most convenient method of calculating dividend paid is as follows:

		£
Current Liability Balance Sheet figure for proposed dividend @ 31/3/91		30,000

Add
All dividends paid and proposed
for 1991/92   90,000

Subtract
The final dividend for 1991/92 proposed
but not paid shown as a <u>current liability</u> @ 31/3/92   (40,000)
DIVIDEND ACTUALLY PAID OUT IN THE YEAR   80,000
                                                               ======

Summary - <u>Heading</u> - Returns on Investment and Servicing Finance

This heading deals with interest income and interest payments as
well as dividends. However, it is the cash paid and received
that is recorded.

<u>Heading 3</u> - Tax Paid

You must remember that taxation charged against profit for the
year will <u>not</u> be paid in the same year. Taxation is paid on the
profit in years later than the current year. The amount of tax
paid needs to be calculated in questions. The best approach is
as follows.

i)   Add all the tax liabilities in the balance sheet at the
        start of the year together (including deferred tax,
        advanced corporation tax and corporation tax).

ii)   To (i) above add the amounts recorded as due in respect
        of the current year, recorded in the profit and loss
        account.

iii)   Deduct the end of year liability from the sum of (i)
        and (ii) above. This will give you the figure of tax
        paid for the year.

Example Tax Paid

	31 March	
	1991 £	1992 £
Corporation Tax Due	110,000	140,000
Balance on deferred tax a/c	10,000	8,000
ACT payable	15,000	30,000

The profit and loss account for the year reveals tax due of
£120,000. The amount paid is therefore as follows:

	£
Amount due 31/3/91	135,000
Plus amount due for 1991/92	120,000
	225,000
Less	
Amount outstanding 31/3/92	178,000
Amount paid in 1991/92	77,000
	======

The amount to be recorded in the cash flow statement is therefore £77,000.

Summary - Heading 3 - Tax Paid

Care needs to be taken to establish the tax paid rather than the taxation payable. Tax payments are normally made in subsequent years and therefore it is important to consider the necessary calculations to arrive at the tax paid figure.

Heading 4 - Investing Activities

This heading deals with the following cash movements.

- Payments to acquire intangible fixed assets.
- Payments to acquire tangible fixed assets.
- Receipts from the sale of tangible fixed assets

This heading has been covered when the topic of operating activities was discussed. It is here that the proceeds from sales and the payment for capital spending needs to be recorded.

Heading 5 - Financing

This heading deals with the following:

- issue of ordinary share capital;

- issue of debentures;

- repurchase of debenture loans;

- expenses paid in connection with share issues.

These items are normally relatively easy to find from comparing the opening balance sheet with the closing balance sheet and identifying the movement. There will of course be some complication, like for instance where bonus shares have been issued and no cash is involved.

The Cash Flow Statement (FRS1) example format.

The following statements are provided to enable the reader to see the basic requirement with example figures.

ABC Plc - Example Figures

Cash Flow Statement for the Year Ending 31 March 1992

	£000	£000
Net cash from operating activities		6,500
RETURNS ON INVESTMENT AND SERVICING OF FINANCE		
- Interest received	3,000	
- Interest paid	(1,000)	
- Dividends paid	(1,250)	750
TAXATION		
Tax paid		(1,100)
INVESTING ACTIVITIES		
- Payments to acquire tangible fixed assets	(1,300)	
- Receipts from sale of fixed assets	300	
Net cash outflow from investing activities		(1,000)
Net cash inflow before financing		5,150
FINANCING		
Issue of share capital	100	
Redemption of debenture loan	(1,000)	(900)
Increase in cash and cash equivalents		4,250

Notes Required for Cash Flow Statement

- Reconciliation of operating profit to net cash inflow from operating activities.

This note would start with the figure for profit for the year and take account of:

- changes in stock, debtors and creditors;
- effect of book entries.

Note 1 The Note might appear as follows:

	£	£
Operating profit		7,100
Add Depreciation	1,200	
Loss on sale FA	100	1,300
Less Increase in stock	(500)	
Increase in debtors	(400)	
Decrease in creditors	(1,000)	(1,900)
Net cash inflow from operating activities		6,500

Notes would also be required which should show the change in cash equivalents and these might be as follows:

Note 2   Analysis of the cash and cash equivalents shown in the balance sheet

	1992 £000	1991 £000	Change £000
Cash at bank and in hand	500	700	(200)
Short term investments	24,455	20,000	4,455
Bank overdraft	(10)	(5)	(5)
	24,945	20,695	4,250

Note 3   Analysis of change in cash and cash equivalents for 1991/92

	£000
Balance @ 1/4/91	20,695
Net Cash inflow 1991/92	4,250
Balance @ 31/3/92	24,945

Note 4   Analysis of changes in financing during 1991/92

	Share Capital Including Premium £000	Debenture Loan £000
Balance @ 1/4/91	6,900	10,100
Cash inflow (outflow)	100	(1,000)
Balance @ 31/3/92	7,000	9,100

At this stage we can undertake some reasonably comprehensive examples.

The next two examples are provided to enable the process of preparing the statements to be understood.

Exercise 4.1

Example 1 is called "Pork Pie" and is a reasonably simple example.

Exercise 4.2

Example 2 is called "Supertec Plc" and is much more difficult example complicated with taxation and dividends.

These examples are followed by examination questions which students can practice upon.

Example Question 4.1

Pork Pie Plc

The balance sheet of Pork Pie Plc for this and the previous years are as follows:

The managing director finds it difficult to understand why in a year of profitable trading the firm's bank account has become overdrawn.

BALANCE SHEET

	Year Ended 30.9.91		Year Ended 30.9.92		
	£000	£000	£000	£000	£000
SOURCES OF CAPITAL FUNDS					
Share Capital					
£1 ordinary shares		500		500	
10% preference shares				250	750
Revenue Reserve		250			500
		750			1,250
		===			=====
EMPLOYMENT OF FUNDS					
Fixed Assets					
Land		500			960
Plant and Machinery	900			600	
Less: accumulated dep'n	500	400		200	400
Current Assets					
Stock	600			700	
Sundry debtors	500			860	
Cash at bank	200			___	
	1,300			1,560	
Less: current liabilities					
Sundry Creditors	1,390		1,100		
Bank overdraft		(90)	200	1,300	
					260
Total assets less current liabilities		810			1,620
Less: amounts falling due after more than one year-10% Debentures		60			370
		750			1,250
		====			======

Machinery purchases of £200,000 were made in the year and depreciation for the year has been provided in the above figures. Some old machines which originally cost £500,000 were sold. Accumulated depreciation on these totalled £400,000 and cash received was equal to the written down value of the machines.

NB Debenture interest due for the year and paid was £30,000
Bank interest due and paid for the year was £12,000.

Required: Prepare a cash flow statement in accordance with FRS1.

Tutorial Answer - Pork Pie Plc

The first step is to prepare the note required to support the heading known as **"net cash flow from operating activity"**.

The steps to be taken are as follows:

* Establish the profit for the year

* Adjust the profit to remove book entries

* Adjust the profit to remove items shown on the face of the cash flow statement

* Convert profit to cash via adjustments for increases and decreases in stocks, debtors and creditors.

Identify Profit for Year

Profit can be found by identifying the change in revenue reserves. This sum is £250,000.

Remove Book Entries from the Profit for the Year

The best way of identifying book entries for depreciation and profits and loss on sale of assets is to draw up fixed asset accounts and disposal accounts. The following is the fixed asset account and disposal account for Machinery.

	Fixed Asset Plant and Machinery				Depreciation Account Plant and Machinery		
	£000		£000		£000		£000
1/10/91 bal b/fwd	900	Dispoal	500	Disposal	400	1/10/91 bal b/fwd	500
purchases		bal c/fwd	600				
CASH	200						
	1,100		1,100				
	=====		=====				

	Disposal Account Plant and Machinery		
	£000		£000
Fixed Asset a/c	500	Depreciation a/c	400
		Cash	100
	500		500
	====		====

NB There are therefore no Profits or Losses on disposal.

Calculation of Depreciation Charged to the Profit and Loss Account

The ledger account for depreciation has not been closed off. At present the balance is £100,000. However, on the closing balance sheet the account balance is £200,000. Therefore the missing entry in the depreciation account must be as follows:

	DR £	CR £
P&L Account	100,000	
Accumulated depreciation		100,000

This is the missing entry, the action required on the cash flow statement is to add back this sum to the profit figure.

Adjust the profit to remove items to be shown on the face of the cash flow statement

The Pork Pie Plc has no taxation or dividends in the question to make it a simple example.

It is necessary to remove the amount of interest due from the profit and loss account, and record interest paid on the face of the cash flow under the heading "Returns on Investment and Servicing Finance".

The amount of interest to be added back to profit in this year are £30,000 for debentures and £12,000 for bank interest.

Convert profit to cash via adjusting for changes in stock debtors and creditors

Stocks have increased from £600,000 to £100,000 an increase of £100,000. This effectively is an application of cash i.e an outgoing.

Debtors have increased from £500,000 to £860,000 an increase of £360,000. This is effectively as outflow financing debtors and results in less cash received than recorded in the profit statement.

Creditors have reduced from £1,390,000 to £1,100,000 a reduction of £290,000. This is effectively an outflow of cash from paying cash to creditors.

We can now prepare the note on Net Cash Flow from operations as follows:

Note 1   **Net Cash From Operating Activities**

	£000	£000
Profit for the year		250
<u>Add back</u> book entry for depreciation		<u>100</u>
		350
<u>Add back</u> charges for interest		
- debentures	30	
- bank interest	<u>12</u>	
		<u>42</u>
		392

Adjustment for changes in stock, debtors, creditors

- increase in stock	100 (-)		
- increase in debtors	360 (-)		
- reduction in creditors	<u>290</u> (-)	<u>750</u> (-)	

Net cash out flow from operating activities	358 (-)

Preparation of Cash Flow Statement

It is now possible to prepare the statement as follows:

<u>Cash Flow Statement for Pork Pie Plc for the year ending 30/9/92</u>

		£000	£000
1	Net Cash outflow from		358 (-)
2	Return on investments and servicing finance		
	- debenture interest paid	30 (-)	
	- bank interest paid	<u>12</u> (-)	42 (-)
3	Taxation paid		nil
4	Investing Activities		
	Purchase of fixed assets		
	Land	460 (-)	
	Plant and Machinery	200 (-)	
	Proceeds from sale	100 (+)	560 (-)
5	Financing Activities		
	issue of Preference Shares	250 +	
	debentures raised	<u>310</u> +	560 (+)
	Change in cash and cash equivalents		400 (-)

This cash flow statement can be reconciled as follows:

Note 2   **Analysis of Cash and Cash Equivalent shown in the Balance Sheet**

	1992 £000	1991 £000	Change £000
Cash at bank	–	200	(200) A
Bank overdraft	200	–	(200) A
	200	200	(400) adverse

Note 3   **Analysis of Change in Financing during 1991/92**

	Share Capital £000	Debenture Loans £000	Preference Shares £000
Balance @ 30/9/91	500	60	–
Cash inflow (outflow)	–	310	250
Balance @ 30/9/92	500	370	250

The presentation of this answer shows the actual cash flow statement in between the notes. This was obviously for explanation purposes and the statement itself is a prime financial statement to be shown along with the Profit and Loss Account and the Balance Sheet.

The next example is Supertec Plc and is rather more difficult, it is useful to consider a further problem before attempting the question related to Development Costs.

Development Costs

Development Costs can under strict rules be capitalised in the balance sheet of a company. In the question Supertec development cost have been paid during the financial year. At the same time some development costs have been depreciated in the Profit and Loss Account.

The entry to the Profit and Loss Account is a book entry the actual payments can be found by considering the change in the reported balance sheet amount for such costs, after taking account of the depreciation entry for such costs.

An Example

XYZ Co extract from Balance Sheet

	1992 £000	1991 £000
Intangible assets -Development Costs	150	110

The XYZ Company had charged £10,000 to P&L account related to depreciation of assets classified as development costs.

To work out the cash payments we need to understand, that had the £10,000 depreciation not been provided, the closing balance would have been £160,000 the increase being £50,000. Therefore cash paid would have been £50,000.

The action required for cash flow purposes is therefore to add back the depreciation charge in the calculation of the **"Net Cash Flow from Operating Activity"**, and show the cash paid as an investing activity.

Exercise 4.2 Example Supertec Plc

The following are extracts from the financial statement of Supertec Plc, a company engaged in development and sale of computer software.

Balance Sheet as on 31 March

	1992		1991	
	£000	£000	£000	£000
Fixed Assets				
Development Costs		107		93
Freehold land		1,200		900
Plant and Machinery		390		423
Investments (at cost)		240		250
		1,937		1,666
Current Assets				
Stock	670		580	
Debtors	410		520	
Short-term investments	114		56	
Cash	13		29	
	1,207		1,185	
Current Liabilities				
Bank overdraft	159		436	
Trade creditors	390		350	
Taxation	55		40	
Proposed dividend	30		25	
	634		851	
Net Current Assets		573		334
		2,510		2,000
12% debentures		(500)		(600)
		2,010		1,400

	1992	1991
	£000	£000
Capital and Reserves		
Share capital		
50p ordinary shares	1,200	1,000
Reserves		
share premium	100	50
Land revaluation	300	-
Undistributed profit	410	350
	2,010	1,400

Profit and Loss Appropriation Account for the year ended 31 March 1992

	£000	£000
Net profit before tax		160
Tax		60
Profit after tax		100
Dividends		
Interim (paid)	10	
Final (proposed)	30	
		40
Retained profit for the year		60

Notes: The following items provide essential information for the preparation of the cash flow statement.

1 Profit for the year is after charging: £000

    Depreciation on plant and machinery   77
    Development expenditure   6

2 During the year, plant with a Net Book Value of £50,000 was sold for £98,000. The assets had originally cost £200,000.

3 Debenture interest paid and payable was £66,000.

4 Investment income received and receivable was £11,000.

Approach Required to this Question

The first step is to try to prepare the note required to convert operating profit to net cash inflow from operating activity. This requires the following:

Profit includes book entries for

- depreciation;
- development expenditure;
- profit on the sale of plant.

We must remove these from profit.

The next step is to remove from profit and loss items which will appear elsewhere on the cash flow statement:

- interest paid;
- investment income.

Finally the adjustment for matching need to be accounted for to establish real payments and receipts. This involves adjusting for:
- stock;
- debtors;
- creditors.
Note 1 can now be shown and the workings are shown for the cash flow statement.

Note 1

Reconciliation of Operating Profit to Net Cash Inflows from Operating Activities.

	£000	£000
Operating profit for 1991/92 before tax		160
Remove interest paid and received-paid	66	
-received	(11)	55
ADD BACK		
Depreciation on P&M	77	
Development expenditure	6	83
<u>Deduct</u> profit on sale**		(48)
ADJUSTMENT for working capital		
Stock increased	(90)	
Reduced debtors	110	
Increased creditors	40	60
NET CASH INFLOW FROM OPERATING ACTIVITY		310

Workings

SALE OF ASSET - PLANT

Net Book Value
(fixed Asset A/C - Depreciation)

1/4/91 bal b/f	423,000	Net Book Value sale	50,000
*		Depreciation for the year	77,000
Capital Investment Cash		bal c/d	390,000
			517,000

Profit on sale is as follows:

	£000
Cash proceeds	98
<u>Less</u> Net Book Value	50
**Profit on sale	48

* This figure is derived as the only figure missing on the Net Book Value Account and is £94,000 capital investment.

	£000	£000

Working Dividends Paid

	£000	£000
Dividends proposed 31/3/91		25
Dividends during 1991/92		
- Paid	10	
- Proposed	30	40
		65
Less		
Proposed dividend liability on balance sheet @ 31/3/92		30
Dividend Paid		35

Working Tax Paid

	£000
Taxation liability 31/3/91	40
Tax due 1991/92	60
	100
Less	
Taxation liability 31/3/92	55
Tax Paid	45

Working Development Costs

	£000
Development Costs @ 31/3/91	93
Less	
Charged to P&L a/c in 1991/92	(6)
	87
Less	
Development costs @ 31/3/92	107
Cash Paid	20

Supertec Plc

Cash Flow Statement for the Year Ending 31 March 1992

	£000	£000
NET CASH FLOW FROM OPERATING ACTIVITIES		310
RETURN ON INVESTMENT AND SERVICING OF FINANCING		
- Investment interest received	11	
- 12% debenture interest paid	(66)	
- Dividends paid	(35)	
	─────	(90)
TAXATION		
Tax Paid		(45)
INVESTING ACTIVITIES		
- Payments to acquire fixed assets	(94)	
- Payments regarding development	(20)	
- Receipts - sale of investments (assume no profit or loss)	10	
- Receipts - sale of plant and machinery	98	(6)
	─────	─────
Net cash inflow before financing		169
FINANCING		
Issue of Share Capital	200	
Share premium	50	
Repayment of debenture	(100)	
	────	150
		─────
Increase in cash and cash equivalents		319
		===

Note 2   **Analysis of the cash and cash equivalents shown in the balance sheet**

	1992 £000	1991 £000	Change £000
Cash at bank	13	29	(16)
Short term investments	114	56	58
Bank overdraft	(159)	(436)	277
	(32)	(351)	319

Note 3   **Analysis of change in cash and cash equivalents for 1991/92**

	£000
Balance @ 1/4/91	(351)
Net cash inflow 1991/92	319
Balance @ 31/3/92	(32)

Note 4   **Analysis of change in financing during 1991/92**

	Share Capital Including Premium £000	Debenture Loan £000
Balance @ 1/4/91	1,050	600
Cash inflow (outflow)	250	(100)
Balance @ 31/3/92	1,300	500

Examination Question 4.1

The following are extracts from the financial statement of Fastfood Plc.

Balance Sheets as on 31 March

	1992 £000	1992 £000	1991 £000	1991 £000
Fixed Assets				
Development costs		10		–
Freehold Land		1,400		1,100
Plant and machinery		500		400
Investments (at cost)		30		50
		1,940		1,550
Current Assets				
Stock	200		150	
Debtors	320		100	
Cash	100		20	
	620		270	
Current Liabilities				
Trade Creditors	120		240	
Taxation	40		20	
Proposed dividend	30		15	
	190		275	
Net Current Assets		430		(5)
		2,370		1,545
12% debentures		200		100
		2,170		1,445

	1992 £000	1991 £000
Capital and reserves		
Share capital		
50p ordinary shares	1,200	1,100
Reserves		
Share premium	470	295
Land revaluation	300	–
Undistributed profit	200	50
	2,170	1,445

Profit and Loss Appropriation Account for the year ended 31 March 1992

	£000	£000
Net profit before tax		240
Tax		50
		___
Profit after tax		190
Dividends		
Interim (paid)	10	
Final (proposed)	30	
	___	
		40
		___
Retained profit for the year		150
		___

Notes:

1   Profit for the year is after charging: £000

	£000
Depreciation on plant and machinery	50
Development expenditure	nil

2   During the year, plant the a Net Book Value of £55,000 was sold for £16,000. The assets has originally cost £70,000

3   Debenture interest paid and payable was £13,500

4   Investment income received and receivable was £4,000

Examination Question 4.2

Dog Plc

The financial statements of Funds Ltd are summarised below:

Balance Sheets as at	31.3.91 £000	31.3.91 £000	31.3.92 £000	31.3.92 £000
Share capital and reserves				
Called-up share capital		700		1,000
Share premium account		-		94
General reserve		100		120
Profit and loss account		160		200
		960		1,414
		====		=====
Fixed Assets				
Freehold premises		200		294
Plant and machinery		200		250
		400		544
Current Assets				
Stocks	500		900	
Debtors	250		300	
Balance at bank	300		70	
	1050		1270	
Current liabilities				
Creditors	290		400	
Net Current Assets		760		870
		1,160		1,414
Debenture loan		200		-
		960		1,414
		======		=====

Changes in fixed assets

	Freehold Premises £000	Plant and Machinery £000
Cost		
as at 31 March 1991	210	400
additions	100	170
	310	570
Less cost of assets disposed of during the year	-	70
As at 31 March 1992	310	500
	====	====

	£000	£000
Depreciation		
As at 31 March 1991	10	200
Depreciation charged in the year	6	70
	16	270
Less depreciation provided in respect of		
assets disposed of during the year	-	20
	16	250

As at 31 March 1992

Profit and Loss Account for the year ended 31 March 1992

Profit before dealing with the following items		146
Less Depreciation	76	
Loss on sale of fixed assets	10	
		86
Profit for the year		60
Transfer to general reserve		20
Balance brought forward		40
Balance carried forward		160
		200

Debenture interest for 1991/92 was £10,000 and has been included in the profit calculation.

Required:

A Cash Flow Statement for Dog plc in the format required by the FRS1, for the year ending 31 March 1992.

Examination Question 4.3

The Financial statement of Squiff Limited are summarised below:

Balance Sheets as at 31 March	1991 £000	1992 £000
Fixed Assets		
Freehold premises	700	800
Motor vehicles	100	120
	800	920
Current Assets		
Stock	400	800
Debtors	200	150
Bank	250	85
	850	1,035
Creditors: amounts falling due within one year		
Trade creditors	230	410
Net Current Assets	620	625
Total assets less current liabilities	1,420	1,545
Creditors: amount falling due after one year		
Debenture loans	200	100
	1,220	1,445
Capital and Reserves		
Ordinary share capital	700	800
Share premium account		100
General reserve	400	400
Profit and loss account	120	145
	1,220	1,445

Movements on Fixed Asset Accounts

	Freehold Premises at cost £000	Motor Vehicles at cost £000
As at 31 March 1991	700	160
Additions	100	100
	800	260
Less: Cost of assets disposed during year		40
At at 31 March 1992	800	220

Depreciation of Motor Vehicles

£000

```
As at 31 March 1991                               60
Depreciation charged in year                      60
                                                 ----
                                                 120

Less: depreciation provided in respect
      of assets disposed of                       20
                                                 ----
As at 31 March 1992                              100
                                                 ----
```

Profit and Loss Account for the year ended 31 March 1992

```
Profit before dealing with the following         100
items

Less: depreciation                                60
      loss on sale of fixed assets                15
                                                 ----
Profit for the year                               25
                                                 ----
```

Debenture interest already charged to the P&L a/c was £15,000.

Required:

A Cash Flow Statement in accordance with FRS1.

Examination Question 4

Caroline Brown Ltd

The summarised balance sheets of Caroline Brown Ltd for each of the two years ended 31 December 1991 and 1992 are set out below.

	At December	
	1991	1992
	£	£
Fixed Assets:		
Cost	90,000	140,000
Depreciation	30,000	54,000
	60,000	86,000
Current Assets:		
Stocks	42,500	55,700
Debtors	28,750	34,200
Bank	19,250	7,300
	90,500	97,200
Less: Creditors falling due within one year		
Creditors	27,500	37,800
Corporation Tax	12,000	15,000
Proposed Dividends	6,000	12,000
Loan	10,000	-
	55,250	64,800
Total Assets Less Current Liabilities	95,250	118,400
Financed by:		
Share Capital and Reserves		
Share Capital and £1 Ordinary shares	30,000	40,000
Share premium	-	5,000
Distributable Reserves	65,250	73,400
	95,250	118,400

Notes:

1   The loan was repaid at par during the year ended 31 December 1992.

2   10,000 be £1 Ordinary shares were issued at a premium of 50% during the year ended 31 December 1992.

3   Fixed assets were sold during the year under review for proceeds of £7,000. They had a cost value of £10,000 and the disposal gave rise to a figure of £1,000 for depreciation over - provided.

4   The Corporation Tax outstanding at 31 December 1991 was settled during the year ended 31 December for a payment of £12,500.

5   No interim dividend was paid during the year.

Required:

A Cash Flow Statement for Caroline Brown Ltd for the ended 31 December 1992.

Chapter 5

Company Accounting an Introduction

Introduction

The subject of company accounting requires extensive knowledge if accounts are to be prepared in accordance with the Companies Acts and best accounting practice.

It is considered appropriate to provide three chapters on this subject. The first is an introduction which explains the basic legal constitution of companies, a general explanation of terms used in company accounting.

Examples are provided which do not require the full published form of company accounting but introduce the basic layout of the financial statements.

A second chapter on company accounting follows which concentrates on the minimum requirements of the Companies Act with precise formats and consideration of the notes required to published accounts. The requirements of FRS3 are also included.

The third chapter provides information on complexities of company accounting such as taxation, and a number of examination questions and answers.

Approach in the Chapter to Company Accounting

The topic will be approached as follows:

* An outline is given of the general terms used in Company Accounting;

* Accounting for the issue of Company Shares is considered;

* A simple question preparing company accounts is provided;

* Questions are provided for students to test themselves.

This chapter will therefore introduce the basics of company accounting assuming little knowledge exists on the topic for the reader.

Limited Companies

Students studying for accounting may have only looked at company accounting briefly in previous courses leading to this stage. However the rules and principles of preparing company accounts are similar to those of sole traders and partnerships, in that, the same underlying concepts need to be employed.

There are, however, some differences in the accounts of limited companies, of which the following are probably the most important.

Company Legislation

The legislation governing the activities of limited companies is very extensive. The Companies Act 1985 as amended by the Companies Act 1989 specifies the accounting records that must be kept and that the annual accounts will be filed with the Registrar of Companies to enable public inspection to take place. Businesses which are not incorporated enjoy comparative freedom (non limited companies) while limited companies are required to produce their annual accounts in a standard form and have a professional audit provided, which advises the shareholders whether the accounting statements show a true and fair view.

Public and Private Companies

There are two classes of limited company:

Private Companies

These companies are normally family companies, which do not and cannot invite members of the public at large to invest in their equity (ownership).

Private companies are more likely to be small businesses and often, as these companies expand, their need for finance is such that it is difficult for them to continue their growth without the availability and access to public investment.

Public Companies

While public companies are much fewer in numbers each public company is generally made larger in size. These companies have the words "Public Limited Company" at the end of their name - shortened to PLC. These companies invite shareholdings from the public and their shares are traded on the stock exchange. Therefore, a companies statements of accounts will revel its status private, or public as follows:

> Pleasure Services PLC   = Public Company
> Pleasure Services Limited = Private Company

Need for Legislative Regulation

Company legislative is more necessary than legislation to regulate non in-corporated businesses because companies will be managed by directors who may not be owners of the business, and therefore it is essential that the shareholders interest is protected and that adequate financial statements are prepared for the shareholder which reflect the real position of the company. In other business forms it is more likely that the managers will be the owners.

It must be recognised that a company has separate legal status, unlike the partnerships and sole trader businesses.

Limited Liability

Companies offer limited liability to their owners. This means that the <u>maximum</u> amount an owner stands to lose in the event of a company becoming insolvent is the amount of equity held in the company. It is not possible for the shareholders possession to be taken to provide for unpaid debts, therefore limited companies offer a major advantage over the liability of the owners when compared to un-incorporated businesses.

Statutory Registers

Companies are required to maintain the following statutory books and records.

Accounting Records which should disclose the financial position of the company's financial position and include

a)   day-today entries of money received and spent;
b)   records of the companies assets and liabilities;
c)   stock records;
d)   adequate records capable of producing true and fair view accounting statements.

Register of Statutory Books

Theses include:

Register of all shareholders
Register of debenture holders
Register of directors and company secretaries
Register of directors' interests

Capital and Reserves of a Company

The capital and reserves section of company accounts is significantly different from unincorporated businesses and students need to become familiar with different terms.

Share Capital

The proprietor's capital in a limited company is known as **share capital**. When a company is set up for the first time it issues shares which are paid for by investors who became **shareholders of the company.**

Shares may be issued in units of say £1.00 shares or £0.50p or whatever seems appropriate. The face value of the share is known as the nominal value. If a company were established with an authorised capital of £200,000 this could be made up in many ways as follows:

a)   200,000 shares of £1
            or for example
b)   400,000 shares of £0.50p

The amount (price) at which shares are actually issued will depend on the marketability of the shares and may exceed the nominal value. If this occurs and for example shares with a £1 nominal value are issued at £1.50 the following entries would be made:

	DR	Cr
Bank	£1.50	
Share Capital		£1.00
Share Premium Account		50

Assuming the shares were fully paid for on issue the share premium amounts to £0.50. The share premium account is a non distributable reserve and belongs to all shareholders. Therefore the share premium is shown as part of the capital of the company along with the share capital and is part of the shareholders' equity.

Authorised, Issued, Called-up and Paid-up Capital

A distinction must be made between authorised, issues, called-up and paid-up share capital.

a) Authorised (or nominal) capital is the maximum amount of share capital that a company is empowered to issue. The amount of authorised share capital varies from company to company, and can change by agreement (between the members of the company, who can agree to alterations in the amount of authorised share capital during general meetings).

For example, a company's authorised share capital might be 15,000,000 ordinary shares of £1.50 each. This would then be the maximum number of shares it could issue, unless the maximum were to be changed by agreement.

b) Issued capital is the nominal amount of share capital that has been issued to shareholders. The amount of issued capital cannot exceed the amount of authorised capital.

Continuing the example above, the company with authorised share capital of 15,000,000 ordinary shares of £1.50 might have issued 14,000,000 shares. This would leave it the option to issue 1,000,000 more shares at some time in the future.

When share capital is issued, shares are allotted to shareholders. The term 'allotted' share capital means the same thing as issued share capital.

c) Called-up capital. When shares are issued or allotted, a company does not always expect to be paid the full amount for the shares at once. It might instead call up only a part of the issue price, and wait until a later time before it calls up the remainder.

For example, if a company allots 500,000 ordinary shares of £1, it might call up only, say, 80 pence per share. The issued capital would be £500,000 but the called up share capital would only be £400,000.

d) Paid-up capital. Like everyone else, investors are not always prompt or reliable payers. When capital is called up, some shareholders might delay their payment (or even default on payment). Paid up capital is the amount of called up capital that has been paid.

For example, if a company issued 500,000 ordinary shares of £1 each, calls up 80 pence per share, and receives payments of £390,000, we would have:

Allotted or issued capital	£500,000
Called-up capital	£400,000
Paid-up capital	£390,000
Called-up capital not paid	£ 10,000

The balance sheet of the company would then include called up capital not paid on the assets side, as follows:

	£
Called-up capital not paid	10,000
Cash (called up capital paid)	390,000
	400,000
called-up share capital	
500,000 ordinary shares of £1,	
with 80p per share called up	£400,000

The Board of Directors

A company might have a large number of shareholders, or only a few. No matter how many there are, they delegate authority for the day-to-day management of the company to its directors, who are directly responsible to the shareholders for what they do. (In some companies, the directors of the company and its shareholders might be the same people). There must also be a company secretary. Company policy is decided at regular meetings of the board of directors.

It is important to note that whereas the salary of a sole trader or a partner in a partnership is not a charge in the P & L account, but is an appropriation of profit, the salary of a director (is a P & L account expense) even when the director is also a shareholder of the company. The director being treated as an employee.

Dividends

Shareholders who are also directors of their company will receive a salary as a director. They are also entitled to a share of the profits made by the company.

Profits paid out to shareholders are called dividends. Dividends are appropriations of profit after tax. A company might pay dividends in two stages during the course of their accounting year;

a)   in mid year, after the half year financial results are known, the company might pay an interim dividend.

b)   at the end of the year, the company might pay a further final dividend.

The total dividend for the years is the sum of the interim and the final dividend. Not all companies by any means pay an interim dividend. Interim dividends are, however, commonly paid out by public limited companies.

At the end of an accounting year, a company's directors will have proposed a final dividend payment, but this will not yet have been paid. This means that the final dividend should be appropriated out of profits and shown as a current liability in the balance sheet.

The terminology of dividend payments can be confusing, often dividend payments are expressed in terms of pence per share. The XYZ company decided to pay a dividend on its ordinary share capital of 10p per share; the company had 1,000,000 £1 ordinary shares and therefore the dividend equalled £100,000.

Ordinary Shares and Preference Shares

At this stage it is relevant to distinguish between the two types of shares most often encountered, preference shares and ordinary shares.

Preference shares are now rather old-fashioned and rarely issued, although they do have occasional resurgences of popularity. They carry the right to a final dividend which is expressed as a percentage of their nominal value e.g. a 6% £1 preference share carries a right to an annual dividend of 6p. Preference dividends have priority over ordinary dividends; in other words if the directors of a company wish to pay a dividend (which they are not obliged to do) they must pay any preference dividend first. Otherwise, no ordinary dividend may be paid.

The rights attaching to preference shares are set out in the company's constitution. They vary from company to company but typically:

a)   preference shareholders have a priority right over ordinary shareholders to a return of their capital if the company goes into liquidation.

b)   preference shares do not carry a right to vote.

c)   if the preference shares are cumulative,it means that before a company can pay an ordinary dividend it must not only pay the current year's preference dividend, but must also make good any arrears of preference dividends unpaid in previous years.

Ordinary shares are by far the most common type of shares. They carry no right to a fixed dividend but are entitled to all profits left after payment of any preference dividend. Generally, however, only a part of such remaining profits are distributed, the rest being kept in reserve. The amount of ordinary dividends fluctuates although there is a general expectation that it will increase from year to year. Should the company be wound up, any surplus is shared between the ordinary shareholders. Ordinary shares normally carry voting rights.

Ordinary shareholders are thus the effective owners of a company. They own the 'equity' of the business, and any reserves of the business belong to them. Ordinary shareholders are sometimes referred to as equity shareholders. Preference shareholders are in many ways more like creditors (although legally they are members, not creditors). It should be emphasised however that the precise rights attached to preference and ordinary shares vary from company to company; the distinctions noted above are generalisations. But the ordinary shares are those which carry most risk and are often referred to as risk capital.

Dividends, Ordinary Shares and Preference Shares: example

Tarzan Ltd has issued 50,000 ordinary shares of 100 pence each and 10,000 7% preference shares of £2 each. Its profits after taxation for the year to 30 September 1992 were £8,000. The board of directors has decided to pay an ordinary dividend which is 50% of profits after tax and preference dividend.

Therefore the amount in total of dividends and of retained profits on ordinary shares is as follows:

	£
Profit after tax	8,000
Preference dividend (7% of £2 x10,000)	1,400
Earnings (profit after tax and preference dividend)	6,600
Ordinary dividend (50% of earnings)	3,300
Retained profit (also 50% of earnings)	£3,300

The ordinary dividend is 6.6 pence per share (£3,300 ÷ 50,000 ordinary shares).

The appropriation of profit would be shown as follows:

	£	£
Profit after tax		8,000
Dividends - preference	1,400	
- ordinary	3,300	
		4,700
Retained profit		£3,300

The Market Value of Shares

The nominal value of shares will be different from their market value, which is the price at which someone is prepared to purchase shares in the company from an existing shareholder. If you own 1,000 £2 shares in Tarzan Ltd you may sell them to XYZ for £2.60 each.
This transfer of existing shares does not affect Tarzan Ltd's own financial position in any whatsoever apart from changing the register of members, the company does not have to bother with the sale at all. There are certainly no accounting entries to be made for the share sale.

The profit or loss made is due to the valuation of the shares on the market fluctuating and belongs to the individual concerned.

Accounting Entries for the Issue of Shares

The accounting entries for the issue of shares are best demonstrated by an example. The process of issuing shares is often complicated by shareholders not paying for the shares issued to them at some stage in the process. This can then result in the shareholder forfeiting any rights to those shares and forgoing any refund of any part payment made on the shares.

The following example of small limited is provided for illustrative purposes. In this example the shares are paid for in stages. The stages normally allowed for payment are as follows:

> a sum payable with the application for shares, (known as the application stage);

> a sum payable when the shareholder is advised that he / she has been successful in applying for shares, and as been allotted shares (known as the allotment stage);

> sums payable on certain agreed dates. These are known as calls. There maybe any number of calls. If there were two calls for funds, they would be termed first call, and final call;

Exercise 5.1
Example : Small Ltd

> Small plc wish to issue 250,000 £1 ordinary shares, 60p (including 10p premium) per share payable on application, 20p on allotment and the final 30p on call, 300,000 applications were received. The Directors rejected small applications of 50,000 shares and allotted the remainder.

You are required to show the journals recording the issue.

	DR £	CR £
The first step is to record the cash received		
Bank a/c	180,000	
(300,000 x 0.60p)		
Application a/c		180,000

being the amount received from the issue on application including those later to be rejected.

	DR £	CR £
The next step is to refund applications rejected		
application a/c	30,000	
(50,000 x 0.60p)		
Bank a/c		30,000

being the refund of money received on applications which were subsequently rejected.

The next step is to transfer the applications into share capital accounting

```
        Application a/c              150,000
             Share capital                      125,000
             Share premium a/c                   25,000
```

being the closure of the applications account and the setting up of share capital and share premium account. It is alternatively acceptable to combine the application and allotment account.

The next step is to record the receipt of allotment payments and transfer them to share capital accounts

```
        Bank a/c                      50,000
        (250,000 x20p)
             Allotment a/c                        50,000
```

being the cash received on allotment of the shares

```
        Allotment a/c                 50,000
             Share capital a/c                    50,000
```

being the recording of the share capital and the closure of the Allotment a/c.

The next step is to record cash received on first and final call

```
        Bank a/c                      75,000
        (250,000 x 30p)
             Call a/c                             75,000
```

being the final amount due on the shares which are now fully called up.

The final step is to transfer the call received to share capital

```
        Call a/c                      75,000
             Share capital a/c                    75,000
```

being the closure of the call account and the transfer to share capital a/c.

The Balances of Small Plc would therefore be as follows:

```
                                         £
        Current Asset
        Bank Balance                  275,000
                                      _____

        Financed By:
        Share capital
        250,000  @ £1                 250,000
        Share premium a/c              25,000
                                      _____
                                      275,000
                                      _____
```

Complications on Issuing Shares

However, the issue of shares is unlikely to run as smoothly as this. We now consider a few-what if, situations, using the same example. The Directors may have decided not to reject any applicants requests for shares, but to allocate shares pro rata as follows:

> 300,000 requests therefore allocate 5 shares for every 6 requested. This scales down the requests for shares to application possible from 300,000 to 250,000.

It may also be the case that no money will be refunded to applicants, but that excess receipts will be off set against allotment. Under this scenario the following transactions would have been recorded.

	DR £	CR £

First step record the cash received

	DR £	CR £
Bank a/c (300,000 @ 60p)	180,000	
Applications a/c		180,000

being cash received from application

Next step transfer excess funds on application to allotment

	DR	CR
Application a/c	30,000	
Allotment a/c		30,000

being the transfer of monies received on application to the allotment a/c

Next step transfer funds on application to share capital accounts

	DR	CR
Application a/c	150,000	
Share capital a/c		125,000
Share premium a/c		25,000

being the closure of the applications account and the creation of the share capital and share premium accounts.

Next step would be to record the cash received on allotment from shareholders

	DR £	CR £
Bank a/c (250,000 x20p-12p)	20,000	
Allotment account		20,000

being the amount due from shareholders on allotment less the amount already received.

Final step transfer all allotment funds to share capital

	DR	CR
Allotment account	50,000	
Share capital		50,000

being the amount to be allocated to share capital from the allotment account. If a combined application and allotment account had been operated the entries would have been easier, avoiding the transfer from applications to allotment.

What if, some of the cash due on the call had not been paid by some shareholders and after a warning the Directors declared the shares forfeited.

Example - Small Plc

After the call was made the money due on 5000 shares was not received. After due notice the shares were declared forfeit. These shares were subsequently reissued at a fully paid price of 75p.

Obviously all journal entries upto the call would be the same as previously described, but from there on the following journals would record the entries.

	DR £	CR £

Step 1 record cash received on Call

	DR £	CR £
Bank a/c (250,000-5,000) @ 30p	73,500	
Call a/c		73,500

being the cash received on the Call, which is less than planned.

Step 2 Transfer the whole sum receivable to share capital until shares are officially announced forfeit

	DR £	CR £
Call a/c	75,000	
Share Capital a/c		75,000

being the recording of the share capital in issue even though the cash has not all been received. Subsequently the forfeited shares will be removed from share capital.

	DR £	CR £

Step 3 write out the shares which are forfeit

	DR £	CR £
Share capital a/c 5,000 @ £1	5,000	
Forfeiture share a/c		5,000

being the removal of shares that have been declared forfeit to the forfeiture share account.

Step 4 transfer the balance left on the Call account to the forfeiture account

           Forfeiture share account   1,500
                Call a/c   1,500

     being the closure of the call account transferring the unpaid
     sum to the forfeiture account.

Step 5 transfer the balance on the forfeiture account to a forfeiture re-issue account

The forfeiture account now looks as follows:

	£		£
Call A/c	1,500	Share capital a/c	5,000
Balance from forfeiture to			
forfeiture re-issue	3,500		
	5,000		5,000
	=====		======

Step 6

Now the forfeiture re-issue share account can be opened as
follows:

                                            £   £
           Forfeiture share a/c   3,500
                Forfeiture re-issue share a/c   3,500

     being the opening of the forfeiture re-issue share a/c as
     previously demonstrated in the ledger account.

Step 7 re-establish the share capital at nominal value

           Forfeiture re-issue share a/c
           (£1 x 5000) =   5,000
                Ordinary share capital   5,000

     being the re-issue of shares, although the cash received
     will be only 75p per share.

Step 8 record the cash received from re-issue

           Bank a/c (5,000 x 75p)   3,750
                Forfeiture re-issue share a/c   3,750

     being the cash received from the re-issue

Now we can look at the forfeiture re-issue share a/c as follows:

Forfeiture Re-Issue Share A/c

	£		£
Ordinary share a/c	5,000	Forfeiture share a/c	3,500
		Cash	3,750
			7,250

We can now transfer the excess amount received for the share to the share premium account.

	DR £	CR £
Forfeiture re-issue share a/c	2,250	
Share premium a/c		2,250

What if the Directors had decided not to reissue the Forfeiture Shares?

In this case the forfeiture share account would have been opened as before, and the amount underpaid on the Call would have still been transferred into it along with the shares nominal value as follows:

Forfeiture Share Account

	£		£
Call A/c	1,500	Ordinary share Capital a/c	5,000
			————
			5,000
			======

At this stage the Forfeiture Share account shows the share nominal value less unpaid monies on Call. The difference is the amount received for which no capital account now exists. This sum can be transferred to a capital reserve account as follows:

	DR £	CR £
Forfeiture share a/c	3,500	
Capital reserve		3,500

A summary of the ledger accounts is as follows:

This is based on the issue of shares / the repayment of excess applications and the forfeituring of 5000 shares which are eventually reissued at 75p.

Bank Account

	£		£
Applications	180,000	Applications	30,000
Allotment	50,000		
Cash	73,500		
		Balance c/d	277,250
Forfeiture re-issue account	3,750		————
	————		
	307,250		307,250
	=========		=========

Applications Account

	£		£
Bank a/c	30,000	Bank a/c	180,000
Ordinary share	125,000		
capital account			
Share premium account	25,000		
	180,000		180,000

Allotment Account

	£		£
Ordinary share	50,000	Bank account	50,000

Call Account

	£		£
Ordinary share		Bank account	73,500
capital account	75,000	Forfeiture share a/c	1,500
	75,000		75,000

Ordinary Share Capital Account

	£		£
Forfeiture share a/c	5,000	Applications	125,000
		Allotment	50,000
		Call	75,000
Balance c/d	250,000	Forfeiture re-issue share a/c	5,000
	255,000		255,000

Share Premium Account

	£		£
		Applications	25,000
Balance c/d	27,250	Forfeiture re-issue share a/c	2,250
	27,250		27,250

The issue of shares can be seen to be problematic from an accounting point of view when the issue does not run as smoothly as anticipated. Of course in practice this is often the case.

In practice a shareholder who does not pay the Call will be warned that if the Call is not paid within a specified time, the shareholder will not be able to retain the shares. After that specified time a notice will be sent to advise the shareholder that the shares will be re-issued. The shareholder at that stage may still be able to apply for the refund of sums paid on the shares less the cost of resale, and any losses on resale. If the shareholder still fails to acknowledge the shareholding the shares will be forfeit and no funds returned to the original shareholder.

Debenture Loans

Limited companies may issue debenture stock ('debentures') or loan stock. These are long term liabilities described on the balance sheet as loan capital. They are different from share capital in the following ways:

a)   shareholders are members of a company, while providers of loan capital are long term creditors;

b)   shareholders receive dividends (appropriations of profit) whereas the holders of loan capital are entitled to a fixed rate of interest (an expense charged against revenue);

c)   loan capital holders can take legal action against a company if their interest is not paid when due, whereas shareholders cannot enforce the payment of dividends;

d)   debentures or loan stock are often secured on company assets.

The holder of loan capital is generally in a less risky position than the shareholder. He has greater security, although his income is fixed and cannot grow, unlike ordinary dividends. As remarked earlier, preference shares are in practice very similar to loan capital, not least because the preference dividend is normally fixed.

Interest is calculated on the nominal value of loan capital, regardless of its market value. If a company has £500,000 (nominal value) 10% debentures in issue, interest of £50,000 will be charged in the profit and loss account per year. Interest is usually paid half yearly; examination questions often require an accrual to be made for interest due at the year end.

For example, if a company has £500,000 of 10% debentures in issue, pays interest six monthly in arrears on 30 June and 31 December each year and ends its accounting year on 30 September, there would be an accrual of three months' unpaid interest (3/12 x £50,000) = £12,500 at the end of each accounting year that the debentures are still in issue.

The accounting entries would require the following:

	DR £	CR £
Profit and Loss Account	12,500	
Current liability		12,500

being the allocation of interest outstanding on debentures
to the profit and loss account, to ensure it is recorded in
the period to which it relates, and the creation of a
current liability in the balance sheet as at that date.

Preparation of Company Account

The following question and answer are provided to enable students
to grasp the fundamentals of preparing a company accounting
statements. Students should be able to follow the basic concepts
from the explanation of items in this chapter. and the knowledge
acquired earlier in studying on unincorporated bodies.

Exercise 5.2
Fully Worked Example – PC PLC 2.1

Preparation of Limited Company Account an example

At this stage it is probably a good idea to prepare an answer to
a basic question and the following exercise and tutorial answer
is provided.

Exercise 5.2

The following trial balance was extracted from the books of PC
PLC as at 31 December 1992

	DR £	CR £
Called up share capital –		
ordinary shares of £1.25 each		30,000
10,000 5% preference shares @£1 each		10,000
Debenture Interest	6,000	
Debtors and Creditors	8,500	6,500
Sales		182,000
Purchases	161,000	
Rents and Rates	900	
Light and Heat	300	
Salaries and Wages	8,500	
Bad Debts	200	
Provision for Bad Debts 31.12.1991		600
10% Debenture		60,000
Profit and Loss Account		7,000
General Reserve		5,000
Stock in Trade 31.12.1991	16,000	
Insurance	150	
General Expenses	920	
Bank Balance	17,230	
Motor Vans @ Cost 31.12.1991	10,000	
Motor Expenses	1,000	
Freehold Premises	85,000	
Rent Received		600
Provision for Depreciation – Premises 31.12.1991		10,000
– Motor Vans 31.12.1991		4,000

The following information is available:

1   Stock in Trade @ 31.12.1992 was £50,000

2   Payment for the Preference share dividend for the year will
     be made during January 1993, along with the 10% recommended

ordinary share dividend.

3   The provision for bad debts is to be reduced to £400.

4   The vans are to be depreciated by 10% on the cost of assets held at 31.12.1992.

5   £1,000 is to be provided for this years depreciation of freehold premises.

6   On 1 January a motor van was scrapped it has originally cost £2,000 and accumulated depreciation was £1.750.

7   Corporation tax due, amount to £3,500 and will be paid in 1993.

Required:

Prepare a Trading Profit and Loss Account for 1992 and a balance sheet as at 31.12.1992.

Tutorial Answer – PC PLC

Students should always make sure they understand the notes to the question. My own technique is to journalese the notes to ensure I do not forget to perform the necessary adjustments. Therefore each note will be addressed in turn.

Note 1

The Stock in Trade figure is given at the close of business and is required to be taken into account to ensure that the cost of goods sold is calculated accurately and to be used for balance sheet purposes. These notes show the debits and credit required.

	DR £	CR £
Current Asset - Balance sheet stock	50,000	
Reduce purchases in the trading account		50,000

being the adjustments for end of year stock.

Note 2

This note informs us that the dividends proposed to ordinary share holders and preference share dividends will be paid after the end of the accounting year.
It is necessary to:

a)   record these charges in the Profit and Loss account appropriation section

b) create current liabilities

	DR £	CR £
Profit and Loss Appropriation account		
Preference dividend	500	
Ordinary dividend	3,000	
Current Liabilities		
Preference dividend		500
Ordinary dividend proposed		3,000

Note 3

The current provision for bad debts can be found in PC's trial balance and is £600. We are instructed to reduce the provision to £400. Therefore we need to:

	DR £	CR £
Provision for bad debts	200	
Profit and Loss Account		200

being the adjustment for the reduction of bad debts provision.

Note 4

Depreciation. This should be a familiar adjustment for students, however Note 6 tells us of a disposal, and requires adjustment by this note for a 10% provision on the cost of motor vans held at the 31.12.1992 as follows:

Motor vans cost   = £10,000 Less disposal note 6. £2,000 = £8,000
Depreciation @ 10%= £800

	DR £	CR £
Profit and Loss Account depreciation	800	
Motor Van depreciation account		800

being the annual charge for depreciation of motor vans.

Note 5

This note advises of the depreciation to be provided on freehold premises. Students should acknowledge this will relate to the building and not the land. Land is not depreciated.

	DR £	CR £
Profit and Loss account depreciation	1,000	
Premises depreciation account		1,000

Note 6

This note requires the removal of an asset from the accounts and the calculation of the profit or loss on disposal.

It is advisable to demonstrate by way of ledger accounts as follows:

Motor Vans Account				Motor Vans Depreciation			
£		£			£		£
a) balance b/fwd 10,000		b) disposal 2,000		b) disposal 1,750		balance b/fwd 4,000 (a)	

a)   bring forward opening balances

b)   transfer asset values of motor van sold to a disposal account

c)   bring into account any cash received in this case none the van was scrapped.

d)   calculate whether the asset cost is covered by depreciation plus proceeds if not transfer loss to Profit and Loss account.

Disposal Account			
£			£
b) Motor van account 2,000		b) depreciation	1,750
		d) loss to Profit and loss account	250
2,000			2,000
=====			======

Note 7

Corporation tax is payable but will not be paid in this financial year therefore we must charge it to profit and loss and create a creditor.

	DR £	CR £
Profit and Loss	3,500	
Creditor for Corporation Tax (Inland Revenue)		3,500

WE CAN NOW PREPARE THE ACCOUNTING STATEMENTS

PC PLC Trading Profit and Loss Account for the year ending 31 December 1992

	£	£
Sales		182,000
Opening Stock	16,000	
Plus Purchases	161,000	
	177,000	
Less Closing Stock	50,000	
		127,000
Gross Profit		55,000
Add reduced provisional bad debts		200
		55,200
Plus rent received		600
		55,800
Less expenses		
Debenture interest	6,000	
Rent and Rates	900	
Light and heat	300	
Salaries and wages	8,500	
Bad debts	200	
Insurance	150	
General expenses	920	
Motor expenses	1,000	
Loss on scrapped vehicle	250	

	800		
Depreciation			
Motor Vans	800		
Premises	1,000	1,800	20,020
Profit before tax			35,780
Taxation			3,500
Available for Appropriation			32,280
Preference dividend		500	
Ordinary dividend	3,000		3,500
			28,780
Profit and Loss Account b/fwd			7,000
Profit and Loss Account c/fwd			35,780

PC PLC Balance Sheet as at 31 December 1992

Fixed Assets		Cost £	Dep £	Net £
Freehold Premises		85,000	11,000	74,000
Motor Vans		8,000	3,050	4,950
		93,000	14,050	78,950

Current Assets

Stock		50,000	
Debtors	8,500		
Less Provisional	400	8,100	
Bank Balance		17,230	
		75,330	

Less Current Liability

Creditors	6,500		
Tax	3,500		
Ordinary dividend	3,000		
Preference dividend	500	13,500	61,830
			140,780
Less debentures			60,000
			80,780
			=======

Financed by:

Called-up shares

24,000 £1.25 ordinary shares		30,000
10,000 5% £1 preference shares		10,000
General reserve		5,000
Profit and Loss Account	35,780	80,780
		======

Interpretation of the Answer to PC PLC

The answer is set out in the type of fashion a student
considering company accounting can recognise as being similar to
the preparation of unincorporated organisations accounting
statements.

However, company accounting would never have this level of detail
given for expenses on the face of the profit and loss account.
The profit and loss account format is shown in full in the next
chapter, but as a starting point the profit and loss account
would look something like the following:

XYZ Company Profit and Loss Account for the year ending 31 March
1993

	£	£
Turnover		1,000,000
Cost of sales		(500,000)
Gross profit		500,000
Selling and Distributing Costs	200,000	
Administrative Costs	150,000	(350,000)
Operating Profit		150,000
Investment income	1,000	
Debenture interest	51,000	(50,000)
Net profit		100,000
Dividends		(50,000)
Retained Earnings for the year		50,000

At this stage the important items to note from the layout
provided is as follows:

> *The layout is still not complete as required by the
> Companies Act for example taxation is not provided.

> *The expenses are grouped into three categories:

>> Cost of sales;
>> Selling and Distribution;
>> Administrative;

It is necessary to split costs into these three categories, and
to enable students to take the process of preparing company
accounts one step further a question and answer is provided.

The answer is more in line with proper presentation requirements
than PC PLC was, but is still not as required by the Companies
Acts, and Financial Reporting Standard 3.

Exercise 5.3

Old Harlow PLC prepares accounts annually to 31 March. The following is a summary of the balances taken from the company's books as at the year ended 31 March 1993.

	£
Freehold Land and Buildings (Cost)	1,450,000
Fixtures and Fittings (Cost)	65,000
Motor Vehicles (Cost)	90,000
Accumulated Depreciation at 1.4.92:	
Freehold Land and Buildings	64,000
Fixtures and Fittings	22,000
Motor Vehicles	52,000
Stock at 1.4.92	49,500
Short-term Investments	8,030
Trade Creditors	74,200
Bank Overdraft	1,640
Issued Share Capital	1,200,000
Profit and Loss Account (Credit balance)	182,400
10% Debentures (repayable 1998)	300,000
Sales	982,800
Purchases	428,300
Salaries and Wages	164,000
Motor expenses	85,000
Advertising	63,200
Sundry Overheads	51,000
Director's Remuneration	40,000
Interest Payable	28,200
Investment Income	890
Interim Dividend Paid	24,000
Trade Debtors	346,100
Provision for doubtful debts	12,400

The following information is also available:

1) The authorised share capital is £1,500,000.

2) The share capital, issued and fully paid, consists of 2,400,000 ordinary shares of 50p each.

3) Interest payable consists of:
Debenture interest	£25,000
Bank Overdraft Interest	£ 3,200

   Bank overdraft interest is to be treated as an Administration Expense.

4) The cost of the land is £800,000.

5) Depreciation is to be provided on cost at the following rates:
Buildings	5%
Fixtures and Fittings	10%
Motor Vehicles	25%

6) Expenses are to be apportioned as follows:

	Cost of Sales	Admin	Selling and Dist
Depreciation:			
Buildings	50%	40%	10%
Fixtures and Fittings	20%	60%	20%
Motor Vehicles	5%	5%	90%
Salaries and Wages	40%	40%	20%
Motor Expenses	5%	5%	90%
Sundry Overheads	10%	45%	45%

7) Bad debts of £15,000 are to be written off (a selling and distribution overhead) and the Provision for Doubtful Debts should be 3% of the remaining debtors.

8) A final ordinary dividend of 1.5p per share is proposed.

9) Stocks at 31 March 1993 were valued at £64,000 at cost.

Required:

Prepare a Profit and Loss Account for the year to 31 March 1993 and a Balance Sheet as at that date. Both statements should conform to the requirements of legislation and good accounting practice.

Old Harlow PLC profit and Loss Account for the year ended 31 March 1993

	£	£
Turnover		928,800
Cost of Sales 1		(507,425)
Gross Profit		475,375
Saving and Distribution Costs 2	(232,783)	
Administration Costs 3	(154,025)	(386,808)
Operating Profit		88,567
Investment Income	890	
Debenture Interest	(30,000)	(29,110)
Net profit		59,457
Dividends		
Interim (Paid)	(24,000)	
Final (Proposed)	(36,000)	(60,000)
Transferred to P&L Account		(543)
Profit and Loss a/c balance b/fwd		182,400
Profit and Loss a/c balance c/fwd		181,857

Old Harlow PLC Balance Sheet as at 31 March 1993

	£	£	
Fixed Assets			1,405,500
Current Assets			
Stock	64,000		
Investments	8,030		
Debtors	321,167		
	393,197		
Less Creditors: Amounts falling are within one year	(116,840)		
Net Current Assets			276,357
Total Assets less current liabilities			1,681,857
Less Creditors: Amounts falling are after more than one year			(300,000)
			1,381,857
			==========
Capital and Reserves:			
Issued shared capital			1,200,000
Profit and Loss Account			181,857
			1,381,857
			==========

Notes

1   Cost of sales   £
    Purchases   428,300
    Increase in Stocks   (14,500)
    Salaries and Wages   65,600
    Motor expenses   4,250
    Sundry Overheads   5,100
    Depreciation (Buildings)   16,250
    Depreciation (Fixtures and Fittings)   1,300
    Depreciation (motor Vehicles)   1,125
                                                   ─────────
                                                   507,425

2   Selling and Distribution Costs:
    Salaries and Wages   32,800
    Motor Expenses   76,500
    Advertising   63,200
    Sundry Overheads   22,950
    Bad Debts   15,000
    Decrease in Provision for Doubtful Debts   (2,467)
    Depreciation (Buildings)   3,250
    Depreciation (Fixtures and Fittings)   1,300
    Depreciation (Motor vehicles)   20,250
                                                   ─────────
                                                   232,783

3   Administration Costs:
    Salaries and Wages   65,600
    Motor expenses   4,250
    Sundry overheads   22,950
    Directors' Remuneration   40,000
    Interest on bank overdraft   3,200
    Depreciation (Buildings)   13,000
    Depreciation (Fixtures and Fittings)   3,900
    Depreciation (Motor Vehicles)   1,125
                                                   ─────────
                                                   154,025

4   Interest Payable   £
        10% Debentures   30,000

5	Land Building	Fixture Fittings	Motor Vehicles	Total
Cost	1,450,000	65,000	90,000	1,605,000
Accumulated Deprec				
1.4.90		64,000	22,000	52,000	138,000
Depreciation for year	32,500	6,500	22,500	61,500
31.3.91				
	96,500	28,500	74,500	199,500
Net Book Value	1,353,500	36,500	15,500	1,405,500

6   £
        Short Term Investments   8,030

7	Debtors	331,100
	Provision for Doubtful Debts (3%)	(9,933)
		321,167
8	Trade Creditors	74,200
	Debenture Interest Due	5,000
	Proposed Ordinary Dividend	36,000
	Bank Overdraft	1,640
		116,840
9	10% Debentures (1998)	300,000
10	Authorised share capital	1,500,000
	Issued Share Capital	
	2,400,000 50p ordinary shares	
	issued as fully paid	1,200,000

Interpretation of Old Harlow Plc

The answer to Old Harlow starts to introduce the necessary
requirements of Company accounting and students will recognise
the use of notes for the first time. The notes required by the
Companies Act and accounting standards are extensive. The Old
Harlow question deals with the notes only up to the point
necessary to explain the answer, and is not as extensive as
required in practice.

Examination Questions

A few examination questions are provided to enable students to
test their abilities regarding the preparation of company
accounts at the level required in this chapter.

Conclusion

This chapter has introduced the subject of company accounting and
provided simple examples of accounting required. The chapter is
intended to enable students to progress from the preparation of
unincorporated organisation accounts to the special requirements
of companies. The chapter introduces the need for a different
format for the profit and loss account and notes to the accounts.

The next chapter deals extensively with the requirements of
proper statements of accounts, which are prepared in compliance
with legal provisions and accounting standards.

Examination Question 5.1

The following information was extracted from the books of Spellbrook Ltd as at 31 May 1993.

Trial Balance as at 31 May 1993	£000	£000
Ordinary shares of 25p each fully paid		200
8% £1 Preference Shares fully paid		100
12% Debentures		200
General Reserve		70
Balance on Profit & Loss Account at 1 June 1992		50
Freehold property at cost	300	
Depreciation of buildings at 1 June 1992		10
Plant and equipment at cost	280	
Depreciation of plant & equipment at 1 June 1992		120
Stock at 1 June 1992	150	
Provision for doubtful debts at 1 June 1992		10
Purchase	2,790	
Sales		3,450
Debenture Interest paid	12	
Wages and Salaries	214	
Light and heat	30	
Rates and insurance	70	
Printing postage and stationery	50	
Preference dividends	8	
Interest on Bank overdraft	15	
Goodwill	181	
Bank overdraft		30
Cash in hand	10	
Debtors	280	
Creditors		150
	4,390	4,390

You are also given the following information:

1 Depreciation for the year to be made:
   25% on cost or revaluation of plant and equipment
   2% on freehold property (land cost £100,000)

2 The Freehold property was revalued at £500,000 by Pee and Aye, Chartered Surveyors. This revaluation is to be reflected in the accounts and this year's depreciation is to be based on revaluation.

3 Amount still outstanding in respect of electricity is

estimated at £8,000 and rates, and insurance prepaid amounted to £24,000.

4   Stock at 31 May 1993 was valued at £176,000.

5   The directors recommend the provision for
          1   a final dividend of 5p per ordinary share;
          2   audit fee of £15,000;
          3   a transfer to general reserve of £30,000.

6   All shares rank for dividend.

7   Debenture interest for the year is also to be provided **for.**

You are required to prepare in as good a form as possible:

a)   the profit and loss account for the year to 31 **May** 1993 **and**

b)   a balance sheet as at the date

Examination Question 5.2

The following trial balance was extracted from the books of Pleasure Services PLC as at 31 December 1988

	DR £	CR £
Called up share capital		
Ordinary shares of £1 each		45,000
15,000 5% Pref Shares @£1 each		15,000
Debentures interest	3,500	
Debtors and Creditors	9,500	
Sales		2,500
Purchases	263,000	381,000
Rents and Rates	1,900	
Light and Heat	2,300	
Salaries and Wages	28,500	
Bad Debts	1,200	
Provision for bad debts 31/12/87		600
10% Debenture		35,000
Profit and Loss Account		18,600
General Reserve		5,000
Stock in Trade 31/12/87	30,000	
Insurance	650	
General Expenses	1,920	
Bank Balance	12,230	
Motor Vans @ cost 31/12/87	12,000	
Motor Expenses	1,500	
Freehold Premises	145,000	
Rent received		500
Provision for Depreciation- Premises 31/12/87		5,000
- Motor Vans 31/12/87		5,000

The following information is available.

1 Stock in Trade @ 31/12/88 was £40,000

2 Payment for the Preference share dividend for the year will be made during January 1989, along with the 25% recommended ordinary share dividend.

3 The provision for bad debts is to be reduced to £200

4 The vans are to be depreciated by 15% on the cost of assets held at 31/12/88.

5 £1,500 is to be provided for this years depreciation of freehold premises

6 On the 1 January a motor van was scrapped it had originally cost £4,500 and accumulated depreciation was £1,500.

7 Corporation Tax due amounts to £12,000 and will be paid in 1989.

Required:

Prepare a trading profit and loss account for 1988 and a balance sheet as at 31/12/88.

Examination Question 5.3

Rum Drum Plc issue the following shares on the 1 January 1992, requiring payment in the following stages.

400,000 Ordinary shares of £1 nominal value. To be issued at £1.50p.

- 50 pence on application (including 25p premium)

- 50 pence on allotment (including 25p premium)

- 50 pence on first and final call

Applications for 600,000 shares were received. The Directors decided to scale the allotment down to 4 shares for each 6 applications. No money to be refunded, but cash received on application to be offset against monies requested on allotment.

One shareholder fails to pay the first and final call on 10,000 shares. After warning letters are sent to the shareholder without response, the Directors decide to declare the shares forfeit and cancel 5,000 shares, while re-issuing the other 5,000 shares. The re-issued shares are sold for £1.40 per share.

You are required to:

Show the journal entries and ledger accounts for these transactions. You should keep the applications account separate from the allotment account.

CHAPTER 6

Content of Published Accounts

Introduction

This topic involves the use of a good deal of knowledge, and for students the recall of a significant volume of information. There are many factors which affect the presentation requirements of financial statements and information as follows:

* Financial Reporting Council

The Financial Reporting Council Standards require disclosure of many factors in the notes to the accounts. The basic approach is that any material item which affects the understanding of the accounting statements must be disclosed in the published accounts.

In addition the presentation of the profit and loss account which had generally been dictated by the Companies Act 1985 is also affected by the Financial Reporting Standard 3 (FRS 3) which requires specific disclosure on the face of the profit and loss account.

The Accounting Standards board which is a constituent company of the Financial Reporting Council have also issued a discussion document on providing more meaningful written explanations in the published accounts. This document is entitled "Operating and Financial Review".

Therefore a significant impact is made by the Financial Reporting Council , and advice and regulation is being added as part of a continuing process of improving the quality of financial reporting.

* The Companies Acts

The Companies Acts provide standard formats for the presentation of Financial statements, as well as extensive specific disclosure requirements to be recorded in the notes to the accounts.

It is vital at this stage that students do however appreciate the true and fair view override. The true and fair view statement is required to be provided by independent external auditors is of vital importance. When a company is reporting to shareholders, the shareholders must be given the audit report which will either confirm the true and fair view or otherwise as the case may be.

When auditors are considering expressing their opinion in this context they must consider whether the accounts comply with pronouncements of the Financial Reporting Council and its constituent companies,i.e. have the Financial Reporting Statements (FRSs) and Standard Statements of Accounting Practice (SSAPs) been applied where appropriate.

If the application of the SSAPs/FRSs conflict with the legal provision then the requirement of true and fair view is more important than the statutory provision. This is known as the true and fair override.

The presentation of company accounts therefore fully acknowledges the statutory provisions as well as the pronouncements of the Financial Reporting Council.

*   The Directors' Report

The Companies Act requires that a directors' report is provided as part of the overall financial report given to the shareholders. The content of the report is prescribed and certain factors must be included.

It is therefore important that the requirements of the directors' report are considered.

*   Requirements of the Stock Exchange

If a company wishes to be listed on the Stock Exchange it must comply with the requirements of the Stock Exchange yellow book. These are over and above the Companies Act requirements. The details of these therefore needs to be considered.

I summary therefore it can be concluded that the main influences on presentation of published information are as follows:

   * Financial Reporting Council

   * Company Law

   * Stock Exchange requirements

It must be added that these are influenced by the European Directives and the International Accounting Standards.

Structure of this Chapter

The approach taken in this chapter is first to consider what the filing requirements are with the Registrar of Companies. Then to consider the Financial Reporting Council's pronouncements of the required form of published accounts. The Companies Act Standard formats can then be considered in a modified form as required by the Financial Reporting Council.

PUBLICATION OF COMPANY ACCOUNTS

Published Accounts
Statutory accounts are part of the price to be paid for the benefits of limited liability. Limited companies must produce such accounts annually and they must appoint an independent professional to audit and report on them. Once prepared, a copy of the accounts must be sent to the Registrar of Companies, who maintains a separate file for every company. The Registrar's files may be inspected, for a fee, by any member of the public. This is why the statutory accounts are often referred to as published accounts.

It is the responsibility of the company's directors to produce accounts which show a true and fair view of the company's results for the period and its financial position at the end of the period. The board evidence their approval of the accounts by the signatures of two directors (now one ca. 1989) on the balance sheet. Once this has been done, and the auditors have completed their report, the accounts are laid before the members of the company at the general meeting. When the members have adopted the accounts they are sent to the Registrar for filing.

Registrar of Companies

The role of the Registrar of Companies is to provide the accurate and up to date company information to which the public is entitled. By law all private limited companies must file a copy of their accounts at Companies House within ten months of the end of their financial year. Public limited companies have seven months in which to file. All late filings risk the danger of penalties imposed by Companies House and any adverse affect on their credit rating.

The Registrar of Companies is part of the Department of Trade and Industry, and is also an Executive Agency. From July 1992 the Registrar of Companies has sought to enforce powers contained in the Companies Act which have introduced penalties of up to £5,000 for defaulting companies. The penalties imposed are as follows:

TABLE - PENALTY DUE TO DELAY IN FILING ACCOUNTS

DELAY	PUBLIC LIMITED COMPANY £	PRIVATE LIMITED COMPANY £
Not more than 3 months	500	100
More than 3 months but not more than 6 months	1,000	250
More than 6 months but not more than 12 months	2,000	500
More than 12 months	5,000	1,000

All accounts filed must be signed in the appropriate places.

In April 1990 sections of the Companies Act 1989 were introduced which required accounts to be signed as follows:

- the balance sheet should be signed by one director (the name must also be stated);

- the directors' report will need to be signed by a director or by a Company Secretary. Again the name must be stated;

- the Auditor's report must state the names of the auditors and be signed by them.

These provisions are contained in the Companies Act 1985 as substituted by sections 7, 8 and 9 of the Companies Act 1989.

The requirement that the accounts show a true and fair view is paramount; although statute lays down numerous rules on the information to be included in the published accounts and the format of its presentation, any such rule may be overridden if compliance with it would prevent the accounts from showing a true and fair view.

The documents which must be included in the accounts laid before a general meeting of the members are:

(a) a profit and loss account (or any income and expenditure account in the case of a non-trading company);

(b) a balance sheet as at the date to which the profit and loss account is made up and notes to those statements and accounts;

(c) a cash flow statements and primary statements required by FRS 3;

(d) a directors' report;

(e) an auditors' report addressed to the members (not to the directors) of the company;

(f) the group accounts in the case of a company which has subsidiaries at the year end date.

The European Community Fourth directive introduced the concept of small and medium sized companies,which was incorporated into the Companies Act.

Small or medium-sized private companies are entitled to certain exemptions. Although they must prepare a full set of statutory accounts for approval by the members the accounts they send to the registrar may be in a summary form (the statutory term is modified accounts). Such companies must balance the expense of preparing two different sets of accounts against the advantage of publishing as little information about themselves as possible. despite the risks of assisting trading rivals by publishing full accounts, many small companies may decide that that is preferable to the expense of producing two different sets of accounts and may therefore not take advantage of the filing exemptions.

The Rules Regarding Filing Exemptions

Exemptions exist for small and medium-sized companies. The definition of company size is as follows:

> To qualify for exemption in a particular year, the company must satisfy <u>at least</u> two of the following criteria, for both the year in question <u>and</u> the preceding year.

TABLE - CRITERIA FOR DEFINITION OF COMPANY SIZES

CRITERIA	SMALL	MEDIUM-SIZE
Turnover not exceeding	£2.0 million	£8.0 million
Balance sheet not exceeding	£975,000	£3.9 million
Average number employees (on a weekly basis) not exceeding	50	250

<u>NB:</u> Balance sheet total = total of all assets <u>without</u> deduction for any liabilities.

Interpretation of the Rules

Once a company is established as small or medium-sized its status will not be changed until the second year that it does no satisfy its original status. The following provides an example which demonstrates this point:

Example - XYZ company was a small company in 1989 and the company accounts and information show the following:

XYZ Company	Small Statutory limit	Year		
		1990	1991	1992
Turnover	£2m	£3m	£3.4m	£6.0m
Balance sheet total	£0.975m	£1.4m	£3.2m	£0.9m
Employees	50	52	60	48

- 142 -

Status of XYZ Company

1990 In 1990 the company will remain a small company even though it failed all three tests. This is because XYZ was designated a small company in 1989 and must fail to meet that categorisation for two successive years.

1991 The XYZ company will be redesignated as a medium-sized company having met the criteria for two successive years.

1992 The XYZ company will continue to be designated as a medium-sized company. This is of course due to the fact that despite meeting the small company criteria in 1992 it did not in the preceding year.

What Do These Filing Exemptions Involve?

The following table sets out the filing exemptions which are available to small and medium-sized companies.

Large Company Reporting Requirement	Small company	Medium-sized Company
Directors' Report	Not required	Required
Profit and Loss Account Standard Format	Not required	Abbreviated format can start with gross profit
Balance Sheet Standard Format	Abbreviation permitted. Not all information required	Standard format required
Notes to Financial Statements	Abbreviated. Limited information required	Abbreviated. Limited information required, but more than small companies
Cash Flow Statements FRS 2	Not required	Required

Can All Companies File for Exemption?

Not all companies can file for exemption. In particular the following companies cannot file for exemption.

(i)   A Public Company;
(ii)   Banking or Insurance companies;
(iii)   An authorised person under the Financial Services Act 1986.

Conclusion on Filing Exemptions

All companies must produce full financial statements and comply with all legal requirements, and regulating requirements. They must also report the full information required to their own shareholders.

Small and medium-sized private companies may take advantage of provisions within the Companies Act to file abbreviated accounts with the registrar of companies.

Issue of Summary Financial Statements to Shareholders

Under the Companies Act 1989 a provision was introduced permitting Public Listed companies to send summary financial statements to their shareholders.

Summary statements can only be provided if the following conditions are satisfied.

*   The companies memorandum and Articles of Association must permit summary statements to be sent out.

*   The company must establish that individual shareholders are prepared to accept summary statements, and do not wish to receive the full accounts and reports.

*   Summary statements must be provided within the statutory seven months from the end of the financial year.

*   The summary statements must be approved by the Board and the original statements signed.

*   A statement must be included in the summary as follows:

        "This summary financial statement does not contain sufficient information to allow a full understanding of the results and state of affairs of the company (or group) to be obtained. For further information the full accounts, audit report and directors' report should be consulted."

        Effectively this statement is a warning to shareholders that the summary is inadequate for the purposes of interpreting results.

*   The summary statements must make it clear that the full accounts and report are available free of charge. A reply paid card request form should be provided.

In order for the company to satisfy itself that shareholders do not wish to receive the full accounts, the company should

-    Obtain a written notification from the shareholder confirming full accounts and reports are not required. this should be obtained 28 days before the annual report is sent out.

or

-    Having given shareholders examples of the full set of accounts compared to the summary, and having given members the opportunity to return a paid reply envelope assume that the shareholder will accept the summary.

The Form and Content of Summary Financial Statements

The information provided in the summary statements included the following:

*   An abridged report including the following

     - review of Business
     - Post balance sheet events
     - future developments
     - full list of directors

*   An abridged Profit and Loss account (although much is still required).

*   A summary balance sheet requiring only Alpha letters on the statutory format to be provided.

Previous Year Figures

The previous year's corresponding figures must be provided in the summary statements.

Important Items To Be Included

It is important that the following are clear

(i)   A directors' note stating that the information provided is a summary.

(ii)   A statement from the auditor confirming that the summary is consistent with the full accounts.

(iii)   If the accounts are qualified a statement from the auditor regarding the qualification.

(iv)   A statement of an audit criticism regarding reconciliation or whatever.

Reporting Financial Performance FRS3

This financial reporting standard is aimed at improving financial reports to avoid some of the problems experienced when considering financial results.

Financial results have been misleading in many respects where the companies have for example misinterpreted the rules on dealing with extraordinary items. Or results have been unclear as a result of discontinuing operations, and costs of restructuring, and profits and losses on the disposal of fixed assets.

FRS3 attempts to avoid these problems in the future and to achieve this aim, provides some fundamental changes to traditional financial statements and accounting practice. These changes are as follows:

* New advice is given regarding extraordinary items and prior year adjustments (SSAP 6);

* The earnings per share calculation is raised (SSAP 3);

* A layered format is to be used for the profit and loss account to highlight a number of important components;

* A statement of total recognised gains and losses is required as a primary financial statement;

* A note of historical cost profits and losses is required as a memorandum item;

* A reconciliation of movements in shareholders' funds is required;

Each of these items can be explained in turn to provide a reasonably thorough explanation of the FRS 3.

New Advice Regarding Extraordinary Items and the Calculation of Earnings Per Share

The FRS does not completely rule out extraordinary items which are not part of ordinary operations, but builds on the advice given by the urgent Issues Task Force in making it quite clear that for example with restructuring costs, if they are related to a discontinued operation then they will be put into the Profit and Loss account under that category, but will not be extraordinary.

In fact the FRS states that all exceptional items should be shown in the profit and loss account under the appropriate standard heading and that the following items should be treated as exceptional and shown separately on the face of the Profit and loss account:

- Profits and losses on the sale or termination of an operation;

-    Costs of fundamental reorganisation or restructuring having
     a material effect on the nature and focus of the reporting
     entities operations;

-    Profits and losses on the disposal of assets.

Extraordinary items have been used wrongly in the past by
companies to record costs which should have been considered part
of ordinary activities. The reason for this was partly due to
the fact that the earnings per share, which is used by analysts
to advise investors looked better due to the earnings per share
being based on profit before extraordinary items.

The FRS amends the calculation of the earnings per share as
follows:

    "The profit in pence attributable to each equity share,
    based on profit of the period after tax, minority
    interest and extraordinary items and after deducting
    preference dividends and other appropriations in
    respect of preference shares, divided by the number of
    equity shares in issue and ranking for dividends in
    respect of the period."

This new definition makes the creative use of extraordinary items
redundant, and will therefore hopefully remove distortions.

The FRS does not prevent additional earnings per share
calculations at other levels of profit, but requires that if
another method is used as well as the FRS method it is used
consistently, and the FRS figure is shown at least as prominently
as any additional version. Furthermore the addition version if
used should be explained and reconciled to the FRS method.

A Layered Format Approach to the Profit and Loss Account to Highlight Important Items

Diagrammatical Presentation of the Profit and Loss Account

Continuing   Discontinued

Normal Operations   Normal Operations

Split between continuing   Profit and losses on sale or and
discontinuing as   termination, costs of fundamental
as appropriate   reorganisation. profits and losses
                            disposal of fixed assets

Extraordinary items

-    Continuing operations and acquisition should be clearly
     distinguished from discontinued operations.

-    Profits and losses on the sale or termination of an
     operation, costs of fundamental reorganisation or
     restructuring and profits or losses on the disposal of fixed
     assets should be shown on the face of the profit and loss
     account.
-    Extraordinary items will be extremely rare but if present

should be shown on the face of the profit and loss account <u>not</u> divided between continuing and discontinued operation

The FRS considers extraordinary items to be rare, and as such does <u>not</u> provide any examples of what might be considered to be extraordinary.

<u>Example of Presentation FRS 3</u>

	Continuing operations	Acquisitions	Discontinued operations	Total	Total
	1993	1993	1993	1993	1992 as restated
	£million	£million	£million	£million	£million
Turnover	550	50	175	775	690
Cost of sales	(415)	(40)	(165)	(620)	(555)
	----	----	----	----	----
Gross profit	135	10	10	155	135
Net operating expenses	(85)	(4)	(25)	(114)	(83)
Less 1992 provision			10	10	
	----	----	----	----	----
Operating profit	50	6	(5)	51	52
Profit of sale of properties	9			9	6
Provision for loss on operations to be discontinued					(30)
Loss on disposal of discontinued operations			(17)	(17)	
Less 1992 provision			20	20	
	----	----	----	----	----
Profit on ordinary activities before interest	59	6	(2)	63	28
Interest payable				(18)	(15)
				----	----
Profit on ordinary activities before taxation				45	13
Tax on profit on ordinary activities				(14)	(4)
				----	----
Profit on ordinary activities after taxation				31	9
Minority interests				(2)	(2)
				----	----
[Profit before extraordinary items]				29	7
[Extraordinary items] (included only to show positioning				-	-
				----	----
Profit for the financial year				29	7
Dividends				(8)	(1)
				----	----
Retained profit for the financial year				21	6
				=====	=====
Earnings per share				39p	10p
Adjustments				Xp	Xp
[to be itemised and an adequate description to be given]					
				----	----
Adjusted earnings per share				Yp	Yp
				----	----

[Reason for calculating the adjusted earnings per share to be given]

This example shows clearly the following:

                                                                    £m
    Profit on ordinary activities before interest
    - continuing operations   59

While the results of acquisitions are shown separately and the
figure for the profit on acquisitions is as follows:

    Profit on ordinary activities before interest
    - acquisitions   £6 million

The total profit on continuing and acquisitions is therefore £65
million. However a £2 million loss was incurred on discontinued
operations. this is intended to give a better view of the future
performance potential of the company.

It should be noted that the analysis of continuing operations
from discontinued is only given down to the level of profit on
ordinary activities before interest.

It is important that the terminology used is understood, and for
this purpose the following terms are defined.

Discontinued operation

To be included in the category of discontinued operations a sale
or termination must have a material effect on the nature and
focus of the reporting entity. This could be as a result of
either withdrawal from a particular market (whether class of
business or geographical) or from a material reduction in
turnover in its continuing markets.

The FRS gives an example which is useful in understanding the
concept of discontinued operations. If a hotel company which had
traditionally served the lower end of the market sold its
existing chain of hotels, and purchased up market hotels. The
company would have materially changed the nature and focus of its
operations, and the sale of the lower end of hotels would
constitute a discontinued operation.

Had the hostel chain simply been involved in purchasing and
selling material assets as part of the routine maintenance of its
portfolio of assets the activity would be classified as
continuing operations.

Similarly a company selling or downsizing its operations to
achieve productivity improvements, or other cost savings is part
of the entities continuing operations.

In addition the FRS states that to be classified as a
discontinued operation the assets, liabilities, results of
operations and activities must be clearly distinguishable,
physically, operationally and for financial reporting purposes.

A Statement of Total Recognised Gains and Losses is Required as a Primary Financial Statement

Statement of total recognised gains and losses

	1993	1992 as restated
	£million	£million
Profit for the financial year	29	7
Unrealised surplus on revaluation of properties	4	6
Unrealised (loss)/gain on trade investment	(3)	7
	-------------	-------------
	30	20
Currency translation differences on foreign currency net investments	(2)	5
Total recognised gains and losses relating to the year	28	25
		====
Prior year adjustment (as explained in note x)		
total gains and losses recognised since last annual report		

Note of historical cost profits and losses

	1993	1992 as restated
	£million	£million
Reported profit on ordinary activities before taxation	45	13
Realisation of property revaluation gains of previous years	9	10
Difference between a historical cost depreciation charge and the		
actual depreciation charge of the year calculated on the revalued amount	5	4
	-------------	-------------
Historical cost profit on ordinary activities before taxation	59	27
	===================	===================
Historical cost profit for the year retained after taxation,		
minority interests, extraordinary items and dividends	35	20
	===================	===================

Reporting Requirements of the Companies Act

The Companies Act 1985 sets out the formats required for the balance sheet and the profit and loss account. The balance sheet is not amended by FRS 3, while the profit and loss account format is affected. The first step therefore is to consider the format of the balance sheet.

Balance Sheet Published Format Required

The Companies Act 1985 sets out two formats for the balance sheet.

(a) Vertical
(b) Double sided

The style used is invariably the vertical format. Therefore the format shown in this book will be the vertical format.

When looking at the presentation required it should be noted that some headings are prefixed by a capital letter (A, B, C, etc.,) while other headings are prefixed by a Roman numeral (I, II, III, etc.,) and finally some headings are prefixed by an Arabic number (1, 2, 3, etc.,). These prefixes do not have to appear on the published balance sheet, but are provided in the Companies Act to signify their relative importance from a presentation point of view.

The following extract from the published form can be used to illustrate the point.

Demonstration of the Importance of Prefixes

<u>Example</u>

     C   Current Assets

         I.   Stocks

              1. Raw materials and consumables
              2. Work in progress
              3. Finished goods
              4. Payments on account

        II.   Debtors

              1. Trade debtors
              2. Amounts owing by groups
              3. etc

Items C must appear on the published balance sheet as must all Alpha items. Item I stocks must also appear on the balance sheet, but the detail of 1, 2, 3 and 4 can be provided in a note to the published accounts. Therefore the extract shown above will appear as follows on the face of the balance sheet.

     <u>Current Assets</u>
        Stocks   (note 6)
        Debtors   (note 7)

Note 6 will then show the detail which has been relegated from the face of the balance sheet to the notes to the accounts.

The order of items on the balance sheet may never be varied, and the Alpha and Roman prefixed items must always be shown.

The full balance sheet format can now be shown reproduced from the Companies Act 1985.

PRO FORMA BALANCE SHEET

Vertical format

A CALLED UP SHARE CAPITAL NOT PAID*   X

B FIXED ASSETS
   I   Intangible assets
         1. Development costs   X
         2. Concessions, patents, licences, trade
           marks and similar tights and assets   X
         3. Goodwill   X
         4. Payments on account   <u>X</u>

```
                                                                    X
    II    Tangible assets
          1. Land and buildings                          X
          2. Plant and machinery                         X
          3. Fixtures, fittings, tools and equipment X
          4. Payments on account and assets in
             course of construction                      X
                                                                    X
    III   Investments
          1. Shares in group companies                   X
          2. Loans to group companies                    X
          3. Shares in related companies                 X
          4. Loans to related companies                  X
          5. Other investments other than loans          X
          6. Other loans                                 X
          7. Own shares                                   X
                                                              X
                                                                          X

C CURRENT ASSETS

    I     Stocks
          1. Raw materials and consumables               X
          2. Work in progress                            X
          3. Finished goods and goods for resale         X
          4. Payments on accounts                        X
                                                                    X
    II    Debtors
          1. Trade debtors                               X
          2. Amounts owed by group companies             X
          3. Amount owed by related companies            X
          4. Other debtors                               X
          5. Called up share capital not paid*           X
          6. Prepayment and accrued income*              X
                                                                    X
    III   Investments
          1. Shares in group companies                   X
          2. Own shares                                  X
          3. Other investments                           X
                                                              X
    IV    Cash at bank and in hand                        X
                                                              X
D REPAYMENTS AND ACCRUED INCOME*                          X
                                                              X

E CREDITORS: AMOUNTS FALLING DUE WITHIN ONE YEAR
          1. Debenture loans                              X
          2. Bank loans                                  X
          3. Payments received on account                X
          4. Trade creditors                             X
          5. Bills of exchange payable                   X
          6. Amounts owed to group companies             X
          7. Amounts owed to related companies           X
          8. Other creditors including taxation
             and social security                         X
          9. Accruals and deferred income*               X
                                                             (X)
F NET CURRENT ASSETS (LIABILITIES)                                  X

G TOTAL ASSETS LESS CURRENT LIABILITIES                             X
```

```
b/f                                                        X        X
H CREDITORS: AMOUNTS FALLING DUE AFTER MORE THAN ONE YEAR
          1. Debenture loans                      X
          2. Bank loans and overdrafts            X
          3. Payments received on account         X
          4. Trade creditors                      X
          5. Bills of exchange payable            X
          6. Amounts owed to group companies      X
          7. Amounts owed to related companies    X
          8. Other creditors including taxation   X
             and social security                  X
          9. Accruals and deferred income*        X
                                                           X
I PROVISIONS FOR LIABILITIES AND CHARGES
          1. Pensions and similar obligations     X
          2. Taxation, including deferred taxation X
          3. Other provisions                     X
                                                           X
J ACCRUALS AND DEFERRED INCOME*                            X
                                                                   (X)
                                                                   £X
K CAPITAL AND RESERVES                                     £       £
   I      Called up share capital                                  X
   II     Share premium account                                    X
   III    Revaluation reserve                                      X
   IV     Other reserves
          1. Capital redemption reserve           X
          2. Reserve for own shares               X
          3. Reserves provided for by the articles
             of association                       X
          4. Other reserves                       X
                                                           X
   V      Profit and loss account                                  X
                                                                   £X
```

*These items may be shown in either of the positions indicated.

Companies Act 1985 Presentation Requirement of the Profit and Loss Account as Modified by FRS 3

The format of the profit and loss account also uses Alpha, Roman and Arabic numerals. the meanings are the same as those for the balance sheet.

Four formats are provided, however only two formats are vertical the other two being double sided. the profit and loss account when published in company accounts is invariably provided in a vertical format, and therefore this book will concentrate on those formats.

Format 1 - Operational Format

Format 1 is the most widely used format for the profit and loss account. It is interesting to note that all items listed are prefixed by an Arabic number. this means that in theory all items could be relegated to the note. In practice this is not possible.

Many profit and loss account items need to be shown to comply with other provisions of the Companies Act. the statements produced in this book include three items added at the end which while not included in the standard format are required by company Act specific requirements these are as follows:

- Dividends paid and proposed
- Transfers to (from) reserves

Format 2 - Type of Expenditure Format

This format is less popular than format 1 and many of the points raised about format 1 are also relevant to format 2.

The Formats Need to Be Modified for FRS 3

The formats are produced in this book, but they are now semi redundant. The FRS 3 has taken over from these statutory formats. When producing a profit and loss account you must adhere to the statutory format as much as possible, but you must ensure that the disclosures required by FRS 3 are provided.

Therefore the two statutory formats are followed by the two standard formats in FRS 3.

PRO FORMA PROFIT AND LOSS ACCOUNT - STATUTORY FORMAT

Format 1 - Operational Format

		£	£
1.	Turnover		X
2.	Cost of sales		(X)
3.	Gross profit (or loss)		X
4.	Distribution costs	X	
5.	Administrative expenses	X	
			(X)
			X
6.	Other operating income		X
			X
7.	Income from shares in group companies	X	
8.	Income from shares in related companies	X	
9.	Income from other fixed asset investments	X	
10.	Other interest receivable and similar income	X	
			X
			X
11.	Amounts written off investments	X	
12.	Interest payable and similar charges	X	
			(X)
	Profit and loss on ordinary activities before taxation		X
13.	Tax on profit (or loss) on ordinary activities		(X)
14.	Profit (or loss) on ordinary activities after taxation		X
15.	Extraordinary income	X	
16.	Extraordinary charges	(X)	
17.	Extraordinary profit (or loss)	X	
18.	Tax on extraordinary profit (or loss)	(X)	
			X
			X
19.	Other taxes not shown under the above items		(X)
20.	Profit (or loss) for the financial year		X
	Dividends paid and proposed		(X)
	Transfers to (from) reserves		(X)
	Retained profit (or loss) for the financial year		£X

The unnumbered captions do not appear in the standard formats, but with the exception of retained profit or loss for the financial year, their disclosure on the face of the profit and loss account is required elsewhere in the CA 1985 (Sch 4 para 1(6) and 1(7)).

Format 2 - Type of Expenditure Format - Statutory Format

		£	£	£
1.	Turnover			X
2.	Change in stocks of finished goods and work in proress			(X)
3.	Own work capitalised*			X
4.	Other operating income			X
				X
5.	(a) Raw materials and consumables	X		
	(b) Other external charges	X		
			X	
6.	Staffcosts:			
	(a) Wages and Salaries	X		
	(b) Social security costs	X		
	(c) Other pension costs	X		
			X	
7.	(a) Depreciation and other amounts written off tangible and intangible fixed assets	X		
	(b) Exceptional amounts written off current assets	X		
			X	
8.	Other operating charges		X	
				(X)
				X
9.	Income from shares in group companies		X	
10.	Income for shares in related companies		X	
11.	Income from other fixed asset investments		X	
12.	Other interest receivable and similar income		X	
				X
				X
13.	Amounts written off investments		X	
14.	Interest payable and similar charges		X	
				(X)
	Profit and loss on ordinary activities before taxation			X
15.	Tax on profit (or loss) on ordinary activities			(X)
16.	Profit (or loss) on ordinary activities after taxation		X	
17.	Extraordinary income		X	
18.	Extraordinary charges		(X)	
19.	Extraordinary profit (or loss)		X	
20.	Tax on extraordinary profit (or loss)		(X)	
				X
				X
21.	Other taxes not shown under the above items			(X)
22.	Profit (or loss) for the financial year			X
	Dividends paid and proposed			(X)
	Transfers to (from) reserves			(X)
	Retained profit (or loss) for the financial year			£X

*Own work capitalised represents the amount of work or costs which are incurred in producing a product which is to be treated as a fixed asset.

Profit and loss account example 1 - Financial Reporting Standard 3

	1993 £million	1993 £million	1992 as restated £million
Turnover			
Continuing operations	550		500
Acquisitions	50		

	600		
Discontinued operations	175		190
		775	690
Cost of sales		(620)	(555)
		-----------	-----------
Gross profit		155	135
Net operating expenses		(104)	(83)
Operating profit			
Continuing operations	50		40
Acquisitions	6		

	56		
Discontinued operation	(15)		12
Less 1992 provision	10		
		51	52
Profit of sale of properties		9	6
Provision for loss on operations to be discontinued			(30)
Loss on disposal of discontinued operations	(17)		
Less 1992 provision	20		

		3	

Profit on ordinary activities before interest		63	28
Interest payable		(18)	(15)
		-----------	-----------
Profit on ordinary activities before taxation		45	13
Tax on profit on ordinary activities		(14)	(4)
		-----------	-----------
Profit on ordinary activities after taxation		31	9
Minority interests		(2)	(2)
		-----------	-----------
[Profit before extraordinary items]		29	7
[Extraordinary items] (included only to show positioning		-	-
		-----------	-----------
Profit for the financial year		29	7
Dividends		(8)	(1)
		-----------	-----------
Retained profit for the financial year		21	6
		===========	===========
Earnings per share		39p	10p
Adjustments [to be itemised and an adequate description to be given]		Xp	Xp
		-----------	-----------
Adjusted earnings per share		Yp	Yp
		-----------	-----------

[Reason for calculating the adjusted earnings per share to be given]

Profit and loss account example 2 – Financial Reporting Standard 3

	Continuing operations	Acquisitions	Discontinued operations	Total	Total
	1993	1993	1993	1993	1992 as restated
	£million	£million	£million	£million	£million
Turnover	550	50	175	775	690
Cost of sales	(415)	(40)	(165)	(620)	(555)
Gross profit	135	10	10	155	135
Net operating expenses	(85)	(4)	(25)	(114)	(83)
Less 1992 provision			10	10	
Operating profit	50	6	(5)	51	52
Profit of sale of properties	9			9	6
Provision for loss on operations to be discontinued					(30)
Loss on disposal of discontinued operations			(17)	(17)	
Less 1992 provision			20	20	
Profit on ordinary activities before interest	59	6	(2)	63	28
Interest payable				(18)	(15)
Profit on ordinary activities before taxation				45	13
Tax on profit on ordinary activities				(14)	(4)
Profit on ordinary activities after taxation				31	9
Minority interests				(2)	(2)
[Profit before extraordinary items]				29	7
[Extraordinary items] (included only to show positioning				-	-
Profit for the financial year				29	7
Dividends				(8)	(1)
Retained profit for the financial year				21	6
Earnings per share				39p	10p
Adjustments [to be itemised and an adequate description to be given]				Xp	Xp
Adjusted earnings per share				Yp	Yp

[Reason for calculating the adjusted earnings per share to be given]

Summary of General Disclosure Requirements

Once a company has chosen the format it wished to use for its profit and loss account and balance sheet it must adhere to it for subsequent financial years unless, in the opinion of the directors, there are special reasons for a change. Details of any change and the reason for it must be disclosed by note to the accounts.

Each item in the standard formats is prefixed by capital letters and Roman and Arabic numbers. these prefixes do not have to be shown in a company's published accounts but are given in the Act for ease of reference.

The following points should be borne in mind:

(a)   any item preceded by a letter or a Roman number must be shown;

(b)   items preceded by an Arabic number may be amalgamated;

     (i)   if their individual amounts are not material;
    (ii)   if amalgamation facilities the assessment of the company's state of affairs (but then the individual items must be disclosed by note);

(c)   items preceded by Arabic numbers may be:

     (i)   adapted (e.g. title altered) or
    (ii)   rearranged (in position);

(d)   any item required to be shown in greater detail than required by the prescribed format;

(e)   a company's balance sheet or profit and loss account may include an item not otherwise covered by any of the items listed, except that the following must not be treated as assets in any company's balance sheet:

     (i)   preliminary expenses;
    (ii)   expenses of and commission on any issue of shares or debentures;
   (iii)   costs of research.

Although all profit and loss captions are preceded by Arabic numbers, this does not mean that the entire account can be relegated to a note. The following items must be disclosed on the face of the profit and loss account:

(a)   profit or loss on ordinary activities before taxation;
(b)   transfers to or from reserves;
(c)   dividends paid and proposed.

Corresponding amounts for the balance financial year must be disclosed for all items appearing in the balance sheet or profit and loss account, or in the notes to the accounts. Where a corresponding amount is not comparable with the current year's figure, (e.g. owing to a change in accounting policy), it must be adjusted. In examination questions it is unlikely that you will be required to present corresponding amounts.

A caption in the standard formats need not be disclosed at all if both the current and corresponding amounts are nil. Immaterial items do not need to be separately disclosed: they may be amalgamated with some other appropriate heading.

The FRS 3 is now the format to follow, with reference to the statutory format.

Notes to the Published Accounts of Companies

Notes are required to be provided along with the financial statements as part of the annual report. The notes required are the minimum required by the Companies Act. However, notes are required to comply with SSAPs and FRS as well.

The purpose of the notes is to provide valuable information which assists in helping the reader of the accounts make a judgement about the results of the company.

The notes are normally listed in number order as follows:

A general Note 1. Accounting policies are required to be shown in the notes to the accounts.

Note 2 onwards is taken from the first item on the profit and loss account needing disclosure down to the last item on the profit and loss account. The profit and loss account note might end with prior year adjustments for example note 10.

Note 11 onwards might be those required for the balance sheet starting at fixed assets and ending with reserves say note 20.

Other notes then follow such as the note required regarding capital commitments and the FRS 3 notes regarding statements of historic cost.

Example of Details Required in Notes

1. Accounting Policies

It would be normal to find the following notes regarding accounting policies.

Depreciation

A statement of the method of depreciation used, and the useful lives used on different classes of assets.

Accounting Standards

a statement that accounting standards have been observed in the preparation of financial statements.

Stocks and Work in Progress

the basis of valuation of stocks and work in progress.

Changes in Accounting Policy

It is essential that any changes in accounting policies adopted are disclosed and the impact quantified.

Other Items of Importance

many other items can be disclosed but it would largely be dependent on the circumstances related to the individual company and an attempt to assist in the presentation of a true and fair view.

2. Turnover

A note should be provided regarding the amount included in the accounts for different classes of business. The turnover should also be analysed between geographical markets as follows:

        Class of business;
             - retailing
             - betting and gaming
             - building

        Analysis of markets;
             - UK
             - USA
             - Europe

However, where the directors feel that disclosure would be seriously prejudicial to the interests of the company the information can be omitted. However the omission must be noted.

3. Operating Costs and Revenue

This note can be extensive. If distribution costs and administrative expenses are not shown on the face of the profit and loss account as is often the case a note is required which provides the details. Formats for disclosure are included in FRS 3 as follows:

Notes to the financial statements
Note required in respect of profit and loss account example 1

	1993 Continuing £million	1993 Discontinued £million	1993 Total £million	1992 (as restated) Continuing £million	1992 (as restated) Discontinued £million	1992 (as restated) Total £million
Cost of sales	455	165	620	385	170	555
Net operating expenses						
Distribution costs	56	13	69	46	5	51
Administrative expenses	41	12	53	34	3	37
Other operating income	(8)	0	(8)	(5)	0	(5)
	89	25	114	75	8	83
Less 1992 provision	0	(10)	(10)			
	89	15	104			

The total figures for continuing operations in 1993 include the following amounts relating to acquisitions: cost of sales £40 million and net operating expenses £4 million (namely distribution costs £3 million, administrative expenses £3 million and other operating income £2 million).

Note required in respect of profit and loss account example 2

| | 1993 | | | 1992 (as restated) | | |
	Continuing £million	Discontinued £million	Total £million	Continuing £million	Discontinued £million	Total £million
Turnover				500	190	690
Cost of sales				385	170	555
Net operating expenses						
Distribution costs	56	13	69	46	5	51
Administrative expenses	41	12	53	34	3	37
Other operating income	(8)	0	(8)	(5)	0	(5)
	89	25	114	75	8	83
Operating profit				40	12	52

The total figure of net operating expenses for continuing operations in 1993 included £4 million in respect of acquisitions (namely distribution costs £3 million administrative expenses £3 million and other operating income £2 million).

In addition details of income needs to be provided as follows:

- rents received net of outgoings
- details of exceptional income

Expenditure specifically required to be disclosed by the Companies Act and SSAPs/FRSs is as follows:

- depreciation charged
- auditors remuneration
- hire of plant and machinery
- research and development costs
- details of exceptional charges
- leasing transactions including operational lease rentals

4. Employees

In respect of all employees

(a)   The average number of employed within each employment
      category (calculated on a weekly basis)

      For example (including directors)

	No.
- Production staff	1,100
- Sales and administrative	450
	1,550

      The amount paid is then required to be disclosed if not
shown on the face of the profit and loss account analysed over

         (i) Wages and salaries

(ii) Social Security Costs
(iii) Pensions.

5. Directors

Disclosure is required of all emoluments provided to directors. These would include:

  (i) Fees of directors
 (ii) other emoluments, i.e. golden hellos
(iii) Various other payments such as compensation for loss of office; transfer fees; pension to former directors

Further Disclosures

(a)   The chairman emolument must be disclosed and the highest paid director, if not the emolument of the chairman.

(b)   number of directors in each ascending £5,000 band of emolument excluding pension contribution.

(c)   The number of directors waiving emoluments must be disclosed and the aggregate amount waived.

An example might be as follows

All directors	1992	1991
£0 - £5000	1	-
£5001 - £10000	2	3
£10001 - £15000	1	1
£30000 - £35000	1	

NB   You do not need to list bands which have no directors in that banding.

6. Investment Income and Interest Payable

Disclosure of income from listed investments is required.

Loans and overdraft wholly repayable with 5 years must be distinguished from all other longer term loans.

7. Tax on Profit of Ordinary Activity

Companies must disclose in the notes to the accounts

a)   The basis of computation of UK corporation tax and any special circumstances surrounding taxation such as:

    - charges for:- UK corporation tax, UK income tax, overseas tax, tax credit on franked investment income, irrecoverable ACT.

8. Extraordinary Items and Exceptional Items

FRS 3 has redefined the type of items which can be considered extraordinary. The vast majority of items previously seen under this heading will be treated as exceptional items, and would be shown separately in the notes if they help to facilitate the true and fair view statement.

If an extraordinary item did occur and we have no real
example then it would need to be fully explained in the notes to
the accounts.

9. Dividends

Although the statutory formats of accounting statements in the
Companies Act do not make reference to the entry for dividends on
the face of the profit and loss account, the Act specifically
requires dividends to be disclosed, along with the aggregate
amount of any dividends paid and proposed.

10. Prior period Adjustments

The FRS 3 requires the following treatment of prior period items.

> "Prior period adjustments should be accounted for by
> relating the comparative figures for the preceding
> period in the primary statements and notes and
> adjusting the opening balance of reserves for the
> cumulative effect. the cumulative effect of the
> adjustments should also be noted at the foot of the
> statement of total recognised gains and losses of the
> current period. the effect on the results of preceding
> year should be disclosed where practicable."

11. fixed Assets (Intangibles, Tangibles and Investments)

For all items shown under "fixed assets", there must be shown:

(a)   in respect of cost or valuation:
    (i)   amount at commencement of year
    (ii)   movements during year:
        1. additions
        2. revaluation surpluses
        3. costs of disposals
        4. transfers between categories
    (iii)   amount at end of year

(b)   in respect of depreciation
    (i)   accumulated provisions at commencement or year
    (ii)   movements during year:
        1. depreciation provisions on disposals
        2. provision for year
        3. other movements (such as revaluation adjustments)
    (iii)   accumulated provisions at end of year

(c)   in respect of land and buildings, separate analysis of:
    (i)   freeholds
    (ii)   long leaseholds (50 years or more to run)
    (iii)   short leaseholds (less than 50 years to run)

(d)   in respect of capitalised development costs
    (i)   reasons for capitalisation
    (ii)   period of write off

(e)   in respect of acquired goodwill
    (i)   period of write off

        (ii)   reasons for choosing that period

(f)   in respect of investments shown as fixed assets, any amounts
       written off their value or any such provisions written back,
       so far as is not disclosed in the profit and loss account.

Additional disclosure requirements are applicable to fixed assets
shown at a valuation, as follows:

(a)   for all assets other than listed investments:
       (i)   the years and the amounts of each valuation
       (ii)   for a valuation during the financial year:
              1. name or qualification of valuers
              2. bases of valuation

(b)   where the company adopts the Alternative Accounting Rules,
       explained in Chapter 2 (assets included at current cost or
       at valuation), there must be disclosed, in addition:
       (i)   the comparable amounts determined according to the
              historical cost accounting rules, or
       (ii)   the differences between those amounts and the
              carrying amounts actually shown in the balance sheet.

12. Investments (Shown as Fixed or Current Assets)

(a)   analysis between those:
       (i)   listed on a recognised stock exchange
       (ii)   others

(b)   market value of listed investments where different from book
       value and stock exchange value if less than market value.

A note must be given of the tax which would be payable if
the investments were sold at the valuation figure (SSAP 15).

In respect of an investment comprising

(a)   10% or more of the nominal value of any class of shares, or

(b)   share capital having a total book exceeding 10% of its own
       assets

the following must be disclosed:

(a)   name of the undertaking

(b)   country of incorporation if outside Great Britain or country
       of registration if incorporated in Great Britain and
       different from country or registration of reporting company
       and address in unincorporated, and

(c)   description and proportion of each class if shares held.

In addition, in respect of an investment representing more that
20% of the allotted share capital:

(a)   aggregate capital and reserves at the end of its most recent
       financial year ending during or within that of the reporting
       company and

(b)   the profit and loss of the investee for that year.

(a)   for investments accounted for under the equity method of
       accounting (i.e. associated undertakings, see SSAP 1) or

(b)   for an investment in a subsidiary where the reporting
       company is a wholly owned subsidiary incorporated in Great
       Britain or the subsidiary's accounts are included in the
       group accounts.

14. Current Assets

(a)   Stocks

       The formats require separate amounts for all significant
       stock categories.

       It is also necessary to disclose the difference, if
       material, for each category between carrying value and
       replacement cost.

(b)   Debtors

       The formats require analysis of debtors under a number of
       headings (see formats).

       Analysis is also required between debtors falling due:

       (i)   within one year, and
       (ii   outside one year.

(c)   Investments

       See section 12 above.

14. Current Liabilities

Interestingly, the term "current liabilities" has been replaced
in Formats by "creditors: amounts falling due within one year".

The formats require analysis under various headings.

In the vertical format, creditors are shown under two headings.
In the "debit/credit" format all creditors appear under a single
heading but analysis is required between items falling due within
one year and outside one year.

There is a separate heading for "other creditors including
taxation and social security". amounts for taxation and social
security should be shown separately, thus effectively creating
two headings. In addition, the Act requires that the amount of
any provisions for taxation other than deferred taxation shall be
stated". the logical treatment would therefore seem to be to
disclose:

(a)   corporation tax payable
(b)   PAYE and social security balances.

Details should be given of secured creditors, stating type of
creditor (according to the format), amount secured and the nature
of the security. For example, £100,000 of the bank overdraft is
secured by a fixed charge on the company's freehold".

15. Creditors Falling Due After More Than One Year

For each item under creditors, it is necessary to disclose the aggregate amount of debts not wholly repayable within five years

(a)   by instalment
(b)   otherwise

The aggregate amount of instalments due after five years must also be shown.

For each item falling to be disclosed above, there must be disclosed the repayment terms and the rate of interest.

For each liability heading in the balance sheet, there must be disclosed:

(a)   aggregate amount of secured liabilities and
(b)   an indication of the nature of the securities given.

For debentures issued during the year, there must be stated:

(a)   reasons for issue
(b)   classes of debentures issued
(c)   for each class, the amount issued and the consideration received

Disclosure must also be made of redeemed debentures available for re-issue.

Details should also be given of all secured creditors.

16. Provisions for Liabilities and Charges

The most usual item under this heading will be deferred taxation.

Deferred taxation balances must be separately disclosed.   (This requirement complied with SSAP 15)

17. Accruals and Deferred Income

The most usual item under this heading will be government grants.

18. Called Up Share Capital

The following information must be disclosed:

(a)   authorised share capital

(b)   number and aggregate nominal value of allotted shares of each class

(c)   in respect of redeemable shares
      (i)   earliest and latest dates for redemption
      (ii)   whether redeemable in any event or at the option of the company or of the shareholder
      (iii)   premium on redemption

(d)   for shares allotted during the year:

      (i)   reasons for allotment

```
        (ii)    classes of shares allotted
        (iii)   for each class, the number allotted, their aggregate
                nominal value and the consideration received

(e)    in respect of share options issued:

        (i)     number, description and amount of shares
        (ii)    period of option
        (iii)   price at which option exercisable.
```

19. Reserves

Movements on all reserves must be disclosed.

The requirements to disclose information regarding by Notes 18
and 19 has been built upon by FRS 3 which requires a statement of
reconciliation of the movement of shareholders funds, a suggested
format included in FRS 3 is as follows:

Reconciliation of movements in shareholders' funds

	1993	1992 as restated
	£million	£million
Profit for the financial year	29	7
Dividends	(8)	(1)
	21	6
Other recognised gains and losses relating to the year (net)	(1)	18
New share capital subscribed	20	1
Goodwill written-off	(25	0
Net addition to shareholders' funds	15	25
Opening shareholders' funds (originally £375 million before deducting prior year adjustment of £10 million	365	340
Closing shareholders' funds	380	365

Reserves

	Share premium account £million	Revaluation reserve £million	Profit and loss account £million	Total £million
At beginning of year as previously stated	44	200	120	364
Prior year adjustment			(10)	(10)
At beginning of year as restated	44	200	110	354
Premium on issue of shares (nominal value £7 million)	13			13
Goodwill written-off			(25)	(25)
Transfer from profit and loss account of the year			21	21
Transfer of realised profits		(14)	14	0
Decrease in value of trade investment		(3)		(3)
Currency translation differences of foreign currency net investments			(2)	(2)
Surplus on property revaluations		4		4
At end of year	57	187	118	362

Note: Nominal share capital at end of year £18 million (1992 £11 million).

21. <u>Capital Commitments, Contingent Liabilities and Financial Commitments</u>

The Act requires disclosure of:

(a)   Commitments for capital expenditure (to be incurred in subsequent accounting periods)

   (i)   aggregate amount contracted for
   (ii)   aggregate amount authorised but not contracted for.

(b)   Contingent liabilities so far as not provided for:

   (i)   amount of liability
   (ii)   legal nature
   (iii)   whether any security has been provided by the company.

(c)   Financial commitments, in particular:

   (i)   any charge on the company's assets to secure the liabilities of any other person.

   (ii)   pension liabilities, showing separately
           1.   those provided for in the accounts
           2.   those not so provided.

           Separate analysis is required of past directors' pensions.

   (iii)   other financial commitments which

           1.   have not been provided for and
           2.   are relevant in assessing the company's state of affairs.

22. <u>Earnings Per Share</u>

It may be that an alternative computation to the earnings per share is provided by a company. Any alternative must be fully explained in the notes to the accounts, and a reconciliation to the FRS 3 method provided.

This section on notes to company accounts has been prepared in an attempt to provide a reasonably comprehensive guide. it will provide a very useful course of reference for students. however, it is impossible in a publication such as this book to deal with the requirement in a complete way. For example, the ICAEW publish a check list for companies which includes:

- Company Law;
- Accounting standards;
- Stock Exchange requirements.

This document is 60 pages long. Therefore please bear in mind the extensive requirements in this book are not compete in every detail.

We can now proceed to consider the requirements of the directors'

report. It is of course important to know not just the pure
accounting disclosure requirements, and the Director's report is
provided to inform shareholders of the business performance and
progress.

The Requirements for a Directors' Report

A directors' report is required by the Companies Act, and must
include a minimum amount of information.

It should be noted that companies cannot avoid disclosure
requirements for the accounting statements or notes by disclosing
information in the director's report.

The auditor must be given the opportunity to consider the
Directors' report and the auditor must comment on the report if
any information provided by the directors is not in the auditor's
opinion consistent with the company accounts.

Minimum Contents of the Directors' Report

*   Results and dividends. The directors must recommend the
    divided to be paid and advise shareholders of any transfers
    to reserves.

*   Business review. The report should provide information of
    the business performance of the principle activities and
    developments.

*   Details of the acquisition of the companies own capital.

*   Market value of land and buildings - where different from
    book value.

*   Fixed assets - details of significant changes.

*   Research and development. A report on the activities
    related to the year.

*   Future developments. A report on the plans or proposals for
    future development and the likely trends of development.

*   Events since the year end. Important events which have
    occurred since the year end.

*   A list of the interests of directors in the shares of the
    company.

*   Political and charitable contributions.

*   Employment policy where employees exceed 250 during the
    year, related to
    - training;
    - career development of disabled persons.

    Information concerning involvement of employees in
    management.

*   Details of the arrangements in force for securing health,
    safety and welfare of employees.

*   Professional indemnity insurance. Where the company have
    arranged insurance cover it should be disclosed in the
    directors report.

*   The directors' report is approved by the board and signed
    either by a director or more commonly the company secretary.

Standards of Reporting

The references provided in the directors' report in this
chapter are in note form, but the reporting requirements are
quite extensive.

The Financial Reporting Council are considering the information
being given in company accounts and the Accounting Standards
Board have issued a discussion document "Operating and Financial
Review".

Operating and Financial Review

This document states that the financial reporting of major
companies would be enhanced by the inclusion in annual reports of
an operating and financial review (OFR).

However, the ASB believe that an OFR standard could only be
achieved by consensus rather than regulation. The OFR would
include the following:

> - a commentary on the operating results;
> - a review of the financial needs and resources;
> - a commentary on shareholders return and value.

The content of these sections is given in the discussion document
as follows:

Commentary on the operating results

The purpose of this aspect of the OFR would be to enable
management to explain to the user of the financial statements the
main influences and uncertainties affecting the enterprise's
results and operating cash flows, by major segment, and thus
assist the user in making his own assessment of likely future
results. The commentary should not assume a special knowledge of
the enterprise or of the industry in which it operates, but
should nevertheless not omit specific information merely because
its significance will only be fully understood by the more
informed user.

The review would be a "top-down" assessment of the results of the
enterprise as a whole, dealing in more detail with particular
segments in that context, rather than being an amalgamation of
individual segment reports without considering the impact of each
on the overall enterprise. It should focus on those matters that
affected the period and are not expected to recur, and on those
that did not affect the period but are expected to affect future
periods.

It is envisaged that the review would include the following:

(a) a discussion of the overall results of,and cash generated
     by, operating activities, focusing on those business

segments or other divisions of the enterprise that are
relevant to an understanding of the operating activities as
a whole; in particular, changes in turnover and trading
margins should be discussed and reference should be made to
products or services designed to protector enhance earnings
or market share;

(b)   a discussion of the man risks and uncertainties relating to
       the operation activities as a whole, and individual business
       segments and divisions as necessary for an overall
       understanding, including matters such as:

       - sensitivity to the economic and business environment,

       - dependence on major customers, suppliers or products,

       - dependence on scarce raw materials or expertise of
         uncertain supply,

       - termination or expiry of patent, licences or franchises,

       - currency and commodity price risk and their day to day
         management,

       - environmental protection costs and possible liabilities;

(c)   a discussion of the impact on overall results and cash flows
       of both discontinued activities and new activities;

(d)   a discussion of the impact on overall results and cash flows
       of acquired businesses, including their integration with
       existing activities;

(e)   a discussion of the extent to which the growth in earnings
       has been affected by inflation;

(f)   an indication of the influence of exchange rate changes on
       the results and a discussion of their effect on comparisons
       with previous years' results;

(g)   a discussion of the enterprise's expenditure on research and
       development and other revenue investment.

Review of financial needs and resources

The purpose of this aspect of the OFR would be to enable
management to explain to the user of the Annual Report the
enterprise's liquidity and solvency, including the financing
requirements resulting from its capital expenditure plans,
together with the approach to managing interest rate, foreign
exchange rate and commodity price fluctuations on an overall
basis.

It is envisaged that this review would include the following:

(a)   a discussion of the enterprise's current capital structure,
       explaining the purpose and impact of financing transactions
       entered into during the period covered by the financial
       statements and up to date of signing; and major fixed assets
       or investment acquisitions and disposals during this period;

(b) a discussion of the enterprise's approach to managing
     interest rate risk and foreign currency exchange rate risk;

(c) a discussion of the enterprise's current liquidity, giving
     details of peak borrowing requirement and borrowing
     facilities. The discussion should include confirmation that
     the enterprise can meet its short term cash requirements
     from existing borrowing facilities without breaching
     covenant or other borrowing restrictions or, if this is not
     the case, details of the restrictions and the action being
     taken to remedy the situation. It should also include
     details of any restrictions on the enterprise's ability to
     transfer funds from one part of the enterprise to meet the
     cash needs of another part of the enterprise;

(d) a summary of the enterprise's fixed and working capital
     investment plans, distinguishing, if practicable, between
     expenditure intended to maintain existing businesses and
     that intended to expand existing businesses or develop new
     business areas;

(e) a summary of the enterprise's internal and external sources
     of funds available to meet its capital expenditure plans,
     its working capital requirements and other financial
     commitments, and an assessment of its long term solvency.

Commentary on shareholders' return and value

The purpose of this aspect of the OFR would be to enable
management to explain to the user of the annual report the
relationship between operating results and shareholders' earnings
and dividend payments; and the relationship between the financial
statements and the overall value of the enterprise.

It would be helpful for the user to understand how value to
shareholders has been enhanced. It is, therefore, envisaged how
value to shareholders has been enhanced. it is, therefore,
envisaged that the OFR would include a commentary from the
shareholders' perspective, including:

(a) a discussion of the increase or decrease in dividends paid
     and proposed in comparison with the increase or decrease in
     operating profit, profit attributable to members, total
     gains and losses and earnings per share (indicating other
     influences on the level of dividend), together with a
     discussion of return on assets and return on equity;

(b) a commentary on strengths and resources of the enterprise
     whose value is not, or not adequately, reflected in the
     balance sheet (such as brands and other similar items) and
     changes in such items over the period; however, it is not
     intended that an overall valuation of the enterprise be
     given, nor, in the case of listed companies, for net asset
     value to be reconciled to market capitalisation.

PRESENTATION OF THE OFR

Whether or not presented as a separate section of the annual
report, the OFR should clearly be seen to be the responsibility
of all the directors. If it is formally referred to in the
Directors' Report it could meet the Companies Act requirement to

give a fair review of the development of the business of the
company or group during the year and of its position at the end
of it, but would go much further than is normally considered
necessary to meet the requirement; if part of the Directors'
Report, all directors would be formally responsible for the OFR.
It is not intended that any distinction be made between those
parts of the OFR that are considered to be necessary to meet the
Companies Act requirements and those giving additional
information.

Conclusion

This chapter has attempted to provide extensive details of
the requirements of the Companies Act and the accounting
standards. It has considered the major changes required to the
face of the profit and loss account by Financial Reporting
Standards 3 (FRS 3). The disclosure requirements in the notes to
the company accounts and the directors' report have been
considered. Finally the future of financial reporting through
the OFR has been contemplated. This OFR has now been issued as a
statement by the Financial Reporting Council, but is not FRS
standard. It simply encourages best practice in external
reporting by consensus.

CHAPTER 7

Examples of Company Accounting

Introduction

This chapter of the book deals with some further basic accounting required to understand company accounting at the level needed for attempting testing examination questions.

The chapter deals with accounting for revaluation and taxation then questions and answers are provided on the preparation of the primary statements required and the notes to company accounts.

Complications - Company Accounting

Students will undoubtedly come into contact in examples with revaluation adjustments and taxation and these are now dealt with before a fully worked example is provided.

Revaluation reserve

A revaluation reserve must be created when a company revalues one or more of its fixed assets. Revaluations frequently occur with freehold property, as the market value of property rises. The company's directors might wish to show a more 'reasonable' value of the asset in their balance sheet, to avoid giving a misleading impression about the financial position of the company.

When an asset is revalued, the difference between:

(a)   the revalued amount of the asset and

(b)   its net book value in the company's accounts before the revaluation takes place, is credited to a revaluation reserve.

Depreciation is subsequently charged on the revalued amount.

Example: revaluation reserve

X Ltd purchased land and buildings for £20,000 ten years ago; their net book value (after depreciation of the buildings) is now £19,300. A professional valuation of £390,000 has been given, and the directors wish to reflect this in the accounts.

The revaluation surplus is £390,000 - £19,300 = £370,700. The entry to be made is therefore:

	£	£
Dr Freehold property	370,700	
Cr revaluation reserve		370,300

The balance sheet will then include:

	£
Reserves	
Revaluation reserve increased by	370,700
Fixed assets	
Freehold property (at valuation) increased by £370,700 to £390,000	390,000

An unrealised profit (such as the £370,700 above) is generally not distributable.

Taxation in Company Accounts

The treatment of taxation in company accounts is a complicated subject and difficult to learn, because a knowledge of tax law is required and an understanding of the accounting treatment of tax in company accounts.

This section explains taxation only to level required to prepare company accounts for publication purposes.

Requirements Related to Taxation in Company Accounts

In order to fully understand the requirements of taxation in practice a good knowledge of the following would be necessary:

- The Company Act 1985 as amended by CA 1989.
- SSAP's 15 Accounting for deferred taxation and 8 the treatment of taxation under the imputation system in the accounts of companies.

It is assumed that VAT SSAP 5 would have already been extensively covered.

This section will deal first with the imputation system and corporation tax on company profits, then attention will be paid to the treatment of deferred taxation.

Corporation Tax

Companies are required to pay corporation tax on their taxable profits and taxable profit is a different profit than accounting profit.

Accounting profit is arrived at by taking income from trading into account and deducting operating and other expenses. Some expenses are not allowed for tax purposes, such an entertainment. Depreciation is not allowed for tax purposes, capital allowances are given instead.

Assessing the level of taxation therefore involves the construction of accounting information in accordance with tax law, once this has been agreed the amount of the tax liability can be calculated as a percentage of taxable profit.

The corporation tax rate varies according to the size of the company small companies @ 25% others @ 35%. a good deal of effort is required to establish the tax liability and it may be changed in negotiations with the Inland Revenue.

Payment of Corporation Tax

In general companies pay the corporation tax liability nine months after the end of the accounting period. More generous arrangements are being phased out, which applied to companies trading before 1 April 1965.

The delay in payment by companies of their tax liability results in the profit and loss account being charged with an estimated tax liability and a creditor being created. This tax liability is normally referred to as mainstream liability.

Advance Corporation Tax - ACT

If a company pays a dividend to shareholders during an accounting period it normally would be required to make an advance payment of corporation tax. This means that some of the mainstream liability would be paid before the nine months after the accounting period has elapsed.

The calculation of ACT involves assessing how much dividend is being paid and calculating the basic rate income tax that the company is imputed to have given shareholders as a tax credit.

For example the company pay dividends to shareholders amounting to £15,000. Shareholders would receive their dividend and would also accept a tax credit at the standard tax rate, meaning that basic rate tax has been paid.

Therefore the company dividend of £15,000 is equivalent to paying shareholders £20,000 less tax @ 25% of £5,000.

This figure of £5,000 can be found by applying the ACT fraction to the dividend paid. The ACT fraction is in this case 25/75, i.e. the income tax basic rate divided by one hundred less the income tax basic rate. If the income tax rate was 30% the ACT fraction would be 30/70.

The £5,000 tax credit or ACT is paid by the company to the inland revenue, on a quarterly basis fourteen days after the following dates 1 March, 30 June, 30 September, 31 December, or if nearer fourteen days after the annual balance sheet date.

Illustrative Example

Tarzan Ltd calculate taxable profits to be £2.5 million and proposed a dividend of £1,200,000. Calculate the corporation tax liability and the amount of ACT.

Corporation tax liability @ 35% = £875,000 on £2.5 million taxable profit.

Advanced corporation tax = £1,200,000 x 25/75 = £400,000

Therefore the accounting treatment required is as follows:

	Dr £	Cr £
(a) Profit and loss account	875,000	
Creditor corporation tax		875,000

being the tax liability for Tarzan Ltd.

(b) The amount of ACT <u>if it had been paid in cash</u> would have been
as follows:
(i) ACT recoverable   400,000
    Cash   400,000

or

however if the dividend had only just been proposed the
entries would be as follows:

(ii) ACT recoverable   400,000
    ACT payable   400,000

Therefore if ACT had been paid only £875,000 less £400,000 would
have been subsequently payable to the Inland Revenue.

Deferred Taxation

The reason for deferred taxation is that timing differences occur
due to the taxation system. For example capital allowance at one
time could be obtained @ 100%. This meant that the tax burden
was reduced in the year of the capital investment significantly
and yet in accordance with the matching concept should only have
been brought into account as the burden is charged to the
profit statement.

However, the tax authorities pay no regard to depreciation and
therefore a timing difference occurred. the deferred taxation
concept was to charge extra tax to profit and loss account in
line with the deprecation policy in the first year of allowance
and reverse the process over the depreciable life of the asset.
This system continues today even though 100% capital allowances
have been gradually phased out. However, although the size of
deferred tax adjustments are less significant these days if
assets are written down for tax purposes at different rates from
depreciation rates applied in the accounts, timing difference
will arise.

For example a motor vehicle is purchased for £6,000 the capital
allowance is 25% but depreciation only 10% on cost.

The capital allowance of 25% or £1,500 reduces the tax burden by
say 35% £525. However, the depreciation charge is only £600
which if allowable would reduce the tax burden by 35% £210.
Therefore a deferred tax adjustment in year 1 of £315 should be
effected as follows:

	Dr £	Cr £
Profit and loss account taxation	315	
Deferred tax account		315

Solls Soyce Ltd Exercise 7.1

This first question is provided to demonstrate the requirements
to deal with the complications of taxation, and although working
notes are shown in the answer to the question is not complemented
by complete notes as required by the Companies Act.

FULLY WORKED EXAMPLE SOLLS SOYCE

QUESTION

Solls Soyce Ltd had the following trial balance at 31 December 1992

	£	£
Ordinary share capital		280,000
7% preference shares		40,000
Sales		753,400
Cost of sales	556,540	
Debenture interest	1,000	
Stock in trade at 31 December 1992	78,290	
Preference dividend	1,400	
Taxation:		
corporation tax at 1 January 1992		20,000
deferred tax		10,000
advanced corporation tax paid	300	
Wages and salaries	45,370	
Motor vehicles - at cost	36,000	
Fixtures and fittings - at cost	52,800	
Provision for depreciation on		
motor vehicles		11,600
Provision for depreciation		
on fixtures and fittings		4,560
Investment income: £		
quoted 700		
unquoted 2,100		2,800
Debtors and creditors	81,060	44,808
Freehold land - at cost	256,000	
Profit and loss account balance at		
1 January 1992		12,140
Bad debts written off	1,880	
Quoted investments	8,000	
Unquoted investments	15,600	
General expenses	61,810	
Balance at bank	21,258	
Share premium account		10,000
General reserve		8,000
5% debentures, redeemable 1998		20,000
	---------	---------
	1,217,308	1,217,308
	---------	---------

Notes

1. The directors recommend an ordinary final dividend of 10%.

2. £18,000 is to be transferred to general reserve.

3. Depreciation is to be provided:

    > Fixtures and fitting: 10% on cost
    > Motor vehicles: 15% on cost

    £800 of the depreciation on fixtures and fittings is to be treated as a manufacturing cost; all other depreciation is to be divided equally between administration and distribution.

4. £8,500 of the general expenses related to distribution costs; the remainder related to administrative expenses.

5. Wages and salaries include £5,600 manufacturing wages and £19,280 administrative salaries; the remainder are distribution costs.

6. The freehold land is to be revalued to £300,000.

7. The quoted investments consist of shares in UK companies, which had a market value of£12,000 on 31 December 1992. the unquoted investments consist of short-term loans to local authorities.

8. Taxation of £12,000 is to be provided on profits for the year.

9. The amount shown on the trial balance in respect of corporation tax represents the provision made for the year ended 31 December 1991. The tax liability for that year has been finally agreed at £18,000 and is payable on 31 March 1993.

10. The deferred tax provision is to be increased to £11,000.

11. The rate of corporation tax is to be taken as 50% and the income tax rate as 30% in all relevant years.

12. The authorised share capital is as follows:

    500,000 ordinary shares of £1 each.
    100,000 7% preference shares of £1 each.

13. It is necessary to provide for the balance of the preference dividend to be paid.

REQUIRED

(a) Produce a profit and loss account for the year ended 31December 1992 and a balance sheet as at 31 December 1992, presenting these statements as far as is possible from the information given in the format of the Companies Act 1985. (Notes to the accounts are not required.)

(b) Draft the note that would be included in the accounts in compliance with the Compliance Act 1985 in respect of the taxation charge in the profit and loss account.

ANSWER Exercise 7.1

Solls Soyce Ltd Profit and Loss Account for year ended 31.12.92

	£	£
Turnover		753,400
Less: Cost of sales		562,940

		190,460
Less:		
Distribution costs	33,930	
Administrative expenses	79,410	113,340
	------	-------
Operating profit		77,120
Other income (Investments)		2,800

		79,920
Debenture interest		1,000

Profit on ordinary activities before taxation		78,920
Taxation		11,000

Profit on ordinary activities after taxation		67,920
Transfer to General Reserve	18,000	
Dividends: Paid: Preference	1,400	
Proposed: Preference	1,400	
Ordinary	28,000	48,800
	------	------
Unappropriated profits for the year		19,120
Unappropriated profits b/f		12,140

Unappropriated profits c/f		31,260

Workings:

1. Cost of sales

	£
Per trial balance	556,540
Wages and salaries	5,600
Depreciation: fixtures and fittings	800

	562,940
	-------

2. Distribution costs:

Wages and salaries	20,490
General expenses	8,500
Depreciation: motor vehicles	2,700
fixtures and fittings	2,240

	33,930
	------

3. Administrative expenses:

Wages and salaries	19,280
Bad debts	1,880
General expenses	53,310
Depreciation: motor vehicles	2,700
fixtures and fittings	2,240

	79,410
	------

4. See answer to part (b) of this question.

Solls Soyce Ltd Balance Sheet as at 31.12.92

	£	£
Fixed assets		
Tangible assets		362,960
Investments		23,600

		385,560
Deferred asset		
ACT recoverable		12,600
Current assets	180,608	
Creditors falling due within one year	104,808	

Net current assets		75,800

Total assets Less current liabilities		473,960
Creditors: Amount falling due after		
more than 1 year	31,700	
Provisions for liabilities and charges		
Deferred Tax	11,000	42,700
	------	-------
Net assets		431,260

Representing	£
Share capital and reserves	
Share capital	320,000
Share premium account	10,000
Revaluation reserve	44,000
General reserve	26,000
Profit and loss account	31,260

	431,260

Notes to the accounts

1. Tangible assets:

	Cost or Valuation £	Accumulated Depreciation £	Net £
Land and buildings	300,000	–	300,000
Fixtures and fittings	52,800	9,840	42,960
Motor vehicles	36,000	17,000	19,000
	-------	------	-------
	388,800	26,840	361,960
	-------	------	-------

    Freehold land was revalued during the year from £256,000 to £300,000

2. Investments:

	£
Quoted (market value £12,000)	8,000
Unquoted (short-term loan to local authorities)	15,600

	23,600
	------

3. Current assets: £

     Stock   78,290
     Debtors   81,060
     Bank   21,258

                                                     180,608

These notes have been shown purely to help students understand
the answer. The question specifically says notes to the accounts
are not required.

Solls Soyce Ltd - Answer to Part (b)

The note required for taxation would be as follows:

Taxation
                                                          £
UK Corporation Tax at 50% on profits for the year   12,000
Amount over-provided for the previous year   (2,000)
Increase in deferred tax provision   1,000

                                                       11,000
                                                       ======

(Note mainstream liability for 1992 has been reduced by £300
ACT.)

To ensure student fully understand the Tax Treatment the
following extensive note is provided. This would not be required
in this detail in the accounts.

Note to CIPFA P1 student regarding tax treatment in Solls Soyce
Ltd

Note 1   The trial balance shows the following:
                                         Dr   Cr
                                         £   £
Corporation tax at 1 Jan 1992   20,000*
Deferred tax   10,000
ACT paid   300

Note 2   Tax for the year ending 31 Dec 1991 as provisional been
made in 1991 accounts and was £20,000* but has now been agreed at
£18,000. therefore the liability in the trial balance is too
high, by £2,000.

Note 3   This year assessment of corporation tax is £12,000. This
must be provided for in the P & L account, and a long term
creditor created.

Entries in Accounts

Reduce liability for note 1   Dr   Cr
                                             £   £
Creditor tax 1991   2,000
     P & L account over provision   2,000

P & L account corporation tax   12,000
     Creditors   12,000

*will be reduced for ACT paid £300.

Deferred Tax

The deferred tax account in the trial balance is £10,000 and this now needs to be increased to £11,000.

Entries in Accounts	Dr £	Cr £
P & L account deferred tax	1,000	
Deferred tax		1,000

ACT

Dividends amount to £29,400	- preference	£ 1,400
	- ordinary	£28,000

		29,400

ACT therefore is £29,400 x 30/70 = £12,600

Entries in the accounts	Dr £	Cr £
ACT recoverable	12,600	
ACT payable on proposal dividends		12,600

This could have been debited to the deferred tax account as an alternative.

ACT paid of £300 will be taken off of the balance sheet liability for mainstream corporation tax,

Summary of the Treatment

On the final balance sheet the following figures will appear.

Creditors Amount falling due within one year.

Corporation tax £18,000 (20,000 - 2,000)
ACT payable on proposed dividends £12,600

Creditors Amount due more than one year.

Corporation tax £11,700 (£12,000 - £300)

Charges to P & L Account

Corporation Tax 1992	£12,000	
Corporation Tax 1991	£(2,000)	over provided
Increase deferred tax	£ 1,000	

	11,000	
	======	

Motor Mouth PLC - Exercise 7.2

This next question requires consideration of the FRS 3 with regard to the following:

- The sale of a vehicle
- The treatment of a discontinued operation.

Motor Mouth PLC is a small company which has been trading for many years as electrical contractor. the book-keeper has extracted the attached trial balance at 31 December 1992. During November 1992, a decision was taken to withdraw from the business of repairs to appliances and concentrate on industrial electrical contracting.

The following information may be relevant.

a) There are three directors: Major, Lilley and Lamont. Lamont is part-time only and is paid a salary of £6,000. Major is Chairman and shares the balance of salaries equally with Lilley.

b) The company has an authorised £1m of ordinary shares of 50p each and £100,000 5% preference shares of £1 each.

c) Adjustments are to be made for the following:

   i)   A final dividend of 3.5p per share.
   ii)   Closing stock at cost of £381,000.
   iii) Corporation tax of £48,000 for the current year.
   iv)   Director's fees of £4,000 each.
   v)   Office expenses prepaid £2,000.
   vi)   Vehicle expenses accrued £3,000.
   vii) Depreciation for the year is at rates of 12.5% on cost for plant and equipment and 25% on cost for vehicles No depreciation is provided on land and buildings.

d) Land and buildings were revalued by XY and Co., Chartered Surveyor at £105,000 on 31 December 1992. This value is to be incorporated into the accounts.

e) A general provision of 2% is to be made in respect of the outstanding debtors.

f) The suspense account represents sale proceeds of a vehicle which was three years old, when sold on 1.1.92 and which originally cost £4,000. no other entry has been made in respect of this transaction.

g) Corporation tax for previous year has now been agreed at £30,000 and is payable on 1 January 1993.

h) Bank interest of £2,000 is included in office expenses.

i) Included in the trial balance are the following items related to repairs to appliances. Cost of sales £600,000, administrative expenses £50,000, selling expenses £75,000. Turnover was £675,000.

You are required to prepare a Profit and Loss Account for the year ending 31 December 1992 and a Balance Sheet as at that date, to comply with the minimum requirements of the Companies Acts and FRS3 so far as possible from the information given.

Do not invent information.

Motor Mouth PLC

Trial Balance as at   31.12.92

	Dr	Cr
5% Preference shares		56,000
800,000 Ordinary shares		400,000
General reserve		30,000
Unappropriated profits		81,500
Freehold property, at cost	80,000	
Sales staff salaries	63,000	
Plant and equipment, at cost	62,000	
Motor vehicles, at cost	58,000	
Accumulated depreciation at 1.1.92 Plant and Equipment		17,000
Accumulated depreciation at 1.1.92 Motor vehicles		12,000
Corporation tax		28,000
Office staff salaries	57,000	
Debtors and creditors	486,000	301,000
Interim pref. dividend	1,400	
Interim Ord. dividend	21,000	
Stock at 1.1.92	421,500	
Purchases	1,492,000	
Sales		1,894,000
Bank overdraft		16,650
Directors' salaries	54,000	
Office expenses	23,000	
Vehicle expenses	18,000	
Suspense account		750
	---------	---------
	2,836,900	2,836,900
	=========	=========

Tutorial Answer to Motor Mouth Plc

Treatment of Notes to the question

a)   This note provides information which will be required to be provided in the notes to the accounts of Motor Mouth. The information needed is in respect of the amounts earned by directors, and needs to be combined with other remuneration of the directors.

       Total directors salary £54,000 of which Lamont   £6,000
                                              Major   £24,000
                                              Lilley   £24,000

b)   The authorised capital of the company is needed for the notes to the accounts.

c)   Adjustments.

       i)   Final dividend can be computed by multiplying the

number of shares called up by the dividend per share as follows:

800,000 ordinary shares x 3.5p per share = £28,000

This sum can be charged to the profit and loss account in the appropriate place, and shown in the balance sheet as a current liability as follows:

	Dr	Cr
P & L account	28,000	
current liabilities		28,000

ii) The figure of closing stock is needed to compute the cost of goods sold. This can be calculated as follows:

	£
Opening stock	421,500
Plus purchases	1,492,000

	1,913,500
Less closing stock	381,000

	1,532,500

add any items related to the cost of good sold in later notes namely depreciation of plant.

iii) Corporation tax needs to be charged to the profit and loss account and show as a current liability. However this is complicated by having to make an adjustment due to note (g).

	Dr	Cr
P & L account	48,000	
Non current liability		48,000

Notice that the corporation tax is not a current liability but a liability exceeding 1 year. This can be established on the basis that last year's tax liability has not yet been due for payment.

iv) Directors fees of £4,000 each need to be added to the charges for administration in the profit and loss account. These amounts also need to be considered in conjunction with note (a) above when considering the bands of remuneration for directors, which needs to be shown in the notes to the accounts.

	Dr	Cr
P & L account - admin expense	12,000	
Current liabilities		12,000

v) Office expenses have been prepaid and therefore the following entries are required.

	Dr	Cr
Prepaid expense	2,000	
Office expenses		2,000

vi) Vehicles expenses accrued need to be adjusted.

	Dr	Cr
Vehicles expenses	3,000	
Current liability		3,000

vii) Depreciation is to be provided as follows:

Plant and Equipment	12.5% on cost
Vehicles	25 % on cost

Plant and Equipment therefore is depreciated as follows:

£62,000 @ 12.5% = £7,750

	Dr	Cr
	£	£
Profit & loss account		
Cost of goods sold	7,750	
depreciation account		7,750

Depreciation of vehicles is a little more difficult because a vehicle has been sold according to note (f).

It is necessary therefore to deal with note (f). This note explains that a vehicle had been sold for £750, and had originally cost £4,000 having been depreciated for three full years. The following ledger accounts can be shown to demonstrate the adjustments.

Motor Vehicle Account

	£		£
bal b/fwd	58,000	Disposal	4,000

Depreciation Motor Vehicle

	£		£
Disposal	3,000	bal b/fwd	12,000

```
              Disposal Account
                £                       £
----------------------------------------------------------
F asset         4,000  │ Depreciation   3,000

                       │ Cash             750

                       │ Loss to P & L    250
                -----  │                -----
                4,000  │                4,000
                =====  │                =====
```

The loss on the disposal account although not material to
the accounts will be shown separately on the face of the
profit and loss account, to show the intended treatment
required of profits and losses on disposal by FRS 3.

(d) Land & buildings were revalued and the entry required is as
     follows:

	Dr £	Cr £
Land & building	25,000	
Revaluation reserve		25,000

The value of land and building will now be shown at £105,000
being £80,000 previously shown plus this £25,000. This
information will also need to be shown in the notes.

(e) This note requires a provision to be created for doubtful
     debts at 2% of outstanding debtors. The following entries
     are required.

	Dr £	Cr £
Profit & loss - Administrative expense	9,720	
Provision for doubtful debts		9,720

The provision has been calculated as follows:
     £486,000 @ 2% = £9,720

(f) This note has been dealt with at the same time as note
     c(vii).

(g) Corporation tax for the previous year has now been agreed at
     £30,000. However, the trial balance indicates that the
     accounts are only showing a liability of £28,000. It can be
     assumed therefore that the previous year's accounts have
     been undercharged by £2,000. Therefore the following
     adjustment is required:

	Dr £	Cr £
Profit & loss account	2,000	
Current liability		2,000

When this note is combined with note c(iii) the total charge
for tax will be £48,000 + £2,000 = £50,000.

(h) Bank interest paid needs to be shown separately on the face of the profit and loss account. There has been an error in charging interest to the office expense account which needs to be corrected as follows:

	Dr £	Cr £
P & L account bank interest	2,000	
Office expense		2,000

(I) This note enables discontinued activities to be identified. These activities must be shown separately on the face of the profit and loss account, and will feature in the notes required for net expenses.

Motor Mouth Plc Profit & Loss Account for the year ending 31 December 1992

	Continuing £	Discontinued £	Total £
1. Turnover	1,219,000	675,000	1,894,000
Cost of sales	940,250	600,000	1,540,250
Gross profit	278,750	75,000	353,750
2. Net operating expenses	124,220	125,000	249,220
Operating profit (loss)	154,530	(50,000)	104,530
3. Loss on sale of vehicle	250	---	250
Profit (loss) on ordinary activities before interest	154,280	(50,000)	104,280
4. Interest payable			2,000
5. Profit on ordinary activities before tax			102,280
6. Tax on profit on ordinary activities (48,000+2,000)			50,000
Profit on ordinary activities after tax			52,280
7. Dividends - ordinary shares 49,000 - Preference shares 2,800			51,800
Retained profit for the financial year			480
Earnings per share*			6.19p

* Earnings per share based on profit after tax and preference dividend as per FRS 3, i.e. £52,280 - 2,800 = £49,480

800,000 ordinary shares

Motor Mouth Balance Sheet as at 31 December 1992

		£	£	£
Fixed assets				
Tangible assets (8)				173,750
Current assets				
Stocks	(9)	381,000		
Debentures	(10)	478,280	859,280	
Creditors:				
Amounts falling due within 1 year (11)		392,050	467,230	
				640,980
Creditors:				
Amounts falling due after more than 1 year (12)			48,000	
				592,980
Capital and Reserves				
Called up share capital (13)				456,000
Other reserves				30,000
Revaluation Reserve (14)				25,000
Profit & Loss Account				81,980
				592,980

PRIMARY STATEMENT

Statement of total recognised gains and losses

	1992	Previous year not available
	£	£
Profit for the financial year	49,480	
Unrealised surplus on revaluation of property	25,000	
Total gain since last annual report	74,480	

Note on Historic Cost Profit and Loss

There are no material differences between the historic profit and loss and that profit reported because

(i)   Assets subjected to revaluation are not depreciated
(ii) Assets sold were not subjected to revaluation

Reconciliation of Movements in Equity Shareholders Funds (can be primary statement or a note).

		£
Profit for the financial year		52,280
dividends - pref.	2,800	
- ord.	49,000	51,800
		480
Other recognised gains or losses		25,000
Ordinary shareholders funds capital b/fwd		511,500
		536,980

Reserves

	General £	Revaluation £	P & L a/c £	Total £
1. At beginning of the year	30,000	-	81,500	111,500
2. Transfer from P&L a/c	-	-	480	480
3. Surplus on property revaluation	-	25,000	-	25,000
Reserves at year end	30,000	25,000	81,980	136,980

Nominal Share Capital £400,000

Cash Flow Statement for the year ending 31 December 1992

Not enough information available to produce a cash flow statement.

Notes to the Accounts

Accounting Policies

Based on - Depreciation at cost P&M 12.5%
                                    MV   25 %

- Bad debts provision 2%
- Stocks at cost

1. Turnover

We have little information about the sales in terms of different markets, or geographical operations. We cannot therefore provide any note of any consequence.

2. Net operating expenses.

FRS 3
Note required in respect of profit and loss account (to provide breakdown of distribution costs admin expenses other operating income)

Net operating expenses

	Continuing £	Discontinuing £	Total £
Distribution	22,500	75,000	97,500
Administrative	101,720	50,000	151,720
Other operating income			
Total	124,220	125,000	249,220

Admin expenses	£	Selling & Distribution	£
Bad debts provision	9,720	Sales staff salaries	63,000
Office expenses	19,000	Vehicle expenses	21,000
Directors' fees	12,000	Depreciation vehicles	13,500
Directors' salaries	54,000		------
Office salaries	57,000		97,500
	-------		------
	151,720		
	-------		

3. Profits or losses on the disposal of fixed assets

An asset was sold at a loss of £250 which has been shown as a separate item in accordance with FRS 3. It is not really a material item but demonstrates the idea of FRS 3 in reporting such asset sales on the face of the profit and loss account.

4. Interest Payable

The interest payable is in respect of bank interest and amounts to £2,000.

5. Profit on Ordinary Activities before tax

The profit before tax has been calculated after charging the following items.

		£
Depreciation Plant & machinery		7,750
Motor vehicles		13,500

Total		21,250
		======

Salary costs & Director costs

Staff costs including directors   £186,000
(not enough information to provide wages; NI; pensions)

	£
Directors - salary	54,000
- fees	12,000

- total	66,000

Chairman received	28,000

Earnings bands	£5,000 = £10,000	1
	£25,000 - £30,000	2

6. Taxation

The corporate tax rate was x%, and the charge to profit and loss is as follows:

	£
Corporation tax estimate current year	48,000
Under provision previous year	2,000

	50,000
	======

7. Dividends

dividends approved and provided for are as follows:

	5% preference £	Ordinary shares £	Total £
Interim dividends	1,400	21,000	22,400
Final dividends	1,400	28,000	29,400
	------	------	------
	2,800	49,000	51,800

Ordinary dividends were 2.625p Interim and 3.5 Final dividend.

8. Tangible Assets

	Freehold property £	Plant & equipment £	Motor vehicles £	Total £
Balance @ 1/1/92	80,000	62,000	58,000	200,000
Additions	-	-	-	-
Disposals	-	-	(4,000)	(4,000)
Revaluation	25,000	-	-	25,000
	105,000	62,000	54,000	221,000
Depreciation @ 1/1/92	-	17,000	12,000	29,000
Disposals	-	-	(3,000)	(3,000)
Charge for the year	-	7,750	13,500	21,250
	Nil	24,750	22,500	47,250
Net book value	105,000	37,250	31,500	173,750

9. Stocks

This note would normally show the different categories of stock
but in this case we only appear to have one class of stock.

10. Debtors

	£	£
Debtors are made up as follows:		
Debtors	486,000	
Provision for doubtful debts	9,720	476,280
Prepaid expense		2,000
		478,280

11. Creditors Amounts falling due within 1 year

	£
Creditors	301,000
Accruals	3,000
Directors' fees	12,000
Proposed dividends	29,400
Taxation	30,000
Bank overdraft	16,650
	392,050

12. Creditors amounts falling due after more than 1 year

	£
Taxation payable	48,000

13. Called up share capital

The company has an authorised £1 million ordinary shares of 50
pence each, and £100,000 of 5% preference shares @ £1.

Capital called up is 800,000 ordinary shares @ 50p totalling
£400,000. Preference shares in issue amount to £56,000 @ 5%.

14. Revaluation Reserve

The revaluation reserve is related to the revaluation of land and
buildings by the XY & Co. Chartered Surveyors at £105,000 on the
31 December 1992.

Exercise Question 7.3

1. In 1974 JM, who was engaged in the wholesale trade, had an opportunity to buy a whole building for £170,000 (plus the usual costs). The building was too big for his own business and was beyond his resources, but there was not doubt that in time the surplus space in the property, in excess of his own requirements, could be let. He therefore approached AB and CD for financial assistance and a company was formed, JM Ltd., with an authorised capital of £500,000 in £1 Ordinary shares, to run both the wholesale business and the property. JM himself became Managing Director and was also the Chairman. AB and CD took little part in the day to day management but were directors, while in 1976 EF was engaged as assistant to JM and at the end of that year became a director; there have been no other changes in the constitution of the board.

    Attached is the trial balance of JM Ltd. at 31 December 1992 prior to making final adjustments for preparing the company's accounts for the year ended on that date. No dividends have been paid before 1992, but in anticipation of a more substantial profit in that year, an interim dividend has been paid in October.

    (a) (i) Depreciation for 1992 has <u>not</u> been applied before the trial balance was taken out and must be provided for. The straight line method has always been used - at 10% on Fixtures and Fittings and at 20% on Motor Vehicles.

         (ii) No depreciation has so far been provided on the Freehold property - indeed it has recently increased in value and a formal valuation by XY, FRICS, gave a figure of £400,000. The directors were quite surprised at this figure and have decided that it should be incorporated in the books and accounts of the company as the value of the property.

    (b) Fees for the directors are to be provided at £2,500 each. Salaries, already included in the figure for Salaries and Wages, are made up as follows:

	£
Paid to JM, Managing Director	£17,500
Paid to AB	3,000
Paid to CD	3,000
Paid to EF, Asst. Managing Director	12,000
Paid to GH, Marketing Executive	10,500
Paid to IJ, Chief Accountant	9,500
Paid to other salaried staff	26,897
	£82,397

    There is a pension scheme for all these salaried persons, the company contributing 10% of salaries paid, this being charged in the general expenses. General expenses also includes National Insurance contributions of %5 of Salaries and Wages paid (see note g).

(c)   A small fabrics treatment business was acquired by JM
      Ltd on the 1 July 1992. The assets and liabilities
      have been brought into the trial balance at fair value
      and a payment made for the net assets has been made.
      However, the payment agreed for the net assets was
      £1,000 more than their fair value. JM personally paid
      this £1,000 (the only item not included in the trail
      balance) because the directors did not want to create
      any goodwill in the accounts. JM expects reimbursement
      and you should treat the amount as a net loss on
      purchase.

      The small fabrics business' revenue income and
      expenditure included in the trial balance is as
      follows:

| | Dr | Cr |
	£	£
Sales		55,000
Cost of sales	12,000	
Distribution	15,000	
Administration	12,000	

      Orders have been placed for new equipment to the value
      of £55,000, and delivery is expected in February 1993.

(d)   (i)   The provision against Bad Debts should be
             increased to 2.5% of the total of outstanding
             debtors.

      (ii)   The closing stock was £182,574, at cost on a FIFO
             basis. Its replacement cost was £220,000.

      (iii) Provision should be made for auditors fees of
             £1,000 and expenses of £500.

(e)   (i)   Corporation Tax on profits of the year (at 50%)
             must be provided - a sum of £40,000.

      (ii)   Assume the balance on the Corporation Tax a/c
             represent an underprovision for the prior year.
             Ignore all other tax implications.

(f)   A final dividend for 1992 is to be recommended of the
      same amount as the interim dividend (£8,750).

(g)   Salaries and wages should be allocated as follows, cost
      of sales 60%, distribution costs 30% and administrative
      expenses 10%. Heating, lighting and rates and general
      expenses should be allocated on the same basis. Charge
      hire of plant to distribution cost and allocate
      depreciation of fixtures and fittings as follows, costs
      of sales 80%, administrative 20%.

(h)   Creditors at £34,581 comprise trade creditors £30,000,
      PAYE £2,000 and other creditors £2,581.

YOU ARE REQUIRED:

**To produce, in a suitable style for publication, Profit and loss
Account, Balance Sheet and appropriate notes regarding the year**

to 31 December 1992, to comply with the <u>minimum</u> requirements of the Companies Acts, and FRS 3.

<u>Note</u>:   If you have to do workings and calculations in respect of your answer, these should be done in recognisable form and included in your submission.

JM Ltd.   Trial balance at 31 December 1992 before final entries

Ordinary Capital		350,000
Profit * Loss a/c		23,476
Dividends	8,750	
Fixtures and Fittings	85,380	
Motor Vehicles	82,850	
Freehold property	180,400	
Stock (1 Jan 1992)	172,226	
Accumulated Depreciation (Fixtures)		29,475
Accumulated Depreciation (Motors)		45,350
Purchases	434,864	
Salaries and Wages	177,769	
Warehouse Heating, Lighting & Rates	7,635	
Expenses relating to let property	3,540	
General Expenses	55,259	
Hire of Plant	2,360	
Motor Expenses	9,256	
Advertising, etc.	5,525	
Creditors total		34,581
Debtors Total	77,334	
Provision for Bad Debts		710
Bank Interest	2,039	
Sales less returns		782,765
Rents of Property		18,350
Corporation Tax	11,005	
Bank Balance		31,485
	1,316,192	1,316,192

Tutorial Answer JM Ltd

Treatment of the Notes

Note 1.

This note provides historic background to the private company and will enable us to consider whether its size will permit exemption from the detailed filing requirements of the Company's Act.

In addition the note tells us that JM is Chairman, and Managing Director, while three other Directors are engaged by the Company.

(a)   (i)   Depreciation is calculated as follows:

Motor vehicles 20% of £82,850 = £16,570
Fixtures and fittings 10% of £85,380 = £8,538

(ii) The property is revalued to £400,000

	Dr £	Cr £
Freehold property	219,600	
revaluation reserve		219,600

(b) This note enables the salaries and wages to be identified
     and pension and national insurance to be calculated.

	£	Pension £	NI £	Total
Salaries	82,397	8,240	4,120	94,757
Wages	95,372	--	4,769	100,141
	177,769	8,240	8,889	194,898

Plus directors fees
£2,500 x 4 =

	£	Pension £	NI £	Total
	10,000	--	--	10,000
	187,769	8,240	8,889	204,898

(c) This note provides information which needs to be disclosed
     on the face of the profit and loss account in respect of
     acquired operations in accordance with FRS 3.

     The note also identifies a net loss on acquisition which
     must be shown on the face of the profit and loss account.
     Additionally a capital commitment of £50,000 needs to be
     mentioned in the notes to the accounts.

(d) (i) The provision for doubtful debts needs to be adjusted
          to 2.5% of outstanding debtors. This involves the
          following calculation.

          Debtors £77,334 x 2.5% =   £1,933
          Less current provision of   710

          Increase provision required   1,223
                                       =====
          Dr profit and loss account admin expense
          Cr provision for bad debts account

     (ii) This is an interesting note, in that the closing stock
          is given of £182,574, but an unrecognised gain is
          identified which will need to feature in the statement
          of gains and losses required by FRS 3.

          Calculation of the cost of goods sold is as follows:

	£
Opening stock	172,226
Purchases	434,864
	607,090
Less closing stock	182,574

          Stock
                Costs of goods sold 424,516*
                                    =======

<u>NB</u> * Before other allocated costs.

(iii) The following entries are required

	Dr £	Cr £
Administrative expenses	1,500	
Current liabilities		
(accrued expenses)		1,500

Also the audit fee must be shown in the notes of the accounts.

(e)(i)&(ii) The tax position is complicated by a debit balance on the trial balance. this can only occur due to the payment of tax exceeding the provision made in the previous year.

This can be illustrated as follows:

estimated tax payable in 1991 could have been £20,000. this sum would have been debit to the 1991 profit and loss account and credited to the corporation tax account being a liability. Subsequently tax was paid of £31,005. This would have involved the debit of the corporation tax account and the credit of cash.

This balance of £11,005 therefore needs to be charged to the 1992 profit and loss account along with this year's estimated taxpayable.

The entries would be as follows:

	Dr £	Cr £
P & L account current year	40,000	
P & L account underprovision 1991	11,005	
Corporation tax account		51,005

NB   At the end of the year the corporation tax account will have a credit balance of £40,000. This representing the unpaid tax for 1992.

(f)   Adjust the accounts for the final dividend as follows:

	Dr £	Cr £
P & L account dividend proposed	8,750	
Current liability		
dividend proposed		8,750

(g)   <u>Allocation of Costs Over Appropriate Headings</u>

	Cost of Sales £	Distri- bution £	Admin- istration £	Total £
Salaries & Wages	122,939	61,469	20,490	204,898
Heating & Light & Rates	4,581	2,291	763	7,635
General expenses	22,878	11,439	3,813	38,130
Hire of plant	--	2,360	--	2,360
Depreciation f & f	6,830	--	1,708	8,538
	157,228	77,559	26,774	261,561

(h)   This note is required for the calculation of final creditors and to provide detail for the notes to the accounts.

Tutorial Answer JM Ltd 7.1

JM Ltd Profit and Loss Account for the year ending 31 December
1992

		Continuing	Acquired	Total
		£	£	£
1.	Turnover	727,765	55,000	782,765
	Cost of sales	569,744	12,000	581,744
	Gross profit or (loss)	158,021	43,000	201,021
2.	Net operating expenses	96,597	27,000	123,597
3.	Loss on acquisition	–	1,000	1,000
	Profit before interest			76,424
4.	Interest			2,039
5.	Profit on ordinary activities before tax			74,385
6.	Corporation tax			51,005
	Profit after tax			23,380
7.	Dividends			17,500
	Retain earnings for the year			5,880

| * | Earnings per share | | | 6.68p |

$$* \quad \frac{23,380}{350,000} = 6.68p$$

JM Ltd Balance sheet as at 31 December 1992

		£	£	£
Fixed Assets				
8.	Tangible	468,297		
Current Assets				
9.	Stocks	182,574		
10.	Debtors	75,401	257,975	
Current Liabilities Amounts Falling Due				
11.	Within one year		127,316	130,659
	Net Assets			598,956
Capital and Reserves				
	Called up share capital		350,000	
12.	Revaluation reserve		219,600	
	Profit & loss account		29,356	598,956

Notes to the Accounts

1. Turnover

   No analysisis provided

2. Net operating expenses

	Continuing £	Acquired £	Total £
Distribution	93,910	15,000	108,910
Administrative	17,497	12,000	29,497
Other income	(14,810)	--	(14,810)
	96,597	27,000	123,597

3. The loss reported of £1,000 is the excess of fair value paid on the purchase of assets related to the operation of fabric purchased.

4. Interest

5. Profit on ordinary activities before tax

   The profit has been calculated after charging.

	£
Depreciation	25,108
Hire of plant	2,360
Auditors remuneration	1,000
Staff costs wages & salaries	187,769
(including directors)	
Social security	8,889
Pensions	8,240
Directors remuneration	37,275
fees	10,000
pension	3,550
The chairman earned	21,000

Director bandings		
1,000 - 5,000	2
15,000 - 20,000	1
20,000 - 25,000	1

6. Taxation

   50% rate and make up

	£
UK corporation tax	40,000
Underprovision	11,005
	51,005

7. Dividends

	£	
Ordinary paid	8,750	
proposed	8,750	17,500

8. Fixed Assets

	Freehold property	Fixtures & fittings	Motor Vehicles	Total
	£	£	£	£
bal b/fwd	180,400	85,380	82,850	348,630
Additions	--	--	--	--
Revaluations	219,600	--	--	219,600
Disposals	--	--	--	--
	400,000	85,380	82,850	568,230
Depreciation				
bal b/fwd	--	29,475	45,350	74,825
additional provided	--	8,538	16,570	25,108
	--	38,013	61,920	99,933
Net book value	400,000	47,367	20,930	468,297

9. Stocks

The stocks provided in the balance sheet have been valued at F1FO. However, they have a current replacement cost of £220,000. This unrecognised gain appears in the gains and losses statement.

10. Debtors

Debtors are made up as follows:	£
Trade debtors	77,334
less 2.5% provision	1,933
	75,401

Notes to the accounts

Net Operating Expenses

	Continuing	Acquired	Total
	£	£	£
Distribution	93,910	15,000	108,910
Administrative	17,497	12,000	29,497
Other operating income	(14,810)	--	(14,810)
	96,597	27,000	123,597

Workings other operating income	£
Rent income	18,350
Expenses	3,540
	14,810

Workings see note (g)

	Cost of Sales £	Distri- bution £	Admin- istration £	Total £
Note (g)	157,228	77,559	26,774	261,561
goods (d) (ii)	424,516	--	--	424,516
Motor vehicle deprec.	--	16,570	--	16,570
Motor expenses	--	9,256	--	9,256
Advertising	--	5,525	--	5,525
Increase prov. bad debts	--	--	1,223	1,223
Note (d) (iii)	--	--	1,500	1,500
	581,744	108,910	29,497	720,151

JM Statement of Total Recognised Gains and Losses

	£
Profit for the financial year	23,380
Unrealised surplus on revaluation	219,600
Unrealised gain on stock	37,426
Total gain since last annual report	280,406

Historic cost no significant difference

	£
historic profit before tax	74,385

Reconciliation of Movements in Shareholders Funds

	£
Profit for the financial year	23,380
Less dividends	(17,500)
Unre revaluation	219,600
	225,480
Capital b/fwd	373,476
	598,956

Reserves	P & L a/c £	Revaluation £	Total £
bal b/fwd	23,476	--	23,476
additions during year	5,880	219,600	225,480
	29,356	219,600	248,956

Nominal capital = £350,000

11. Creditors falling due within one year

	£
Creditors	34,581
JM	1,000
Corporation tax	40,000
Proposed dividends	8,750
Bank overdraft	31,485
Accrued expenses	1,500
Directors fees	10,000
	127,316

12. <u>Revaluation Reserve</u>

The freehold premises were revalued by XY FRICS and the figure of £400,000 has been brought into the balance sheet as a results.

13. <u>Capital Commitments</u>

A commitment exists to purchase capital equipment at a cost of £55,000 early in 1993. This is required for the fabric treatment business.

Examination Question 7.1

Stream Plc was formed eight years ago to develop, produce and market micro-computers and associated software. Expansion in both areas has been very rapid and the company estimates that in the last year the split between hardware and software in terms of both turnover and profit is 70% and 30% respectively. 15% of the company's turnover was exported and 12% of the company's profit was earned during the year. 19% of Company's share capital is owned by Quick Inc., and American Company. The trail balance at 31 December 1993 is given below.

You ascertain the following information which may or may not be relevant.

i)   At the start of the year there were 20,000,000 ordinary shares of 25p on issue. During the first half of the year a 1 for 4 bonus issue was made. No entries were made in the books to record this and the directors wish to maintain the maximum amount of distributable reserves. The new shares rank for the final dividend only.

ii) The investments in the trial balance are shown at cost and represent temporary surplus funds. Market value of these listed investments is £4.7 million.

iii) The stock as at 31 December 1993 was classified under with net realisable values as stated in £000s.

	Cost	Net Realisable Value
Category A	3,800	3,750
Category B	1,000	1,100
Category C	3,600	4,000
Stock at 31.12.93	8,400	8,850

iv) The directors have placed contracts for building an extension to the company's existing premises for £250,000. Work will begin on 31.3.94.

v)   There are only four directors whose salaries, included in wages and salaries, were as follows:

	£
Managing Director-Chairman	50,000
R & D Director	30,000
Marketing Director	35,000
Financial Director	40,000

vi) The following items outstanding at the end of the year have not been allowed for:

	£
Auditor's remuneration	100,000

vii)   Equipment and machinery are depreciated at 10% straight
          line and should be charged to Costs of Sales, office
          fixtures and fittings are depreciated at 20% straight
          line and should be charged to Administration Costs, and
          motor vehicles are depreciated at 25% straight line and
          should be charged to Distribution Costs. During the
          year a motor vehicle was purchased for £10,000.

          No depreciation is charged on freehold land but 2%
          straight line is charged on buildings.

Stream Plc

Trial Balance as at 31 December 1993

	DR £000s	CR £000s
Ordinary share capital		5,000
Share premium		5,000
Retained profits		3,000
Freehold land	4,000	
Freehold buildings	6,000	
Equipment/machinery	2,000	
Office fixtures and fittings	500	
Motor vehicles	100	
Depreciation at 1.1.93		
Freehold buildings		300
Equipment/machinery		500
Office fixtures and fittings		200
Motor vehicles		50
Investments	4,500	
Purchases	25,000	
Stock at 1.1.93	7,200	
Selling expenses	1,950	
Distribution expenses	1,200	
Repairs costs under guarantee expended	250	
Office expenses	1,850	
Sales		42,000
Debtors	3,500	
Creditors		2,100
Dividend paid	200	
Corporation tax for 1992		2,500
Research and Development	2,000	
Cash at bank	400	
	60,650	60,650

viii)   Included in the various expenses are the following:

	£000s
Wages and Salaries	2,200
Pension contributions	220
NHI contributions	400

Contribution to charity	100

ix)   Provide 5% of outstanding debtors for repairs guarantee. The repairs cost under guarantee can be charged against this provision.

x)   Research and development expenses include:

	£000s
Pure research	300
Development of hardware	1,450
Development of software	250

xi)   The Corporation tax liability on all the current year's profits is estimated at £6,000,000.

xii)   The directors recommend a final dividend of 1.5 pence per share.

Required

Prepare the Profit and Loss Account for the year to 31 December 1993 and the Balance Sheet as at that date to comply with the Companies Acts and the relevant SSAPs and FRS 3. A cash flow statement in accordance with FRS1 is also required and the Stream Plc Balance Sheet for 1992 is attached, page 4, for that purpose.

Stream Plc

Balance Sheet as at 31 December 1992

	£000s	£000s
Fixed Assets:		
Tangible Assets		11,540
Current Assets:		
Stock	7,200	
Debtor	2,100	
Investment	4,500	
Cash	510	
	14,310	
Amounts falling due within one year:		
Creditors	10,350	
Taxation	2,500	
	12,850	
Net Current Assets		1,460
Total Assets less current liabilities		13,000
Total Assets less liabilities		13,000
Equity and reserves:		
Called up share capital		5,000
Share premium account		5,000
Retained profits		3,000
Total capital employed		13,000

CHAPTER 8

Introduction to Local Government Accounting
and External Reporting

Introduction

Local authorities are experiencing unprecedented changes in the way that they offer services to the community. Central Government are following the concept established in the late 1980s/early 1990s of focusing local authorities on enabling services to be delivered to users, rather than necessarily providing the services themselves.

Shift of Emphasis

This shift of emphasis has been seen much in evidence in legislation. Examples to name but a few are the provisions of the National Health Service and Community Care Act 1990, which sets out a role for local authorities buying in care, and in fact at the extreme could even see transfer payments to people needing care, which would enable self purchase. Competitive competition for local authority services recently extended to white collar services under the provisions of the Local Government Act 1992. This is another example of the emphasis being on buying services rather than providing them directly. Many more examples can be demonstrated to support this trend.

Review of Local Government Structure

The Local Government Commission have been established to undertake a review of the structure of local government. The aim here intended to provide authorities appropriate to the area where services are being offered, and organised in acknowledgement of local preferences for which authorities should provide the services. This process at the time of writing is at an early stage, and there are already signs that the government may change course on the review.

The Tax Burden of Providing Local Services

We have seen the demise of the rating system, followed by the introduction of the community charge. The community charge being unpopular and politically unsustainable, resulting firstly in an introduction of community charge grant, which was a switching from locally raised taxes to an increase in VAT, set at £140 per charge payer, and secondly the removal of the community charge and the introduction of the council tax.

The Drive for Greater Accountability

Throughout this period of change the buzzwords have come and gone, but the accounting system and external financial reporting requirements have had to change to accommodate the growing emphasis on accountability.

Objectives of this Local Government Section of this Book

The sections devoted to Local Government accounting in this book are going to demonstrate the response of accounting practice to the challenge of improving accountability. This chapter will lay out the statutory requirements of local government accounting and discuss the voluntary codes which CIPFA have produced. The chapter will consider the need for external reporting. Chapters that follow will address the following issues:

- **Chapter 9 - Capital Accounting** and the new proposals for charges to be made for both depreciation and the cost of capital, while ensuring the impact on local taxation is not affected;

- **Chapter 10 - Revenue Accounting** including the recent developments to the standard classification as a result of the work by CIPFA, regarding Accounting for Education 1992 and Accounting for Social Services 1993;

- **Chapter 11 - Statements of Support Service and Trading Accounts** required as a result of the compulsory competition requirements for white collar staff;

- **Chapters 12 & 13 - Accounting for the Collection Fund and consolidation issues including cash flow.** These sections looks at the council tax and resultant changes to accounting for the Collection Fund. The new cash flow statement is also included in Chapter 12.

How are Local Authority Accounts Regulated?

Local authority accounts are of course subject to external audit by the Audit Commission. The Audit Commission was established by the Local Government Finance Act 1982. Under the provisions of that act, the Commission appoints auditors, after consultation, to local authorities.

The audit undertaken requires a statement to be issued by the auditor to establish whether the accounting statements 'presents fairly' the financial position and transactions of the authority.

In addition to the requirement for the auditor to give an opinion on the accounting statements, the auditors may issue reports in the public interest to bring attention to matters of great concern, which may not necessarily be material in terms of the opinion given.

What do the External Auditors consider when Expressing Their Opinion

Many factors too numerous to mention are involved in this process. However, the most important aspect from the preparation of accounts point of view is as follows:

- Proper accounting practices are required to be observed for the preparation of statements of accounts in accordance with the statutory framework established for England and Wales by regulation 7 of the Accounts and audit regulations 1983 (as amended) by section 41 and 42 of the Local Government and Housing Act 1989.

What are Considered to be Proper Practices?

Sections 41 and 42 of the LGHA 1989 require all expenditure of a
local authority to be accounted for in accordance with proper
practice. Section 66 explains that proper practices are "those
accounting practices which the authority are required to follow
by virtue of any enactment; or which, whether by reference to any
generally recognised publish code, or otherwise, are regarded as
proper accounting practice to be followed in the keeping of
accounts of local authorities".

Section 66 also explains that in the occurrence of a conflict in
accounting practice arising between statute and any accepted
code, then the statute would be regarded as proper practice.

Proper practices can therefore be divided into
- statutory proper practice
- non-statutory proper practice.

What Statutory Proper Practices are Most Relevant?

The Account and Audit Regulations are the most relevant statutory
provision which needs to be considered.

Under the provisions of section 23 of the Local Government
Finance Act 1982 the Secretary of State took the power to
prescribe the form, preparation and certification of local
authority accounts and accounting statements.

The power has been used to issue the Accounts and Audit
Regulations 1983. The Accounts and Audit Regulations set general
requirements as follows:

- A summarised statement of Income and Expenditure for each
  fund that a body is required by statute to keep a separate
  account.

- A summarised statement of capital expenditure
  differentiation between services and showing the sources of
  finance.

- A consolidated balance sheet.

- Any balances of funds not consolidated.

- A statement of source and applications of funds.

- A statement of main principles and any changes in practice
  which significantly affect the statements.

These major requirements are of course in some detailed respects
a little out of date. for example the regulations require a
statements of source and application of funds. In practice this
is no longer provided, because the codes of practice, i.e. non-
statutory codes require a cash flow statement. The immediate
worry comes to mind surely this is an instance of a code being
used in preference to a statutory requirements. However, this is
not the case, the code simply changes the format of reporting
cash movements, and therefore is not considered to be any
different to the statutory requirement.

What Non-Statutory Proper Practices are Most Relevant?

The most important non-statutory practices are those which are supported by the Accounting Standards Board of the Financial Reporting Council.

The Accounting Standards Boards is fully explained in earlier chapters of this text. However, it is primarily responsible for regulating the accounting provision of companies through the issue of Financial Reporting Standards.

With regard to accounting of other bodies and organisations the Accounting Standards Board approve recognised bodies for the purpose of establishing statements of recommended practice (SORPs). The body so designated then sets about the task of establishing accounting practices in line with the general requirements of best accounting practice. the Accounting Standards Board will appoint a project manager to consider SORPs and if acceptable issue a negative assurance. The negative assurance is a statement that nothing is contrary to best accounting practice.

The Public Sector designated standard of recommended practice setting body is the CIPFA/LASAAC Joint Committee. CIPFA representing its public sector accounting interests, and LASAAC concerned with the impact in Scotland.

This joint CIPFA/LASAAC Committee has the following terms of reference:

   (i)   to monitor the work of the ASB and to identify its implications for local authorities;

   (ii)   to Liaise with the ASB as necessary on the development of proposed SORPs;

   (iii) to prepare and issue exposure drafts of proposed SORPs for comment by interested parties;

   (iv)   to review and analyse comments received on exposure drafts and to ensure that due account is taken of this in preparing proposed SORPs for submission to the ASB;

   (v)   to publicise its work to both local authorities and the wider accounting profession.

Exposure Draft of a Revised Code of Practice on Local Authority Accounting in Great Britain

The most recent production of material from the CIPFA/LASAAC Joint Committee is this exposure draft. the exposure draft provides a proposed code of practice which will supersede the second code of practice on local government accounting published by CIPFA in 1992, and the existing SORP on the application of SSAPs to local authorities.

This exposure draft was given negative assurance on 22nd July 1993 by the Accounting Standards Board. The exposure draft will now become a SORP and will be published at the same time as this book in September 1993.

The contents of the exposure draft is as follows:

- Accounting Concepts
- Accounting Policies
- The Statement of Accounts

Accounting Concepts

The accounting concepts require local authorities to follow fundamental principles of accounting in particular the code requires the four fundamentals of matching, prudence, consistency and going concern to be adhered to.

This in fact means that local authorities will have to account for capital expenditure on an accruals basis. This will be required from 1 April 1994.

In addition the concept of substance over form is strongly promoted this is where the accounting requirement should be established to accommodate the substance of the situation rather than the narrower form of the legal agreement. An example of this is where assets are subject to a finance lease, and therefore not owned by the local authority, but for all practical purposes the asset is in substance owned by the authority. In such a case the accounting should reflect the situation as if the authority own the asset.

Compliance with the Code

The code of practice is not intended to be a straight jacket with regard to the accounting principles and requires compliance where material to the fair presentation of the financial position.

The accounting policies referred to in the code require authorities to comply with relevant accounting standards. It is therefore expected that the accounting Standards Board rules regarding the following are employed:

- Extraordinary and exceptional items
- Grants
- Lease arrangement
- foreign currency transactions
- Pension costs
- Research and Development
- Stocks and long term contracts
- Value added tax
- Post balance sheet events

In each of these cases wherever possible the authority should apply best accounting practice.

In addition the code covers Local Government related issues such as:

- Capital accounting and the requirements for charges to be made to revenue for depreciation and the cost of capital (see Chapter 9 for more details).

- The application of the Standard classification regarding revenue accounting (see Chapter 10 for more details).

- Accounting for Support Services and overheads (this is considered in Chapter 11).

The code of practice therefore sets out a framework of the accounting fundamentals to be followed by authorities.

The Statement of Accounts

In its statements of accounts, an authority should disclose the information, the accounting statements and the notes as required by the code of practice. The form and minimum content of each required statement is provided by the code. An authority may add such additional information or statements as are necessary to ensure fair presentation of its financial position and transactions.

The Statement of Accounts Comprises:

1. An explanatory foreword

2. A statement of accounting policies

3. The accounting statements

4. Notes to the accounts

An Explanatory Foreword

1. The purpose of the foreword is to offer interested parties an easily understandable guide to the most significant matters reported in the accounts. It should provide an explanation in overall terms of the authority's financial position, and assist in the interpretation of the accounting statements. it should also contain a commentary on the major influences affecting the authority's income and expenditure and cash flow, and information on the financial needs and resources of the authority.

2. It is not the purpose of the foreword to comment on the policies of the authority, rather to explain the financial facts. Content and style are left to local judgment.

3. It is important that the foreword is concise, and restricted to significant matters. It should include the following items which are likely to be significant to the understanding of the accounts. These recommended topics are not intended to restrict the content of the foreword.

    (a) An explanation of which statements follow, their purpose and the relationship between them.

    (b) Service expenditure, capital financing costs, income from grants, local taxpayers and other sources, compared in overall terms to the budget.

    (c) A brief note of any material assets acquired or liabilities incurred. If these are unusual in scale, having regard to the normal activities of the authority, or for any other reason, the circumstances should be explained.

(d) An explanation of any material and unusual charge or credit in the accounts. This should be provided whether the charge is made as part of the cost of services or as an adjustment to the cost of services.

(e) Any significant change in accounting policies. The reason for the change, and the effect on the accounts, should be explained.

(f) Any major change in statutory functions which has a significant impact on the accounts. In addition, a comment on planned future development in service delivery, including a summary of revenue and capital investment plans, distinguishing between expenditure intended to maintain existing levels of service provision and that intended to expand existing services or develop new services.

(g) A brief note of the authority's current borrowing facilities and capital borrowing, outlining the purpose and impact of financing transactions entered into during the year and major fixed asset acquisitions and disposals.

(h) A summary of the authority's internal and external sources of funds available to meet its capital expenditure plans and other financial commitments.

The Accounting Statements

The accounting statement required are as follows:

- **Consolidated Revenue Account.** The account required is shown in the capital accounting chapter of this book, and the format used is that proposed by the code of practice.

- **Housing Revenue Accounts**

- **Summary Direct Service Organisation Revenue and Appropriation Accounts**

  These two accounting statements are not included in this text, but the subjects are covered in the text book "Advanced Public Sector Accounting" also published by Allen Accountancy.

- **Collection Fund.** There are two formats provided for a collection fund one for England and Wales, the other for Scotland. The details of England and Wales, and examples are provided in a Chapter 13 of this text.

- **Consolidated Balance Sheet.** This statement is provided in the examples in the capital accounting chapter of this book.

- **Cash Flow Statements.** This is a major change from the previous code of practice, and is in a format rather like FRS 1. Full detailed and examples are provided in a later chapter of this book.

-       **Superannuation Fund Accounts**

These statements are for a statement of revenue income and expenditure plus a net assets statement. These formats are covered in "Advanced Public Sector Accounting" also published by Allen Accountancy.

Annual Reports

The requirement for local authorities to produce statements of accounts is therefore provided in both statutory requirements and through the recognised accounting codes of practice which are given negative assurance by the Accounting Standards Board.

There is however no statutory requirement for local authorities to produce an annual report as such, although Section 2 of the Local Government and Planning Act 1980 does empower the Secretary of State for the Environment to issue a code or codes of recommended practice as to the publication of information by local authorities about the discharge of their functions.

Section 3 of the Local Government Planning & Land Act 1980 gives additional power to the Secretary of State to regulate the manner, form and regularity of their publications and Section 4 gives a further power to direct bodies to publish information.

A Code of Practice - Publication of Annual Reports by Local Authorities

A code was produced in 1981. The code was prepared by CIPFA and the Society of Local Authority Chief Executives (SOLACE). The code was issued by the Secretary of State.

Aims of the Code

The intention of the Code of Practice is to ensure as far as possible a broad consistency of practice, and a maximum standard of content is provided with the overall objective of:

(i)   giving local taxpayers clear information about local government activities;

(ii)   to make it easier for electors, taxpayers and other interested parties to make comparisons and judgments on performance of their local authorities;

(iii)   to help councillors from judgments about the performance of their own authority.

Recommendation Contained in the DOE Code for Annual Reports

The following information was suggested for inclusion in the annual reports.

Although authorities will have complete discretion as to the layout of their Report, it should contain the following information including for the appropriate authorities, details of general fund services, housing, trading services and direct labour organisation activities.

1.   Details of revenue expenditure and income for the year ended
      31 March, as follows:

      -     an indication of how in overall terms the financial
            outturn compared with the budget, and an explanation of
            major variances;

      -     a service analysis of gross revenue expenditure and
            income;

      -     net expenditure by service for the year compared with:

            (i)   the original estimated plus inflation (or where
                   these are not available, the revised estimate).

            (ii)   the actuals for the previous year.

            (iii) comments on any changing pattern of expenditure
                   between services within the authority and any
                   corporate strategy underlying this.

2.   A summary of capital expenditure by service and a statement
      showing the sources of finance for the total capital
      expenditure during the year, e.g. borrowing, reserves,
      leasing. progress of any major capital projects showing
      future commitments (including manpower) and any anticipated
      savings.

3.   A summary subjective analysis of gross revenue expenditure
      and income for the year, also showing approximate rate
      (Council Tax) income by each main class of heridament.

4.   General statistics for major services showing, for example:

      -     the scale of service provision
      -     the client group served, and numbers (where applicable)
      -     usage of service
      -     measures of cost

      in comparison with the previous year.

5. A set of key service indicators selected by the authority
(including those specified in the list in the table) which where
possible measure performance, including productivity where
appropriate, using information at least for the year of account.
Where indicated in the table and otherwise as appropriate, the
figures for the authority should also be compared with actual and
average figures of other authorities based at least on the
figures for the year preceding the year of account. But
authorities may also wish to make such comparison on a more
recent, estimates, basis as well.

TABLE - PERFORMANCE MEASURES

FIRE SERVICE   (net) cost per 1000 population
                                proportion of area in high fire risk
                                categories

```
PUBLIC PASSENGER
(County Councils only)
TRANSPORT                    passenger journeys per week per 1000
                             population(County Councils only)

HIGHWAYS                     maintenance cost per kilometre:
                             principal roads
                             maintenance cost per kilometre:
                             principal roads

HOUSING - HRA                gross rent as a proportion of total
                             costs management and maintenance: cost
                             per dwelling per week (excluding special
                             management) rent arrears as percentage
                             of rent collectible for the year

HOUSING CONSTRUCTION         construction cost per dwelling completed

LIBRARIES                    (net) cost per 1000 population

TOWN AND COUNTRY
PLANNING                     (net) cost per 1000 population

RECREATION                   (net) cost per 1000 population

REFUSE COLLECTION            (net) cost per 1000 population

REFUSE DISPOSAL              (net) cost per 1000 population

SPECIFIED TRADING
SERVICES                     *revenue: gross cost ration (see Note 2)

GENERAL ADMINISTRATION       *change in numbers of support staff over
                             previous year (see Note 2)
```

Note 1
Authorities should select and amalgamate services according to
local priorities for the purpose of publishing the two general
statistics, net cost and manpower per 1000 population. They
should however publish these statistics in the particular cases
where those indicators are specified in the list.

Note 2
For statistics marked thus *, authorities should only publish
comparisons with other authorities, or with averages, where they
consider it relevant to do so.

6.   A year-end manpower statement summarised by staff category
      and by service, drawing comparisons with the previous year,
      and giving an indication of any significant seasonal
      fluctuations.

7.   References to any publicly available audit report since the
      previous year's Annual Report, including any auditor's
      comments on the Report.

8.   Details of how interested parties may follow up matters
      arising from the Annual Report, with a timetable showing key
      dates in the financial and management planning process.

9.   (Where the Abstract of Accounts is not included in the
       Annual Report):

       -     a summary revenue account;

       -     the consolidated balance sheet including explanatory
             notes;

       -     a summary statement of the accounting policies of the
             authority, including its observance or otherwise of any
             accounting standards, CIPFA accounting guidelines and
             the Accounting Code of Practice

The Department of the Environment's Code of Practice also suggest
supplementary information which authorities should endeavour to
provide as follows:

1.   Further statistical and financial information of the
       following kinds:

       -     a basic profile of the authority including demographic
             statistics and other relevant and available background
             'environmental' statistics;

       -     any changes reflected in the *current* year's budget
             including where available, statistics and comparisons
             with other authorities based on the current year's
             estimates.

2.   -   where appropriate, comparisons with neighbouring
             authorities;

       -     statistical and financial trends over the past five
             years, including an illustration of trends in volume
             terms, together with planned *future* direction of major
             policies over the medium term with supporting
             statistical data.

3.   Details of investigation and review procedures, for example
       the methods used by the authority to review its existing
       policies and base expenditure, efficiency and policy
       investigations carried out during the year, and areas where
       further investigations are planned.

4.   Further details of manpower policies, including a reference
       to productivity and incentive bonus schemes and their
       review.

5.   An explanation of local authority terminology, accounting
       practices and other information for non-specialists.

Other Important Requirements for Local Authority Financial Reporting

In addition to the external reporting required by statutory and
non-statutory rules of proper practice, additional requirements
do exist. On the 16 July 1993, the CIPFA Council agreed an
institute statement on financial reporting

The full details of the institute statements are obviously available from CIPFA. However, the statement set out to establish an obligation on members to observe and apply best practice.

The statement recognises the responsibility of CIPFA members to provide accounting statements which the public can rely on having incorporated:

- sound financial accounting and reporting;
- integrity of accounting information;
- good presentation of accounts;
- dissemination of accounting information;
- a tight process of preparing account information.

CIPFA members are required to comply with the CIPFA statement, and are reminded that the provisions of the Accounting Standards Board are applicable in principle to local authorities.

The Director of Finance should ensure that the work of preparing the financial statements is planned, monitored and controlled. the statement requires Directors of Finance to make their best endeavours to make it possible for the financial statements to be published no later than seven months after the end of the financial year.

In addition the Director of Finance should ensure that financial information is available as early as possible to the board or elected representatives.

Summary statements, produced for inclusion in any annual report, should not distort, or give a selective picture of the financial position of the organisation, but remains a fair presentation of the full financial statements.

Financial statements should be distributed to all interested parties and potential users should be made aware of how to obtain copies.

The Integrity of the Financial systems

The institute statement makes it clear that adequate financial records need to be retained to ensure:

* transactions can be verified
* regular reporting is practised
* system of recording material commitments operates
* any processing errors are identified and corrected promptly
* an adequate system of internal control is in operation
* procedures are in place to ensure reconstitution of records is possible.

This is not an exhaustive list but provides the general gist of the institute statement, for complete information see the statement.

Other Forms of External Reporting

This chapter has concentrated on the external reporting of an accounting nature, and the statutory requirements. However, very often a formal annual report and accounting statements are not the best methods of achieving widespread information to the public electors.

The following methods/means are additional ways of providing external information.

- local newspapers
- local government leaflets
- open government, reports, agenda, and minutes of committee meetings, etc.
- community forums
- local structural plans
- corporate/policy plans
- public consultation meetings
- council tax leaflet

It is important not to lose sight of alternative ways in which both financial and non-financial information is disseminated to interested parties.

Summary

This chapter has proved an introduction to the requirements of external reporting. It should provide the basis on which more detailed accounting requirements can be considered.

The external requirement has been considered and the term proper practice, and its meaning in both statutory and non-statutory regulations.

Annual reports have been considered and the details of the code of practice.

CIPFA's institute statement has been identified as an important additional aspect for CIPFA members to consider.

Finally very briefly alternative forms of providing external information are considered.

CHAPTER 9

LOCAL AUTHORITY ACCOUNTING
NEW CAPITAL ACCOUNTING PROPOSALS

INTRODUCTION

Local authority capital accounting has been the source of great dilemma to local authority accountants and CIPFA for a number of decades. The oldest reference I could find related to the capital accounting regime was in 1968, when Maurice Stonefrost criticised the system.

A seemingly endless number of reports on the subject have been commissioned over the years, and this has culminated in the proposals of the Capital Accounting Working Group (CAWG). These proposals have been incorporated into the exposure draft of a revised code of practice on Local Authority accounting published in February 1993 which received negative assurance from the Accounting Standards Board on the 22 July 1993.

This exposure draft will become a statement of recommended practice (SoRP). The exposure draft includes a reference to the new capital accounting proposals and required the new proposals to be implemented as proper practice from 1 April 1994.

This chapter is devoted to the subject of capital accounting in local authorities and sets out to cover the topic as follows:

*   An explanation of the categories of capital assets to be found in local authorities' accounts.

*   The accounting entries which are required to finance capital spending. These represent the old systems of accounting

*   Consideration of the shortcomings of accounting for assets purely related to their financing, and therefore establishing the need to find a new system of capital accounting

*   Outline the objectives of any new accounting system, and consider the proposals made by the Capital Accounting Working Group.

*   Worked examples are provided to enable the new system to be understood.

*   Finally, examination questions are provided.

An Explanation of the Categories of Capital Assets to be found in Local Authority Accounts

Fixed assets are defined largely by the Central Government system of capital expenditure controls exercised over local authorities.

The basis of the capital control system is that any expenditure incurred by an authority must be charged to revenue <u>unless</u> it falls within one of the categories of fixed assets.

Capital expenditure is the acquisition of tangible assets, or expenditure which adds to, and not merely maintains, the value of an existing asset. It therefore follows that such expenditure will provide benefits for more than one year. Such expenditure shall be capitalised and categorised as a fixed asset.

The definition of capital expenditure covers the following:

*   Acquisition, reclamation, enhancement or laying out of land

*   Acquisition, construction , preparation, enhancement or replacement of roads, buildings and other structures

*   Acquisition, installation or replacement of movable or immovable plant, machinery and apparatus, and vehicles and vessels.

The term enhancement means:

*   Work undertaken to lengthen substantially the useful life of the asset; or

*   Work undertaken to increase substantially the open market value of the asset; or

*   To increase substantially the extent to which the asset will be used in providing services for the authority.

Circular 11/90 states that enhancement may therefore include:

*   Widening of roads, bridges and enlargement of recreational facilities;

*   Installation of central heating or double glazing;

*   Structural maintenance of roads, re-roofing of buildings, installation of new engines in vehicles;

but should not include repairs or painting, replacement of missing roof tiles or filling pot holes, which are ongoing maintenance works which do not provide enhancement.

De Minimis Levels for Capital Expenditure

Classification of assets as capital fixed assets in local authorities has since the Planning and Land Act 1980 been the subject of a de minimis rule. This is that items which meet the requirement to be classed as fixed asset need not be subject to Government control if the cost of each item is below an agreed sum and therefore immaterial. In such cases the cost is not capitalised in the balance sheet, but is classed a a revenue expense.

The de minimis limit was £5,000 in 1980, but the new control system introduced in 1990 excludes leases and contracts worth up to £10,000 for the purpose of presenting information in the balance sheet. However, CIPFA's code of practice practitioners guide issued in 1991 allows for local authorities to determine a higher limit up to £20,000 across all services, or for those services with large capital programmes, again having regard to materiality.

The de minimis level should be set at the beginning of the year and then applied consistently.

Deferred Charges

Deferred charges are related to spending of a capital nature which does not result in a tangible fixed asset. Examples are as follows:

- charges related to the deferred cost of stock issue discounts and expenses
- charges related to the granting of improvement grants
- charges related to section 40(b) of the LGHA 1989
- charges created to counter balance debt outstanding on assets sold.

These deferred charges are subject to an annual writing off to revenue account. The new capital accounting system modifies the treatment of deferred charges and this will be explained later in the chapter.

Categories of Fixed Assets

The activities of local authorities are diverse and therefore they tend to hold a vast amount of assets. The following categories are required, the titles in ITALICS are new categories required from the 1 April 1994 to be introduced with the new accounting system.

1. Council dwellings
2. Other land and buildings
3. Infrastructure
4. Vehicle, plant, furniture and equipment
5. *Community assets*
6. *Non-operational assets*

Category 1 - Council Dwellings

This category includes housing committee property plus car parking, sheltered accommodation to the extent accounted for through the Housing Revenue Account (HRA). In all cases costs associated with fixed equipment, furniture and plant are included.

Category 2 - Other Land and Buildings

This category includes all land and buildings which are operational and not included in any of the other categories. All fixed equipment furniture and plant would also be included in this heading where fixed to the land and buildings. To give a clearer idea of the type of assets that would be included here the following are suggested: office buildings; schools; libraries; sports centres; swimming pools; day centres; residential homes; theatres; depots and workshops; cemeteries and crematoria; off street car parks. This list is obviously not exhaustive.

Category 3 - Infrastructure Assets

This category includes facilities provided to enable other developments to take place, The assets included here are almost certainly needed to be retained to enable the operational assets to be available, and are not saleable by nature. Examples include: roads including all capital works on roads such as traffic management schemes, road widening etc.; street lighting; water and drainage work; sea defences; bridges; some environmental improvements.

Category 4 - Vehicle Plant Furniture and Equipment

This category includes items which are not fixtures associated with land and buildings or housing property. Therefore these items would normally be movable. The following types of assets would be included under this heading: vehicles; mechanical plant; computers; fixtures and fittings; street furniture.

Category 5 - Community Assets

This category is a new category introduced as a result of the new proposals on capital accounting. The type of assets intended to be included in this heading include the following: parks and open recreation areas; historic buildings; works of art; museum exhibits; civic regalia. the category has been created because these assets are of benefit to the community in perpetuity and need not be valued at current replacement cost under the new capital accounting proposals.

Category 6 - Non-Operational Property

This category is another category which has been created as a result of the new capital accounting proposals. The assets are items which are not in operation and are being held for investment purposes or for future development. The following are examples: land awaiting development; commercial property; investment property; surplus assets.

Requirements for the Balance Sheet

Local authorities are no longer required to keep or present balance sheets for separate services they operate. Each service will have its own revenue account for ongoing income and expenditure, and these will be brought together in a summary consolidated statement. The Housing Revenue Account is required to be ringfenced (held separately) and therefore a statutory HRA will continue to be included separately in the published financial statements. However, only a single consolidated balance sheet is required.

Financing Capital Expenditure - a Brief Explanation of the Old System, Known as Debt Charge Accounting

Up until the 1 April 1994 the debt charge system of accounting for capital expenditure has been employed in local authority accounting. This system is going to be partially replaced by a new system of capital accounting linked to a more commercial accounting approach of depreciating assets.

The old debt charge system cannot however be forgotten and disregarded for ever. This is due to the fact that the new capital accounting system is an attempt to provide more meaningful costs in service revenue accounts, to improve asset management and accountability, while reversing out the impact of these extra charges over and above the old debt charge system in the summary revenue account.

It will typically be the case that the new system of capital accounting will result in far greater charges to the revenue account than would have been made under the old debt charge system. The change is not intended to increase the burden on Council Tax payers. The Government are also not prepared to find more resources for local government purely due to a change in accounting practice. This means that when it comes to charging for local authority services to the Council Tax payer the tax charge must be set at the level required by the old debt charge system and hence the need for reversal entries in the summary revenue account. Students and practitioners must therefore continue to be aware, and account centrally for, the financing of capital expenditure in the old debt charge fashion as well as operating the new system of charges for capital.

Debt Charge System of Accounting for Capital Financing

The debt charge system of financing capital expenditure involves a combination of different sources of finance. The three most important sources are as follows:

- direct revenue finance;
- use of capital receipts;
- loans finance;

Each of these methods will be dealt with in turn. It should be noted that other forms of financing do exist such as the use of renewals funds and capital funds. However, for the purposes of keeping this section reasonably simple the three main methods are the only ones fully explained.

Method 1 - Direct Revenue Financing

Financing capital expenditure direct from the revenue account, and this is often referred to as " Direct Revenue Financing" (DRF) or "Revenue Contributions to Capital Outlay" (RCCO). The term RCCO is an older term for this financing method.

The effect of charging capital expenditure direct to the revenue account is that the whole cost of capital falls on the current beneficiary of the services. This is against the accounting convention of the matching principle where benefits are required to be charged over the asset life, or alternatively charges are made over years reflecting the wearing out of the asset.

Accounting Entries for Direct Revenue Financing

The double entry system for this item <u>would have been</u> as follows:

		Dr £	Cr £
Step 1	Purchase of Fixed Asset for £125,000		
	Fixed asset account category (1-6)	125,000	
	Capital cash		125,000

being the purchase of the fixed asset and the use of capital cash to pay for the capital transaction.

		Dr £	Cr £
Step 2	Charge the cost to Revenue account		
	Revenue Account Service Committee	125,000	
	revenue cash		125,000

being the charge to the service committee revenue account all in the first year.

Step 3

Demonstrate that the service committee has fully financed the asset purchased, via the use of a capital discharged account known as DRF or RCCO.

	Dr £	Cr £
Capital cash	125,000	
DRF/RCCO		125,000

being the recording of the fact that the capital has been financed by the committee direct through the revenue account.

<u>NB</u> It is important to note that these journals indicate that separate cost transactions are retained between revenue and capital transactions. These days of computerised accounting systems would automatically account for the cash movement and therefore these journals are shown purely from the point of completeness.

Effect of These Entries on The Balance Sheet

The balance sheet presentation for direct revenue financing leaves us with the following picture:

	£000
Fixed assets	125
Less capital discharged	125

Amount to be financed	nil

It should become immediately apparent to observers who have some knowledge of private sector accounting that this presentation in the balance sheet is completely different from the commercial approach.

The amount to be financed in future is nil because the whole sum of capital spending has been charged to the revenue account. However, in commercial accounting the figure for capital discharge would not appear, and a depreciation to date figure would be provided. The result would be that the asset would be shown at net book value. The following might be the presentation if the asset life were ten years, with no residual value.

Commercial Presentation - Fixed Assets

	£000
Fixed assets	125.0
Less	
Accumulated depreciation	12.5
Net book value	112.5

The commercial approach is considered to be much more informative reflecting an approximation to the net value of the asset being held.

Method 2 - Use of Capital Receipts

Local Authorities have the ability to raise significant cash resources from selling assets. When an asset is sold it results in the generation of a cash receipt which is termed to be a capital receipt.

The government have in the past regulated the use of capital receipts, and intend to in the future. At present an authority can use the whole of new capital receipts for capital spending. However, this came about by the autumn statement of November 1992, and is due to revert back to a restrictive arrangement at the end of 1993. If the use of capital receipts reverts back to the most recent control arrangement pre-autumn 1992, capital receipts from selling council housing will results in 25% being unable for capital spending while 75% are required to be reserved for debt redemption. Non-housing receipts are subject to 50% being usable and 50% being reserved.

Capital receipts are recorded by increasing the cash account and the reserve account know as capital receipts unapplied. The entries are as follows:

presume an asset sale resulted in cash received of £200,000

	Dr £	Cr £
Capital cash	200,000	
capital receipt unapplied		200,000

This being the cash proceeds received and placed in the capital receipt unapplied reserve account. At present it can all be used.

The capital receipt may subsequently be used to finance capital expenditure and had this occurred where the purchased capital asset was £125,000 the following entries would have been generated.

Step 1

	Dr £	Cr £
Fixed asset account category (1-6)	125,000	
Capital cash		125,000

being the purchase of the asset and the use of capital cash to pay for the purchase.

Step 2   Finance the purchase from capital receipts unapplied

	Dr £	Cr £
Capital receipts unapplied	125,000	
Capital receipts applied (CRA)		125,000

This involves the removal of the capital receipt used to finance the capital expenditure from the capital receipt unapplied account, indicating less capital receipts left to be used. However, the use of capital receipts has fully financed the purchase of capital spending, and in accordance with local authority practice under the debt charge regime, needs to be shown in a capital discharged account showing that the asset has been financed. This capital discharged account is known as capital receipts applied.

Effect of the Entries on the Balance Sheet

The balance sheet presentation for capital receipts used to finance capital spending would have been as follows:

	£000
Fixed assets (category 1-6)	125
Less capital discharged	
- capital receipts applied (CRA)	125

Amount to be financed	nil

Here once again the asset as a nil balance, due to the fact all capital has been financed in year 1, but without any charge to revenue.

Revenue Impact of the Use of Capital Receipts

The revenue account is not charged with any amount related to the purchase of the fixed asset. The manager of services may not recognise the full cost of keeping the asset because no cost is being borne in the expenditure account of the service. Once again this method of accounting for the purchase of fixed assets does not comply with the matching concept.

Method 3 - Loan Finance

Loans are raised in accordance with the council's Basic Credit Approvals and supplementary credit approvals for new capital spending. These approvals are made by the Government to local authorities, and enable local authorities to raise loans. The level of loan raised is tightly controlled by the Government.

However, if an authority raises a loan to finance capital spending then debt charges are incurred and <u>would have been</u> charged to the revenue account. The process can be described as follows: an asset was purchased for £125,000, and the council raised a loan to finance the capital expenditure.

Step 1
	Dr £	Cr £
Fixed asset account category (1-6)	125,000	
Capital cash		125,000

being the purchase of the fixed asset and the reduction of capital cash used to finance the capital transaction.

Step 2
	Dr £	Cr £
Capital cash	125,000	
Loans outstanding		125,000

This being the recording of the loan raised for the purpose of financing capital expenditure.

At this stage although a loan has been raised, there has been no repayment of the loan, and therefore the service committee has not discharged its liability to pay for the asset. Therefore until such repayments take place there will be no capital discharge account required.

Step 3 - Repay the Loan Outstanding

In local authority accounting it has been the practice to charge the principal repayment of the loan to the revenue account along with the interest charge. The principal repayment must be at least "the minimum revenue provision" MRP. This amount, in simplistic terms, is 2% of the loan for Housing and 4% for other capital spending.

	Dr £	Cr £
Loan outstanding	5,000	
Capital cash		5,000

This being the repayment of the loan outstanding based on 4% of the loan outstanding. The repayment is in fact a notional entry to the loans pool, but this fact will be explained later.

Step 4 - Charge the Revenue Account for the Principal Repaid

	Dr £	Cr £
Revenue Account	5,000	
Revenue cash		5,000

being the charge to the service committee revenue account for the principal repayment, and the transfer of revenue cash to capital cash to reimburse capital cash for the loan repayment.

Step 5 - Demonstrate that the Revenue Account has Financed Capital Expenditure

	Dr £	Cr £
Capital cash	5,000	
Capital discharged loans redeemed		5,000

This entry shows the reimbursement of capital cash and the recording of the fact that the revenue account has financed capital expenditure. In this case the capital discharged account was called loans redeemed.

Effect of the Entries on the Balance Sheet

The balance sheet presentation where fixed assets have been financed by loans is as follows:

	£000
Fixed assets (category 1-6)	125,000
Less capital discharged	
- loans redeemed	5,000

Amount to be financed	120,000

Under this method of financing capital expenditure there is some matching taking place here. An annual charge is being made of 4% which may or may not reflect the wearing out of the asset. In addition, not shown here is the charge for interest payment reflecting the cost of capital.

Summary of the Debt Charge System of Capital Accounting and Consideration of its Shortcomings

The debt charge system is a term which covers many different methods of financing capital expenditure. The three methods demonstrated in this chapter are the three most commonly used. Each method has a different impact on the revenue costs reported by service committees.

This can be demonstrated by the following table.

Method of Finance	Impact on Revenue Account
Direct Revenue Financing	All cost borne in first year
Use of Capital Receipts	No cost borne in revenue expenditure
Loan Finance	An annual cost related to principal repayment plus interest

The result of this system of accounting is that services provided do not reflect a fair or consistent charge for capital expenditure, and this in turn makes any comparison with previous years costs impossible from the accounting statements for revenue accounts.

Any comparison of costs between local authorities cannot include the charges for capital because of the inconsistencies. this means that assets and their use are excluded from unit cost analysis. Value for money studies related to the use of unit costs overlook the costs associated with holding assets.

Individual managers may not be concerned with the level of non-operational assets held, or the level of under utilised assets in operation, because they may not be carrying a revenue cost related to the assets. This could occur when capital receipts have been used to finance the asset for example.

The asset values net of capital discharged shown in the balance sheet have only one meaning, which is that the total represents the amount of assets to be financed by future loan repayments. The net figure gives no insight to the book value of the assets. If we consider the examples used in this chapter to demonstrate the double entry we can identify the following.

Balance Sheet Presentation

Account	DRF/RCCO	Method of financing used — Capital receipts	Loans
	£	£	£
Fixed assets	125,000	125,000	125,000
Less			
Capital discharged			
DRF	125,000	---	---
CRA	---	125,000	---
Loans redeemed	---	---	5,000
	-------	-------	-------
Amount to be financed	nil	nil	120,000
Financed by:			
Loan outstanding	---	---	120,000
	-------	-------	-------
	nil	nil	nil
	-------	-------	-------

The net figure for fixed assets less capital discharged is clearly reflecting the method of financing employed. This results in the net figure being no reflection of assets values held by the local authority.

Assessment of the Debt Charge System of Capital Accounting

The debt charge system provides for basic stewardship of costs paid for capital. The system fails to fulfil the needs of a practical and useful capital accounting system on the following grounds.

- Inconsistent impact on the revenue account of the costs of capital

- Misleading messages can be provided to managers

- Lack of comparability hinders unit cost analysis and readily available cost comparison over years.

- The overall effect is less than adequate accountability for the use of assets

- Balance sheet presentation is unrepresentative of the real assets in use and their values

- The system is not able to provide an accounting structure required for the changing environment in which local authorities find themselves.

This last point can be expanded upon by reference to the Government established requirements for Direct Service Operations, and the inevitable move toward compulsory competition for white collar services.

Regime for Direct Service Operations

Although the accounting for this topic is not included in this book, it can be found in "Advanced Public Sector Accounting", also published by Allen Accountancy. The accounting regime involves the need to make a rate of return on a current cost accounting basis. this also involves the computation of depreciation. At present local authorities facilitate the accounting requirement by use of memorandum accounting information, which is not part of the actual accounting systems

This may be acceptable for one or two services, but is not likely to be acceptable as and when CCT spreads, as it will do, more extensively within local authorities.

Public Sector Accounting Practice

It is often also argued that other parts of the public sector are already operating accounting rules that involve commercial style accounting for capital assets, and this is undoubtedly true. In this book the NHS and Central Government are shown to use current cost information and depreciate assets on that basis. However, in my view this does not necessarily mean that is a case for applying this regime to local authorities. However, it cannot be denied that the debt charge system if woefully inadequate and needs replacement.

An Outline of the Objectives of Any New Capital Accounting System of Local Authorities

In my view the objectives of a new capital accounting system need to be established before considering the proposed system. The following objectives have therefore been established for the purpose of evaluating the proposals made. Having stated these objectives which are my objectives, not necessarily those of CIPFA. The new proposals will be explained, and readers will need to come to their own conclusions regarding how successful the new proposals are in meetings the objectives.

The Author's Objectives for Capital Accounting are as follows:

1. The system must provide consistent charges to the revenue account for costs of capital, unrelated to the financing method. This will enable better unit cost analysis and aid the quest for value for money.

2. The charges to revenue must fairly reflect the real costs of holding assets.

3. The system should be clearly defined to enable all local authorities to adopt comparable capital accounting entries.

4. Messages given to managers regarding assets should be clear and reflect the cost of holding assets. For good asset management responsibility for the asset and their costs must fall on cost centre managers.

5. The proposals should be achievable at reasonable cost, be as simple as possible, to ensure the system results in practical benefits, and is adhered to by all local authorities.

6. Academically the system should be supportable. It must represent best practice.

7. The proposals should be able to cope with the changing nature of local government, and the compulsory competition challenge.

8. Balance sheet values should be of use and reflect the authority's asset values.

9. There should be no impact on the charges levied under the Council Tax due solely to a change in capital accounting techniques.

These objectives are wide ranging and it may be that all are not achievable under any system proposed. however, at least we have a clear view of the requirements.

The Proposals of the Capital Accounting Working Group. A New System of Accounting for Capital by Local Authorities

This section provides a summary of the proposals included in the CIPFA published report on this subject. For full details the report is obviously available from CIPFA. This section is intended to contribute towards the knowledge and research of the system and not to infringe CIPFA's copyright.

Accruing for Capital Spending

The first point which is worthy of note is that in future local
authorities will be required to accrue for capital spending. In
the past local authorities have recorded capital spending on a
payment and receipts basis. The change to an accruals
arrangement will have an impact on the first year of
implementation, in that capital spending will include more than a
full year's expenditure. However, CIPFA have discussed the
proposal with officials at the DOE and an adjustment with
creditors is envisaged to ensure local authorities do not suffer
any practical difficulties.

Valuation of Fixed Assets

Fixed assets are to be valued at current value or historic cost
depending on the classification of the asset. Current value is
defined as the assets replacement cost, or the cost of its
nearest equivalent, adjusted to reflect the condition of the
asset.

Current Value Assets

The following classifications of assets are to be subject to
current value: land associated with operational property;
operational buildings; operational equipment;and non-operational
property.

However, certain short lived assets such as vehicles , plant and
equipment, may be valued at historic cost as a proxy for current
cost where the difference between current value and historic cost
is not material.

Assets which are carried in the balance sheet at current value
are required to be revalued at intervals not greater than 5
years.

Historic Cost Assets

The following assets may be valued at historic cost:

- Infrastructure assets
- Community assets
- Assets under construction
- Vehicles, plant and equipment where there is no material
  difference
- Between current value and historic cost.

Charges to the Revenue Account - Asset Rents

The system is based on charges to the revenue account for
capital, in the form of an asset rent. The asset rent should be
made up of, at least, depreciation where appropriate and cost of
capital charge. the requirement is such that councils which have
adopted an asset rent system in advance of the requirement should
be able to comply with the rules, without major changes.

Rules Regarding Depreciation of Assets

Depreciation is to be provided on the carrying value of the asset where appropriate. Not all assets required to be depreciated.

Land does not need to be depreciated in line with the rules of commercial accounting.

Infrastructure and community assets will not need to be depreciated if properly maintained.

Depreciation will not be required where the local authority make regular repairs and maintenance to extend the assets useful life in existing use.

Depreciation will not be required where an asset is deemed to have an infinite useful life. this is defined as being more than 20 years.

It may transpire that depreciation is limited to reasonably few assets. however where assets are depreciated it should be based on the carrying value of the asset, and the depreciation provision should be used to write down the asset in the balance sheet.

Rules Regarding Charges for the Cost of Capital

As explained above in addition to the depreciation charge a calculation will be required on all assets for notional interest also to be included as a charge to the revenue account.

The notional interest charge will be 5% where assets are valued at current values, representing a real rate of return. Where assets are included at historic cost a prescribed market rate of interest will be used, for example a PWLB rate.

In fact it is the notional interest charges that are likely to be the major element of the asset rent. These charges are of course purely notional.

Asset registers need to be maintained to form the basic data on which capital charges are made.

Impact on The Council Tax

Where capital charges exceed the current debt charge system a reversal will be required in the summary revenue account.

Guidance on Charges to Services

The CAWG report states that "as a minimum, such charges are to be made to individual services as defined in CIPFA's standard classification of income and expenditure, central support services and statutory trading accounts, including DSOs. Local authorities are free to choose whether to pass these charges down to individual cost centres, and if so, on what basis. However, there is no requirement to do so".

These rules represent a broad summary of the proposals. In the CAWG a fuller account is given of why some of these decisions

have been taken. The very next problems is how to account for
these items in practice.

Detailed Accounting Requirement

When the detailed accounting requirement is considered the
system, which in principle is relatively straightforward, become
more difficult to understand. This is partly due to a complex
method adopted to reverse the tax impact out of the consolidated
revenue account. The detail involves coming to terms with the
following:

- Treatment of the Housing Revenue Account
- Preparation of the Asset Restatement Account
- Preparation of the Capital Financing Reserve
- Preparation of the Asset Management Account
- Preparation of the Capital Receipts Unapplied Account
- Consideration of Deferred Charges.

Each of these problems will be discussed in turn to enable an
understanding of the purpose of the item to be understood, before
a fully worked example is provided.

Treatment of the Housing Revenue Account

The HRA must be charged with capital charges equating to the
capital financing costs calculated in accordance with the
statutory requirement. The HRA will therefore be charged with
that amount. The HRA is also to be included in with the
consolidated summary revenue account to a limited degree. This
will become apparent when the example which follows later in this
chapter is explained.

Preparation of the Asset Restatement Account

This account is new to local authority accounting and will be
used to facilitate the following:

- The account will be debited or credited as a result of
  decreases or increases in asset values.

- When assets are sold the net book value will be transferred
  to this account. the cash received will be credited to
  capital receipts unapplied.

- Any deferred charges written off will be effectively
  transferred to this account. This is in respect of deferred
  charges related to asset previously sold on which debt is
  outstanding. Under the new system deferred charges of this
  type will not be retained.

The balance on this account is shown under the financed by
section on the balance sheet.

Preparation of the Capital Financing Reserve

The Capital Financing Reserve is primarily a replacement for the
capital discharged accounts. It also holds the reserved capital
receipts set aside for future debt redemption. In practice, the
account is marginally more complicated than this, the entries

might typically include the following:

Credit entries from - Direct Revenue Financing
                    - Capital Receipts applied
                    - Minimum Revenue Provision/Loans redeemed*
                    - Reserved Capital Receipt

*   the additional complication here is that the revenue account
     is charged with the minimum revenue provision adjusted by
     the amount already provided for depreciation. for example
     if depreciation amounts to £1.5 million and the minimum
     revenue provision would have been £2.5 million. Then the
     entry in the capital financing reserve for MRP would only be
     £1 million because the credit of £1.5 million can be found
     in the depreciation account netted off of fixed assets.

The capital financing reserve can be found on the balance sheet
under the Financed by section.

Preparation of the Asset Management Account

The asset management account is combined with contribution to the
capital financing reserve to effect the reversal of the impact of
asset rents on the Council Tax payer. This can best be
demonstrated with the use of some example figures.

Example   The service committee revenue accounts of the Downtown
           District Council have been charged with asset rents
           made up as follows:

Downtown asset rents

                         £10 million notional interest charges
                         £ 3 million depreciation

     Total asset rents   £13 million
                         ===========

Downtown's charges for capital under the debt charge system would
have been as follows:
     External interest   £ 6.1 million
     Direct revenue funding   £ 2.1 million
     Minimum revenue provision   £ 4.1 million

                                  £12.3 million
                                  =============

Interpretation of these Figures

This example shows that as a result of the new system £700,000
too much would be charged to Council Tax payers unless a
reversal is carried out.

The reversal will be carried out in two parts, and be shown on
the face of the summary revenue account. The Asset Management
account reverses the impact of the imbalance of real interest to
notional interest. While the impact of the minimum revenue
provision and direct revenue funding are adjusted through the
capital financing reserve. This can be illustrated as follows:

Example from the Summary Consolidated Revenue Account

	£	£
Net cost of services(including asset rents of 13 million)		32.0 million
Asset management account		
Depreciation	3.0 million	
External interest	6.1 million	
Less assets rents charged	(13.0) million	(3.9) million
Net operating expenditure		28.1 million
Contribution to capital reserves		
Provision for replacement of external loans		1.1 million
Direct financing of fixed assets		2.1 million
Amount to be met from Central government Grants and local taxation		31.3 million

This example may appear confusing but you should note two facts which might improve your understanding. First the change between net cost of service and amount to be met from taxation is £700,000 which of course is the amount to be reversed related to the excess of asset rents compared to the debt charge system.

Secondly the adjustment in the capital financing reserve is not the full minimum revenue provision because depreciation remains as a charge on the summary consolidated revenue account. Therefore the charge for minimum revenue provision supplement, is purely a topping up process, and could in fact work in reverse if the MRP were less than the Depreciation charge.

Preparation of the Capital Receipts Unapplied Account

This account remains part of the Financing shown in the authorities balance sheet and is made up as follows:

	- capital receipts unused brought forward;
Add	- new capital receipts received
Less	- the set aside sums transferred to capital receipts applied/capital financing reserve;
Less	- the amount used to finance capital expenditure

Consideration of Deferred Charges.

Deferred charges related to assets previously sold are to be transferred to the asset restatement account. Other deferred charges will be retained and written off to revenue over a specified period.

Summary of Charges for Capital Accounting

The capital accounting proposals involve the establishment of fixed assets either at current values or historic cost.

Many assets will be exempt from a depreciation charge under certain circumstances. however notional interest charges have to be provided on all assets.

The probable overall effect will be greater asset rent charges to the revenue accounts than would have been the case under the debt charge system. This in turn is subject to a complex reversal via the asset management account, which is shown on the face of the consolidated revenue account, and the contributions to capital financing reserve.

This chapter has provided details of the proposal, and has attempted to explain the main accounting changes it should now be possible for a complete question to be considered.

Fully Worked Example - Quickstart District Council

This question has been developed by the author to fit the worked example figures in the CAWG's report. It has been modified to avoid confusion over a few items. However, in general the question outlines a scenario that fits the CAWG's worked example. this means that the question is based on no depreciation being provided for land and buildings or council dwellings. This may appear to be an exceptional occurrence, but in fact it is the example provided in the CAWG's report to guide local authorities regarding the ways the system can operate.

Additional examination questions provided are wholly original, the author considered it appropriate for the fully worked example to follow the CIPFA CAWG's proposal to enable students to accept the example as being practically based, and reflective of the approach many authorities may take.

Question - Fully Worked Example Quickstart District Council

Exercise 9.1
Example question 1 - New Capital Accounting System

The following balances were extracted from the books of the Quickstart District Council as at 31 March 1994

	Fixed Assets Cost £000s	Less Capital Discharged £000s	Unfinanced Balance £000s
Council Dwellings	103,421	34,140	69,281
Other Land and Blds.	12,225	4,240	7,985
Vehicle Plant & Eq.	2,693	750	1,943
Infrastructure	5,772	3,820	1,952
Non Operational	2,800	300	2,500
	126,911	43,250	83,661

	HRA £000s	General Fund £000s
Loans outstanding	27,576	19,882
Capital receipts	30,012	12,953
Deferred charges	1,270	1,666
Revenue reserves	300	12,589

Transactions for 1994/95

	Expenditure £000s	Income £000s
Housing Revenue Account	13,557	20,144
Housing General Fund	2,100	200
Leisure	3,100	1,500
Environmental Health	1,020	50

```
Others                           3,850      250
                                 -------------------
                                 23,627    22,144
```

Other Items

	HRA £000s	General Fund £000s
Minimum Rev. Provision	1,431	1,038
Loans Repaid	1,175	750
Cash Proceeds Sale FA	8,000	1,000

NOTES

1. The General Fund services should be charged with the following asset rents.

	Depreciation £000s	Notional £000s	Total £000s
Housing General Fund	200	850	1,050
Leisure	570	2,560	3,130
Environmental Health	100	410	510
Others	263	875	1,138
	1,133	4,695	5,828

2. Quickstart District Council have decided that their HRA properties do not require to be depreciated. This is on the basis that the life of the stock exceeds 20 years and that the stock is well maintained. However under item 8 determination the HRA should be charged interest of £4,887,000. This figure can be considered equivalent to an asset rent and is not the amount of interest chargeable on the old loans pool arrangements.

3. The following revaluation adjustments need to be made to the unfinanced balances as at the 31 March 1994. This will effectively bring assets up to Net current replacement cost.

	£000s
Council Dwellings	20,719
Other land & Blds.	42,015
Non Operational	37,500

4. Vehicle Plant & Equipment, and infrastructure assets are brought into the new system at historic cost. Under the CIPFA proposals the unfinanced balance as at 31 March 1994 will be sufficient to achieve this.

5. Current assets and current liabilities as at the 31 march 1995 will be £38,736,000 and £16,975,000 respectively.

6. Assets disposed of during 1994/95 had the following net book values.

	£000s
Council Dwellings	11,879
Other land & Blds.	160
Vehicle P & E	28
	12,067

7. The depreciation in note 1 above was made up of £1,031,000 Vehicle Plant & Equipment, and £102,000 infrastructure.

NB: Other Land and Buildings were not depreciated because they were deemed to be of infinite life.

8. Capital expenditure during the year was made up as follows:

Capital Expenditure	£000s	
Council Dwellings	16,590	
Other land & Blds.	1,057	
Vehicle P & E	618	
Deferred Charge	720	General Fund
Infrastructure	176	
Total	19,161	

	HRA £000s	General Fund £000s
Financed by:		
Direct Revenue Funding	-	500
Capital Receipt	7,262	453
Loans Raised	9,328	1,618
Total	16,590	2,571

9. Deferred charges on the HRA are all in respect of assets previously sold, where debt remained outstanding. These are to be written off to the Fixed Asset Restatement Reserve.

    Deferred charges on the General fund relate to expenditure on intangible assets. These are retained in the balance sheet and written off over a specific period. This year's write off is £192,000 and has been included in the transactions.

10. The amount to be reserved for the redemption of debt from capital receipts is 50% for the General fund and 75% for the HRA.

11. The real repayment of interest amounted to £2,115,000 and £3,456,000 for the General Fund and HRA respectively.

12. Collection Fund revenues to be brought into account for 1994/95 are £13,048,000.

You Are Required To:

Prepare the Consolidated summary revenue account for the Quickstart District Council for the year ending 31 March 1995, and a consolidated balance sheet as at the 31 March 1995.

TUTORIAL ANSWER QUICKSTART DISTRICT COUNCIL

Probably the best way of approaching this very complex question is to try to prepare the first section of the Consolidated Revenue Account for 1994/95.

This can be achieved by recording the expenditure and income and including the asset rent figures as follows:

Quickstart District Council Extract of Consolidate Summary Revenue Account for the year ending 31 March 1995

	Expenditure	Income	Net
	£000	£000	£000
(2,100 + 1050) Housing General Fund	3,150	200	2,950
(3,100 + 3130) Leisure	6,230	1,500	4,730
(1,020 + 510) Environmental Health	1,530	50	1,480
(3,850 + 1138) Other Services	4,988	250	4,738
	15,898	2,000	13,898

NB: (includes asset rentals of £5,828,000)

Net cost of general fund services			13,898
(13,557 + 4,887 note (ii)) Housing Revenue Account	18,444	20,144	(1,700)
Net cost of services			12,198

At this point the consolidated summary revenue account is recording the cost of all services based on charges made for asset rents.

Calculation of Asset Rents

This example provides for asset rents which are not based on the real procedures for calculating the notional interest. Please therefore just accept the figure as being correct. if you were to try to calculate the general fund interest for example you would discover that it is based on the revalued assets figure before considering current year capital expenditure and also uses a rate of 5% which is not correct because assets based on historic cost carry a larger interest % burden.

This note is provided to avoid confusion and misunderstanding.

Removal of HRA Surplus

We now need to remove the HRA surplus which is ringfenced in its own account, and cannot be considered to be part of the general fund balance. In addition the asset rents have got to be replaced by real cost of capital. This involves a good deal of effort as follows:

What is the Actual Cost of Capital

Under the old accounting regime the accounts would have been charged with the following amounts:

	£000
Direct Revenue Finance	500
Minimum Revenue Provision	2,469
Interest	5,571
Total	8,540

Therefore as a result of the new capital accounting system asset rents exceed the old charge method. This can be proved by adding up the asset rent as follows:

	£000
General fund - depreciation	1,133
General fund - interest	4,695
HRA - interest	4,887

	10,715
	======

Therefore the excess (£2,175,000) needs to be reversed out of the consolidated summary revenue account. CIPFA achieve this via the use of two accounts which appear on the face of the consolidated revenue account. These accounts are:

- Asset Management Account
- Capital Reserve Account

I will explain the accounting for these accounts in turn.

Asset Management Account

The Asset Management Account is credited with the asset rentals that are charged to the revenue account.

The account is then charged with the real interest payments and depreciation. Therefore the account appears as follows:

Asset Management Account

	£000		£000
		Revenue Account Asset rents General	
Depreciation a/c	1,133	Fund - depreciation	1,133
Actual interest	5,571	- interest	4,695
Balance to summary revenue account	4,011	HRA - interest	4,887
	------		------
	10,715		10,715
	======		======

The account can only become logic if we assume for the moment that the debit for depreciation is the same as the minimum revenue provision (unfortunately it is not, but it will explain later). The asset management account would then be arguably explainable as follows:

	£000
Asset rents	10,715
Less	
Old system costs	6,704
(1133 + 5571)	
Amount to be reversed to ensure a nil impact on	------
the Council Tax	4,011

This statement of the asset management account is not wholly correct because depreciation will not equal the minimum revenue provision, and direct revenue funding is not included in the above analysis even though it is a cost under the old system. The reason for this is that CIPFA have chosen to carry out the reversal of the tax impact in two accounts and the remaining entries are entered onto the summary revenue account as transfers to a capital reserve account known as the capital financing reserve.

The charges to the consolidated summary revenue account are as follows:

- charge for Direct Revenue Financing
- adjustment for the difference between depreciation and the minimum revenue provision (MRP)

In Quickstart the direct revenue financing equals £500,000, while the difference between depreciation and the MRP is as follows:

	£000
Minimum revenue provision	2,469
Less	
Depreciation charge	1,133

Adjustment required to summary revenue account	1,336
	=====

We can now continue to produce the consolidated summary revenue account as follows:

	£000	£000
Net cost of services		12,198
(NB: this includes 10,715,000 of asset rents)		
Asset Management Revenue Account:		
Depreciation	1,133	
External interest	5,571	

	6,704	
Less		
Asset rents charged to services	(10,715)	(4,011)
	--------	-------
Net operating expenditure		8,187
Contribution to Capital Reserves		
Provision for repayment of external loans	1,336	
Financing fixed assets	500	1,836
	------	------
		10,023

If we now consider the combined effect of the asset management account, and the contribution to capital reserve the following becomes apparent.

	£000
Asset management account	(4,011)
Contribution capital reserve	1,836

Net effect of summary revenue account	(2,175)
	=======

This represents the reversing of the tax impact of the new capital accounting system.

having explained the logic behind these accounts we can now complete the consolidated revenue account by carrying out the following:

- Removing HRA surplus from the general fund balance
- bringing in collection fund revenues
- bringing in last year's general fund surplus brought forward

In order that the whole consolidated summary revenue account can be seen the previous extracts will be repeated to show the full statement.

Quickstart District Council Consolidated Summary Revenue Account for the year ending 31 March 1995

	Expenditure £000	Income £000	Net £000
General fund			
- Housing General Fund	3,150	200	2,950
- Leisure	6,230	1,500	4,730
- Environmental Health	1,530	50	1,480
- Other services	4,988	250	4,738
	------	------	------
	15,898	2,000	13,898
Housing Revenue Account	18,444	20,144	(1,700)

Net cost of services			12,198
Asset Management Account			
Depreciation	1,133		
External interest charges	5,571	6,704	
	-----	-------	
Less Asset rents charged to revenue		(10,715)	(4,011)

Net operating expenditure			8,187
Transfer to HRA surplus to HRA reserves			1,700
Contribution to capital reserves			
- Provision for repayment of external loans		1,336	
- Financing of fixed assets		500	1,836
		-----	-------
Amount to be met from Central government grants and local taxpayers			11,723
Collection fund reserves			13,048

Net general fund surplus			1,325
Balance brought forward on general fund revenue reserve as at 1/4/94			12,589

Balance as at 31/3/95			13,914
			=======

Preparation of the Balance Sheet for Quickstart District Council, as at 31 March 1995

Note		£000	£000
1.	**Fixed Assets**		
	Council Dwellings	94,711	
	Other L & B	50,897	
	VPF + E	1,502	
	Infrastructure	2,026	
	Non Operational	40,000	189,136

2.	**Deferred charge**		2,194
	Current Assets	38,736	
	Less		
	Current liabilities	16,975	21,761
		------	-------
			213,091
	Long term loans outstanding		56,479

			156,612
			=======
3.	Financed by:-		
4.	Fixed Asset Restatement Reserve		86,897
5.	Capital Financing Reserve		16,051
6.	Usable Capital Receipts		37,750
7.	Revenue Reserves Plus HSG		15,914
	(13,914 300 + 1700)		-------
			156,612
			=======

Quickstart Fixed Asset Statement

Note 1	Council Dwellings	Other land & buildings	VPF + E	Infra	Non operational	Total
	£000	£000	£000	£000	£000	£000
Not b/fwd	69,281	7,985	1,943	1,952	2,500	83,661
Revaluation	20,719	42,015	-	-	37,500	100,234
	90,000	50,000	1,943	1,952	40,000	183,895
Capital Exp.	16,590	1,057	618	176	-	18,441
Sale of FA	(11,879)	(160)	(28)			(12,067)
	94,711	50,897	2,533	2,128	40,000	190,269
Depreciation	-	-	1,031	102	-	1,133
	94,711	50,897	1,502	2,026	40,000	189,136

Note 2 Intangible Assets - Deferred Charges

	HRA £000	GF £000	Total £000
Amount in old system	1,270	1,666	2,936
New expenditure	-	720	720
	1,270	2,386	3,656
Less written of to			
Fixed asset restatement	(1,270)	-	(1,270)
Revenue account	-	(192)	(192)
	nil	2,194	2,194

Note 3 Loans outstanding

	HRA £000	GF £000	Total £000
Loans o/s b/fwd	27,576	19,882	47,458
New loans raised	9,328	1,618	10,946
	36,904	21,500	58,404
Less loans repaid	1,175	750	1,925
	35,729	20,750	56,479

Note 4 Fixed Asset Restatement Reserve

	£000
Revaluations	100,234
Less	
Deferred charges written out	1,270
Book value of assets sold	12,067
	86,897

Note 5 Capital Financing Reserve

	£000
DRF	500
balances MRP (2,469 - Dep 1,133)	1,336
CRA	7,715
Reserve capital receipts	6,500
	16,051

Note 6 Usable Capital Receipts

	HRA £000	GF £000	Total £000
B/fwd	30,012	12,953	42,965
Add new receipts	8,000	1,000	9,000
	38,012	13,953	51,965
Less CRA	7,262	453	7,715
Less reserved	6,000	500	6,500
			37,750

Note 7 - Revenue Reserves and Housing Revenue Account Extract

	£000	£000
Income		20,144
Operating costs		13,557
External interest	3,456	
Minimum revenue provision	1,431	4,887
	------	------
Surplus for the year		1,700
Housing revenue account balance		
@ 1/4/94		300
		------
balance as at 31/3/95		2,000
HRA surplus as at 31/3/95		2,000
General fund surplus as at 31/7/95		13,914

Total revenue reserves consolidated balance sheet		15,914
		======

Conclusion to Exercise Quickstart District Council

This exercise should give a good overview of the process of producing final accounts under the CAWG's proposal. It does not, however, provide fine detail of the workings of the system.

To ensure that a more detailed understanding is obtained further exercises are provided which deal with specific aspects of the proposals.

Example Question 2 - Calculation of Asset Rents

Exercise 9.2
Tinytown City Council provide the following information regarding capital accounting for their services.

Capital Charge Information

Notional interest rate to be used for assets at current value is 5%, while on assets held at historic cost is 10%.

Depreciation is provided on costal defence and vehicle plant and equipment only at 5% and 15% respectively.

Balance Sheet as at 31 March 1994

	Historic cost £000	Capital discharge £000
Land & buildings	45,000	15,000
Costal defences	5,000	2,000
Vehicles Plant & Equipment	8,000	6,000

Revaluation

Land and buildings have been revalued to £38,000,000 net current replacement cost. The average life being in excess of 35 years with no property having a life of 20 years or less.

Capital Expenditure

During the year 1994/95 £200,000 was spent on acquiring new land and buildings. While £100,000 was spent on vehicles.

Transactions for the year	£000
Net costs of services (excluding asset rents)	15,200
Minimum revenue provision	800
External interest	1,200
DRF/RCCO	200

You are required to:

i)   **Calculate the asset rents for the year 1994/95.**

ii) **Prepare the asset management revenue account.**

iii) **Prepare the consolidated summary revenue account.**

iv) **Show the closing asset values for balance sheet purposes.**

Tutorial Answer to Tinytown Example Question 2

i)
Capital charges - notional interest
Land & buildings
Land & buildings £38 million plus half the capital spending multiplied by 5%

$$= £38,000,000 + \frac{£200,000}{2} = £38,100,000 \times 5\% = £1,905,000$$

Costal Defences

Under the CIPFA proposals the historic cost can be taken to be the unfinanced balance. This is £3,000,000 as at 1 April 1994. Add to this balance half the capital spending for 1994/95 for the purposes of calculating notional interest and depreciation.

Calculation of Capital Charges for Costal Defence

$$£3,000,000 + \frac{£100,000}{2} = £3,050,000$$

Notional interest = 10% x £3,050,000 = £305,000
                                       ========

Depreciation = 5% x £3,050,000 = £152,500
                                 ========

Vehicles Plant & Equipment

Notional interest = 10% x £2,000,000 = £200,000
                                       ========

Depreciation   = 15% x £2,000,000 = £300,000
                                     ========

Summary of Asset Rents - Tinytown

	Notional interest £	Depreciation £	Total £
Land & buildings	1,905,000	–	1,905,000
Costal defence	305,000	152,500	457,500
Vehicles Plant & Eq.	200,000	300,000	500,000
Total	2,410,000	452,500	2,862,500

ii) & iii)

Tinytown Consolidated Summary Revenue Account for the year ending 31 March 1995

	£	£
Stated net cost of services		15,200,000
Add asset rents not included		2,862,500
Actual net cost of services		18,062,500
Asset management revenue account		
- external interest	1,200,000	
- depreciation	452,500	
	1,652,500	
Less asset rents	(2,862,500)	(1,210,000)
Net operating expenditure		16,852,500
Contribution to capital reserves		
Provision for repayment of external loan		347,500
Financing of fixed assets DRF		200,000
Amount to be met from Government grants and local taxpayers		17,400,000

The answer can be checked by calculating the difference between the asset rent and the debt charge system this amount should equal the difference between net cost of service and the amount finally chargeable to taxpayers.

	£
Asset rent	2,862,500
Less	
debt charge system (800 + 1,200 + 200)	2,200,000
	662,500
Actual net cost of services	18,062,500
Less	
chargeable to local taxpayers	17,400,000
	662,500

Tinytown Balance sheet Extract of fixed Assets as at 31/3/95

```
Fixed Assets                                          £
Other land & buildings                             38,200,000
Costal defences (3,000,000 + 100,000 - 152,500)     2,947,500
Vehicle Plant & Equipment (2,000,000 - 300,000      1,700,000
                                                   ----------
                                                   42,847,500
                                                   ==========
```

Example Question 3
Exercise 9.3

1. The ABC Council spends capital sums of £21,000,000 on
    housing, of which £17 million is on the provision for new
    accommodation, while £4 million is in respect of repairs.

2. The ABC Council also spends £10 million on new schools but
    at the end of the year has a capital creditor for £1
    million.

3. A barter deal was undertaken during the year where an open
    education site is valued in the accounts at £350,000 was
    swapped for an historic building valued at £400,000.

4. An operating lease on a special computer gadget was agreed
    for a 1.5 year period at a total cost of £170,000.

5. A work of art was purchased for £200,000.

6. A machine was purchased to count coins for £2,000.

**You are required to consider the treatment of these items under
the new capital accounting rules**

Tutorial Answer Example Question - Exercise 9.3

Part 1

The questions raised here are as follows:

> The new building on housing is certain to be capital and
> will be capitalised in the category council dwellings.
> Presumably the assets will last more than twenty years and
> therefore not need to be depreciated.

> However, will the repairs meet the requirements of capital,
> do they enhance the building and extend their useful life?
> It will very much depend on the type of repairs undertaken.
> it might be necessary to treat some of the repairs as
> revenue.

Part 2
This point is easily resolved the new building is capital, and
would be classed as other land and buildings. The assets are
probably going to last more than 20 years, and therefore need not
be depreciated, but will need to be included in the calculation
of notional interest.

The amount to be capitalised is £11 million because the accrual needs to be recognised.

Part 3
The barter deal must be reflected in the balance sheet. This will involve a transfer from education other land and buildings account of £350,000 to the assets restatement reserve account, while the historic building will have to be introduced as a community asset at cost of £400,000 offset by an entry in the fixed asset restatement reserve account.

Part 4
The operational lease would not be considered to be capital unlike finance leases. The costs related to the operational lease would be charged to the revenue account.

However, it would be necessary to provide a note in the balance sheet of the outstanding repayments due on the operating lease.

Part 5
Interestingly the purchase of a work of art is not considered capital under the government capital expenditure controls. however, it would be capitalised in the balance sheet as a community asset.

Part 6
The machine will undoubtedly last more than one year but it is under the de minimis level, and subject to the council's policy would normally be treated as revenue expenditure and not capitalised.

Conclusion Capital Accounting Chapter

Hopefully, this chapter has provided comprehensive coverage of the subject, and the examples helped to consolidate the information transmitted.

It should be possible for a judgment to be made regarding the new system, and whether or not it meets the objectives set.

It should also be possible for the following examination question to be attempted successfully.

But most importantly hopefully the logic behind the proposals will be understood. this is particularly important because the interaction of these proposals with other chapters is evident, and an understanding required.

Examination Question 9.1 - New Capital Accounting System

The following balances were extracted form the books of the Cheeseham London Borough as at 31 March 1994.

	Fixed Assets Cost	Less Capital Discharged	Unfinanced Balance
	£000s	£000s	£000s
Council Dwellings	57,400	21,400	36,000
Other Land and Blds.	33,000	11,500	21,500
Vehicle Plant & Eq.	6,250	1,250	5,000
Infrastructure	9,300	3,300	6,000
Non Operational	3,200	200	3,000
	109,150	37,650	71,500

	HRA	General Fund
	£000s	£000s
Loans outstanding	16,500	22,400
Capital receipts	38,638	8,500
Deferred charges	520	500
Revenue reserves	3,500	15,690

Transactions for 1994/95

	Expenditure	Income
	£000s	£000s
Housing Revenue Account	18,200	23,417
Education	24,100	22,200
Social Services	16,300	11,500
Highways	47,200	16,150
Others	49,200	50,250
	155,000	123,517

Other Items

	HRA	General Fund
	£000s	£000s
Minimum Rev. Provision	430	900
Loans Repaid	1,815	7,200
Cash Proceeds Sale FA	12,000	3,000

NOTES

1. The General Fund services should be charged with the following asset rents.

	Depreciation	Notional	Total
	£000s	£000s	£000s
Education	180	2,700	2,880
Social Services	120	1,100	1,220
Highways	300	600	900
Others	120	800	920
	720	5,200	5,920

2. Cheeseham London Borough have decided that their HRA properties do not require to be depreciated. This is on the basis that the life of the stock exceeds 20 years and that the stock is well maintained. However under item 8 determination the HRA should be charged interest of £5,100,000. This figure can be considered equivalent to an asset rent and is not the amount of interest chargeable on the old loans pool arrangements.

3. The following revaluation adjustments need to be made to the unfinanced balances as at the 31 March 1994. This will effectively bring assets up to Net current replacement cost.

	£000s
Council Dwellings	11,200
Other land & Blds.	53,500
Non Operational	47,695

4. Vehicle Plant & Equipment, and infrastructure assets are brought into the new system at historic cost. Under the CIPFA proposals the unfinanced balance as at 31 March 1994 will be sufficient to achieve this.

5. Current assets less current liabilities as at the 31 March 1995 should be the balancing figure.

6. Assets disposed of during 1994/95 had the following net book values.

	£000s
Council Dwellings	10,500
Other land & Blds.	200
Vehicle P & E	500

	11,200

7. The depreciation in note 1 above was made up of £550,000 Vehicle Plant & Equipment, and £170,000 infrastructure.

NB: Other Land and Buildings were not depreciated because they were deemed to be of infinite life.

8. Capital expenditure during the year was made up as follows:

Capital Expenditure	£000s	
Council Dwellings	10,300	
Other land & Blds.	3,100	
Vehicle P & E	200	
Deferred Charge	100	General Fund
Infrastructure	500	

Total	14,200	

	HRA £000s	General Fund £000s
Financed by:		
Direct Revenue Funding	-	200
Capital Receipt	4,900	600
Loans Raised	5,000	3,500
	------	------
Total	9,900	4,300

9.   Deferred charges on the HRA are all in respect of assets previously sold, where debt remained outstanding. These are to be written off to the Fixed Asset Restatement Reserve.

     Deferred charges on the General fund relate to expenditure on intangible assets. These are retained in the balance sheet and written off over a specific period. This year's write off is £50,000 and has been included in the transactions.

10. The amount to be reserved for the redemption of debt from capital receipts is 50% for the General fund and 75% for the HRA.

11. The real repayment of interest amounted to £1,100,000 and £2,300,000 for the General Fund and HRA respectively.

12. Collection Fund revenues to be brought into account for 1994/95 are £41,200,000.

You Are Required To:

Prepare the Consolidated summary revenue account for the London Borough of Cheeseham for the year ending 31 March 1995, and a consolidated balance sheet as at the 31 March 1995.

Examination Question 9.2

The balance sheet of
Stardown District Council included the following:

Fixed Assets	£000
Council Dwellings	25,200
Other land and buildings	15,400
Community assets	7,100
Vehicles	3,200
Fixed asset restatement reserve	17,300
Capital receipts unapplied	7,400

Carry out the following adjustments in the notes and restate the
above accounts. No entries have been made at all for these
items.

Notes

i)   An area office was demolished. The net book value was
      £75,000. The site was sold for £50,000 and cash was
      received.

ii)   Council house sales amounted to £7,100,000 the net book
      value amounted to £3,100,000.

iii) Sale of (non HRA) land raised £500,000. The net book value
      was £300,000.

iv)   A building valued at £200,000 in the above balance has been
      revalued to £700,000 due to the development of a superstore.
      this is a permanent change which is going to be realised in
      the near future.

CHAPTER 10

Accounting for Local Authorities Revenue Transactions

Introduction

Local authorities perform services which are varied and managed by different committees of the local council. Each committee is constructed from interested members of the council. An election process is undertaken to determine the chair and vice chair of each service committee. The chair and vice chair of committees will normally also serve on the Policy and Resources committee participating in more general debates regarding the level of the council tax and allocation of resources among service committees.

Each service committees is therefore responsible for the management of services it provides. Decisions of the service committee are ratified by the full council which operates in a rubber stamping capacity.

The main building block of local authority accounting is therefore revenue accounts of income and expenditure for each service committee.

Standard Classification of Service Committee Revenue Accounts

CIPFA have developed and maintained a voluntary code of standard accounting practice known as the standard classification.

The purpose of the standard classification is to provide a common and therefore consistent basis for producing published and statistical financial information of a stewardship or control nature. There are two main levels to the standard classification as follows:

- objective classification
- subjective classification

Objective Classification

CIPFA requires its members to adopt wherever possible the recommended objective classification for service and divisions of service. However, those recommendations at sub division level and below are only advisory and authorities are permitted to have regard to their own particular circumstances in determining how to record these lower levels of analysis.

An Example of the Levels is as follows:

```
Service                   = social services
Division of service       = children and families
Sub division of service   = Purchasing costs
(suggest analysis only)
```

Subjective Analysis

The subjective analysis is the detailed analysis of costs which is required across all services provided by local authorities.

The most recent analysis provided in the CIPFA document accounting for Social Services 1993 sets out nine standard subjective groupings as follows:

Employees
Premises related expenditure
Transport related expenditure
Supplies and services
Third party payments (formerly agency and contracted services)
Transfer payments
Support services
Capital financing costs
Income

Recent Revisions to the Standard Classification

CIPFA's most recent service subject to review was in 1993 the following gives a list of those reviewed since the last wholesale review which took place in 1985.

- Accounting for Social Services 1993
- Accounting for Education 1992
- Housing and Other Services (revised) 1989

Services that have not been reviewed since 1985 are as follows:

- Highway and Transportation
- Home Office Services

Significance of New Standard Classification

The reviews that have taken place are significant, because they reflect the changing nature of local authorities in providing and purchasing services. Education's guide was amended largely because of the local management of schools initiative which results from the Education Reform Act 1988. Changes to the Social Services classifications were as a direct result of the changing role of Social Services due to the NHS and Community Care Act 1990.

However, what is particularly important about these documents is not just the change in classifications themselves but the emergence of a revised approach to identifying support services costs. We find that a new classification of costs in addition to corporate management is not chargeable down to cost centres and trading operations. This heading is known as service strategy and regulations. More detail will be provided on this topic in the next chapter dealing with trading accounts for support services.

Example of the Objective Analysis

The following is a full analysis of the service and division of service for social services.

Service	Division of Service
Social services or social work	Service strategy & regulation
	Children & families
	Report to the Children's panel (Scotland only)
	Elderly
	People with a physical or sensory disability
	People with learning disabilities
	People with mental health needs
	Offenders services (Scotland only)
	Social services management & support services

The standard objective analysis enables statistics to be gathered related to standard service provision. Each authority can, from this information, with the help of unit cost information provided by the Audit Commission, consider their spending against similar local authorities.

Detail of the Subjective Analysis

Each of the nine previously mentioned 'standard grouping' are split into greater detailed divisions known as 'sub groups' and detail headings. It is important to recognise that standard grouping and sub groups are required to be used by CIPFA institute members, and carry the status of an institute statement. The detailed headings are advisory and authorities are permitted to have regard to their own particular circumstances in determining the detail headings appropriate.

The following gives a general explanation of each standard grouping, sub grouping and recommended optional detailed headings.

STANDARD GROUPING	SUB GROUPS	OPTIONAL DETAILED RECOMMENDATION
1. Employees	Direct employee expenses	Employee type
		or
	Indirect employee expenses	element of cost

Under this standard grouping the Direct Employee Expenses includes salaries, wages, employers national insurance and superannuation contributions. All staff must be recorded here whether they are full time, part-time, or temporary.

Indirect employee expenses are those expenses which are wholly associated with staff employment as follows: relocation costs, interview and training expenses, advertising, severance payments and pension enhancements.

CIPFA's employee detailed recommendation, proposes that the detailed analysis could be either the employee type, i.e. operational , support staff, kitchen and canteen staff, etc. Alternatively the details might analyse payment between such detailed headings as gross pay, national insurance, superannuation, and allowances.

STANDARD GROUPING	SUB GROUPS
2. Premises related expenditure	Repairs, alteration and maintenance of buildings
	Energy
	Rents
	Rates
	Water services
	Fixtures & fittings
	Apportionment of expenses of operational buildings
	Cleaning & domestic supplies
	Premises insurance
	Contributions to premises related provisions

The optional detail is left completely to local authorities to determine, but for example energy would make electricity, gas, fuel, etc. More advice is given to clarify in which headings costs should be recorded. For example, cleaning and domestic supplies does not include cleaning equipment which should be charged to equipment, furniture and materials under the supplies and services standard grouping 4.

STANDARD GROUPING	SUB GROUPS
3. Transport related expenditure	Direct transport costs
	Recharges
	Contact hire and operation issues
	Public transport/car allowance
	Transport insurance

Where transport costs are incurred directly by the service committee the majority of costs would be recorded as direct transport costs. The recharge sub group heading relates to pool vehicles, while external providers of transport would be classified under contract hire or operational lease.

STANDARD GROUPING	SUB GROUPS
4. Supplies and services	Equipment, furniture and materials
	Catering
	Clothing, uniforms and laundry, printing, stationery, etc.
	Services
	Communications and computing
	Expenses including members allowances
	Grants and subscriptions
	Contribution to provisions
	Miscellaneous

The standard grouping covers a vast number of expenses. An important point to note from a student's point of view is the fact that the miscellaneous heading can be found here. Often in examination questions a special expense will appear which is not easily identifiable from the standard listings. In these cases rather than waste time attempting to allocate the cost, it may be more practical to record these few items as miscellaneous.

STANDARD GROUPING	SUB GROUPS
5. Third party payments	Independent units within the Council (DSOs) Other local authorities Health authorities Government departments Voluntary associations Other establishment Private contractors Other agencies

This standard classification grouping was formerly known as agency and contracted services. The heading can be confusing. It is intended to record payments for a specific objective undertaken by either an internal independent service deliverer, or an external service deliverer. Examples would include the payment of grant to a voluntary organisation to provide residential care. Another example would be the payment to a contractor for refuse collection

However, where the payment relates to a type of expenditure, for example repairing vehicles or building repair, the cost should be recorded under the standard grouping appropriate to the expense in these cases transport and premises standard groupings respectively.

STANDARD GROUPING	SUB GROUPS
6. Transfer payments	None defined

These payments are made to individuals where no goods or services are received in return by the authority. Examples are as follows:

-   Assistance in cash and kind to children in care (S17) Childrens Act 1989

-   Education costs include payments to pupils for clothing, music scholarships, free meals granted. General grants, etc.

-   In Housing services benefits granted to tenants and private sector rent allowances are transfer payments.

STANDARD GROUPING

7.   Support Services

Advice on sub groupings is provided under this standard grouping
by function as follows:

Sub groupings which apply across the board of services is not
considered appropriate.

accountants; architects; buildings & offices; cashiers; committee
administration; contracting; couriers; energy management;
engineers; information technology; insurance; internal auditors;
lawyers; management services; office catering; payroll; personnel
officers; press officers; post room; printers; purchasing;
quantity surveyors; receptionists; security guards; stores;
surveyors; telephonists; transport/fleet management; typists;
valuers.

This list is the most up to date list available published in
CIPFA's trading accounts guidance. However, it is not
exhaustive, and can be added to wherever and authority provide a
support activity which may be turned into a trading organisation.

This category should be used where units are operating as trading
or internal business units rather than within supplies and
services or third party payments.

Standard Grouping

8.   Capital Financing Costs

These costs relate to items which meet the definition of being
capital related, in that they are charges resulting from the
capitalisation of non-current expenditure.

Capital accounting is undergoing radical change as a result of
new proposal by CIPFA. The current standard classification does
not at present reflect these changes which are to be implemented
in 1994/95. The following is a breakdown of charges to revenue
accounts for 1993/94 and thereafter under the new system.

Sub groups 1993/94 Old System	Sub groups 1994/95 New System
Loans pool - principal & interest	Asset rents including at least a charge for depreciation, where appropriate, and notional interest
Finance Leasing charges	
Direct Revenue Financing (RCCOs)	
Debt Management expenses	

For further information on capital accounting read the previous
chapter. However, asset rents will form the basis of the charge
to revenue accounts.

STANDARD GROUPING

9.   INCOME

All income received by the service *from external users or by way of charges or recharges to internal users.*

Sub-Groups

Government grants	Specific and special government grants
Other grants, reimbursements and contributions	Revenue income received to finance a function/project jointly or severally undertaken with other local authorities. Value of costs recharged to outside bodies including other committees.
Customer and client receipts	Sales of products, materials, data technology or surplus commodities. Fees and charges - for services, use of facilities, admissions, lettings. Rents - tithes, acknowledgements, way leaves and other land and property based charges of a non-casual nature.
Interest	
Recharges	Value of costs *recharged to internal users. This does not include charges made for services provided under SLAs or similar (TAGs) agreements by units operating as independent trading units. Such units should record income from internal customers under fees and charges above.*

Conclusion Subjective Analysis

This section has set out in a good deal of detail the requirements of classification both objective and subjective. It is normally the subjective classification which feature most in examination questions.

The next part of this chapter deals with the preparation of revenue accounts for different activities operated by local authorities.

Requirement to Produce Revenue Accounts in the Financial Statements

The CIPFA Accounting Code of Practice does not require individual revenue accounts to form part of the statement of accounts for local authorities. Only one statement is required for the purpose of revenue accounting in the statement of accounts, and that is the consolidated summary revenue account.

The consolidated summary revenue accounts is drawn up from the individual revenue accounts of the local authority services. This chapter sets out the different types of revenue account that need to be prepared for two reasons. firstly that these revenue accounts represent the building blocks of local authority accounts, and all local authority students need to be able to prepare them, and secondly examination questions often involve using revenue accounting information.

Types of Revenue Accounting

The following type of accounts are often required.

- individual committee revenue accounts
- trading format revenue accounts
- consortia revenue accounts
- statement of support service costs/support service trading accounts
- special services revenue accounts
- consolidated summary revenue account

Individual Committee Revenue Accounts

With effect from the 1 April 1994 revenue accounts of local authorities will be required to be charged with asset rents. the asset rent as a minimum will include depreciation, where appropriate, and notional interest charges. The asset rent will replace the old system of debt charge accounting. It will therefore not be necessary to record the charges for principal, interest and direct revenue financing in the individual revenue account.

The new accounting code of practice does not require individual committees to produce a balance sheet and under the new capital accounting rules this would be inappropriate. The only balance sheet required to be produced for publication is the consolidated balance sheet. Therefore questions in this chapter on revenue accounting for individual revenue accounts will not require a full balance sheet.

The individual revenue accounts produced relate to services which are deficit financed. Such services as Education, Leisure and social Services, for example. The presentation of the revenue account in this book remains double sided. the main reason for this is to distinguish the format from trading format revenue accounts.

Trading Format Revenue Accounts

These format are prepared for services which are able to generate significant income, and the local authority may wish to pursue a breakdown or profit making policy. the trading services to which these formats relate are <u>not</u> only those subject to compulsory competition.

Trading services which are subject to CCT are dealt with later in this book in the next chapter. Due to the current proposals for white collar CCT all formats for trading accounts will be considered in the next chapter.

Consortia Revenue Accounts

These accounting formats are no different to the traditional individual revenue accounting format. However, they involve the added complication of dealing with personal accounts.

In these questions a number of parties contribute to the running cost of the service, and personal accounts are maintained for each contributor. An example will be provided in this chapter.

Under the new capital accounting proposals, contributors towards the jointly provided service would have to be prepared to finance the asset rents charged, unless adjustments are made to ensure these are removed and the impact of the higher asset rents are not effective on the consortia members. An example is provided which attempts to identify and account for these problems.

Statement of Support Service Costs/Support Service Trading Accounts

The proposals for white collar CCT are dealt with extensively in the next chapter. However, the government no longer intend to pursue a requirement for internal trading accounts. The current publication of accounting information is intended to take the form of a statement of support service costs (SSSC). This statement will be discussed in more detail along with the format for trading accounts and their benefits in the next chapter.

Special Service Revenue Accounts

Special service revenue accounts is a term used to describe revenue accounts not developed for standard services. These include the Housing Revenue Account which is a ringfenced account which must be accounted for separately from other services. Another special service revenue account is the superannuation fund which again is not part of standard service committee accounting. The accounting for these special services can be found in "Advanced Public Sector Accounting", also published by Allen Accountancy.

Consolidated Summary Revenue Account

The consolidated summary revenue account has been explained in the previous chapter dealing with capital accounting, examples have been provided to enable students to consider the accounting required.

Examples of the Accounting for Revenue Accounts

Example 1.   Individual service revenue account for Uppercrust
             Parks Recreation and Leisure Services Committee.

Exercise 10.1

Question
The following are the Transactions of income and expenditure of
the Parks Recreation and Leisure Services Committee of the
Uppercrust District Council for the year ending 31 March 1995
were as follows:

Transactions during the year

	£
Employees National Insurance Contributions	24,000
Salary Costs	165,000
Printing Stationery and Postage	16,500
Rent	12,300
Rates	6,500
Repairs and Maintenance of Grounds	34,200
Electricity	3,500
Equipment and Tools	2,800
Support Services	61,500
General Office Expenses	15,800
Use of Transport	29,500
Vehicle Insurance and Tax	16,200
Miscellaneous Expenses	5,300
Training Costs	1,800
Agency Costs	31,000
Fees and Charges	198,000
Water Rates	16,200
Asset rent - depreciation	62,000
- notional interest	94,000
Sales	17,800
Grants to Voluntary Organisations	9,200
Capital Expenditure	265,000

Note 1

The Capital Expenditure was financed £50,000 from revenue,
£75,000 from the capital fund and £140,000 from loans. Although
the cash balance as at 31 March has been adjusted for this
transaction, no other entry has been made in the accounts. The
capital expenditure has been taken into account when the asset
rent was set.

Note 2
This period's Revenue Account will require a General Fund
Contribution of £391,500. you are required to prepare the
Revenue Account for the year ending 31 March 1995.

Tutorial Answer to Uppercrust District Council

This question simply involved the preparation of a service
committee revenue account in a traditional format.

Treatment of Note 1

Note 1 is an explanation of the method of financing capital expenditure. however, we have no need for this information when producing a revenue account for the service. Instead our asset rent is charges to the revenue account. The entries for principal, real interest paid and direct revenue financing are accounted for in the summary consolidated revenue account.

Treatment of Note 2

This note provides us with guidance that the income will not be adequate to meet all expenditure and therefore a contribution from the general fund will be required. the amount stated is £391,500 and should equal the deficit on the revenue account.

We can now prepare the service revenue account as follows:

Parks, Recreation and Leisure Services Committee Revenue Account for the year ending 31 March 1995

Transactions during the year

Expenditure

Employees	£	£	Income	£	£
Direct - Salary	165,000		Customer and client		
Nat Ins	24,000		receipts		
Agency	31,000		- Fees and		
Indirect training cost	1,800	221,800	Charges 198,000		
			- Sales 17,800		215,800

Premises Related Expenses

Repairs and Maintenance	34,200	
Rent	12,300	
Water Rates	16,200	
Rates	6,500	
Energy - Electricity	3,500	72,700

Net expenditure
to Rate Fund   391,500

Transport Related Expenses

Use of Transport	29,500	
Vehicle Insurance and Tax	16,200	45,700

Supplies and Services

Printing Stationery	16,500	
Equipment and Tools	2,800	
General Office Expenses	15,800	
Miscellaneous Expenses	5,300	40,000

Third Party Payments

Grants to Voluntary Organisations	9,200	9,200

	£	£	£	£
Support Services	61,500	61,500		

Capital Financing Costs

Asset rent
- depreciation   62,000
- notional interest 94,000

	156,000	
	£607,300	£ 607,300

Consortia Revenue Accounts

The format for these revenue accounts is no different to that for
individual revenue accounts. However, with consortia revenue
accounts the deficit is split between the sponsors of the
service. Therefore these accounts involve the accounting
necessary for personal accounts.

An example of the services that might be subjected to a consortia
approach is any service where a number of local authorities get
together to provide a service. These could include police
services, computer services or even audit services.

A simple exercise requiring personal accounts is as follows:

Exercise 10.2

The following information is provided by the Joint Audit
Consortia facility of Spectown, Bogtown and Uptown. Any deficit
is shared between the three councils as follows:

	%
Spectown	40
Bogtown	40
Uptown	20

Joint Audit Facility Consortia Revenue Account for the year ending 31 March 1993

Expenditure	£	Income	£
Employees	310,000	Consultancy	30,000
Premises related	15,000		
Transport related	5,000		
Supplies & services	5,000	Deficit to be charged	
Support services	25,000	to sponsors	391,000*
Financing costs leases	61,000		
	421,000		421,000

The sponsors will need to finance the deficit reported on the
revenue account for the year and this will involve crediting the
revenue account as follows:

	Dr	Cr
	£	£
Personal accounts		
Spectown	156,400	
Bogtown	156,400	
Uptown	78,200	

being the amounts chargeable to each authority to finance the joint audit service.

These charges required would not have been known precisely at the 31 March 1995. This is due to a delay in closing the accounts regarding processing payments and receipts, and the need to identify debtors and creditors.

Payments of Contributions by Sponsors

The normal process is for each sponsor to make payments based on an estimate. The amount of cash paid will never equal the amount actually due to be paid, but a settlement can be organised in the following year.

If for example the following monthly payments were made by sponsors to the consortia we can develop the entries, and build up the personal accounts of sponsors.

	Spectown £	Bogtown £	Uptown £
Monthly cash amounts Received and receivable from sponsors	15,000	15,000	7,000

The amounts paid by each sponsor when aggregated over the year would result in the following entries.

	Dr £	Cr £
Joint audit facility cash account	444,000	
Personal accounts		
Spectown		180,000
Bogtown		180,000
Uptown		84,000

being the cash received by the joint audit facility over the year.

Personal Accounts

The position on the personal accounts would therefore be as follows:

Spectown	£		£	Bogtown	£		£	Uptown	£
£									
Rev A/C payment due	156,400	Cash	180,000	Rev A/C payment due	156,400	Cash	180,000	Rev A/C payment due	78,200	Cash	84,000
bal c/fwd	23,600			bal c/fwd	23,600			bal c/fwd	5,800		
	180,000		180,000		180,000		180,000		84,000		84,000
		bal b/fwd	23,600			bal b/fwd	23,600			bal b/fwd	5,800

These accounts show that all sponsors have paid more than required and therefore would appear as creditors in the balance sheet of the Joint Audit Facility.

Off Setting of Service Costs

In addition to the entries recorded in this simple example there would be additional items regarding services provided by the individual sponsors for the consortia.

For example, Spectown might have been responsible for the administrator of the audit function. Spectown might have invoiced the consortia for costs incurred of say £10,000. had this actually happened the consortia would have charged their revenue account, and credited Spectown's personal account. The effect of this entry would have been to share the cost of £10,000 between all sponsors, and reduce the amount of cash payable by Spectown to the consortia.

The following is a more extensive example.

Example Question - Colin

Exercise 10.3

Three local authorities have combined their resources to provide a joint computer service. The consortia is known as Colin (Computer Operations Locally Integrated Network). The local authorities in the consortia are named as follows:

Discham district
Terminham district
Bannerham district

The consortia is organised largely by Discham, with all payments and collections being undertaken by the authority. Terminham is responsible for software development and marketing. Bannerham financed leased transport costs on behalf of Colin.

Each authority can recharge agreed costs to Colin, and then finance the eventual deficit in the following ratios: these ratios are based on perceived volume of usage of the computer service.

Discham 32%; Terminham 28%   Bannerham 40%:

The following information is available for the year ending 31/3/95.

Balances as at 1/4/94

D	£40,000	Dr
T	£12,000	Cr
B	£23,000	Cr

Income and expenditure 1994/95

	£	£
Employees		1,320
Premises		632
Supplies & services		120
Customer & client receipts		530
Operating lease expenditure on equipment		58
Receipts: from D	400	
from T	380	
from B	690	

Additional information.

1.   D has provided an account of administration cost in line
      with approvals to Colin of £210,000.

2.   T has provided an account for software development of
      £340,000.

3.   B has notified Colin of transport operating lease payments
      totalling £300,000. The consortia reimburse B for all costs
      of lease repayment.

4.   T has collected £230,000 from software sales which should be
      passed onto Colin.

5.   All costs undertaken by D,T,B are accounted for through the
      personal accounts held by Colin.

(i)   You are required to: draw up the revenue account of Colin
      and the personal accounts of D, T & B.

(ii) In addition B feel that costs should be shared on the basis
      of population from 1995/96 onwards, explain the implications
      had this principle applied in 1994/95 and consider the
      reaction you would expect from D & T.

      Populations: D 78,000   T 67,000   B 65,000

Tutorial Answer - Colin

Treatment of Notes

Note 1
Discham have invoiced Colin for the administration costs of
operating and organising the consortium. The entries required
would be as follows:

	Dr £	Cr £
Colin revenue account - support services	210,000	
Discham personal account		210,000

It is difficult to decide exactly where to charge the
administration costs, if they had been direct costs they would
have been expended on employees, etc. I decided to call them
support services because I had insufficient information to record
them in any other category.

Note 2

Terminham district have provided software development, and sent Colin the invoice the entries for this are as follows:

	Dr £	Cr £
Colin revenue account supplies & services	340,000	
Terminham personal account		340,000

Note 3

This time Bannerham have provided a service

	Dr £	Cr £
Colin revenue account - transport	300,000	
Bannerham		300,000

being the charging of the consortia for transport costs.

Note 4

This note requires an off setting the reverse to the previous items here Colin is due to receive income from Terminham. The entries required are as follows:

	Dr £	Cr £
Terminham personal account	230,000	
Colin income customer & client receipt		230,000

being the income due from Terminham to the consortia.

Note 5

This note simply confirms the normal arrangement whereby cash does not pass between consortia members for cost undertaken on behalf of the consortia.

Now we can draw up the revenue account.

Part (i)

Colin Revenue Account for the year ending 31 March 1995

Expenditure	£	Income	£	£
		Customer & client		
Employees	1,320,000	receipts (530+230)		760,000
Premises	135,000	Deficit contributions		
Transport	300,000	D	710,400	
Supplies & Services	1,015,000	T	621,600	
Support services	210,000	B	888,000	2,220,000
Gross expenditure	2,980,000			2,980,000

```
Personal Account
Discham            £                                £
─────────────────────────────────────────────────────────────
bal b/fwd 1/4/94   40,000  Rev a/c
                           administration  210,000
Rev account                Cash
amount due        710,400  received         400,000

                           bal c/fwd        140,400
                  -------                    -------
                  750,400                    750,400
                  =======                    =======


Personal Account
Terminham          £                                £
─────────────────────────────────────────────────────────────
Rev A/C amount             bal b/fwd 1/4/94  12,000
due               612,600  Rev A/C
Rev A/C software           computing        340,000
sales             230,000  Cash received    380,000

                           bal c/fwd        119,600
                  -------                    -------
                  851,600                    851,600
                  =======                    =======


Personal Account
Bannerham          £                                £
─────────────────────────────────────────────────────────────
Rev A/C amount             bal b/fwd
due               888,000  1/4/94            23,000
                           Rev account
                           transport        300,000

bal c/fwd         125,000  Cash received    690,000
                ---------                   ---------
                1,013,000                   1.013,000
                =========                   =========
```

Part (ii)

If the method of contribution of sponsors to deficits changes there would be some authorities gaining while others suffer extra costs the effect in 1994/95 would have been as follows:

Authority	Actual Contribution Required £	Population Based Contribution Required £	
Discham	710,400	824,571.43	37.14%*
Terminham	621,600	708,285.71	31.90%
Bannerham	888,000	687,142.86	30.95%
	2,220,000	2,220,000	

* revised percentages based on population.

This would result in Discham and Terminham paying £114,171.43 and £86,685.71 more respectively while Bannerham would gain by paying £200,857.14 less.

Consider the Reaction of Sponsors

Discham and Terminham would undoubtedly be against the proposal. These authorities would fight to retain the current method of financing the deficit. Bannerham are at present paying considerably more than the others, and would have to consider how the consortia could justify charging them the amount in question. Bannerham might have to consider the costs of going it alone if they could not get an agreed reduction. Undoubtedly if the consortia arrangement is to everyone's benefit a revised agreement will eventually be reached.

Problems Associated with the New Capital Accounting system and Consortia Accounting

The examples shown in the questions in this chapter avoid the problems of capital accounting by using operating leases. however, the problem does exist and needs to be considered.

Under the new capital accounting system the assets used by the consortia would be required to be charged to the revenue account with an asset rent rather than the traditional debt charge arrangement. This could result in the consortia partners being required to contribute larger sums, and in turn create a burden on their Council Tax.

The capital accounting regime is not intended to increase the burden on the Council Tax, and therefore I presume an adjustment would be necessary. The CIPFA accounting code of practice does not proved the answer to this problem.

However it could be adjusted on the following basis.

Example - Impact of Asset Rents on Consortia

Exercise 10.4

The following facts are provided by the Joint Computer Consortia.
Provided for A & B councils.

Balances as at 31 March 1994

	£	£
Fixed assets	1,120,000	
Less		
Capital discharged	500,000	620,000
Net current assets		20,000
		640,000
Less loans outstanding		40,000
		600,000
Financed by:		
Capital receipts unapplied		600,000

Transactions for the year 1994/95

		£	£
Revenue expenses			550,000
(excluding capital financing)			
Asset rents	- depreciation	15,000	
	- notional interest	60,000	75,000
Debt charges	- principal MRP		20,000
	- interest		35,000
Customer and client receipt			50,000
Real loans repaid			10,000

Notes

1. Contributions are made equally by authorities A & B.

2. Assets were revalued on the 1 April 1994, although assets
   are to be valued partly at net current cost, and partly
   stated at historic cost the overall impact was to produce a
   figure for fixed assets of £720,000, before depreciation for
   1994/95.

Tutorial Answer

The revenue account of the consortia could be constructed as
follows:

	£		£
Revenue Expenses	550,000	Customer & client	
Assets rents	75,000	receipt	50,000
Gross cost of services	625,000	Contributions	
*Removal of impact of		A	277,500
notional charges	20,000	B	277,500
	605,000		605,000

* Removal of impact is made up of credit from the asset management amount of £25,000 and a debit to the capital financing reserve of £5,000.

The revenue account impact has been reversed on the face of the revenue account by carrying out the capital accounting adjustments on this account rather than the summary consolidated revenue account.

This method is therefore consistent with CIPFA's proposals, but due to the circumstances is carried out at the lower level of the consortia revenue account.

Basically to achieve this through the debit and credits of double entry accounting we need to carry out the following:

- credit asset rents to an asset management revenue account.

- debit real charges for interest to the asset management account.

- Transfer depreciation for the year out of the asset management account into the accumulated depreciation account.

These entries in the asset management revenue account leave us with the difference between notional interest and actual charges for interest. In this question the amount is £25,000. This means that too much has been charged in the asset rent if we are to preserve a neutral effect on the Council Tax.

However, the depreciation charge is only £15,000 where as the minimum revenue provision is £20,000. Therefore the asset rent is too low on this element. Therefore and extra charge is made to the revenue account for this £5,000 by debiting revenue account and crediting the capital financing reserve account. the overall impact on reversing charges for asset rents is as follows:

	£
1. Reduction for excess interest	(25,000)
2. Charge for balance of minimum provision	5,000

	20,000
	=======

The following show the accounting entries and the closing balance sheet.

Joint Consortia Balance Sheet as at 31 March 1995

	£	£
Fixed assets	720,000	
Less depreciation	15,000	705,000

Net current assets		20,000

		725,000
Less loans outstanding		20,000

		705,000
		=======
Financed by:-		
Capital receipts unapplied		600,000
Fixed asset restatement reserve		100,000
Capital financing reserve		5,000

		705,000
		=======

<u>NB</u>   Accounting for adjustments

Fixed Asset Restatement Account

	£		£
Net value fixed asset	620,000	Fixed asset account Revaluation	720,000
bal c/fwd	100,000		
	-------		-------
	720,000		720,000
	=======		=======

Asset Management Account

	£			£
<u>Debt charges</u>		Asset rent rev a/c		
Interest	35,000	- depreciation	15,000	
		- notional interest	60,000	75,000

Transfer to depreciation	15,000			
Rev a/c reversal	25,000			
	------			------
	75,000			75,000
	======			======

Loans outstanding

	£		£
Loans repaid	20,000	bal b/fwd	40,000
bal c/fwd	20,000		
	------		------
	40,000		40,000
	======		======

Capital financing reserve

	£		£
		MRP provision for external loans	
bal c/fwd	5,000	rev a/c	5,000
	-----		-----
	5,000		5,000
	=====		=====

Conclusion - Accounting for Consortiums

This type of question could be a very useful one to set in examinations. The reason being that the question can incorporate the problems of dealing with the standard classification for revenue expenditure and income, the difficulties or personal accounts, and the requirements of the new capital accounting provisions.

Accounting for the Repairs and Renewals Fund

Another complication which is often built into a revenue accounting question is the treatment of the repairs and renewals fund.

The use for Repairs and Renewals funds are reasonably widespread and are a very useful method of accounting for costs which are difficult to predict.

Local Government and Housing Act 1989

Section 41 of the Local Government and Housing Act 1989 created some concern about whether repairs and renewals funds remained a valid and legal means of accounting for income and expenditure. this was due to the wording of the section which required all expenditure and income incurred by a local authority to be recorded in its revenue account. This problem can be explained after considering the operation of the funds.

Operation of Repairs and Renewals Fund (R&R Fund)

R & R funds are established to avoid problems of accounting for expenditure which is difficult to predict. an example might be catering equipment at a large Day Centre. In the early years of operating the centre it may be necessary to spend a great deal of money on repairing and renewing equipment. However, after a certain period of time large sums may be required to repair and renew equipment. From a budgeting point of view we experience years of underspending and years of overspending. The calculation of the annual amount to be included in the estimate requiring very detailed consideration.

An alternative is to set up a R&R fund. The principle being that as assessment of spending requirements is considered over a longer period than a single year. the following provides some figures in an example to demonstrate this point.

<u>Example of R & R Fund</u>

The manager of a day centre has assessed the needs to repair and replace equipment over the next five years, and feels that at today's prices £50,000 would be adequate.

The accountant for the day centre decided to set up a R & R fund and the following table reveals how the fund operated over the five year period.

Year	Budget	Actual Expenditure	Variance		Fund balance at year end
	£	£	£		£
1	10,000	4,000	6,000	(F)	6,000
2	10,500	7,000	3,500	(F)	9,500
3	11,025	6,000	5,025	(F)	14,525
4	11,580	15,000	3,420	(A)	11,105
5	12,160	12,800	640	(A)	10,465
	55,265	44,800	10,465		

<u>Budget Column</u>

The budget column represents the charge made to the service committee revenue account. The reason for the budget provision increase is due to the incremental budgeting system, whereby a percentage is added each year to account for inflationary pressure. The sums charged are placed into the repairs and renewals fund.

<u>Actual Expenditure</u>

The actual expenditure is the amount spent during the financial year on the repair and renewal of equipment. The actual costs are charges to the renewals fund, and <u>not</u> to the revenue account.

<u>Variance</u>

The variance is the difference between amounts set aside in the renewals fund from the revenue account budget, and actual costs absorbed by the fund. the variance is added to, or taken from the fund balance, depending on whether the variance is favourable (F) or adverse (A).

<u>Fund Balance</u>

The fund balance can be seen to grow over the early years and diminish a little towards the end of the five year period. maybe when the budget is reviewed the amount provided will be reduced to bring the fund size down a little over the next five years.

<u>Further Complications on Operating R & R Funds</u>

It will often be the case that any balance left on the fund will be entitled to be credited with interest income. This encourages fund holders to retain funds and builds up the fund.

Capital expenditure may be financed from the fund although the

fund is a revenue fund. The capital expenditure may be within
the £10,000 de minimis expenditure limit of the capital control
system. Alternatively the council may operate a higher de
minimis level for the purpose of capitalisation.

Both these issues can be considered in turn.

Do R &R Funds Meet the Requirements of the LGHA 1989?

In order that the provisions of S41 are met all expenditure must
be charged to revenue account. In the case of R & R fund, actual
expenditure is charged to the R & R fund rather than the revenue
account. However, the revenue account has previously been
charged with a contribution. therefore S41 is deemed to be
satisfied but a timing difference is simply apparent.

However, with regards interest income the normal approach now
taken to comply with S41 is that interest income is credited in
the first place to the revenue account and then passed onto the
fund in the form of larger contributions.

Capital Spending from the R & R Fund

If the capital spending takes place from the R & R fund this does
not really involve major problems. the fund is decreased in size
as a result, and a capital asset needs to be created. However,
the new capital accounting rules will change the accounting
slightly.

Example − Capital spending from the R & R Fund

£20,000 is spent on a new industrial oven at a day centre.   The
following entries are necessary.

	Dr	Cr
	£	£
Fixed assets		
− Vehicle plant & equipment	20,000	
Capital cash		20,000

being the purchase of the asset.

	Dr	Cr
Repairs & Renewals fund	20,000	
Revenue cash		20,000

being the financing of the purchase of the fixed asset.

	Dr	Cr
Capital cash	20,000	
Capital financing reserve		20,000

being the reimbursement of capital cash and the demonstration
that capital financing has taken place.

The asset will, as in the case of all assets, be subject to an
asset rent which will be charged to revenue account and reversed
out in the summary revenue account.

Example Question - Renewals Fund

Exercise 10.5

Leisure services committee have established a repairs and
renewals fund which has a balance of £300,000 as at 31 March
1994. During 1994/95 a further contribution is made of £17,000.
Actual costs of repairing equipment were £32,000, and unusually a
replacement of a single item of equipment amounting to £20,000
took place the replacement is deemed to be capital. £24,000
interest was received by leisure and needs to be passed to be
passed on to the R & R fund in additional contributions.

Prepare the Entries Required in the R & R Fund

The R & R Fund will receive contributions of £17,000 and £24,000
therefore totalling £41,000. The double entry for the fund will
be as follows:

	Dr	Cr
	£	£
R & R Fund Cash	41,000	
R & R Fund balance		41,000

being total contributions from Leisure revenue account.

Actual costs of repairs need to be recorded as follows:

R & R Fund repair costs	32,000	
R & R Fund cash		32,000

being the actual cost of repairs charged to R & R Fund.

The replacement of equipment needs to be recorded as follows:

Leisure service {Fixed asset VP&E	20,000	
accounting entries {		
not R & R Fund { Capital cash		20,000

being the capital expenditure on equipment recorded in leisure
services accounts.

R & R Fund - equipment cost	20,000	
R & R Fund cash		20,000

being the transfer of funds from the R & R Fund to pay for
leisure capital expenditure.

Leisure capital cash	20,000	
Capital financing reserve		20,000

being the recording of reimbursement of capital cash from the R &
R Fund and a record of capital financing.

R & R Fund Balance as at 31 March 1995

	£		£
Actual repair costs	32,000	bal b/fwd	300,000
Equipment renewed	20,000	contributions	41,000
bal c/fwd	289,000		
	-------		-------
	341,000		341,000
	=======		=======

Summary Management of R & R funds are widespread, and they
incorporate the following operations.

1. Annual contributions are made which are charged to the
    revenue account of the appropriate service committee.

2. Often a front end contribution to establish the fund might
    be required.

3. Actual expenditure is met directly from the fund.

4. Capital expenditure can be financed by the fund.

5. The fund can operate and comply with (S41) of LGHA 1989.

6. Interest earned can be passed onto the fund via extra
    contributions.

7. The fund enables managers to calculate contributions over a
    longer term, and avoid budgeting problems.

8. By setting aside sums in the renewals fund, end of year
    panic spending of unspent budgets can be avoided.

Examination Question 10.1

The following balances were extracted from the Social Services
Committee of Capptown County Council's accounting system.

	£000s
Balance @ 1.4.94 Transport R & R Fund	2,000

Income and Expenditure Transactions during the year   **£000s**

Transport running costs	730
Transport major maintenance (charge to R & R)	200
Contribution to transport renewals fund	300
Purchase of vehicles under	
£10,000 not capitalised (charge to R & R)	200
Agency staff costs	4,010
Salaries	12,810
National Insurance	1,410
Superannuation	1,320
Printing and Stationery	210
Rents and rates	370
Cash paid to children in care (S17)	100
Payments to contractors	50
Payments under agency agreement to Vol. Sector	60
Electricity	730
Support services recharge	
- professional services	1,600
- office services	1,400
- service strategy and regulation	230
General Office expenses	420
Sales	110
Fees and Charges	6,540
Asset rent	1,980
Equipment and tools	250
Repairs and maintenance (charge to revenue)	670
Recharges to HRA	1,200
to other committees	320
Trading agreement income	210
Miscellaneous expenses	110
Interest income	55

1. Any deficit on the revenue account will have to be financed
    from the Council's County fund.

2. The stock certificates reveal that physical stock of spare
    parts included in repairs and maintenance (revenue) is
    £50,000 at 31.3.95 and an adjustment should be made for this
    through the revenue account. Opening stock was nil.

3. Late invoices have been submitted relating to 1994/95 for
    electricity in the sum of 20,000.

4. Interest income of £20,000 included in the transactions
    statement, should form extra contributions to the R & R
    fund.

5. The R & R Fund finances major maintenance and vehicles
    purchased only.

You are required to:

Prepare a revenue account for the Capptown County Council Social Services Committee for the period ending 31 March 1995 along with a statement of the R & R fund movements over the year.

Examination Question 10.2

A local authority operates a repairs and renewals fund and at the 1 April 1994 the balances were as follows:

	£
Fund balance	345,000
Investments	75,000
Cash	270,000

The fund has been under utilised over the last few years but during 1994/95 the following transactions took place:

	£	
Purchase of vehicles	75,000	(to be capitalised)
Repairs	120,000	
Interest received	9,000	
Contributions	20,000	

You are required to:

a)   **Prepare the journal entries for the transactions above both in the R & R fund and the service committee accounts. Investment income is to be credited to the revenue account initially but then transferred to the R & R fund as an additional contribution.**

b) **Show the balance on the R & R fund as at 31 March 1995.**

Examination Question 10.3

The following balances were extracted from the Jamtown joint
Police Authority formed by Trafficham and Struckshire Counties.
to be referred to as T & S respectively.

Balances as at 31 March 1994

	£000s	
Other land and buildings	42,300	
Capital receipts unapplied	3,560	
Capital receipts applied	3,200	
Deferred charges	1,210	
Loans outstanding	18,780	
Loans redeemed	16,410	
Capital fund	560	
RCCO	1,650	
Current assets	1,210	
Current liabilities	560	
Personal accounts - T County	70	Dr
- S County	60	Dr
- Government grant	130	Cr

Transactions during the year

Employees	
- members of the Force	32,150
- civilian staff	3,100
- agency staff costs	600
Premises related costs	1,710
Electricity	420
Support services recharge	4,230
Common Police services	140
Supplies and services	1,080
Pension contributions received	3,100
Debt charges	2,470
Equipment and tools	50
Transport related costs	4,170
Miscellaneous expenses	110
Capital expenditure	3,500
Receipts from - T County	12,430
- S County	17,098
Government grant received	27,090

Balances at the 31 March 1995

Creditors	530
Stocks	1,100
Debtors	30
Cash	6,068

1. Fixed assets have a Net current replacement cost of
    £38,200,000.

2. ASSET RENTS have been assessed as follows:

    - Depreciation £350,000
    - Notional interest £4,890,000

3. The capital expenditure was financed by the use of £3m capital receipts and £400,000 revenue contribution to capital outlay, while £100,000 was raised from loan.

4. Any deficit on the revenue account will have to be financed from the Government Grant (50% of all net costs excluding Common Police service), and from T & S deficit contributions of 45% and 55% respectively. The impact of the new rules on capital accounting must be reversed before grant and deficit contribution are calculated.

5. Debt charges include £470,000 repayment of principal (which represents the minimum revenue provision).

6. Late invoices have been submitted relating to 1994/95 for electricity in the sum of 32,000.

7. T County provide computing facilities and their recharge is £800,000 and has not yet been recorded.

8. Payment for Common Police Service is adjusted through the Government Grant account.

You are required to:

Prepare a Revenue Account for the Joint Police Authority for the period ending 31 March 1995 and a balance sheet at that date.

CHAPTER 11

Accounting for Support Services and The Preparation of Trading Accounts

Introduction

This chapter deals with the changing nature of local authority services. It has proved necessary when writing this section to consider the whole foundation of local government activity.

Therefore the chapter approaches this central issue in the following way:

- Consideration is given to the traditional approach to local authority services, and the hidden problems that existed in accounting for the provision of central costs, now known as Support Services.

- Then an outline of the need to establish central costs which need to be recharged to business units/trading accounts, as opposed to central costs which should be retained centrally. This involves analysing the following categories of cost.

  - corporate management
  - service strategy and regulation
  - client agent activities
  - service delivery

- Assess the proposal for white collar CCT, and the latest timetable for change.

- Consider the potential for developing trading accounts, and the draft guidance note 'Trading Accounts for Support Services in Local Authorities' issued by CIPFA.

- Finally consider the government requirement for the statement of support service costs and associated guidance regarding anti-competitive behaviour under section 9 of the Local Government Act 1992, issued in circular 10/93.

The Traditional Approach of Local Authorities Accounting for Central Costs

Central costs have generally been hidden and unaccounted for in the past. This has been due to the general approach that local authorities had taken towards the provision of services. The most important principle had been recording total costs from a stewardship perspective. Competition was never really considered and therefore the degree to which central costs had to be accounted for was far less important.

Survey of Local Authorities in 1975

A survey undertaken in 1975 revealed that of 200 or so authorities participating 120 authorities did not fully recover central costs from service committees. These central services were therefore only accountable for total costs and service departments had no mechanism to assess the service provided related to price.

Where central charges were recovered from service committees the mechanism was very often an end of year recharge, which managers considered to be an uncontrollable cost, and where variations were a mystery.

Reasons for Reluctance to Account Properly for Central Costs

Many reasons were put forward for not fully or accurately recovering central costs from service committees.

These included the time and effort needed to establish a recharging system. Time sheets need to be maintained, recovery bases established and regularly reviewed. A monthly charging system established. Negotiations need to be entered into regarding the level of service required. Many argued that it was all unnecessary extra work when all members really wanted to know was the total cost.

Major Reason for a Change in Approach to Central Costs

Undoubtedly local authorities have moved considerably from the traditional approach described above. The major reason for the change has been the introduction of CCT. When the Local Government Planning and Land Act 1980 introduced Direct Labour Organisations it became apparent that the DLO's could not expect to survive in the long term without ensuring they were competitive. The issue was further concentrated when the Local Government Act 1988 introduced CCT for Direct Service Operations.

CIPFA had consistently recommended full allocation of central costs, but there were strong arguments for charging DSOs only for the costs of operating their service, central costs related to a multi-purpose authority were not really appropriate for charging down to the business units or DSOs.

More recently the announcement of CCT for white collar services has served to twist the screw on central services directly and a re-assessment of central costs has again been considered afresh.

The most recent advise can be found in the draft guidance note "Trading Accounts for Support Services in Local Authorities". Also details can be found in "Accounting for Social Services" both published by CIPFA.

The first questions that need to be answered are as follows:

What are considered to be support services?
Should all support services be charged to business units?

What Services are Considered to be Support Services?

Support services are services which are not front line services but are necessary supporting services to those front line services. Support services are often centrally organised, due to the economies of scale, and concentration of specialisms possible with central provision.

A list of support services is as follows:

Accountants	Internal auditors	Receptionists
Architects	Lawyers	Security guards
Buildings and offices	Management services	Stores
Cashiers	Office catering	Surveyors
Committee administration	Payroll	Telephonists
Contracting	Personnel officers	Transport/Fleet
Couriers	Press officers	management
Energy management	Post room	Typists
Engineers	Printers	Valuers
Information technology	Purchasing	
Insurance	Quantity surveyors	

Each of these support services are becoming more accountable as
compulsory competition is being brought about by the government.
Each service will have to consider operating at minimum cost,
while providing a quality service.

Many of the support services in this list might be provided by
the Treasurer for example: accountants; insurance; payroll to
name but a few. However, should all the costs associated with
accountancy be charged to front line services or business units,
or is there a case to accurately and equitably decided what costs
should be charged?

Should All Support Service Costs Be Charged to Business Units?

This tricky question has lead to a breakdown of costs into a
number of categories as follows:

- corporate management
- service strategy and regulation
- clients agent
- service delivery

Corporate Management

Corporate management costs are not charged to business units.
Corporate management is best defined as being central costs which
are incurred by a multi-purpose authority. These costs are
likely to continue regardless of an individual service being
provided or not by internal service deliverers.

Examples of corporate management costs will help toward the
understanding of what these costs are specifically:

• Corporate Committee Meetings. These meetings are the
council meeting, corporate policy meeting and meeting of
general nature which are required because the council runs
many diverse services.

• Costs of officers which are centrally required and are of a
statutory nature. These costs would include the Chief
Executive, or top paid officer of the council and the
designated chief financial officer under S151.

• Central work on precepts, revenue support grant, standard
spending assessments which is crucial to the council's
overall financial well being, but not specific to an
individual service.

- The preparation of the statements of accounts, the annual report, and corporate budget work.

- Subscriptions to Local Authority associations and costs associated with participation in their work.

- Local election costs.

These costs described here are not exhaustive, further details can be found in CIPFA publications, but they do demonstrate the general rationale. These costs:

- are Central costs;
- are incurred due to the multi-purpose role of local authorities;
- would continue even if the service delivery was by an external agent.

Corporate management costs are not charged to business units, neither are they charged to service committees. These costs are charged as an objective heading in the summary consolidated revenue account.

Service Strategy and Regulation (SSR)

Service Strategy and Regulation are not charged to business units, but are retained within service committee costs under a specific objective heading.

SSR costs are expenses which are incurred by the service department, but represent the department's costs associated with running a multi service operation. These costs follow the same rationale as corporate management costs, but are related to department costs rather than authority wide central costs.

SSRs are therefore costs which would remain for the department even if there were no directly managed services. Once again, some examples may improve the understanding of this concept.

Examples of Service Strategy and Regulation Costs

1. General costs
Staff, accommodation and running expenses which would be needed to be incurred even if no direct services were delivered.

2. Meetings
Costs associated with organising meetings of the main service committee. For example Social Services committee which is required to meet regardless, for example, of whether a business unit, such as the home help service, is delivered by an internal or external provider.

3. Statutory Officers

Costs associated with the appointment of statutory officers. This relates to departmental costs, rather than central officers. An example would be the Director of Social Service. This post must be provided under the Local Authority Social Services Act 1970.

4. Budget Preparation

Top level budget preparation work. This included the costs of compiling summary budget statements, and work allocating resources over objective headings. In addition costs associated with preparation of the summary capital programme.

However, it must be recognised that the costs of preparing budgets and costing specific to a business unit must be charged to the business unit. Keep in mind the costs regarded as service strategy are costs that would continue regardless of whether an internal business unit supplies the service or an external supplier.

5. Regulation Costs
Local authorities are required to perform regulation activities. These activities are required regardless of the party supplying the service. A few examples might be as follows:

- Children Act requirement to carry out vetting of playgroups
- Environmental Health responsibilities regarding inspection of homes in multiple occupation
- The registration and inspection unit required under the NHS and Community Care Act.

These regulation costs are obviously not charged down to business units.

6. Various Other Costs Which Meet the Criteria

The costs which should be included as service strategy and regulation are varied and it would be unwise to attempt to make an exhaustive list. The important points to remember are that costs must be ongoing regardless of the supplier of services. Other items included in CIPFA's advice for example include the following:

- Strategic Information, Research and Planning
- Liaison with outside bodies

Client's Agent Activities

These costs are not to be charged to business units. However, they are costs which are incurred by the authority in providing services to users regardless of internal or external service supply.

The intention is that if for example insurance were a business unit and subject to CCT. The finance division would have to prepare specifications for the work required and arrange for the tendering process to take place. Whichever supplier wins the contract cost would appear as follows:

	£
Insurance supplier	x
Client Agent Support	y

Total	

This insurance supplier is not responsible for paying the client agent's support activity, which of course is only logical.

The Costs of Client Agent's Activity

These costs are associated with preparing the ground for tendering to take place, evaluating the tenders submitted, and monitoring the contract when in operation. The following broad stages might be involved:

- Providing policy advice to identify exactly what service quality and quantity requirements need to be provided

- Preparing the specification to ensure all service requirements are stipulated in detail, for each tenderer to cost

- Identifying potential suppliers who would be acceptable and able to perform a contract to the specification required.

- Conducting the tendering process

- Negotiating contracts or sealing trading agreements

- Monitoring contract compliance

It should be clear that these costs are necessary costs which would be incurred regardless of the supplier being internal or external.

Service Delivery

These costs are the costs involved in actually delivering the service to the user.

The costs here would be spread over the normal standard classification of expenditure. In my view these are best classified as follows:

Direct Costs

Direct costs of performing the service, including direct labour, premises, transport, supplies and services etc.

Inevitably if the service is supplied by an internal delivery function, some costs will need to be apportioned between direct cost of service and support costs. I think whenever practical these should be kept to a minimum by providing a clear split between service delivery and client activity.

Capital Accounting

With regard to the cost of capital from the 1 April 1994 the new capital accounting regime will be required to be reflected in the service delivery account. For full details see Chapter 9 in this book on that subject.

However, it should be acknowledged that charges will be made to the business unit for depreciation where appropriate, and notional interest. These charges will force business user managers to carefully consider the need to retain assets and make full utilisation of assets.

It is intended that the new capital charging regime will results in business units having to break even, rather than make a 5% return on capital employed. This would be logical because the notional interest charge is intended to be 5% on assets valued at net current replacement cost and a real rate (PWLB) for assets held at historic cost.

Summary Support Service Costs

This section of the chapter has explained the latest thinking on recharging central costs. It should be acknowledged that corporate costs and service strategy and regulation costs are costs which will be continued either at the centre at department level. Whereas client agents' activities are the cost associated with facilitating the CCT process. Only service delivery costs will need to be recorded by the business unit. This whole process is aimed at giving the internal deliverer a fair chance of success against external deliverers.

The current terminology being used to describe the two parties to a trading agreement are service deliverer being either external or internal, and service user being the party receiving the service.

Proposals for Compulsory Competition of White Collar Services

In November 1991 the Secretary of State for the Environment issued a consultation paper "Competing for Quality" and in November 1992 announced revised proposals for extending competition to local authority services and a timetable for their implementation. The government has established three working groups covering the general activities to be subjected to CCT. These are:

- Construction related services
- Home Office services
- Professional services

These service working groups are involved in defining the activities to be subject to CCT in detail.

This chapter is going to concentrate on the professional services in the context of being support services. However, for completeness the Home Office services are related in the main to police support services of vehicle maintenance and cleaning of buildings, services which have already been subjected to CCT in local authorities.

Construction related services are architectural, engineering and property maintenance services.

Professional Services

These services are to be subjected to a requirement to test a proportion of the service against competition. The following table gives a breakdown of these services, proportion to be subjected to CCT and comments on the government view regarding aspects of the service.

Service	Activities defined as	Percentage to be initially available for contract	Comment
Housing management	• rent collection • allocation of properties and lettings • enforcement of tenancy agreements • management of vacant properties • management of repair and maintenance • caretaking and cleaning	100%	The government have not included in the defined activity for housing management: - right to buy - control of capital programme - housing the homeless - waiting lists administration.
Corporate and administrative services	• corporate strategy • committee administration • members' services • electoral registration • information services • public relations • land charges • purchasing • printing • secretarial/clerical support	15%	Government has ruled out services relating to electoral and democratic process. Major candidates for CCT are printing and clerical and secretarial support. Purchasing seen as best exposed to competition by allowing users to purchase where best value for money obtained.
Legal services	• corporate advice and ensuring propriety • advocacy and litigation • commercial and contractual work	33%	All areas seen as candidates for CCT with possible exception of corporate advice/ensuring propriety.
Financial services	• financial planning • internal audit • exchequer services • cash collection • payroll administration • accountancy services • investment management	25%	
Personnel services	• human resource planning • employee relations including health and safety and equal opportunities • staff welfare • organisational development • training • recruitment	25%	Government accepts that human resource planning and corporate strategy would be difficult to put out to tender. Reviewing internal structures/staff training should go out to tender on a project basis.
Computing services	• information systems strategy • systems procurement management • systems and software development • systems operation • telecommunications operations	80%	Competition seen as a good thing in this area, by the government. Running of telecommunications systems not included, because governed by a separate Act of Parliament

NB   It should be noted that the percentages to be subject to CCT may change, and no doubt once the process starts the percentage will gradually increase year on year.

Timetable for Compulsory Competition

The first point to note here is that the government has agreed arrangements for CCT during local government reorganisation. This allows local authorities being structurally reorganised exemptions from the statutory requirement to seek competitive tenders before work can be awarded to their own DSOs. Now authorities will be required to have new contracts in operation within 18 months of reorganisation.

Housing Management - Timetable for CCT

The proposed timetable depends upon the housing stock size held by the local authority.

Band I & II   Authorities with less than 15,000 stock will be subject to CCT from 1 April 1996 or 1 April 1997.

Band III & IV   Authorities with 15,000 - 30,000 stock will be required to subject the first 60% of defined activity to CCT from the 1 April 1996 and the remainder the following year or from 1 April 1997 and the remainder a year later.

Band V   Authorities with over 30,000 stock will be required to subject the first 40% of defined activity from 1 April 1996 and the remaining 60% split equally from 1 April 1997 and 1 April 1998.

The proposed timetable for other professional services is as follows:

Service	Date Contracts Commence
Legal	October 1995
Computing	October 1996
Financing	April 1997
Corporate administration	April 1997
Personnel	April 1997

The Threat to Internal Provision

The timescale for the implementation of CCT does enable local authorities to organise their professional services, and face the challenge.

However, for many authorities the amount of work required is immense. There are authorities that still operate with very lax management of support service costs. Authorities are not necessarily aware of the impact of the new capital accounting arrangements on their competitiveness, and finally due to the recession it is true that private sector pay is often lower that the public sector. In conclusion there is a real threat to internal provision and authorities must get their houses in order if they are going to continue delivering services internally.

Potential for Developing Trading Accounts

When the government first announced the intention to apply CCT to white collar services it was presumed that trading accounts would be required. CIPFA started to work up proposals for the development of trading accounts, and this has culminated in the production of draft guidance notes "Trading Accounts for Support Services in Local Authorities", issued April 1993.

However, the government announced that it intends to make regulations under section 23 of the Local Government Finance Act 1982, setting out a new requirements for an internal accounting framework, including a requirement to publish a 'statement of support service costs' for each support service.

For this reason CIPFA is not proposing to issue a code of practice for trading accounts for support services, but prefers to allow local authorities flexibility in operating internal accounting for trading activities.

This section will attempt to:

> Consider the need to produce trading account internal accounts or a means of evaluating performances.

Trading Accounts

Trading accounts are intended to provide the basis within which local authorities can assess costs and income and judge financial performance. Trading accounts will need to be linked with trading agreements, and should be implemented by business units as soon as practically possible.

It is of course necessary to ensure that the costs of capital accounting and support services accounting are well organised.

Fundamentally the trading account expenditure should be based on fairly identified costs, which are as near as possible to the cost of delivering the service. Income should be based on trading agreements between the service deliverer and the service user.

Trading agreements (TAGs) are similar in principle to service level agreements (SLAs). However, TAGs appears to be the current jargon.

If support services can get trading accounts (TACs) operating fully by the 1 April 1994 they will have a period whereby the mechanism can be tested.

Trading Agreements (TAGs)

The trading agreement would incorporate the following principles:

*   The TAG would be for a specific period. At the end of the said period any cost over runs would need to fall on the service deliverer.

* The detailed content of the services would need to be stipulated, along with delivery timescale, regularity and duration of service.

* Quality issues would need to addressed, and agreed.

* Price will need to be agreed, probably after significant negotiation. The service deliverer should ensure the price charged will cover both a proportion of fixed costs and variable costs. While not overcharging which might results in greater reserves being held than necessary.

* The pricing mechanism should be a simple, equitable and comparable with alternative deliverers as possible.

* Add on services might be identified with their associated costs if taken up during the year.

* A basis of review should be establish to enable both service deliverer and service user to consider progress towards fulfilling the terms of the TAGs.

* Charges should be made regularly to enable the user to acknowledge the cost of the service, and monitor performance.

The basis of the charge for TAGs are discussed in the CIPFA trading accounts publication, and three methods are mentioned.

- Charges which are wholly dependent on inputs, such as charges related to hours spent on the work, and actual materials used. This method will be referred to as the INPUT method.

- Charges which are related only partially to Direct Input Costs. this method will be referred to as the PARTIAL method

- Charges related to the OUTPUT. This method involves a lump sum charge which is agreed in advance and stuck to subsequently. It could also include a list of pre-agreed charges on a schedule of rates.

There is however no stipulation regarding the need to charge all TAGs on the same basis. Although it should be noted that competitive work should not be priced in such a way that non-competitive work subsidies CCT work. This cross subsidisation is specifically precluded by the code of practice for compulsory competition.

Treatment of Deficits and Surpluses

The rules governing local government accounting regarding charging ongoing costs to revenue are set out in section 41 of the Local Government and Housing Act 1989. This section requires all income and expenditure to be provided for in revenue accounts.

For this reason deficits on trading accounts must be charged to the fund to which the service related, i.e. general fund.

Deficit should not be charged to the user.

A memorandum note can be retained of deficits with the intention that future surpluses will compensate for deficits made.

Surpluses from trading funds can be used for many purposes the following are possibilities:

- retain for investment in the trading service
- give back to the user in lower charges
- transfer to the general fund
- carry forward in reserves
- or even a profit sharing scheme with employees

The use of surpluses made is not restricted other than by local government law. For example it would not be possible to apply the funds on discretionary spending (S137 1972 Local Government Act) if the council had already reached the limit on spending under that power.

Example Format for Trading Accounts Extracted from CIPFA's Draft Guidance Note "Trading Accounts for Support Services in Local Authorities"

The following format is NOT PRESCRIPTIVE, but merely provides a guide to authorities in establishing the accounting format most appropriate for their authority.

XYZ District Council Insurance unit Trading Account for the year ending 31 March 1994

Charges made under TAGs	£	£
housing	191,429	
highways	53,367	
environmental services	160,311	
leisure	42,458	447,565
Charges to other bodies		
District Health Authority	21,149	
District councils	4,147	25,296
Apportionments		
corporate management**	8,351	
direct services	21,719	30,070
Miscellaneous income		480
TOTAL INCOME		503,411
Direct costs		
salaries	350,654	
contract staff	11,591	
travelling expenses	8,062	
other direct costs	2,298	372,605
Overheads		
Charges payable under TAGs		
accounting services	4,680	
internal audit	2,837	
computer services	15,888	
legal advice	4,395	
management services	4,802	32,602

Other support services

printing & stationery	11,987	
office administration	61,321	
other overheads	8,941	82,249

NET OPERATING SURPLUS FOR YEAR		15,955

**   This represents work done by the support service for Corporate Management

Standard Classification

My own preference would be to record income in the way suggested by the Trading Account format with the addition of some headings related to the standard classification and with regards to expenditure follow the standard classification for revenue costs. This would mean that payments out under TAGs would be recorded under the heading Third Party Payments. A revised Trading Account format would therefore be as follows:

Revised Trading Account for Support Services

INCOME	£	£	£
Other grants, reimbursements and contributions			
District Health Authority	21,149		
Other District Councils	4,147		25,296
Customer & Client receipts			
Fees & charges			
TAGs			
- Housing	191,429		
- Highways	53,367		
- Environmental Services	160,311		
- Leisure	42,458		
Miscellaneous income	480		448,045

Recharges			
Corporate management	8,351		
Direct services	21,719		30,070

TOTAL INCOME			503,411
EXPENDITURE			
Employees			
- salaries	350,654		
- contract staff	11,591	362,245	

Premises Related Expenditure			
- office accommodation		61,321	
Transport Related Expenditure			
- travelling expenses		8,062	
Supplies and Services			
- miscellaneous direct costs	2,298		
- printing & stationery	11,987		
- other overheads	8,941	23,226	

Third Party Payments			
TAGs			
Accounting services	4,680		
Internal audit	2,837		
Computer services	15,888		
Legal advice	4,395		
Management services	4,802	32,602	487,456
	-------	-------	-------
NET OPERATING SURPLUS FOR THE YEAR			15,955

This revised format uses the standard classification, and would be easily prepared from the accounting system which is hopefully operating the standard classification. For more details on the standard classification see the revenue accounting chapter.

The following example question is provided to demonstrate the mechanism of preparing a trading account for a support service.

Exercise 11.1

Example Question - Midtown District Council **Audit Division**
Trading Information for the year ending 31 March 1995

Transactions during the year	£	£
TAG income Housing		141,000
Leisure		44,500
Environmental health		16,100
Other services		146,810
Salaries & Wages		161,240
National insurance		4,980
Superannuation		4,210
Fuel & light and cleaning materials		16,960
Rates		10,140
Equipment		1,660
Third Party payments TAGS		
- Treasurer	12,100	
- Legal	5,800	
- Computing	17,200	
- Personnel	4,100	
Operational admin building		16,000
General office expenses		18,920
Fees & charges received from XYZ District Council		18,680
Insurance for premises		3,950
Consultancy payment		3,110
Use of transport		18,040
Car allowances		10,000
Travel warrants		7,040

Notes

1. The asset rent chargeable for 1994/95 amounts to £13,000 for notional interest and £6,000 for depreciation. Debt charges amounted to £17,500.

2. Additional charges over and above the TAGs have been agreed, but should be added to the TAGs income, due to being at the rate agreed in the TAGs
    - Housing £3,100
    - Others £2,400

3. Recharges to corporate management, service strategy and client agents advice have been agreed as £14,200, £3,000 and £600 respectively.

4. The charge for operational admin buildings were found to be in error and due to no TAG being in operation an extra charge of 12.5% must be paid.

5. Training costs have been omitted form these transactions for the year, and amount to £3,900.

You are required to prepare in good format.

(a) A trading account for the year ending 31 March 1995.

(b) Comment on the performance and draw attention to any aspects that need special attention.

Tutorial Answer Midtown District Council Audit Services

Part (a)

Treatment of the notes

Note 1

This note required students to recognise that the asset rent is the figure that needs to be included in the trading account. The debt charge figure will find its way into the central account of asset management revenue account, and does not feature in the answer.

Note 2

This note simply requires TAGs income to be adjusted in line with the note.

Note 3

These recharges to corporate management, service strategy and client agent's advice are recorded as recharges out of the trading account. The reason for this is that some expenditure has been incurred by the Audit division which was not related to direct service provision to users.

Note 4

This note demonstrates the problems of not having a TAG related to operational administrative buildings. These extra costs (12.5% £2,000) must be added to expenses.

Note 5

Training costs need to be added to the Audit division expenses, and recorded as an employee indirect cost.

Midtown District Council Audit Division Trading Account **for the** year ending 31 March 1995

INCOME	£	£	£
Other grants, reimbursements **and contributions**			
XYZ District Council			18,680
Customer & Client **receipts**			
Fees & charges			
TAGs			
- Housing		144,100	
- Leisure		44,500	
- Environmental health		16,100	
- Other services		149,210	353,910
		-------	-------
Recharges			
Corporate management		14,200	
Service strategy		3,000	
Client agent's advice		600	17,800
		-------	-------
TOTAL INCOME			390,390

EXPENDITURE			
Employees - Direct Expenses			
Salaries & wages	161,240		
National insurance	4,980		
Superannuation	4,210		

	70,430		
Employees - Indirect Expenses			
Training	3,900	74,330	
Premises related expenditure			
Fuel light & cleaning mats.	16,960		
Rates	10,140		
Operational admin building	18,000		
Insurance premises	3,950	49,050	

Transport related expenditure			
Use of transport	18,040		
Car allowance	10,000		
Travel warrants	7,040	35,080	

Supplies & Services			
Equipment	1,660		
General office expenses	18,920	20,580	

Third Party Payments			
- Treasurer	12,100		
- Legal	5,800		
- Computing	17,200		
- Personnel	4,100		

	39,200		
Consultancy payment	3,110	42,310	

Capital financing costs			
Asset rents			
- depreciation	6,000		
- notional interest	17,500	23,500	344,850
	-------	-------	-------
NET OPERATING SURPLUS FOR THE YEAR			45,540
			=======

Part (b)

The audit division appear to have performed very well having made a considerable surplus of £45,540. A breakeven position would have met the authorities performance requirement.

An important aspect of the trading account is the income generated from TAGs. This is considerable, making up slightly more than 90% of income. If the prices in the trading agreement are competitive then the outlook is all the more promising. Information which is not provided which would be essential to know is the assessment of quality and the degree to which parties to TAGs are satisfied with the service.

With regard to the surplus, is the surplus too big to carry forward or is some required for investment? Does the authority wish to transfer some of the surplus to the general fund?

On the costs side, questions can be raised about the need for a TAG on operation admin buildings.

Probably the most important consideration is related to the length of time TAGs have to run, and the need to sharpen competitiveness to improve the chances of success in retaining the TAG.

Government Requirement for a Statement of Support Service Costs

The government established an Accounting Framework Working Party to consider the internal accounting framework requirements for white collar CCT. It had originally been assumed that trading accounts would be the appropriate mechanism and will undoubtedly be necessary for internal management.

However, the government has decided in the light of consultation, related to the document "Competing for Quality", that it can achieve its objectives more simply than originally anticipated for internal accounting, through a requirement to publish the cost of support services as part of the annual statement of accounts. It is claimed that this alternative approach is intended to achieve the government's management and financial objectives for support services which are:

*   To demonstrate the cost of each of the internal support service costs;

*   To stimulate challenging of these costs;

*   To encourage the development of an internal market, but

*   Without constraining the internal management arrangements of local authorities.

The Statement of Support Service Costs (SSSC) is likely to be an added requirement which many will view as unnecessary. However, the statement is intended to show the total cost of support services , and amounts charged for service delivery to service users. The following is an outline of the format that might be required:

Statement of Support Services **for Financial Users**

Functions of Service Delivery Financial Services	Service Users				
	Housing	Leisure	DSOs	Other Services	Total
Insurance Internal Audit Payroll Payments Debtors and many others	£	£	£	£	£

From this statement it will be possible to establish the total value of work within the ambit of a support service, and with information regarding work subjected to CCT it will be possible to establish the proportion of work and whether the set requirement has been met.

Trading Accounts Requirement

It is very likely that in addition to the statement of support services trading accounts of some form will be necessary. This is likely to be in the form of a revised code of practice produced by the Competition Joint Committee for both blue and white collar services. It is this document that currently provides the internal accounting mechanism for blue collar CCT.

More information on accounting for present Direct Services on the current code of practice can be found in the book "Advanced Public Sector Accounting", also published by Allen Accountancy.

Anti Competitive Behaviour

Many problems have already been addressed in terms of avoiding anti-competitive behaviour, which if unchecked can result in little competition. The most recent additions to the armoury of measures designed to prevent anti-competitive behaviour were issued by circular 10/93. The following is a summary of the measures included.

Local Authority Assets

Local authorities will have to offer prospective tenderers the use of key assets. The assets likely to be included here are DSO depots and DSO shared depots, plus vehicles used by DSOs.

It would appear that in making assets available the local authority can charge market value, current value or provide assets free. Whichever method used the DSO should be at no advantage. For example, if assets are provided free of charge and a tenderer prefers not to use the assets, then in the tender evaluation that tenderer will be given a credit based on the full annual current value.

Packaging of Contracts

Local authorities will be required to package work with the view of encouraging competition. It will not be possible to combine different disciplines to restrict competition. The inference is on small contracts. Although if a large contractor tenders for many small contracts providing best overall value for money is offered, then the large contract can be accepted.

Numbers of Tenderers

This topic is still confusing. EC directives require a minimum of five tenderers to be invited, and enable any greater number to be invited. However, if not enough tenderers meet the requirements of the local authority under EC rules fewer than 5 can be required.

These aspects of anti-competitive behaviour are <u>but a few</u> of the requirements, but demonstrate that the government are alive to the issue.

Summary of Chapter

The chapter has looked at the traditional approach to recording central costs, and the reluctance to change. This change was however inevitable with the different approach taken to local services and seeking competition for services.

The impact of competition requirements has led to a much more analytical approach to central costs to determine cost which are valid to be charged to business units and others which are not relevant to the direct service delivery.

An outline has been given of the proposals for white collar support service CCT, and a timetable for implementation considered. The internal accounting framework has been considered and an accounting example with a tutorial answer provided.

Finally the most recent guidance regarding statements of support service cost have been provided with a brief detail of a few provisions of the anti-competition requirements.

To end the chapter a series of examination questions are provided, but first a note, of the new jargon being used regarding CCT

*   Contractor/client terminology is dropped in favour of:
    - service delivery (previously contractor);
    - service user (previously client).

*   Trading agreements referred to as TAGs replace the term service level agreement.

*   Trading account TACs replace the term operating account or practice account.

*   Trading manager replaces the term support service manager.

*   New terms for central costs not chargeable to trading accounts include;
    - service strategy and regulation and
    - client agent's activity.

Examination Question 11.1

The TUDDY Borough Council have produced some figures for 1994/95 for their computer section. The following list of income and expenditure has been provided.

	Direct costs	Corporate management and SSR, plus client agent activity
	£	£
Employees - salary	520,000	640,000
Light cleaning rate & water	19,000	14,000
Software purchases	52,000	-
National insurance	48,000	61,000
Use of transport	15,100	1,200
Income from local company	3,200	
Receipts fees & charges through TAGs to		
- housing	210,000	-
- community services	55,000	-
- leisure	65,000	-
- other services	215,000	-
Consultancy payment	15,100	
Office expenses	25,000	17,000
Servicing equipment	7,520	1,200
Superannuation contributions	31,000	33,000
Services		
Recharge from: Personnel	6,500	-
Finance	13,500	-
Legal	4,300	-
Sale of software	42,000	-
Purchase of equipment	45,000	-
Printing paper costs etc.	34,000	42,000

Notes 1

Trading assets have been identified and had a net current replacement cots of £655,000 at the beginning of the year, equipment purchased during the year is all considered to be capital.

The computer division has a policy of financing capital entirely from revenue.

Notional interest is calculated on the basis of opening net current cost plus half the capital expenditure during the year.

Depreciation has been calculated to be £75,000.

Note 2

The receipts figures for fees and charges include the following fees and charges which were due in March 1994:

	£
Housing	18,500
Community services	12,000
Leisure	8,000
Other services	17,000

However, charges for March 1995 have not been included. The total trading income expected for 1994/95 for these TAGs were:

	£
Housing	218,000
Community services	70,000
Leisure	75,000
Other services	221,000

You should assume the amount not received for March is responsible for the difference and bring income up to the level required.

Note 4

An error has been made in apportioning salary costs to corporate management the amount should have been £632,000.

Note 5

The list of expenditure included a recharge for finance work. This was subject to a TAG and the contract sum was £11,000. Computer services will not pay any more than the contract sum.

You are required:

(a)   Prepare a Trading Account for the year ending 31 March 1995.

(b)   Provide a statement of debtors as at 31 March 1995.

(c)   Comment on the performance of Tuddy's computer service division.

CHAPTER 12

CONSOLIDATED CASH FLOW STATEMENTS

Introduction

The exposure draft of a revised code of practice on local authority accounting in Great Britain issued in February 1993, (shortly to be reissued as a SORP in September 1993) requires a consolidated cash flow statement to be provided as part of the accounting statements of a local authority.

This new requirement is the second amendment in recent year to the statement which shows how cash has moved during a year, and comparable with the previous year.

Initially back in 1983 when the accounts and audit regulation were issued a statement of source and application of funds was required. This was in line with commercial practice at the time. However, local government accounting requires many adjustments for book entries, and when the first accounting code of practice for local government was published a different statement to record cash movements was required. This statement was known as the statement of capital and revenue movements. However, this chapter will concentrate on the latest requirement - the consolidated cash flow statement.

Financial Reporting Standard 1 (FRS 1)

The first new financial reporting standard issued by the ASB replaced the commercial requirement to provide a source and application of funds statement with a cash flow statement. Chapter 4 of this book is devoted to explaining the requirements of the cash flow statement in a commercial context.

The new cash flow statement is now recommended in a slightly different format for local authorities. The only difference in the cash flow format being greater detail being provided on the face of the cash flow statement required by local authorities.

Interestingly the cash flow statement can be found in the NHS accounting section of this book and the central government section.

The principles that apply to producing the cash flow statement are similar for whichever sector you are preparing a statement. however, the detail is slightly different because of the accounting differences.

The following is the standard format required contained in the new exposure draft.

This consolidated statement summarises the inflows and outflows of cash arising from transactions with third parties for revenue and capital purposes.

Information to be included in the Accounting Statement

Revenue activities
Expenditure
Cash paid to and on behalf of employees
Other operating costs
Housing benefit paid out

Income
Rents (after rebates)
Council Tax income
Disbursements from the Collection Fund (England and Wales)
Non-domestic rate income
Government grants
Revenue Support Grants
DSS grants for rebates
Cash received for goods and services
Other revenue cash payments/income

Servicing of finance

Expenditure
Interest paid
Interest element of finance lease rental payments

Income
Interest received

Capital activities

Expenditure
Purchase of fixed assets
Purchase of long-term investments

Income
Sale of fixed assets
Capital grants received
Other capital cash payments/income

Net cash inflow/outflow before financing

Financing

Expenditure
Repayments of amounts borrowed
Capital element of finance lease rental payments

Income
New loans raised
New short term loans

Increase/decrease in cash and cash equivalents

Information to be disclosed in Notes to the Account

(a) A reconciliation between the net surplus or deficit on the income and expenditure account to the revenue actitivites net cash flow.

(b)   The movement in cash and cash equivalents and the items shown within the financing section of the cash flow statement should be reconciled to the related items in the opening and closing balance sheets for the period.

(c)   Any further narrative or analysis that may assist in interpreting the statement.

(d)   Analysis of government grants.

New Capital Accounting Rules

Under the new capital accounting rules asset rents will be charged to the individual revenue accounts of the local authority. A full explanation is given in the capital accounting chapter in this text. However, what this involves is a charge for depreciation, where appropriate and a charge for notional interest.

Impact of the Asset Rent

The asset rent is of course a non-cash movement and while it is charged to the individual revenue accounts it is eventually reversed out of the consolidated summary revenue account via the asset management account and contributions to reserves.

When preparing a cash flow statement it is important to remove non-cash movements, but this has become very complicated as a results of the new proposals for capital accounting. The following is an example of the summary revenue account to illustrate the point.

Example: Trickham County Council

Trickham County Council Extract Summary Revenue Account for the Year Ending 31 March 1995

	Gross Expenditure £000	Income £000	Net £000
All Service Committees	543,000	320,000	223,000

NB   Included in this figure is £80 million notional interest and £3 million depreciation.

The adjustments for including real interest the minimum **revenue** provision and direct revenue financing are as follows:

	£			
- External real interest	14,000			
- Minimum revenue provision (MRP)	4,000			
- Direct revenue financing	6,000			
	£000	£000	£000	£000
Net cost of services b/fwd				223,000
Asset Management Revenue Account				
Depreciation	3,000			
External interest charges	14,000	17,000		

Less capital charges to service committees		(83,000)	(66,000)	
		-------	-------	
Contributions to capital reserves				
Provision for the repayment of loans		1,000		
Direct financing of assets		6,000	7,000	(59,000)
		-------	-------	-------
Revised net cost of services due to the effect of the asset management				164,000
revenue account and the contributions to capital reserves				=======

Interpretation of Trickham County Council

Trickham County Council have charged a total of £83 million to their revenue accounts for asset rents. however, they are only required to charge tax payers for the traditional methods of financing capital which would have been the £24 million for real interest, principal repayment (MRP)and direct revenue financing. Therefore a reversal is required on the face of the summary revenue account of the difference as follows:

	£000
Asset rents charges	83,000
Less	
Traditional Capital financing charges	24,000

Adjustment for reversal	59,000
	======

The asset management account and contribution to reserves represents a rather elaborate method of reversing the impact of asset rents on the consolidated summary revenue account.

If you are confused you should work through the capital accounting chapter.

We therefore need to establish which figures need adjusting in the question we are dealing with, and which figures are real cash movements and which are not real cash movements.

It could therefore be the case that adjustments are needed for asset rents, or that information is given after asset rents have been reversed out.

What are the Real Cash Movements?

The only real cash movement is for real interest. The entries for asset rents, principal repayments (MRP), and direct revenue financing are all book entries and these are explained as follows:

Financing of Assets from Direct Revenue Funding

Assets financed from direct revenue charges are now accounted to by being charged as a contribution to the capital reserves in the example of Trickham the amount is £6 million.

Consider What Has Actually Happened

EXAMPLE. Trickham £6 million has been spent on Other land & buildings and has been financed by a direct charge to the revenue account shown as a contribution to capital reserve on the face of the summary revenue account. The double entry is as follows:

	Debit £	Credit £
Other land & buildings	6,000,000	
Capital cash		6,000,000

being the purchase/payment of capital expenditure and the use of cash

Summary revenue account	6,000,000	
Capital financing reserve		6,000,000

being the charging of revenue account through the contribution to reserve heading

NB   The direct revenue charge to the summary revenue account does not move cash. ONLY THE ORIGINAL PAYMENT TO PURCHASE MOVES CASH.

THEREFORE DIRECT REVENUE FINANCING IS A BOOK ENTRY.

Financing Assets from Loans

Minimum Revenue Provision

In the example of Trickham, the financing of assets from loan would be determined by the council's credit approval. A minimum revenue provision is required to charge a notional 4% of outstanding credit approvals to revenue.

This minimum revenue provision for repayment of credit/loans is made to the council's consolidated loans pool. The amount is the sum that current tax payers are expected to contribute. However, the real loans raised and repaid are transacted through the council's consolidated loans pool, which records dealings with financial institutions, and the government's National Loans Fund (NLF).

The minimum revenue provision is not a real cash movement. The real cash movements on loans are the loans pool transactions for loans raised and repaid.

Real Interest

The council's loans pool is responsible for paying real interest to financial institutions and the NLF. However, these charges

are passed directly to each service of the council and therefore
the amount of interest charged by the consolidated loans pool
equals real interest.

NB   The minimum revenue provision is NOT A REAL CASH MOVEMENT,
     LOANS REPAID AND RAISED ARE REAL CASH MOVEMENT.

     INTEREST CHARGED BY THE LOANS FUND IS A REAL CASH MOVEMENT.

Conclusion of the Trickham Example

In terms of recording cash outgoing of a revenue nature which is
required under the new cash flow statement. Trickham must ensure
that the revenue actitivites only includes real cash movements.

Gross expenditure was stated at £543,000,000 originally.
However, it should now be clear that from this figure asset rents
should not be included. However, neither should the depreciation
or minimum revenue provision or direct revenue financing.
However, real external interest should be included. Therefore
the following adjustments are needed:

Revenue Activities

	£000
Expenditure	
Gross expenditure	543,000
Less asset rents	83,000

	460,000
Plus	
External interest	14,000

Total cash revenue activity	474,000
Income	
Income summary	320,000

Cash flow from revenue activity	154,000
	=======

However, it might have alternatively been the case that the
figures given for Trickham were such that you did not know the
gross expenditure. If you consider the example from this
perspective it provided an interesting angle as follows:

We know that the net cost of services after the asset management
revenue account are £164,000,000. This means that the impact of
the asset rent has been removed but that the traditional
financing charges have not. To work back to the cash flow from
the revenue activities you simply have to remove the items in the
traditional financing cost which are left in the revenue costs as
follows:

	£000	£000
Revised net cost of services after the reversal of asset rents		164,000
Remove traditional financing		
Minimum revenue provision	4,000	
Direct revenue financing	6,000	10,000
	-----	-------
Cash flow from revenue activities		154,000
		=======

The key to understanding cashflow is to identify real cash movements.

CAPITAL FUND

To add to the complications of local authority accounting some authorities use capital funds for financing capital expenditure. These funds have been established in the past to build up sums for the purposes of financing capital.

Each authority operating a capital fund must determine whether or not the fund should be replenished or not. In most cases authorities require the use of the fund to be recognised as an internal loan arrangement. This means that the revenue account is charged with principal and interest as if a loans pool advance had taken place.

Accounting Entries

An example can help to demonstrate the entries required for the capital fund.

The ABC Local Authority have a capital fund on the 1 April 1994, with the following balances:

	£000	£000
Capital fund balance		1,350
		=====
Assets		
Advances	1,250	
Cash	100	1,350
	-----	=====

During 1994/95 the ABC Council incurred £100,000 on capital spending to be financed from the capital fund.

Entry for Service Committee/General Fund

	Dr £	Cr £
Fixed assets	100,000	
Capital cash		100,000

being the capital expenditure during the year.

Entry in the Capital Fund

	Dr £	Cr £
Advances to committees	100,000	
Capital cash		100,000

being the reduction of capital fund cash replaced by the long term internal debtor known as advances to committees.

Entry in the Service Committee/General Fund

	Dr £	Cr £
Capital cash	100,000	
Loan outstanding - CF		100,000

being the *internal* receipt of cash and creation of a liability to repay the capital fund.

Also during 1994/95 the capital fund charges the general fund service committees with the following sums for principal and interest on advances previously made.

	1994/95 £
Capital fund charges	
- Principal	85,000
- Interest	140,000

The Entries for Interest Are As Follows:

	Dr £	Cr £
Asset management revenue account	140,000	
Capital fund		140,000

The asset management revenue account must be charged because the council have decided to meet these costs from the current year resources. The capital fund entry increases the size of the fund. It should also be noted a revenue cash/capital cash adjustment would technically be required.

The Entries for Principal are as follows:

	Dr £	Cr £

1.   In the General Fund Accounts

	Dr £	Cr £
Loans outstanding CF	85,000	
Capital fund		85,000

being the repayment of internal loans to the Capital Fund.

	Dr £	Cr £
Consolidated summary revenue a/c	85,000	
revenue cash		85,000

being the contribution necessary to capital reserves for the provision of internal loan repayment and the reimbursement of capital cash.

	Dr £	Cr £
Capital cash	85,000	
Capital financing reserve		85,000

being the acknowledgment that capital cash has been reimbursed, and that internal capital financing has taken place.

2.   In the Capital Fund

	Dr £	Cr £
Capital cash	85,000	
Advances outstanding		85,000

being the repayment of advance from the general fund.

Effect of All Entries on the Capital Fund Balance Sheet

		£000	£000
(1,350 + 140)	Capital fund balance		1,490
			=====
	Assets		
(1250 + 100 - 85)	Advances	1,265	
(100 - 100 + 140 + 85)	Cash	225	1,490
		-----	=====

The important point to note here is that:

(a) Interest repaid to the fund increased the fund size, and the entries for a contribution would have a similar effect.

(b) The advance of new funds and the repayment of old advances had no effect on the size of the balance, the reason being they simply involve a shift between assets of the fund from cash to advances or vice versa.

(c) The most important of all points to note, however, is that all these entries are internal, and do not involve the movement of cash. Only the original purchase of the asset is a real cash movement <u>outside</u> of the authority.

<u>NB</u> THE CAPITAL FUND ENTRIES DO NOT MOVE CASH OUTSIDE OF THE ORGANISATION.

Revenue Activities Cash Movements - Reconciliation to Surplus/Deficit

On the face of the new cash flow statement revenue activities are intended to be cash paid and received. Hopefully many questions will provide this information. However, it is more likely that income and expenditure will be provided.

Whatever information is provided it will be necessary to disclose by way of a note, 'A reconciliation between the net surplus or deficit on the income and expenditure account to the revenue activities net cash flow'.

This means that changes in debtors, creditors and stocks will need to be adjusted for. If for example all income items can individually be adjusted to cash, due to a detail of opening and closing debtors then this should be undertaken to ensure receipts only are recorded on the cash flow statement, but where the question is unclear an adjustment in bulk will be required.

In practice these problems should not occur, but in exam questions they are likely to.

It is now possible to attempt a cash flow question and the following fully worked example is provided.

EXERCISE 12.1 - STATEMENT OF SOURCE AND APPLICATION OF FUNDS

The following information has been extracted from the accounts of the West Woldshire County Council.

	31 Mar 1994	31 Mar 1995
Fixed assets	53,649	62,472
Less: Depreciation	(16,173)	(16,673)
	-------	-------
	27,476	33,740
Current Assets	7,636	9,352
Less: Current Liabilities	(7,927)	(7,463)
	-------	------
Net Assets	37,185	47,688
	=======	======

Represented by:
Fixed asset restatement reserve

Long Term Liabilities	10,000	11,000
Loans Outstanding:		
- External	21,591	27,064
Reserves and Funds		
Capital Fund	2,450	3,370
County Fund	1,613	2,490
Capital Receipts/Grants etc.	1,531	2,705
Capital Financing Reserve		1,059
	------	------
	37,185	47,688
	======	======

	£	Cash paid reserved £
Employees Costs	28,172	28,172
Running Expenses	13,629	14,093
Debt Charges	4,199	?
Capital Expenditure financed from revenue	374	?
Contribution to Capital Fund	600	?
Income form Charges etc.	10,663	10,630
Interest on revenue balances	196	180
Precept income	21,548	21,548
Specific government grants	8,246	6,877
Revenue Support Grants	7,198	6,700
Asset rents - deprecation	627	?
- notional interest	5,200	?

Additional information:

(A) Capital expenditure during the year amounted to £7.95m including £216,000 on roads and sewers to enable apiece of land to be sold for development, yielding a capital receipt of £1.39m. The land originally costs £127,000 and was fully depreciated (none to be set aside). The infrastructure costs are to be met from the capital receipt.

(B) £7.5m of new loans were raised during the year. Debt charges paid to the Consolidated Loans Fund amounted to £896,000 principal and £2,783,000 interest. Capital Fund charges were £200,000 principal and £320,000 interest. These charges for principal equal the minimum revenue provision.

(C) Cash in hand was £400,000 @ 31/3/94 and £200,000 @ 31/3/95.

YOU ARE REQUIRED to prepare a source and application of funds statement for the year ended 31 March 1994.

Tutorial Answer - West Woldshire County Council

Step 1

The first step in a cash flow question is to identify what the surplus or deficit for the year has been , and how it has been arrived at by the consolidated summary revenue account.

Therefore the following is the consolidated revenue account:

Working paper **NOT IN REQUIRED FORMAT**

West Woldshire Consolidated Summary Revenue Account for the year ending 31 March 1995

	£ General Exp.	£ Income	£ Net
General fund			
All services			
Employees	28,172		
Running expenses	13,629		
Asset rents	5,827		
Income			
- Government Grant			
- revenue support grant		7,198	
- specific grant		8,246	
- Customer & client receipts			
- fees & charges		10,663	
- Interest		196	
- Precept		21,548	
	-------	-------	
	47,628	47,851}	
Net surplus of general fund services		}	223 cr
Asset Management Revenue Account			
Depreciation	627*		
Loans pool & capital fund			
interest	3,103		
Less			
Asset rents	(5,827)		2,097 cr
Contributions to Reserves			
Provision for repayment of loans		469	
Direct revenue financing		374	
Contribution to capital fund		600	(1,443) dr
		---	-------
Net General Fund Surplus			877 cr
			=======

This working paper shows that the Net General County Fund surplus for the year is £877.000. If you now compare this figure to the County Fund opening and closing balance the following cross check can be made:

	£000
County fund balance 1/4/94	1,613
Surplus for the year	877

County fund balance 31/3/95	2,490
	=====

Step 2

The nest step is to try to prepare the cash flow statement bearing in mind that we have established that at present the net surplus figure excludes the asset rent, but included the charges for principal & interest plus the capital fund.

West Woldshire County Council Cash Flow Statement for the year ending 31 March 1995

Revenue Activities	£	£	£
Expenditure			
Employees	28,172		
Running expenses paid	14,093	42,265	

Income			
Precept	21,548		
RSG grant	6,700		
specific grant	6,877		
Fees & charges	10,630	45,755	
	------	------	
Revenue activities net cash flow			3,490
Servicing of finance			
Interest paid	2,783		
Interest received	(180)		(2,603)
	-------		-------
			887
Capital activities			
Purchase of assets	7,950		
Capital receipts	(1,390)		(6,560)

Net cash flow before financing activities			(5,673)
Financing			
Expenditure			
Loans repaid	2,027		
Income			
Loans raised	7,500		5,473

Decrease in cash and cash equivalents			(200)

Working for Loan Repaid* to find real bonus repaid by the loans pool.

	£000
Balance b/fwd 1/4/94	21,591
Loans raised during year	7,500

	29,091
Less loans repaid	?

Balance c/fwd 31/3/95	27,064
	======

Loans repaid must have been £2,027,000

Step 3

We now need to consider the need to reconcile back from revenue activities on the cash flow statement to the surplus for the year on the County Fund.

To be able to achieve this we need to recognise the difference between the two statements. These differences are as follows:

1. Net cash inflow from revenue activities cannot be directly compared to the surplus on the county fund until interest movements have been included.

   (a) Add net cash flow from revenue activity to the cash paid or received on interest transactions. This can be achieved as follows:

	£
Revenue activities net cash flow	3,490
Plus interest received	
Less interest paid	(2,603)
Figure for cash equivalent of surplus	887

   (b) This figure differs from the surplus due to the following:

   - the surplus is adjusted for book entries related to the financing of capital

   - the surplus is adjusted by debtors, creditors and stock movements.

The following statement therefore compares the cash flow to the surplus.

Reconciliation between the surplus and the revenue activities net cash flow

CASH FLOW FIGURES

	£000	£000	£000
1. Revenue activities net cash inflow		3,490	
2. Adjustment to include:			
- interest paid	2,783		
- interest received	(180)	(2,603)	887

INCOME AND EXPENDITURE ADJUSTMENTS

1. Adjustment for book entries for loans pool			
- principal	896	(896)	
2. Adjustment for book entries capital fund			
- principal	200		
- interest	320		
- contribution	600	(1,120)	
3. Adjustment for direct revenue financing	374	(374)	
4. Change in debtors creditors & stocks	2,380	(10)	
Surplus for the year ending 1994/95		877	

The change in debtors and creditors can be found in total from
the balance sheet or via the individual expenses and income as
follows:

Totals approach - Changes in working capital excluding cash

	1/4/94	31/3/95
	£000	£000
Current assets	7,636	9,352
Less cash	400	200
	-----	-----
	7,236	9,152
Current liabilities	7,927	7,463
	-----	-----
Net current assets excluding cash	(691)	1,689

The total improvement in working capital from the opening to
closing balance sheet is as follows:

	£
opening	(691,000)
closing	1,689,000

Total improvement	2,380,000
	=========

The detail approach would have resulted in the following
analysis:

	Income & expenditure amount £	Cash paid or received £
Expenditure		
Running expenses	(13,629)	(14,093)
Income		
Fees & charges	10,663	10,630
Interest income	196	180
Specific grant	8,246	6,877
RSG	7,198	6,700
	------	------
	12,674	10,294

The total difference being £2,380,000.

Conclusion

The consolidated cash flow statement is very complicated
to understand. However, once the problems have been identified
and understood preparation of the statement is not particularly
time consuming.

The following examination question is provided for the purposes
of practising the techniques involved in producing the statements
required.

EXAMINATION QUESTION 12.1 - SUMMERHAM COUNTY COUNCIL

From the following information extracted from the accounts of the Cuekumbria county Council. You are required to prepare the following:

A cash flow statement in accordance with the Draft Accounting Code of Practice for the year 1994/95.

Consolidated Balance Sheet

31 March 1994 £000s		31 March 1995 £000s
182,943	Fixed assets	188,840
35,463	Less depreciation	36,183
-------		-------
147,480		152,657
12,704	Current assets	15,737
20,926	Current liabilities	15,470
-------		-------
139,258	Net assets	152,924
	Represented by: Long term liabilities	
42,123	Loans outstanding	43,180
	Reserve and funds	
80,000	Fixed asset restatement	82,397
6,742	Capital fund	7,602
--	Capital financing reserve	2,560
4,982	County fund	11,524
5,411	Capital receipts unapplied	5,661
-------		-------
139,258		152,924
-------		-------

Consolidated Summarised Revenue Account

	£000s	Cash payments & receipts £000s
Asset rents - depreciation	720	--
- notional interest	14,200	--
Employees	60,270	60,270
Running expenses	25,420	30,876
Debt charges etc	9,200	?
Income from customers	21,430	20,100
Specific grants	18,200	17,900
Investment income	1,000	1,000
Precept income	56,812	54,900
Direct revenue financing	1,300	?
Cont. to Capital fund	10	?
Grant RSG	5,300	5,179
Transfer to county fund	6,542	?

Notes to the accounts for the year 1994/95

a)   Debt charges were made up as follows:

	Principal £000s	Interest £000s
Consolidated Loans Fund	1,210	6,620
Capital Fund	520	850

b)   Expenditure on capital assets amounted to £3,500,000 and new loans were raised towards their cost of £2,200,000

c)   A piece of land was sold for £500,000 the land had a net current value in the accounts of £603,000. Set aside provision is to be made at 50%.

d)   Cash included in current assets was £950,000 as at 31 march 1994 and £220,000 @ 31 March 1995.

Answer to Examination Question 1

Working paper consolidated summary revenue account

	Gross £	Income £	Net £	
All services				
Employees	60,270			
Running expenses	25,420			
Asset rents	14,920			
Income				
Government grants				
- Revenue support		5,300		
- Support		18,200		
Customer & client receipt		21,430		
Interest income investment		1,000		
Precept income		56,812		
	-------	-------		
	100,610	102,742 }		
		}		
Net Surplus of General Fund Services			2,132	cr
Asset Management Revenue Account				
Depreciation	720*			
Loans pool & capital fund				
interest	7,470			
Less asset rents	(14,920)		6,730	cr
Contribution to reserves				
Provision for repayment of loans		1,010		
Direct revenue financing		1,300		
Contribution to capital fund		10	2,320	dr
		-----	-----	
Net General Fund Surplus			6,542	
			=====	

Cross check summary revenue account

	£000
County fund balance 1/4/94	4,982
Surplus for the year	6,542

County fund balance 31/3/95	11,524
	======

Summerham County Council Cash Flow Statement for the year ending 31 March 1995

	£000	£000	£000
Revenue Activities			
Expenditure			
Employees	60,270		
Running expenses	30,876	91,146	
Income			
Precept	54,800		
RSG grant	5,179		
Specific grant	17,900		
Income from customers	20,100	97,979	
Revenue Activities net cash flow			6,833
Servicing of finance			
Interest paid	(6,620)		
Interest received	1,000		(5,620)
			1,213
Capital activities			
Purchase of assets	(3,500)		
Capital receipt	500		(3,000)
Net cash flow before financing			(1,787)
Financing			
Loans repaid	(1,143)		
Loans raised	2,200		1,057
Decrease in cash and cash equivalents			(730)

Reconciliation between the surplus and the revenue activities net cash flow

CASH FLOW FIGURES	£000	£000	£000
Revenue Activities net cash flow		6,833	
Adjustment for interest cash payment/receipt			
- payment	(6,620)		
- receipt	1,000	(5,620)	1,213
Income & Expenditure Adjustments			
Book entries - loans pool		(1,210)	
- Capital fund			
- principal	520		
- interest	850		
- contribution	10	(1,380)	
- Direct revenue financing		(1,300)	
Adjustment for debtor, creditors & stock		9,219	5,329
Surplus for the year 1994/95			6,542

Loans account	£000
b/fwd	42,123
Plus loans raised	2,200
	44,323
Less repaid	?
bal c/fwd 31/3/95	43,180

* Real loans repaid must have been £1,143,000

- 325 -

CHAPTER 13

Local Government Finance And The Collection Fund

Introduction

Local Government Finance has created major problems for the current Government, and has seen significant changes over the last few year. In 1990 the Community Charge was introduced to replace the domestic rating system, and by the 1 April 1993 had itself been replaced by the Council Tax. This section attempts to provide an outline of the arrangements for Council Tax, and the other major forms of financing local Government. The chapter will therefore consider the following finance.

Local Government Finance

-   Council Tax
-   National Non-Domestic Rates
-   Revenue Support Grant

This chapter will also consider in a second section the accounting for the Collection Fund.

Council Tax

The Council Tax is based primarily on property value, but does contain personal elements. Most dwellings are subject to the Council Tax although their are some exceptions.

The Council Tax is payable on the basis of property values established by the District Valuer. The valuation was based on open market capital values as at 1 April 1991.

Valuation Band	Range of Value
A	up to £40,000
B	over £40,000 and up to £52,000
C	over £52,000 and up to £68,000
D	over £68,000 and up to £88,000
E	over £88,000 and up to £120,000
F	over £120,000 and up to £160,000
G	over £160,000 and up to £320,000
H	over £320,000

Band D is considered to be the average category and the Government expected each authority to set the tax for band D at £485. In an example authority in ESSEX this £485 is split between the amount payable towards the District £72 and the amount to the county approximately £413.

The Government based the figure of £485 on the assumption that the Council would spend at the Government's assessment of standard costs of providing services known as standard spending assessment (SSA).

However local Councils are unlikely to set their Council Taxes at the level prescribed by the Government because they might want to spend more or less than the Government's Standard Spending

Assessment. Any variation from the SSA will increase or decrease the Council Tax.

Council Tax Capping

Councils are permitted to set their Council Tax at levels higher than the amount set by the Government for financing spending, provided they do not breach the capping criteria. If they do breach the capping criteria the Department of the Environment will consider the case of the Council and eventually set a spending level which takes account of the Council's case.

The capping criteria was related to the Council's proposed budget (1993/94) compared to the SSA and the percentage increase of the proposed budget over the current budget (1992/93).

For example, a Council could increase its budget by any percentage it wished providing it did not give rise to a budget requirement over the authorities SSA.

The detailed rules allowed the following:

*   An increase of 0.5% over the 1992/93 budget was permitted providing it did not give rise to spending in excess of 10% of its SSA.

*   An increase of 1% over the 1992/93 budget was permitted providing it did not give rise to spending in excess of %5 above its SSA.

*   An increase of 1.75% over the 1992/93 budget was permitted providing it did not give rise to spending in excess of 1% above its SSAs.

*   An increase of 2.5% over the 1992/93 budget was permitted providing it did not give rise to spending in excess of the SSA.

*   Where an authority proposed a budget 30% or less above the SSA for 1993/94, the authority would have to incorporate no increase in its proposed budget over the 1992/93 budget.

*   Where an authority proposed a budget 60% or less, above the SSA for 1993/94, the authorities budget would have to incorporate a %5 reduction on previous year's budget.

*   The use of the word budget in these paragraphs is related to the amount on which Council Tax is calculated.

An example of the charge capping during 1993/94 would be Harlow District Council. The details are as follows:

EXAMPLE: HARLOW DISTRICT COUNCIL TAX CAPPING

Harlow had an SSA for 1993/94 of £7,801,000, but they had previously been spending £24 million per year, financing significant amounts above SSA from reserves. By 1993/94 the reserves had run out.

Harlow set an original budget of approximately £18 million. This

was above the previous years precept on the Collection Fund by a
massive sum. In 1992/93 the amount which Harlow raised from the
Poll Tax was approximately £11.2 million. this meant that to be
within the capping limit the Harlow Council would have to set a
budget below £11.2 million. After representation by the Council
the outcome was that the Harlow Council were permitted to raise
£11.8 million from the Council Tax, at considerable cost to local
Council Tax payers. No extra Government grant was made
available. It should be clear that the £11.8m was far below the
council's need to continue spending at the 1992/93 level and
hundreds of staff were made redundant and services were cut back.

Which Dwellings Are Not Subject To Council Tax?

Not all dwellings are subject to the Government's Council Tax.
Excluded are properties solely occupied by students, and vacant
properties which:

- are unfurnished (exempt for up to 6 months);
- are owned by a charity (exempt for up to 6 months);
- require or are undergoing structural alteration or major repair
  (exempt for up to 6 months after completion);
- are left empty by someone who has gone to prison, or has moved
  to receive personal care in a hospital or home elsewhere;
- are left empty by someone who has moved in order to provide
  personal care to another person;
- are waiting for probate or letters of administration to be
  granted (and for up to 6 months after);
- have been repossessed;
- are the responsibility of a bankrupt's trustee;
- are empty because their occupation is forbidden by law;
- are waiting to be occupied by a minister of religion.

Are People Entitled to Discounts?

The personal element of the Council Tax does allow for discounts.

The full Council Tax bill assumes there are two adults living in
a dwelling. If only one adult lives in a dwelling their Council
Tax bill will be reduced by a quarter (25%). If a dwelling is
empty the bill will be reduced by half (50%).

Certain people will not be counted when looking at the number of
adults resident in a dwelling if they meet certain conditions:

- 18 and 19 year olds who are at or have just left school;
- full time students, student nurses, apprentices and Youth
  Training trainees;
- patients resident in hospital;
- people who are being looked after in care homes;
- people who are severely mentally impaired;
- people staying in certain hostels or night shelters;
- careworkers working for low pay, usually for charities;
- people caring for someone with a disability who is not a
- spouse, partner, or child under 18;
- members of religious communities (monks and nuns);
- people in prison (except those in prison for non-payment of
  Council Tax or a fine).

Are People Eligible for Benefits?

Council tax benefit is available to people in receipt of income support or on low incomes. Thus people can have their bills reduced by up to 100%.

In addition, people with disabilities will be entitled to have the banding of their house reduced by one band.

How Do Councils Set The Amounts in Each Band of Council Tax

If for example a Council set its Council Tax for band D at £600. The other bands would be determined by established proportions as follows:

if band D is £600

```
                              £
Band A =  6/9 x £600    =   400
Band B =  7/9 x £600    =   467
Band C =  8/9 x £600    =   533
Band D =                =   600
Band E = 11/9 x £600    =   733
Band F = 13/9 x £600    =   867
Band G = 15/9 x £600    =  1000
Band H = 18/9 x £600    =  1200
```

What Part Do The Government Play in Setting Council Tax Levels

The Government have a part to play in how much a individual's Council Tax will be, because the Government determine the level of finance given to the local authority from National Non-Doomestic Rate, and how much is provided from Central Government grant, known as Revenue Support Grant (RSG).

National Non-Domestic Rates

National non-domestic rates are collected by local authorities from Business ratepayers in their areas. The amount collected from the business ratepayer is based on a valuation, multiplied by a national unified charge in the £, multiplied by the valuation.

For example, regardless of where your business is established, providing the area is not an enterprise zone, the amount of business tax payable would be an identical sum, if the valuation were the same. The local Council do not decide how much is collected.

For example, the provisional calculation for the amount that the ABC District Council were required to pay for 1993/94 to the Government for contributions to the national non-domestic rate pool might have been as follows:

TABLE - CONTRIBUTION TO NNDR POOL BY ABC LOCAL AUTHORITY

	£
Aggregate rateable value	71,000,000
	==========
Gross yield based on unified business rate in the £ of 0.416	29,536,000

Less
Transitional arrangement		(100,000)
Mandatory relief	- charitable	(500,000)
	- partly occupied	(300,000)
	- empty premises	(3,500,000)
Discretionary relief	- charitable	(100,000)
Allowance for losses on collection		(250,000)
Cost of collection		(100,000)

Provisional contribution to NNDR Pool		24,786,000
		===========

The ABC District Council in this example have a very high level
of Non-domestic property in their area. It is very unlikely that
the Council will get back anywhere near the amount of business
rate collected to help finance its services. All business rate
payers paid 41.6p in the £ during 1993/94.

For 1993/94 the amount collected for the Government by local
authorities was redistributed back to local authorities on the
basis of their resident populations. In 1993/94 the amount
redistributed to local District Councils was approximately £35
per head of resident population.

The ABC might have had a resident population of 75,000 in which
case the Government would give approximately £2,625,000 back to
the authority to finance its services.

However, the ABC District Council is not the only local authority
providing services within its boundaries because the County
Council are providing the most expensive services such as
Education and Social Services. County Councils receive
approximately £205 per head of resident population. Therefore
ABC business ratepayers pay significantly more for local services
than the finance given to their local authorities to provide
services as follows:

	£	£
Payments into the NNDR Pool		24,786,000
Less		
Business rate income		
- ABC District	2,625,000	
- County	15,375,000	18,000,000
	----------	----------
Excess business rate paid		6,786,000
to the Government		==========

The business rate income to a local authority therefore has no
bearing on the amount collected by the Council, and is generally
considered to be central Government controlled.

Revenue Support Grant

Local authorities also receive revenue support grant. This grant
is calculated by the Government having regard to the level it
believes local authorities should be spending to provide a
standard level of service.

An extremely complicated arrangement exists for calculating each
authorities need for spending.

These Standard Spending Assessments are reasonably logical in principle. A calculation of how much it costs to pay for services it provides. However, the SSAs have been criticised by most commentators of Local Government finance including the Audit Commission. The following extract from a debate in the House of Commons provides an example of how Labour Members of Parliament believe the SSAs are inequitable.

Mr David Clelland, MP for Tyne Bridge, made a statement in the House, including the following extract.

> "This year's revenue support grant settlement once again exposes the partisan nature of the Government's local Government finance regime. Indeed, it goes further; it exposes the whole nature of the Government's approach to local democracy and the sinister way in which our traditional system of Government is being undermined. One instrument which is used for those purposes is the standard spending assessment or SSA, a system which owes more to the prejudices of the Tory party than to any honest attempt properly to assess the needs of individual localities. It is a system which allows the Secretary of State to pick off individual Councils and reward others.
>
> Most casual observers would surely conclude that the needs of the people of Tyne and Wear in terms of local Government services are likely to be at least as high as those living in the heart of the capital. In fact, given the level of unemployment, the decline of industry and the continuing work to remove the scars of our industrial past, most would conclude that our needs are somewhat greater; yet, according to the Government, tory-controlled Westminster's needs amount to £1,200per head of population, while the needs of Labour-controlled Tyne and Wear authorities range from just £661 to £750.
>
> A good example of the partisan nature of the system is the fact that, if Labour-controlled Gateshead were allocated the same level of SSA as Tory-controlled Westminster for just one year. Gateshead's Council Tax could be set at zero for the next three years. It is not a matter of more and more money, as the hon. Member for Harlow suggested earlier. All we want in Gateshead are the same resources that are being applied in Westminster.
>
> The SSA system provides increased help to areas of higher pay and prices, which would appear to conflict with the Government's policy to restrain public sector pay, yet no recognition is made of the need for better public services in areas such as Tyne and Wear, where low incomes and high unemployment are much more prevalent than in Westminster.
>
> If car ownership is low, there is a need for better public transport, and if people cannot afford golf club fees and private health clubs, there is a greater need

for public recreation facilities. However, the system turns that logic on its head, so that the Tory party can direct resources to areas in the south to try to prevent the haemorrhage in its support. The comparison with Westminster demonstrates political manipulation of the system: my hon. Friend the Member for Blackburn (Mr. Straw) drew attention to other examples.

There are other anomalies in the system. For instance, how can a Government who have acknowledged the similarity of the problems faced by Newcastle and Gateshead by creating a partnership area covering both, calculate that Gateshead needs £44 per head, or £9 million less than Newcastle to deal with the same problems? When one take into account the fact that the great city of Newcastle is being forced to cut expenditure by £8 million this year and £12 million between 1994-96, the full scale of the affects of the settlement and the system is realised.

That is due to the inadequacy of the SSA and the fact that it has been reduced by £9 million following the removal of further education responsibilities from the city of Newcastle, although expenditure on those facilities last year was only £6 million. all that will mean reductions in services and increases in unemployment as yet more jobs are lost. The settlement means that more job losses are inevitable.

Comment on the Statement

Obviously this statement is a political statement, but it does demonstrate the type of perceived unfairness in the calculation of SSAs.

Importance of SSAs

The importance of SSAs cannot be over emphasised. This is because the amount of revenue support grant given is based on the SSAs for a local authority.

For example - A District Council with an SSA of £13,000,000 and a resident population of 162,000 might expect to receive the following for 1993/94:

a)   Business rate income of £35 per resident say £5,670,000;

b)   The yield from Council Tax based on an average Council Tax charge required by the Government of say £72 for their tier of Government, producing a total income of £3,995,000;

c)   Revenue support grant of the balance between finance provided by (a) and (b) above and the SSA. In this case £3,335,000.

Summary Finance - District Council

	£
Business rate	5,670,000
Council Tax	3,995,000
Revenue Support Grant	3,335,000
Total	13,000,000

Had the SSA been £2 million more, the revenue support grant would have been £2 million more.

The importance of SSA is central to the whole systems of local Government finance and if it is brought into disrepute then the whole system is subject to criticism.

Calculation of the Yield from Council Tax

In the example above the yield from Council Tax is expected to be £3,995,000. This figure is based on the Government's perception of the amount which should be contributed by the Council Tax payer, i.e. in this example £72 for the lower tier of Government. The County are assumed to receive the difference between £72 and £485 which was the Government's total contribution expected from local tax payers.

The figure of £3,995,000 would have been calculated by assessing the number of properties in each band of tax. Converting them to Band D weight values and taking account of all discount allowable.

For Example

Band	No. of properties subject to Council tax	No. of properties subject to 25% discount	Taxable total
	No.	No.	No.
A	918	200	1,068
B	5,238	1,000	5,988
C	14,034	2,000	15,534
D	30,713	4,000	33,713
E	1,155	–	1,155
F	495	–	495
G	277	–	277
H	4	–	4
	52,834	7,200 *5,400	58,234

This table shows that the number of properties subject to Council Tax at 100% are 52,834. it also shows that 7200 properties are entitled to a 25% discount, and this equals an equivalent of 5,400 full taxable units. The total tax base is therefore 52,834 plus 5,400 which equals 58,234. However, each unit has different tax earning potential and therefore we need to calculate the weighted tax base by converting all units to Band D value as follows:

Band	Tax Base No.	Ratio to Band D	Band D Equivalent
A	1,068	6/9	712
B	5,988	7/9	4,658
C	15,534	8/9	13,808
D	33,713	1	33,713
E	1,155	11/9	1,412
F	495	13/9	716
G	277	15/9	461
H	4	18/9	8
	------		------
	58,234		55,488

Each local authority had to produce calculations to convert its Council Tax base to Band D equivalents.

Process of Calculating Council Tax Bills

The Council Tax is based on a number of factors:

- The number of resident population
- The amount at which the Government set the payment to local authorities of business rate.
- The tax base for Council Tax
- The level of a Council's SSA
- The budget spending set by the Council

To complete this section consider the following example:

How much would the XYZ county Council need to set their Council Tax at, assuming no Council Tax capping?

* XYZ County resident population was 142,000
* The business rate payable to the county is £205 per resident
* The county SSA was £110 million
* The tax base at Band D was 121,065 and the County's share of Council Tax income is £413 of £485 at the SSA.
* The Council plan to send at £120 million

Answer   £

```
Business rate income (142,000 x £205)    29,110,000
Council Tax at SSA (121,065 x £413)      49,999,845
RSG                                      30,890,155 *derived
                                         -----------
                                        110,000,000
                                        ===========
```

However, the XYZ wish to spend another £10 million above SSA. This £10 million must come from Council Tax payers. Therefore the Council Tax will be increased as follows:

$$\frac{£10,000,000}{121,065} = £82.60$$

If the County wishes to spend the extra 10 million it will cost Council Tax payers on extra £82.60, and bring the total charge up to £567.60 per annum (£485 + £82.60). This being split £72 to Districts and £495.60 to the County.

Conclusion

The subject of local government finance is a complex one, and this section of the chapter has attempted to explain the calculations that are required, and give a guide to how Council Tax levels are established. The next part of this chapter deals with the accounting for the Collection Fund.

THE COLLECTION FUND

Introduction

The Collection Fund is an accounting device that was introduced with the community charge. The fund is going to be continued into 1993/94, and has been adapted for the implementation of the Council Tax.

The Collection Fund will have to deal with the residual accounting for the community charge as well as the new requirements for the Council Tax. Only one Collection Fund will operate.

This section of the book sets out to provide details of the requirements for billing authorities to collect the Council Tax in 1993/94, and provide some examples of the accounting requirement.

Major Points to Note

Treatment of Government External Finance

A change in the use of the Collection Fund is that receipts of Revenue Support Grant (RSG) and the National Non-Domestic Rate (NNDR) are to be paid direct to each authority. This is a change from the old Collection Fund arrangements. The billing authority's entitlement to RSG and NDR will be paid into the billing authority's general fund, not its Collection Fund.

Parishes Precepts

The new Collection Fund is used to account for the major precepting authorities. Parishes that normally require much lower level of financing are to precept on the billing authority for the amount they require. however, the billing authority is to meet Parish precepts from its general fund and not its Collection Fund.

Treatment of Interest Payable and Receivable

The billing authority is responsible for the collection of the Council Tax, and must pay precepting authorities according to an agreed schedule the first payment being within five weeks of the financial year, and the last payment within the last eight weeks of the financial. A minimum of ten instalments are required.

It is quite likely that the management of the collecting fund will require temporary investment of funds, and at other times of the year temporary borrowing. All interest payable and receivable is to be accounted for in the billing authorities general fund and not the Collection Fund.

Treatment of Surpluses and Deficits on the Collection Fund

Community Charge Tax Carry Forwards

At the end of the 31 March 1993 any surplus or deficit on the fund will be in respect of the Community Charge. The surplus or deficit at that date is to be borne by the billing authority.

It will therefore be necessary to transfer the deficit/surplus to the billing authority's general fund. During the year transactions will continue belatedly related to the Poll Tax and these are all to be accounted for by transferring the net effect of transactions to the billing authority's general fund.

Council Tax Surplus/Deficit

The Council tax transactions accounted for in the Collection Fund are to be shared between the major precepting authorities.

Precepting authorities would have set their budgets and established the amount of precept required to run their services. The yield from the tax is inevitably going to be different than estimated. However, the Collection Fund must meet the precept. Therefore there will be surpluses and deficits on Collection Funds.

These surpluses and deficits are to be shared by billing and precepting authorities. The surpluses and deficits will be estimated before the end of 1993/94 for 1993/94. Authorities will then adjust their demands on the 1994/95 Collection Fund to take account of their share of the surplus or deficit. The estimated surplus or deficit will be removed in 1994/95 by charging or repaying amounts to the authorities. This process will continue year after year to ensure deficits and surpluses are adjusted in the following year.

Accounting for the Collection Fund

The following accounting entries will need to be made in the Collection Fund.

Income

1. Income from Council Tax Payers. Income from Council Tax would be the amount payable for the year, by Council Tax payers, less the amount of benefit granted by way of reduction of Council Tax bills, and reductions for prompt payments.

    It is important to note here that the Council Tax amount payable would be an amount after allowing for discounts and reductions in respect of transitional relief and disabled relief.

    Transitional relief is given to reduce the impact of Council Tax amount.

2. Income in lieu of Council Tax

3. Aggregate amounts of Council Tax benefits granted by way of reductions in amounts otherwise payable. The income here is financed by the general fund and benefit grant is received from the government into the general fund.

4. Aggregate amounts of reduction is liability to Council Tax in respect of transitional relief. This again is transferred from the general fund where grant is received from the government.

5. <u>Aggregate reductions in amounts of Council Tax payable in respect of prompt payments.</u> Where the billing authority has offered a scheme of discount for prompt payments the benefit of such a share should result in interest savings for the billing authority. The billing authority general fund therefore must provide income to the Collection Fund for the reductions in Council Tax due to discounts.

6. Contributions from the billing authority in 1993/94 to meet the Community Charge deficit, and from 1994/95 onwards contributions from all major precepting authorities to meet the estimated previous years deficit.

7. <u>Income from local non-domestic rate payers, based on the unified business rate.</u> This amount is collected on behalf of the government, and will appear as an expenditure of the fund as well, when it is paid over to the government. You should note this is not the amount of NNDR receivable by the local council for its own use.

8. <u>Refunds of National domestic rate previously paid to the National Non-Domestic Rate pool.</u> This item would occur where the estimate paid over was discovered to be higher than necessary.

9. <u>The billing authority may in exceptional circumstances make a negative demand on the Collection Fund.</u> This could occur where an authority spend so far below their SSA that they do not need to raise a Council Tax. Wandsworth London Borough achieved a nil Community Charge under the old regime.

10. <u>Income in respect of residual amounts from the Community Charge.</u> These will be passed onto the billing authority via an expenditure head.

These ten headings are likely to be required during 1993/94 and possibly into 1994/95, but the Community Charge adjustments will eventually not be required.

Payments Made By The Collection Fund

The payments to be made from the Collection Fund are as follows:

1. Payments to be made to the major precepting authorities in respect of precepts issued by them.

2. Transfer to the billing authorities general fund in respect of the demand made on the fund for providing services.

3. Payment to the major precepting authorities and transfers to the billing authority's general fund in respect of the previous year's estimated surplus, if any.

4. Contribution to the National Non-Domestic Rate pool. This is basically the sum payable to the government having been collected from the business rate payers.

5. The billing authority is entitled to a payment for the cost

of collection of the business rate.

An example of items for the business rate in the Collection Fund would be as follows:

		£
(a)	Income item 7, amount from the local non-domestic rate payers	15,000,000
		==========
(b)	Expenditure item 4, contribution to NNDR pool	14,900,000
(c)	Expenditure item 5. cost of collection paid to general fund	100,000

		15,000,000
		==========

6.   A payments heading would be required for any refunds or adjustments. This heading could also be used for making provisions for Council Tax appeals and non-collection.

Collection Fund Format

The exposure draft of a revised code of practice on local authority accounting in Great Britain does include a standard statement for the Collection Fund both for England and Wales and a separate format for Scotland.

The following is the format for the Collection Fund in England and Wales.

This account reflects the statutory requirement for billing authorities to maintain a separate Collection Fund, which shows the transactions of the billing authority in relation to non-domestic rates and the Council Tax, and illustrates the way in which these have been distributed to preceptors and the General fund. The Collection Fund is consolidated with other accounts of the billing authority.

Information to be included in the Accounting Statement

Income
    Income from Council Tax (showing the amount receivable net of benefits, discounts for prompt payments and transitional relief)

Transfers from General Fund
-    Council tax benefits
-    Transitional relief
-    Discounts for prompt payments

Income collectible from business ratepayers

Contributions

-    Towards previous year's Collection Fund deficit
-    Negative Council Tax
-    Adjustment of previous year's community charges

Expenditure

    Precepts and demands from County and District

Business rate

-    Payment to national pool
-    Costs of collection

Bad and doubtful debts/appeals

-    Write offs
-    Provisions

Contributions

-    Towards previous year's estimated Collection Fund
     surplus
-    Adjustment of previous years' community charges

Movement on fund balance

Information to be disclosed in Notes to the Account

a)   The total non-domestic rateable value at the year end
      and the national non-domestic rate multiplier for the
      year.

b)   The calculation of the council tax base, i.e. the
      number of chargeable dwellings in each valuation band
      (adjusted for dwellings where discounts apply)
      converted to an equivalent number of band D dwellings.

c)   The name of each authority which made a significant
      precept or demand on the fund and the amount included
      for each authority.

EXAMPLE QUESTION - COLLECTHAM DISTRICT COUNCIL

Exercise 13.1

The following information is available for 1993/94 for the
District Council. The question simply required the preparation
of the Collection Fund Income and Expenditure Account, and
identification of items to be recorded in the billing authority's
general fund.

Transactions for the year ending 31 March 1994

	£000
Revenue support grant	10,300
Receipt of cash from NNDR pool	5,100
Council tax income	35,000
Precept Sittingshire C.C.	34,200
Transitional relief	1,100
Council tax benefits	7,100
Payment to NNDR pool	17,300
Income from business ratepayers	17,500
Provision fro council tax appeals	400
Contribution from Collectham DC	
- for deficit Re: 1992/93	700

```
Collectham D.C. demand on fund                    9,200
Income from community charge payers                 100
Cost of collecting NNDR                             200
```

Tutorial Answer

The first step is to try to identity transactions which do not
belong in the collection fund. for example Revenue Support grant
is taken directly to the billing authority's general fund along
with receipts from the NNDR pool.

We can then start to prepare a summary collection fund as
follows:

Collectham District Council Collection Fund for the year ending
31 March 1994

```
                                   £000        £000       £000
Income
  Council tax:
    Income from Council Tax     35,000
    Council tax benefits         7,100
    Transitional relief          1,100      43,200
                                ------      ------
  Contribution from Collectham DC to
  estimated Collection Fund deficit 1992/93    700

  Income in respect of Non-Domestic rate    17,500
  Community charge income for previous years   100
                                            ------
         TOTAL INCOME FOR THE YEAR                      61,500

Expenditure
  Precepts and demands
    - Collectham DC               9,200
    - Sittingshire CC            34,200      43,400
                                ------
Contribution to Collectham DC regarding
Community Charge income 1992/93                100

  Non-Domestic rate             17,300
  Cost of collection               200      17,500
                                ------
  Provision for Council Tax appeals            400
                                            ------
         Total expenditure for the year                61,400
                                                       ------
         Surplus/deficit for the year                     100
                                                       ======
```

Items which would appear in the billing authorities general fund
are as follows:

-    Revenue support grant
-    Receipt from NNDR pool
-    Transitional relief
-    Council Tax benefits
-    Contribution to previous year deficit
-    Transfer of Community Charge income

- Transfer income for cost of collection

Accounting Required in addition to the Collection Fund

The Collection Fund is a summary account of all the dealings necessary between the billing authority and the amjor precepting authorities. It provides a vehicle for collecting and distributing Council Tax. However, the billing authority will need to keep much more extensive accounting records to record the following:

- What arrears and prepayments of Council Tax are there carried forward?

- What arrears and prepayments are there on the collection of NNDR to be carried forward?

- How is the billing authority's general fund affected by the transactions?

The answers to these questions can be demonstrated by the use of examples, but the billing authority would keep additional accounts for both the Council Tax and the National Non-Domestic rate as follows:-

- Council Tax income account. This account is provided to calculate the amount of Council Tax due net of discounts and other reduction. The entries are largely mirrored in the Council Tax payers account which will be shown after the example for Council Tax income.

Council Tax Income Account for the year ending 31 March 1994

	£	£
Council Tax Due		
Band		
A	350,000	
B	2,250,000	
C	12,500,000	
D	7,400,000	
E	300,000	
F	500,000	
G	100,000	
H	10,000	23,410,000
Less reductions		
Discounts	1,350,000	
Reduced assessments	300,000	1,650,000

Less benefits		6,200,000
transitional relief		700,000

Transfer to Collection Fund revenue account		14,860,000
		==========

The figure of £14,860,000 would be the income expected to be found in the collection Fund net of items which need to be shown as income on the face of the Collection Fund revenue account.

The next step is to consider the account which shows the

indebtedness of Council Tax payers. This account to a large
degree is a mirror of the Income account, but includes the cash
received.

Council Tax payers Account for the year ending 31 March 1994

	£	£
Council Tax due		23,410,000
Less reductions		
Discounts	1,350,000	
Reduced assessments	300,000	1,650,000
	---------	----------
Total collectible before benefits & relief		21,760,000
		==========
Less benefits	6,200,000	
Transitional relief	700,000	
Cash received	13,160,000	20,060,000
	---------	----------
Balance c/fwd: arrears	1,900,000	
Less : prepayments	200,000	1,700,000
	---------	----------
		21,760,000
		==========

The Council Tax payers account therefore reveals the indebtedness
of tax payers, and those that have prepaid. This account
represents the debtors account. Most of these entries are simply
contra's to the Council Tax income account.

Entries in the Collection Fund for Council Tax Income

It should be helpful to point out that the Collection Fund will
received the following items:

-       Council Tax collectible £14,860,000 from the Council Tax
        income account.

-       Benefits granted from the General Fund.

-       Transitional relief granted from the general fund.

National Non domestic Rate Income Account

Business rates are collected from local ratepayer and eventually
paid over to the government.

The government pay a sum back to all authorities based on their
resident populations. The cash received by the billing authority
from the government will be accounted for in the general fund and
not the collection fund.

The collection fund is therefore concerned with receiving the
National Non Domestic rate which is necessary to be contributed
to the government, and to pay out that sum less any cost of
collection which will be paid to the billing authorities general
fund.

To achieve this accounting exercise a billing authority will adopt the following:

    National Non Domestic Rate Income Account
    National Non Domestic Rate Ratepayers Account

These accounts are operated in a very similar way to the
council's accounting for council tax income previously described.

The following are examples of the accounts:

Example National Non domestic Rate Income Account

	£000	£000	£000
Amount due from Ratepayers;			
Original debit for rate income		19,100	
Additional debits		2,100	
Empty rate income		320	
Rateable value increases		180	21,700

Less Losses & Reductions			
Rateable value reductions		400	
Mandatory relief		500	
Discretionary relief NNDR proportion		50	
Write offs		200	1,150
		------	------
Billing authorities contribution to NNDR pool			20,550

This account shows the amount that the billing authority are
required to pay to the government in respect of business rate
collectible.

We now need to consider the indebtedness of business ratepayers
and this will be found in the National Non domestic ratepayers
account.

National Non Domestic Ratepayers Account

	£000	£000	£000
Amount due from Ratepayers;			
Original debit for rate income			19,100
Additional debits			2,100
Empty rate income			320
Rateable value increases			180

			21,700
Less Losses & Reductions			
Rateable value reductions		400	
Mandatory relief		500	
Discretionary relief			
NNDR proportion	50		
General fund	100	150	

Write offs		200	1,250
		------	------
			20,450
			======

- 344 -

	£000	£000	£000
Collection cash received	18,900		
Less refunds	100		18,800
	------		------
Balance c/fwd: arrears	1,860		
: prepaid	210		1,650
	-----		------
			20,450
			======

The entries in collection fund should be considered at this point. The collection fund recieves the billing authorities contribution to the NNDR. the collection fund then pays the amount required to the government less the cost of collection which is transferred to the general fund.

The following example question is provided to enable the accounting to be fully considered.

Example Question - Appleton District Council

Exercise 13.2

Appleton district Council has produced the following information for its 1993/94 accounts:

	£
Council Tax income for bands A - H	37,500,000
Council Tax income in lieu amount to	506,000

Allowances and losses on collection were as follows:

	£
Exemption from Council Tax	560,000
Transitional relief	725,000
Council Tax discount	1,500,000

Other information

	£
Precepts to Orchard CC	26,424,000
to Appleton DC	9,801,000
Payment to NNDR National Pool	6,340,000
Council Tax benefit	4,250,000
Revenue support grant	6,430,000
Payment received from NNDR pool	10,500,000
Business rate collectible	
(after deductions for losses & ratepayers)	6,400,000
Cash received from business ratepayers	6,135,000
Interest paid	90,000
Cost of collection business rate	60,000
Business rate refund	50,000
Community charge income 1992/93	155,000
Contribution to 1992/93 deficit by Appleton	600,000
Cash received from Council Taxpayer	29,541,000

Balances as at 31/3/94	Arrears £	Prepayments £
Council Tax	1,440,000	10,000
Business Rate	330,000	15,000

You are required to prepare:

- A list of items to be recorded in the general fund not required in the collection fund.
- The Collection Fund Revenue Account.
- The Council Tax Income and Taxpayers accounts.
- The National Non Domestic Rate income and ratepayers accounts.

Tutorial Answer - Appleton District Council

The first requirement is to prepare a list of items to be recorded in the general fund. These have been included in the question primarily for the purposes of identifying that they are not required in the collection fund.

- Revenue support grant. This item is recorded directly into the billing authorities general fund.

- Payment received from the NNDR pool, again this is recorded directly into the billing authorities general fund.

- Interest paid this is the responsibility of the billing authority and should not be recorded in the collection fund.

Appleton Collection Fund Revenue Account for the year ending 31 March 1994

	£000	£000
Council Tax:		
Income for Council Tax	30,971	
Council Tax benefit	4,250	
Transitional relief	725	35,946

Contribution from Appleton towards collection fund deficit 1992/93		600
Income in respect of Non Domestic rate		6,400
Community Charge income 1992/93		155

Total income for the year		43,101
Expenditure		
Precepts & demands		
- Orchard CC	26,424	
- Appleton DC	9,801	36,225

Contribution to Appleton DC for previous year's Community Charge		155
Non Domestic rate:		
Payment to national pool	6,340	
Cost of collection	60	6,400
	------	------
Total expenditure for the year		42,780
Surplus for the year		321
		======

Council Tax Income Account for the year ending 31 March 1994

	£000	£000
Council Tax due		
- Council Tax	37,500	
- in lieu	506	38,006

Less reductions		
- Discounts	1,500	
- Exemptions	560	2,060

Less benefits	4,250	
Transitional relief	725	4,975

Transfer to collection fund revenue account		30,971
		======

Council Taxpayers Account for the year ending 31 March 1994

	£000	£000
Council Tax due		38,006
Less reductions		
- Discounts	1,500	
- Exemptions	560	2,060
	------	------
		35,946
		======
Less benefits	4,250	
Transitional relief	725	
Cost received	29,541	34,516
Balance c/fwd: arrears	1,440	
Less : prepaid	(10)	1,430
	------	------
		35,946

Appleton's National Non Domestic Income Account for the year ending 31/3/94

	£
Amount due from ratepayers	6,400

This figure is already net of all losses and can therefore be transferred directly into the Collection Fund.

Appleton's National Non Domestic Ratepayers Account for the year ending 31/3/94

	£000	£000
Business rate collectible		6,400,000
		=========
Cash collected	6,135	
Less refunds	(50)	6,085,000

Balance c/fwd: arrears	330,000	
: prepaid	(15,000)	315,000
	-------	---------
		6,400,000
		=========

Conclusion

This chapter has attempted to provide information on the financing of local authorities. The use of the collection fund has been described in detail, and worked examples provided. the chapter now finishes with an examination question.

Examination Question 13.1 - Dogtown District Council

Dogtown District Council has produced the following information for its 1993/94 accounts:

	£
Council Tax income for bands A - H	27,500,000
Council Tax income in lieu amount to	320,000

Allowances and losses on collection were as follows:

	£
Exemption from Council Tax	140,000
Transitional relief	450,000
Council Tax discount	2,510,000

Other information

	£
Precepts to Barkshire CC	15,600,000
to Dogtown DC	4.500,000
Payment to NNDR National Pool	11,200,000
Council Tax benefit	7,105,000
Revenue support grant	3,214,000
Payment received from NNDR pool	4,310,000
Business rate collectible	
(after deductions for losses & ratepayers)	11,460,000
Cash received from business ratepayers	11,135,000
Interest received	90,000
Cost of collection business rate	260,000
Business rate refund	50,000
Community charge income 1992/93	455,000
Contribution to 1992/93 deficit by Dogtown	1,600,000
Cash received from Council Taxpayer	19,000,000

Balances as at 31/3/94	Arrears	Prepayments
	£	£
Council Tax	670,000	40,000
Business Rate	740,000	30,000

You are required to prepare:

- A list of items to be recorded in the general fund not required in the collection fund.
- The Collection Fund Revenue Account.
- The Council Tax Income and Taxpayers accounts.
- The National Non Domestic Rate income and ratepayers accounts.

CHAPTER 14

CENTRAL GOVERNMENT FINANCIAL FRAMEWORK

The purpose of this Chapter is to cover the financial framework in Central Government. The following areas are covered:

- financing of Central Government;

- the composition of Government Expenditure;

- management of public expenditure;

- setting the level of public expenditure PES;

- the Estimate Process;

- the cash limit system;

- monitoring;

- reporting to Parliament;

- budgetary reform;

- changes in structure of Central Government; and

- development of Agencies.

The information is intended to provide you with an overview. You should supplement your knowledge in this area with further background reading.

Financing of Central Government

Central Government maintains two major accounts, a National Loans Fund Account and the Consolidated Fund.

National Loans Fund

The operation of the National Loans Fund is regulated by the National Loans Fund Act 1968. The fund arranges borrowing for:

- Government;

- Nationalised Industries;

- Local Authorities;

- Other Public Corporations (including New Towns and organisations such as the Royal Mint and HMSO); and

- Private Sector bodies (for example Housing Associations).

The Public Works Loans Board is the local authorities arm of the National Loans Fund.

Loans are raised to refinance the National Debt and to finance the Central Government Borrowing Requirement (CGBR). The CGBR consists of net borrowing by the National Loans Fund plus other adjustments, as shown below.

	£ million 1991/92
National Loans Fund	
Consolidated Fund surplus (+)/deficit(-)	-12,715
National Loans Fund net loans (+) and advances(-)	243
Total net borrowing (+) net repayment (-) by the National Loans Fund	12,472
Other central government funds and accounts	
National Insurance Fund	3,120
Exchange Equalisation Account	-1,781
Paymaster General's accounts	-1,724
Accounts managed by the National Debt Commissioners	-176
Northern Ireland funds and accounts	-50
National Savings accrued interest adjustment	701
Other adjustments	347
Total net borrowing (+)/lending(-) by other central government funds and accounts	437
Central Government Borrowing Requirement (+)/Debt Repayment (-)	12,909

The National Loans Fund accounts for receipts and payments within the financial year. The example below sets out a specimen of the Payments and Receipts account. The account distinguishes between transactions which increase or reduce the Central Government Borrowing Requirement/Debt Repayment (CGBR/DR) and those which finance it.

You can see that the example accounts show the NLF was required to finance the Consolidated Fund deficit for the year of £12,715,490,000. If the Consolidated Fund had a surplus, the surplus would be transferred to the NLF account.

National Loans Fund

Account of Receipts and Payments
In the year ended 31 March 1992

	£000
RECEIPTS	
Transactions determining the CGBR	
National Debt	
Interest on Loans	5,925,137
Payment from the Consolidated Fund	8,943,080
Other Receipts	1,822,653
	16,690,870
Loans Repaid	7,536,362
Total	24,227,232
Transactions financing the CGBR	
National Debt: Sums borrowed	241,961,754
Exchange Equalisation Account	5,300,505
International Monetary Fund	59,826
Total	247,322,085
TOTAL RECEIPTS	271,549,317
PAYMENTS	
Transactions determining the CGBR	
Service of the National Debt	16,690,870
Loans Issued	7,293,235
Consolidated Fund Deficit	**12,715,490**
Total	36,699,595
Transactions financing the CGBR	
National Debt: Sums repaid	229,849,722
Exchange Equalisation Account	5,000,000
International Monetary Fund	-
Total	234,849,722
Total Payments	271,549,317

National Debt

The NLF account above shows only the receipts and payments for the year. Supplementary statements to the NLF receipts and payments account are produced which show the change in the National Debt. As at 31/3/91 the Total National Debt was £198,703 million. By 31/3/92 the Total National Debt was £214,528 million. You should note that these liability figures are balance sheet statements and not part of the receipts and payments account for the year.

Public Sector Borrowing Requirement

The Public Sector Borrowing Requirement (PSBR) is made up of CGBR as discussed above plus

     - Local Authority Borrowing Requirement from market and overseas, and

- Public Corporations Borrowing Requirement from market and overseas.

The table below shows the component parts of the PSBR.

		£ billion 1991/92 Outturn	
1	Central Government Borrowing Requirement on own account	11.7	
2	Local Authority Borrowing Requirement	1.7	
3	of which from : central government		0.6
4	market and overseas		1.0
5	Public Corporations' Borrowing Requirement	0.3	
6	of which from : central government		0.6
7	market and overseas		-0.2
8	**Public Sector Borrowing Requirement**	**13.8**	
	Central Government Borrowing requirement (lines 1+ 3 + 6)	12.9	

The policy of the Government is to restrict the level of public sector expenditure in order to reduce the PSBR. However the change in the economic climate has resulted in a swing from Public Sector debt repayment to borrowing. In 1990/91 Central Government Debt Repayment was £2,459 million. In 1991/92 the change in the economy and lower taxation receipts resulted in a Central Government Borrowing Requirement of £12,909 million.

The Consolidated Fund

Receipts from taxation are received directly into the Consolidated Fund. Examples of the types of income are as follows:

- Inland Revenue Taxation Receipts;

- Customs and Excise duty;

- Vehicle Excise duty;

- National Insurance income; and

- Miscellaneous income.

Payments from the Consolidated Fund

There are two types of payment from the Consolidated Fund:

- Standing services; and

- Supply services.

<u>Standing Services</u>

These services are regarded as essential so they do not need annual approval from Parliament. The payments are to independent servants, thus standing services are made to the following groups:

- Judges;

- Comptroller and Auditor General; and

- Other payments for example the Civil list and the expenses of returning officers (Parliamentary elections).

You should be aware of the recent reduction of the Civil List as well as the recent development that Her Majesty the Queen will pay tax on Her income into the Consolidated Fund.

There is a different category of standing service which does not require annual debate. The payments are approved once and for all and include following:

- Payments to the NLF for the service of National Debt;

- Northern Ireland: share of taxes, etc; and

- Payments to the European Communities, etc.

<u>Supply Services</u>

These are the services supplied by government departments. These services are debated by Parliament before the expenditure plans are accepted. The expenditure must be approved by a vote in the House of Commons. The Government proposes the expenditure plans and Parliament is required to approve it.

There are more than 190 Supply Services funded from the Consolidated fund. Examples are :

- Defence;

- Other government departments e.g. Department of Environment, Transport etc;

- National Audit Office; and

- Grants to local government.

Any surplus in the Consolidated Fund account is paid into the National Loans Fund. Any deficit in the Consolidated Fund account for the year is funded by a transfer from the National Loans Fund.

An example of the Consolidated Fund account is shown below. You should note that there was a deficit of £12,715,490,000. This deficit is financed by the National Loans Fund transfer.

Consolidated Fund

Account for Receipts and Payments in the Year ended 31 March 1992

	£000
Receipts	
Tax Revenue	
Inland Revenue	79,509,574
Customs and Excise	61,826,961
Vehicle Excise Duty	2,945,267
National Insurance Surcharge	-
	144,281,802
Repayments from the Contingencies Fund	4,400,000
Other Receipts	27,192,987
Deficit met from the National Loans Fund	**12,715,490**
	188,590,279
Payments	
Supply Services	168,702,687
Standing Services:	
Payment to the National Loans Fund for service of National Debt	8,943,080
Northern Ireland: share of taxes, etc	2,944,844
Payments to the European Communities	3,323,309
Other	121,359
	15,332,592
Issues to the Contingencies Fund	4,555,000
	188,590,279

The main receipts generated by the **Inland Revenue** are from:

- Income Tax;

- Corporation Tax;

- Capital Gains Tax;

- Inheritance Tax;

- Stamp Duties; and

- Petroleum Revenue tax.

The main receipts generated by **Customs and Excise** are from Value Added Tax, Hydrocarbon Oils and Tobacco. Other sources of revenue are from car tax, spirits, beer wine, cider betting and gaming, customs duties, agricultural levies and other duties.

In the examination as part of a central government account question, you may be asked about the inter relationship between the National Loans Fund and the Consolidated Fund. You should understand the principles of the two accounts and the inter relationship between them.

In the above example a deficit on the Consolidated Fund of £12,715,490,000 was met from finance by the National Loans Fund.

The Composition of Government Expenditure Plans

The following is an example of the Government's own expenditure plans. Only the figures for 1992/93 are shown below although estimated outturn figures would also be shown for the year in which the plan is prepared eg 1991/2. The figures are based on a series of totals

Central Government's own expenditure
+
Total Public Corporations (excl. Nat. Industries) eg. grants
= Total Central Government's Own Expenditure

Total Central Government's Own Expenditure
+
Central Government Support for Local Authorities
+
Financing Requirement of Nationalised Industries
+
Reserve
-
Privatisation Proceeds
+/-
Adjustments
= Public Expenditure Planning Total

Public Expenditure Planning Total
+
Local Authority Self Financed Expenditure
+
Central Government Debt Interest
+/-
Adjustments
= General Government Expenditure

The Public Expenditure Planning Total (PEPT) excludes some public sector expenditure but includes the payments by Central Government to other public sector bodies. The General Government Expenditure (GGE) forms the basis of the planning figures in PES. The different sectors of Public Sector expenditure can be classified as follows:

CGOE   Provides clear monitoring of items under the Government's own direct control;

PEPT   Takes account of items not necessarily totally controllable by the Government, for example privatisation receipts which depend on market conditions; and

GGE   Includes local authorities' self financed expenditure which is not controllable other than via capping etc.

The example below sets out the scale of the sums involved:

1992/93	£m
Central Government's own expenditure (pay, grants, subsidies)	167,500
Public Corporations (excluding Nationalised Industries) (Development Corporations , BBC, NHS Trusts)	1,225
Total Central Governments' Own Expenditure	168,775
Central Govt. support for local authorities (Revenue Support Grant NDR payments)	58,458
Financing Nationalised Industries	3,446
Reserve	4,000
Privatisation Proceeds	8,000
Public Expenditure Planning Total	226,629
Public Expenditure Planning Total	226,629
+ Local Authority self financed expenditure	8,500
+ Central Government Debt Interest	16,500
+/- Other Adjustments	4,500
General Government Expenditure	256,400

New Control Total

With effect from 1993/94 the Government aims to achieve its objective of reducing the share of national income taken by public spending, by using a new control total (NCT) which replaces the planning total. Compared with the planning total, the changes in the NCT are; exclusion of cyclical social security and privatisation proceeds; and inclusion of local authority self financed expenditure (LASFE). LASFE is included because the Government influences and restrains it through grant, capping and receipts rules.

Management of Public Expenditure

The management of public expenditure involves the allocation of the total planned spend over different programmes and parts of the public sector. The process has four key stages:

Planning	the Public Expenditure Survey Process, PES, for **medium term** financial planning;
Approval	the Supply Estimate Process for **short term** planning for the next financial year;
Monitoring	the Treasury Financial Information System for **in year** monitoring; and
Reporting	the Appropriation Accounts to Parliament.

Setting the Level of Public Expenditure - PES

Public Expenditure Planning - Plowden.

In 1961 the Government set up a committee chaired by Sir Edward Plowden with a remit to consider the process of public expenditure planning. The report recommended that the Government should carry out regular surveys of public expenditure as a whole, over a period of years ahead.

The Government of the day accepted the Plowden recommendations and established a mechanism of expenditure surveys to be carried out. The Public Expenditure Survey process was established.

Public Expenditure Survey Committee (PESC)

The Public Expenditure Survey Committee was established to evaluate the programmes of public spending required to meet the policies of the government.

The PES process is a series of programmes or draft spending plans prepared by departments. Ministers resolve the bids for resources bearing in mind the constraints to be put on public spending in order to reduce the burden of taxation on the economy.

The PES process has undergone a series of developments from being a programme related plan (without a limit on the cash resources required) to a cash related plan with cash limits on spending targets. The PES process became cash related in 1981/2 . Up to that point plans were always uprated to account for inflation. The key features of the PES process are:

- it is cash related;

- it looks three years ahead; and

- all programmes undergo careful scrutiny.

The tight scrutiny of expenditure is achieved through various initiatives as outlined below.

FMI   The Financial Management Initiative was developed in the early 1980's and involved the delegation of budgets to individual line managers. This resulted in better control of funds because individual managers could control their own budgets and monitor the impact of their spending decisions.

VFM   The National Audit Office carries out Value for Money studies on the economy efficiency and effectiveness with which departments implement the Government's policies, reporting to the Parliamentary Accounts Committee and the department.

Raynor   These studies are carried out by Treasury staff and other appointed experts
Scrutinies   and are designed to examine ways in which departments can improve efficiency and also to examine revenue generating opportunities that the departments should consider.

Work on the PES survey begins each Spring, usually just as the new financial year is beginning. Thus as the 1992/3 year starts the PES process begins to establish the expenditure plans for the 1993/94 year and the following two years. The summary on the next page sets out the broad timetable.

PES Timetable

January	Departments review expenditure
February	Bids are prepared for years 1,2 & 3 ahead
March	Departments consider bids and compare them with the baseline from the previous year
	There may be additional bids or reduced requirements
	Departments receive Treasury guidelines for the expenditure process which includes any special features to be noted in the PES process
	Treasury set the baseline for the new year three
April	Departmental Finance Units present bids to senior management and Ministers
May	Departments send bids to Treasury
June	Discussions between Treasury and Departments over bids. Any reductions are discussed
July	PES report produced by Treasury. Cabinet considers the overall aim and decides on the plan
	Planning total set
August	Departments notified by Treasury of any changes to their bids
September	Departments settle plans for years 1, 2, & 3
October	
November	Autumn Statement to Parliament announcing the agreed totals for public expenditure for years 1,2,& 3
	An economic forecast is included
December	Departments prepare tables for the Departmental Reports (formerly the Public Expenditure White Paper)
January	
February	Departmental Reports set out in more detail aims objectives and targets linking the Public Expenditure plans to the Supply Estimates.
March	Supply Estimates produced for the Departments

The recent changes to the PES process are the new Departmental Reports which replace the old Public Expenditure White Paper and the need for departments to present plans to the Treasury via the responsible Minister. There is less direct negotiation between departments and Treasury.

The Supply Estimates

The Supply Estimate is the first stage in the annual procedure known as the Supply Procedure. The Government requests and then Parliament authorises issues from the Consolidated Fund needed for the bulk of Central Government Expenditure.

The amounts in the Supply Estimates are based on the plans set out in PES but contain more detail.

The Supply Estimates are presented to Parliament in the Spring, usually on Budget Day. Each Supply Estimate or "vote" is accounted for by one department. However a department can have more than one vote. The department's vote can be examined by the relevant select Committee and can be debated in the House of Commons on an Estimate Day.

Appropriation Act

The Appropriation Act gives Parliamentary Authority for the issue of amounts voted by Parliament. The Act is passed each year just before the Summer Recess. The authority applies only to the current financial year. It lapses at the end of the financial year so that any underspend must be surrendered.

The financial year starts on 1st April each year before the Appropriation Act is passed in the Summer. Therefore some form of temporary approval to start spending money from 1st April is needed.

Vote on Account

Parliament does not approve the Estimates until the Appropriation Act in the summer. However Departments need cash to pay bills at the start of the new financial year on 1st April. The Vote on Account gives the authority for issues from the Consolidated Fund to meet expenses from 1st April until the Appropriation Act is passed in the Summer. The Vote on account is usually presented in November of the preceding year. It seeks a provision of about 45% of expenditure authorised in that current year to keep the department going for the first few months of the next year.

Supplementary Estimates

The Government may need to use Supplementary Estimates to ask Parliament for authority for extra expenditure. These can be used at various times of the year and are referred to as Winter Spring or Summer Supplementaries.

A Supplementary Estimate may not request any more cash. For example a department may request permisssion to use Excess Authorised Receipts to fund additional expenditure. Authorised receipts are called Appropriations in Aid. They are used to offset expenditure but can only be used up to the amount in the Estimate. Thus if a department gets more receipts than expected it may wish to amend the Estimate to use these receipts to offset expenditure. Thus the department will get less net grant, more receipts and be able to spend the same cash sum.

<u>Revised Estimate</u>

A revised Estimate can be submitted to replace the original only up to the point the Appropriation Act or Consolidated Act is passed.

<u>Excess Vote</u>

If expenditure exceeds the sum voted in a financial year and no Supplementary Estimate can be sought the department must apply to Parliament for an Excess Vote. The department may be examined by the Public Accounts Committee.

The difference between an Excess Vote and a Supplementary Estimate is that a Supplementary Estimate is a request to Parliament to approve revised expenditure plans **within the financial year.**

An Excess Vote is used by a department **after the financial year**. It is used because after the year has finished it transpires that the department has spent more than the sum approved in the Estimate. Technically although the department has already spent the money, if an excess vote has occurred, it must still get approval from Parliament for the excess expenditure.

A department's Estimate is prepared as a result of the PES planning process. It sets out the plans in more detail and will follow the format shown below.

Class and Vote Number	The **class** contains a group of Estimates covering a department or departments included in the departmental report. The **vote** is an individual Supply Estimate. For example in Class X, The Dept. for Education, there are six votes which make up the class
Title	Identifies the Department e.g.Office of Population Censuses and Surveys
Part 1 Ambit of the Vote	This describes what the expenditure is for, e.g. staff costs and related expenses to carry out surveys and is applied to the Appropriation Act which follows in early Summer
Part 2 Subheads	These are chart of account codes grouped into functions called subheads e.g. Pay subhead, General Admin. subhead etc.. The level of spending is shown for each subhead but Parliament gives authority for the **net** expenditure in the Ambit of the Vote. A Department can vire between subheads but does not need Parliament's authority. It seeks authority from Treasury for virement.

Gross Total (of the Vote)	£14,000,000
Receipts	£10,000,000
Net Grant	£ 4,000,000

Part 3 Extra Receipts   This details extra receipts that are payable to
                                          the Consolidated Fund

The totals of each **vote** in a class add up to a class total. The class total is detailed in the
Departmental Reports. The total of all Departmental Estimates plus adjustments equals the
Public Expenditure Planning Total.

The Cash Limit System

Expenditure programmes are usually set cash limits. The exceptions are those services that are
demand related, for example Social Security Benefits where policy determines the rates to be
applied and the outturn depends on the number of claimants, i.e. the demand.

Where a department is subject to a cash limit, the limit is usually on the gross provision.

Example. A department is voted £10,000,000 and £1,000,000 of authorised receipts. It can
spend up to £10,000,000 and no more. The grant will be £9,000,000 i.e. the net of the gross
estimated spend less receipts. If the department only achieves £500,000 receipts it can only
spend £9,500,000.

As this department is cash limited it cannot spend more than £10,000,000. If it receives say
£2,000,000 of receipts (£1,000,000 more than the authorised sum of receipts) it must surrender
the excess £1,000,000. It cannot use them for example to fund £11,000,000 of expenditure.

A department which underspends must surrender the underspend. The surrender is made the
following financial year after the audit has been completed by the National Audit Office (NAO)
and the sum to be surrendered confirmed. Excess receipts are surrendered to the Consolidated
Fund.

Monitoring

The Treasury Financial Information System or FIS is the monitoring system. It is a single
integrated computer system in which public expenditure plans, Supply Estimates and monitoring
data are held.

The key parts of the FIS system are:

> -profiles of payments and receipts for departmental
> votes and large subheads, maintained on a quarterly
> basis;
>
> -analysis of the public expenditure system (APEX)
> which provides monthly actual cash expenditure and
> details by economic category for example on running
> costs or pay or capital programmes;
>
> - a system of payment returns that compare actual
> outturn with profiled expenditure and annual outturn;
> and
>
> - a computer system which stores profiled figures and
> produces comparison reports.

Actual expenditure details are obtained from two sources; the APEX system operated by the Paymaster General's Office (PGO i.e. the departmental banker) and half yearly outturn return forms from the departments. The APEX system relies on the information that departments provide to the Paymaster General's Office. Thus payment schedules and interdepartmental transfers contain APEX analysis codes as well as the usual transaction details. In this way total expenditures by categories can be monitored by department, vote and globally as required.

APEX is used to summarise the accumulated total of departmental expenditure for central monitoring purposes. It is also used by departments to monitor their own financial systems and check that the correct details have been entered.

Reporting to Parliament

The Accounting Officer is required by statute to prepare an Appropriation Account after the end of the financial year. This is a cash based account of the receipts to and payments from each vote.

The Appropriation Account is covered in more detail in the next chapter. Examination questions frequently ask for the preparation of a set of departmental ledgers and the Appropriation Account. You should note here that the Appropriation Account:

- is signed by the Accounting Officer;

- is prepared on a cash basis;

- compares the cash outturn with the estimate, i.e. the budget and is not therefore part of the double entry;

- contains a note comparing significant variations between outturn and the estimates for each subhead (10% variations or £500,000 whichever is the greater); and

- contains a note on losses and special payments.

The Audit of Government departments is carried out by the staff at the National Audit Office (NAO). The NAO

- is headed by the Comptroller and Auditor General (C&AG). He is responsible to Parliament and not the Government. This enhances his independent status;

- audits the Appropriation Accounts examining the regularity and propriety of the payments and receipts;

- examines the systems of financial control as well as the individual transactions;

- carries out value for money studies on expenditure which look at the economy, efficiency and effectiveness of departmental programmes;

-     under the 1983 National Audit Act has powers to examine
      fringe bodies in receipt of Government money; and

-     reports to the Public Accounts Committee (PAC).

The Public Accounts Committee is a select committee of the House of Commons. It has 15 members and a quorum of 4. It is chaired by a member of the opposition.

The PAC receives reports from the C&AG and can summon Accounting Officers to be examined on matters relevant to the department. The Treasury Officer of Accounts, the C&AG and senior Treasury officials also attend the sessions.

Budgetary Reform

In March 1992 the Chancellor of the Exchequer announced in his Budget Speech that the Government would change the annual budget timetable so that tax and spending proposals could be presented to Parliament at the same time. The logic of the proposal is that spending and the taxation required to fund it can be evaluated together.

Under the system in operation up to 1992/93 the spending programme was announced in the Autumn Statement but the taxation proposals required to fund the programme were not clarified until the following March during the Chancellor's Budget Speech. This procedure was criticised by both the Armstrong Committee on Budgetary Reform (1980) and by the Treasury's Civil Service Committee (TCSC;1982).

In the Chancellor's paper 'Budgetary Reform' Cm 1867, 1992 the Chancellor identified four key advantages of moving to a unified Budget:

*   better decision taking. Ministers will be able to assess spending
        proposals in the light of the economic position and the effects
        on the level of taxation;

*   improved presentation. Producing the revenue and expenditure
        plans together will make the proposals consistent and clear;

*   more informed debate. The improved presentation would focus
        attention in Parliament and among the general public on the
        choices between public expenditure taxation and borrowing;
        and

*   benefits to taxpayers. The earlier announcement of tax
        proposals in the Finance Bill would allow taxpayers to plan their
        affairs and reduce the burden on employers to plan for the
        implementation of the new codes and changes to National
        Insurance Contributions (NIC's).

Details of the new Budget

With effect from December 1993 the Budget Statement to Parliament will cover tax proposals for the next financial year and spending proposals for the next three years. The Budget Statement will be supported by the detail currently put into the Autumn Statement, the Financial Statement and the Budget Report. The main features contained are:

- a summary of the main Budget tax and spending changes;

- analysis of departmental spending plans for the next three years;

- an explanation of key tax and National Insurance measures and their revenue consequences;

- the Government's medium term financial strategy;

- the short term economic forecast;

- detailed material on the likely outturn for the public finances in the current year and the revenue forecasts for the year ahead; and

- details on the costs of tax relief schemes.

The Finance Bill

This will follow the December Budget. It will be published after the Christmas Recess.

Provisional Collection of Taxes Act (PCTA)

This Act allows the Revenue authorities to collect taxes before the Royal Assent with the timing rules geared to a Spring Budget. The Act will be amended to replicate the current provisions but for a December Budget. Royal Assent will be required in May for the December Budget. (Under the old arrangements Royal Assent was required by 5th August for the Spring Budget.)

Implementation of the Budget Proposals

The Government will decide whether taxation changes come into effect immediately or with effect from the new tax year, 6th April. Income tax rates and allowances will continue to take effect from the start of the new tax year.

Legislation will change the point of statutory indexation used to measure personal allowances and capital allowances etc. The original legislation linked allowances to the Retail Price Index in the year to the December preceding the Spring Budget. The Government will amend the point of indexation to an earlier month which can be applied to the December calculations.

National Insurance Contribution changes were announced in the Autumn Statement to give the Contributions Agency at the Department of Social Security time to implement the changes by the following April. From 1993 decisions on tax and NIC's will be brought together and implemented at the same time in April.

Tax Administration

The coding exercise for implementing PAYE will be simplified. Under the old rules code statements issued in January were based on the current tax rules and sometimes required changes after the March Statement. With the Budget announced in early December most of the changes can be set up by 6th April.

Grant Settlements

The White Paper proposes to continue the Government practice of announcing local authority grant settlements in October or early November.

Main Estimates

These will be presented in March before the start of the new financial year seeking authority from Parliament for the spending plans for the year ahead.

Departmental Reports

Details of the public expenditure plans will be published in Departmental Reports and a Statistical Supplement to the Budget early in the New Year.

Short Term Economic Forecasts

These were produced with the Autumn Statement and the Spring Budget. Under the new proposals they will be published with the Budget in December and with the second forecast to be published in the Summer.

New Budgetary Timetable

The new timetable can be summarised as follows:

1992

November	1992 Autumn Statement: expenditure plans 1993-94 to 1995-96
December	

1993

January	
February	Statistical Supplement to 1992 Autumn Statement Departmental Reports
March	Budget 1993 (financial year 1993-94)
April	Finance Bill published
May	
June	
July	Finance Bill Royal Assent
August	
September	
October	
November	
December	Budget (financial year 1994-95 and expenditure plans for 1994-95 to 1996-97)

1994

January	Finance Bill published
February	Departmental Reports
March	
April	
May	Finance Bill 1994 Royal Assent

Changes in the structure of Central Government

The structure and organisation of central government constantly changes to adapt to the policies set by the Government. A complete list of organisational changes is outside the scope of this book. However examples of key changes are:

- the department of National Heritage set up after the 1992 General Election. For 1993/94 year the Department of National Heritage is Class XI with 7 votes including for example, the Museums and Galleries vote, the films, tourism, sport & broadcasting vote and the Royal Palaces and Historic Monuments vote;

- the Department of Energy is now absorbed into the Department of Trade & Industry; and

- parts of the Property Services Agency (design) have been transferred to the Private Sector, namely Tarmac the construction company. The Government Estate is managed by Property Holdings. Departments are able to acquire land and buildings as part of their Departmental Estate. The alternative is for the departments to rent the estate from Property Holdings as part of the Common User Estate (CUE). Property managed by Property Holdings and charged to a department is part of the Property Repayment System (PRS).

Property Holdings

Common User Estate	Departments occupying Common User Estate pay a rental and a maintenance charge to Property Holdings.
Departmental Estate (Freehold)	If the property is on the PRS a rental only applies to the occupying department. If the property is not on the PRS the property is capitalised by the occupying department.
Departmental Estate (Leasehold)	If the property is on the PRS a rental only applies to the occupying department. If the property is not on the PRS the type of lease determines whether the department pays a rental only (operating lease) or capitalises the property (finance lease). The rules of SSAP21 apply.

Development of Agencies

The purpose of this section is to give an overview of the development of Agencies under the Next Steps Initiative. Details on Agency Accounts are covered in the next chapter.

In 1988 the Next Steps Initiative is based on a report by Sir Robin Ibbs aimed at improving the management and quality of service in Central Government. The programme was carried forward until recently by Sir Peter Kemp at the Treasury. The head of the Next Steps team is now Richard Mottram.

The initiative aims to set up smaller units of Government departments as autonomous or semi autonomous agencies that will run their affairs on a more business-like basis.

Executive Agencies can be part of a department (an executive unit) or a department in their own right. Examples of Agencies range from trading funds such as Companies House to On Vote Agencies such as the Veterinary Medicines Directorate or the Public Record Office.

Trading Fund Agencies

Trading Fund Agencies are Agencies which are able to fund their expenditure from revenues raised through operating activities i.e. from fees and charges. There are currently eight Trading Fund Agencies. Included in the trading fund agencies is HMSO which was a trading fund organisation before the Next Steps Initiative, but has Agency Status.

On Vote Agencies

On Vote Agencies tend to rely on a vote from Parliament to fund a proportion of their activities. This is because they can raise only a small proportion of their income from fees. In these circumstances On Vote Agencies can negotiate with Treasury and the responsible Minister for certain flexibilities in the vote financing regime, for example to carry forward allowances on any under spend or permission to use excess authorised receipts raised.

Number of Agencies

There are now 76 Agencies, 30 Customs and Excise Executive Units and 34 Inland Revenue Executive Units established. Executive Units are autonomous units within a larger department which have agency style flexibilities and duties. Together Executive Agencies and Executive Units employ about 290,000 Civil Servants. There are at least another 29 candidates being considered for Agency Status.

Establishing Agencies

The process of establishing an Agency involves the preparation of a comprehensive plan called a framework document. The framework document includes:

- a statement of aims and objectives;

- a planning framework;

- management proposals;

- reporting and accountability procedures;

- finance arrangements;

-   accounting systems; and

-   personnel pay and training arrangements.

The overall aim is to ensure that the Chief Executive of the Agency has the personal responsibility for the success of the Agency and the freedom to manage it. Tough performance objectives are set by Ministers responsible for the Agency and there is effective monitoring of the performance of the Agency.

Statement of Aims and Objectives

The aims and objectives are set out clearly in the framework document and may include:

-   quality of service targets;

-   quantified cost reduction objectives;

-   self financing targets where revenue opportunities are sufficient; and

-   recovery of full costs for some services provided to users where the agency is unable to finance itself fully.

While the Minister responsible for the department sets the objectives, the day to day management required to achieve the objectives is delegated to the Agency.

Planning Framework

Agencies are required to produce a five year corporate plan. The first year is detailed in the Business Plan and indicative targets are included for later years.

The planning details will include:

-   demand analysis forecasts;

-   unit cost targets for measurable services;

-   quality of service targets;

-   fees and charges strategy;

-   manpower and cash resources summary plans; and

-   Information System Strategy details.

Management of the Agency

A Chief Executive is appointed with relevant management and business experience. The Chief Executive may be someone from the private sector with suitable commercial business experience or a suitably experienced senior Civil Servant. The Chief Executive is responsible for:

- the preparation of the Corporate Plan;

- annual bids for finance and resources;

- capital Investment plans and their implementation;

- effectiveness of the Agency;

- efficiency of the Agency; and

- preparation of the Annual Report and Accounts. In the case of On Vote Agencies they will be required to produce accruals accounts in the Annual Report and a reconciliation to the Vote Accounts. The Vote Accounts will still be presented to Parliament in the usual way.

Reporting and Accountability

Agencies work towards achieving the objectives laid down by Parliament and the Minister responsible for the Department which sponsors the Agency.

Written responses to MP's are usually delegated to the Chief Executive.

Public Accounts Committee

The Permanent Secretary will continue to answer questions from the Public Accounts Committee but the Chief Executive should attend the hearing.

Parliamentary Commissioner for Administration

The Parliamentary Commissioner for Administration (the Ombudsman) will be able to report to Parliament on aspects of the administration of Executive Agencies.

Agency Audit

Agencies are audited by the National Audit Office (NAO). In certain cases the NAO may contract out the Audit of Agencies but the final review of the Accounts and the Audit Certificate are signed off by the C&AG.

Agencies are required to produce annual reports containing the accounts. The reports are to be produced before the Summer Recess. This puts pressure on the NAO to complete a large number of audits before the Recess whereas under the normal procedures for Vote Accounts the accounts are not signed off until the Autumn. Under these circumstances Agencies have permission to include draft Vote Accounts with a clear statement to the effect that the NAO have not completed their audit.

Agencies frequently use performance indicators to award performance related pay to their staff. Where such measures are in operation, the NAO audits the performance against targets to ensure that the pay awards disclosed in the accounts are authorised, accurate and valid.

Financing of Agencies

Trading Fund Agencies are financed by **Public Dividend Capital** and or loans from the **National Loans Fund**.

Where the returns from operating activities are likely to vary year on year, **Public Dividend Capital** is used to finance the Trading Fund Agency. This allows for **variable dividends** to be paid to the Consolidated Fund, depending on performance in the year. The Government holds the public dividend shares. This method of finance equates to the share capital finance used in the private sector, where dividends can be varied by the Directors according to the profits the business generates each year.

An example of a Trading Fund Agency financed by Public Dividend Capital is the Royal Mint. Examination of recent Royal Mint Accounts shows how the dividend can vary year on year. For 1990/91 financial year the dividend payable was £14,000,000. In 1991/92 financial year the dividend payable fell to £10,000,000, reflecting the lower turnover in 1991/92.

A loan from the **National Loans Fund** requiring fixed interest payments to be made each year is more suited to a Trading Fund Agency that can ensure a **steady return** from operating activities. In the private sector a company with significant loan finance (a highly geared company) would require more certain operating profits in order to be able to service the debt. Without a more certain profit stream a business would be unlikely to persuade banks etc. to part with the loan.

The Vehicle Inspectorate Agency has a significant proportion of finance from loans. Presumably the number of vehicles requiring statutory inspections is fairly stable therefore the Agency is more able to maintain turnover and profits year on year. The 1991/92 report shows balance sheet finance of long term loans from the Department of Transport to be £14,246,000 as at 31/3/92.

On Vote Agencies are financed each year by a vote approved by Parliament. On Vote Agencies are allowed more flexibility than normal departments funded by a vote. Thus although they continue to be part of the PES system they may be able to negotiate with Treasury to:

- adjust to a net control system to allow extra receipts raised by the Agency to be used to finance extra expenditure rather than be surrendered to the Consolidated Fund;

- carry forward an additional percentage of Capital under spend to the next financial year; and

- carry forward an additional percentage of Running Costs under spend to the next financial year.

Accounting Systems

The systems in operation vary and reflect the diversity of Agency operations. Some On Vote Agencies are financed by several votes from other departments. These Agencies are required to produce accruals accounts but also maintain detailed Vote Account records. Their accounting systems and reported accounts are different from the accounts produced by a Trading Fund Agency which would produce accounts more along the lines of a commercial business.

After an On Vote Agency is set up it continues to produce its Vote Accounts and an Appropriation Account each year. It must also develop its accounting systems to be able to produce accruals accounts within two years of Agency status. By adopting accruals based accounting systems the Agency should:

- produce accounts to a format consistent with Treasury Guidance;

- produce Management Accounts that will ensure effective monitoring of all its resources;

- produce Accounts that can be reconciled to the Vote Account; and

- produce Accounts that will satisfy the audit scrutiny of the NAO, provide adequate security of data and ensure accurate and comprehensive accounts are produced.

Personnel, Pay and Training

Agency Status ensures greater flexibility of operating conditions and more authority is delegated regarding the appointment, promotion and grading of staff. Agencies can recruit certain staff grades directly or use the Recruitment Agency Service (RAS). Increasingly Agencies are establishing their own procedures for recruitment of many different staff grades.

Summary of Agencies

Agencies are a growth area of Central Government. Nearly half the nation's Civil Servants are now working in Agencies.

There are now 76 Agencies and 64 Executive Units in Customs & Excise and Inland Revenue.

Only eight Agencies are Trading Funds. The remainder are financed by a vote. Many On Vote Agencies are at an early stage of development and to date very few have achieved the requirement to produce accruals accounts in addition to their cash based Vote Accounts. All Trading Fund Agencies produce accruals accounts.

All agencies are using the flexibility delegated to them to allow management to use their initiative to improve quality of service and efficiency. The emphasis is on the need to monitor and use resources effectively. The requirement to produce accrual accounts forces On Vote Agencies to maintain asset registers and account for stocks, whereas vote accounting did not require accounting for assets after the year in which the expenditure was incurred. The use of asset registers and stock accounting will encourage better financial planning, costing and use of assets.

The setting of targets by ministers and the monitoring of performance against targets by the NAO is putting pressure on Agencies to improve their quality of service to the public.

Conclusion

This chapter gives a brief insight into the Central Government Framework. You should supplement this material with further background reading.

However by reading this chapter you should understand in outline:

- the financing of Central Government by the National Loans Fund and taxation revenues which are accounted for in the Consolidated Fund;

- the relationship between the National Loans Fund and the Consolidated Fund and the purpose of each account;

- the budgetary process of PES;

- the cash limit system;

- financial monitoring of the Treasury's Financial Information System (FIS) and APEX;

- Departmental Appropriation Accounts and Agency Accounts and their audit by the NAO;

- the proposed new December Budget procedures starting December 1993 which will combine the plans for the next financial year's taxation with the next three year PES details; and

- some key changes to Government structure and the growth in the number of Agencies.

Accounting for Departmental Vote Accounts and Agency Accounts are covered in the next chapter. An outline format for an On Vote Agency is included.

CHAPTER 15

CENTRAL GOVERNMENT ACCOUNTS

The first point to note about Central Government examination questions is that they tend to be easy. The problem for many students is that they are not familiar with the jargon used in Central Government because very few CIPFA students work in Central Government.

However with just a little time spent getting to know the terminology you will see that most questions can be tackled easily and full marks obtained for preparing the accounts. In addition it is worthwhile keeping abreast of Central Government finance because there is a need for accountants in Government departments and agencies and you may wish to take advantage of the career opportunities they offer.

There are three types of accounts that can be set:

- Government Department / Appropriation Account;

- Off Vote Agency Account; and

- On Vote Account.

Government Department / Appropriation Account

This is the most common form of examination question. You will be required to prepare the journals, draw up the ledger accounts and prepare the Appropriation Account.

Most Government Departments are financed by a Vote from Parliament. This is effectively a cash grant for the year and the accounting entries are quite straightforward.

Off Vote Agency Accounts

These accounts are generally trading fund accounts. Off Vote Agencies are organisations which are able to fund themselves from income through a trading activity rather than from a grant. You will be required to draw up a Profit and Loss Account, Balance Sheet and Cash Flow Reconciliation Statement.

You should be familiar with this style of question from your commercial accounting knowledge. The main differences are that these agencies are financed by Public Dividend Capital and advances from the National Loans Fund.

On Vote Agency Accounts

This type of Agency is still linked to the Vote Accounting system. Thus although required to produce accruals accounts as an agency, they must also produce Vote accounts and surrender surpluses each year.

Very few On Vote Agencies have produced auditable accruals accounts and you are unlikely to be asked to produce these.

Other knowledge required

Often examination questions in Central government will test the candidate's knowledge of the relationship between the <u>National Loans Fund</u> and the <u>Consolidated Fund</u>. A full accounts question on this area is unlikely, but you should refer to the previous chapter to make sure you understand the relationship between the two accounts and the purpose of each.

Vote Accounts, Off Vote Agency Accounts and On Vote Agency accounts are covered in the following sections

Central Government Vote Accounts / Appropriation Accounts

There are some key features which distinguish Central Government accounts from commercial accounts:

- accounting is done on a cash basis. there are no accruals etc. This makes examination questions easier because you only have to account for cash payments and receipts;

- there is no fixed asset accounting. This means land, buildings and equipment are not accounted for as balance sheet items nor are they depreciated. Departments only account for the cash paid on fixed assets. they may have asset registers but they do not form part of the accounts; and

- any surplus of grant over actual spend is surrendered the following year. The surplus is not accumulated. A deficit will be set off against next years grant.

In order to prepare the ledger accounts for a Central Government department you need to know about certain key terms. What follows is a list of key terms and the accounting entries required. If you need more information refer to the previous chapter.

Supply Estimate

This is the estimate of the money the department will need for the coming year. The Department will only receive the <u>net total</u> from Parliament.

Supply Estimate

Department of Licences

		£
Gross Total	:	4,000,000
Receipts	:	1,000,000
Net Total		3,000,000

This department will receive the net £3,000,000. It can spend up to £4,000,000 but the shortfall of £1,000,000 must come from receipts, i.e. money the department might get from fees and charges.

Vote on Account

Parliament takes some time to consider the Estimates. They may not be approved at the start of the financial year, 1st April. In the meantime the Department is given money to keep going usually about 1/2 of the net grant, in this case £1.5m . This is the Vote on Account. Entries are:

	Dr. £	Cr. £.
Consolidated Fund	1,500,000	
Parliamentary Grant A/c		1,500,000
being receipt of Vote on A/c		

Appropriation Act

This is passed in the summer. It :

- authorises the issue of the balance of funds needed by departments (the total less the sum advanced in the Vote on Account);

- appropriates the sum for the year for the purposes mentioned in the schedule to the act. the schedule includes the "Ambit of the Vote" (what the money is to be spent on); and

- authorises the department to apply receipts to offset expenditure up to the amount set. In the above example no more than £1,000,000 can be used to offset expenditure. These receipts are called Appropriations in Aid.

Parliamentary Grant Account (PGA). (Income)

This account records the amount of grant available for expenditure. It represents income to the department. The grant is always the net amount a department can spend. In the exam, if you see Gross Expenses of £4,000,000 and Receipts Authorised of £1,000,000, the net grant is £3,000,000.

Consolidated Fund (Debtor)

The Consolidated Fund holds the money that is due to the department. At the start of the year money is due from the Consolidated Fund to the department. It is therefore a debtor when the amount of grant is decided.

Suppose the Department of Licences is granted £4,000,000 less £1,000,000 of authorised receipts. The entries for the net amount are:

	Dr. £	Cr. £.
Consolidated Fund	3,000,000	
Parliamentary Grant A/c		3,000,000

375

Department of Licences

Consolidated Fund		Parliamentary Grant A/c	
£	£	£	£
PGA 3,000,000			C. Fund 3,000,000

Paymaster General (PMG or PGO) (the banker)

The Paymaster General is the banker for the department. Remember when cash goes <u>into</u> bank the entry is <u>debit</u> PGO. The <u>credit</u> is to the Consolidated Fund because this reduces the amount the Fund owes the department.

Suppose the Department of Licences draws £1,500,000 from the Consolidated Fund into the bank (PGO) in order to allow payment of bills.

The entries are:

	Dr.	Cr.
	£	£.
PGO (Bank)	1,500,000	
Consolidated Fund		1,500,000

Department of Licences

Consolidated Fund		PGO	
£	£	£	£
	PGO 1,500,000	C Fund 1,500,000	

Remember in the exam do not get mixed up between the banker, PGO, and the Parliamentary Grant Account, PGA. It is a good idea to write "banker" next to PGO to remind yourself which is which in your ledgers. Also do not be confused if you see the abbreviation PMG for banker. PMG and PGO are the same thing.

Orders Payable

This account is used to record payable orders issued to meet expenses. You might think that money should come out of the bank account, PGO. Indeed it does, but first the credit is posted to a suspense account , orders payable.

Government Departments send payable orders to the payee. The payee will present it for banking, but the banker (Paymaster General) will only pay it if the transaction is recorded on the schedule forwarded by the department. The schedule or <u>warrant</u> is a list of authorised transactions issued separately to PGO thus serving as a control over altered or unauthorised payable orders.

The payable orders account can be used to hold transactions pending clearance. In the exam you may decide it is not necessary to use the account and just make payments via the bank (PGO) in order to save time.

However for completeness the following examples show how the payment works.

The Department of Licences makes a payment of £5,000 for general administrative expenses.

	Dr. £	Cr. £.
(1) General Admin Expenses	5,000	
(1) Orders payable		5,000
being the record of the expense and the issue of the payable order		

Department of Licences

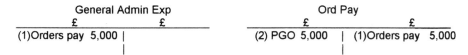

General Admin Exp			Ord Pay	
£	£	£		£
(1)Orders pay 5,000 |		(2) PGO 5,000 |	(1)Orders pay 5,000	

The following week the firm banks the cheque and the Paymaster General makes the payment.

	Dr. £	Cr. £.
(2) Orders payable	5,000	
(2) Paymaster General		5,000
being the payment of cash and the clearance of the payable order		

Department of Licences

```
              PGO
        £               £
                |   Orders pay  5,000
                |
```

The payable orders account is now cleared and the credit comes from the PGO (i.e. cash out).

Suppose a second payment of £3,000 to a firm for general administrative expenses is never banked. the transactions are:

	Dr. £	Cr. £.
(1) General Admin	3,000	
(1) Orders payable		3,000
being the record of the expense and issue of payable order.		

The cheque is never cleared. Three months later the charge to the vote, expense ledger is cleared.

	Dr. £	Cr. £.
(2) Orders payable	3,000	
(2) General Admin		3,000
being the removal of the expense and clearing of orders payable.		

General Admin					Orders Payable				
	£		£			£			£
(1)	3,000	(2)	3,000		(2)	3,000	(1)		3,000

The expense is now cleared from the ledger.

You may find that the operation of the orders payable account is not necessary, if the exam question is quite straightforward. However some questions will require the operation of the orders payable account. I suggest you always operate the account for practice.

Subhead (Expenses Ledger)

A government department will have a whole range of expense codes in the chart of accounts. These are grouped into subtotals called subheads. This is done because Parliament require only certain details, for example, pay costs, other administrative costs, works costs and other capital expenditure.

In the exam you will be given the figures for a subhead as one expense item. Just be aware that it represents several expense codes. For example Salaries = Pay, Superannuation, National Insurance etc.

We treat subheads in the same way that we treat expenses. They are debit entries.

Suppose the Department of Licences pays £50,000 of running cost bills in Subhead B1. The entries are:

	Dr. £	Cr. £.
Running costs (B1)	50,000	
Orders payable		50,000
being the issue of the payment and recording of the expense.		

Then the Payable Order is cleared:

	Dr. £	Cr. £.
Orders Payable	50,000	
PMG (ie bank)		50,000
being the clearance of the payable order and issue of the cash to supplier.		

The Estimates set out the authorised expenditure by subhead. Under certain circumstances departments may apply for virement and transfer allowance from one subhead to another as required.

Appropriations in Aid (A in A) (Authorised Receipts)

These are receipts that a department is authorised to use to offset its expenses. In the Department of Licences example, the grant is £4,000,000 and Authorised Appropriations in Aid (A In A) is £1,000,000. The net grant is therefore £3,000,000 and the department needs £1,000,000 of authorised Appropriations in Aid. The department can only use up to £1,000,000 of authorised receipts to make up the £4m granted spend.

Any excess over £1,000,000 must not be used and must be surrendered to the Consolidated Fund. Any under achievement of receipts will mean the department will not be able to spend £4m. For example if the department received no receipts at all it could only spend £3m.

The entries for receipts are as follows. Suppose the Department of Licences receives £1,000,000 of receipts. The cash goes into the bank (PGO) and is credited to Appropriations in Aid:

	Dr. £	Cr. £.
PGO (Bank)	1,000,000	
A.in A.		1,000,000

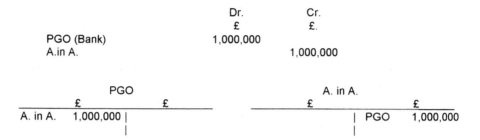

The department now has the extra £1,000,000 it needs in the bank.

The supply estimate sets out the amount of receipts the department is authorised to use to offset against expenditure. Sometimes a department will receive more receipts than it is allowed to use. It must give these receipts back to the Consolidated Fund after the audit of the accounts:

Suppose the Department of Licences actually received £1,500,000 of Appropriations in Aid. The department was authorised to use only £1,000,000 of Appropriations in Aid.

First the receipts are banked.

	Dr. £	Cr. £.
PGO (Bank)	1,500,000	
A.in A.		1,500,000
being the record of the receipts		

After the NAO have completed their audit of the accounts and agreed the amounts the surplus Appropriations in Aid are transferred to extra receipts. The account is called Consolidated Fund Extra Receipts (CFER).

	Dr. £	Cr. £.
A. in A.	500,000	
CFER		500,000
being the transfer of surplus A. in A. to Extra Receipts ready for surrender.		

Suspense Accounts

A government department may keep a series of sub-accounts or "suspense" accounts. These are accounts which are not proper to the Vote or have not yet been identified to the correct part of the Vote.

Examples of suspense accounts are:

- advances to sub accountants (petty cash) used for minor incidental expenses;

- advances to or from other Government Departments in respect of interdepartmental transactions (for example advances by departments to Property Holdings to cover rental charges);

- advances to individuals for travel and subsistence expenses;

- accounts recording losses, overpayments or erroneous payments awaiting recovery;

- accounts recording cash collected or disbursed on behalf of third parties, for example:
  - income tax, national insurance;
  - VAT; and
  - certain EC receipts payable to third parties

- certain advances from the Contingencies Fund.

In an examination question, you are likely to encounter only the first kind of suspense account - advances to sub accountants.

Sub Accountants

The journals for this type of account are straightforward. The sub accountant receives an advance of £900 from the accounting officer to meet certain expenses. Effectively he receives an imprest. The journals are

	Dr. £	Cr. £
Sub Accountant.	900	
PGO		900
being the record of a cash receipt from the PGO to sub accountant.		

Sub Accountant		PGO (Bank)	
£	£	£	£
900			900

Next the sub accountant pays £350 of travel and subsistence expenses. this is recorded in the sub accountant's cash book and the receipts and schedule forwarded to the accounts department to record the expenditure. The journal is as follows

	Dr. £	Cr. £.
Travel & Subsistence	350	
Sub Accountant		350

Travel & Subsistence			Sub Accountant		
£	£		£		£
Sub Account 350			b/f 900	T & S	350

In this way the £350 cash is charged to T&S and the advance to the sub accountant is reduced by £350.

Other Suspense Accounts

Examination questions with any other suspense account transactions are unlikely. However for completeness this section looks at one more common suspense account; the advances for pay.

Many Government Departments use the Chessington Computer Centre (CCC) to operate their payroll function.

CCC require deposits from departments to fund salary costs at the end of the month.

In addition CCC operate advances of pay for certain purposes (e.g. season ticket advances or certain housing allowances) on instructions from departments.

Cash is advanced from the department to CCC to set up a deposit:

	Dr.	Cr.
	£	£.
(1) PGO		500,000
(1) CCC Deposit Account	500,000	

At the start of the month Chessington send a summary statement referred to as the booking minute, summarising the previous months pay transactions.

Example :

	£
Payroll Costs	440,000
Advances	12,000
Recovery of Advances	1,000
Net Cash Movement	451,000
CCC Closing Balance	49,000

For example the booking minute for April would be as follows.

Booking Minute for April 19XX

	Dr.	Cr.
	£	£
Vote (March Salaries)	440,000	
Advances	12,000	
Recoveries		1,000
Bal due to CCC		451,000
	452,000	452,000

The department records the transactions in the books as follows.

	Dr. £	Cr. £.
Salaries Vote	440,000	
CCC		440,000
being record of March salaries paid from cash deposit at Chessington		

	Dr. £	Cr. £.
Pay Advances	12,000	
CCC		12,000
Pay Advance Recoveries		1,000
CCC	1,000	
being record of £12,000 of salaries advanced and recoveries of £1,000		

In April the department makes a payment to CCC as per the booking minute of £451,000 to restore the deposit ready for salaries to be paid at the end of April.

	Dr. £	Cr. £.
PGO		451,000
CCC	451,000	
being the record of the sum paid to restore the CCC deposit		

The ledgers would look like this:

```
               CCC                                    PGO
        £              £                        £              £
MARCH                    |              MARCH                     |
(1)       500,000 | Sal    440,000      b/f    1,500,000 | (1)     500,000
Pay         1,000 | Adv     12,000                       |
Recoveries        | Pay                                  |
                  |                                       |
           _____ | c/d    49,000                _____ | c/d  1,000,000
          501,000 |       452,000              1,500,000 |      1,500,000
APRIL             |                     APRIL             |
b/f        49,000 |                     b/f    1,000,000 | CCC    451,000
PGO       451,000 |                                      |
           _____ | c/d   500,000                _____ | c/d    549,000
          500,000 |       500,000              1,000,000 |      1,000,000
```

```
            Salaries                          Advances of Pay
        £              £                        £              £
MARCH                    |              MARCH                    |
CCC       440,000 |                     CCC       12,000 | CCC      1,000
                  |                                      |
           _____ | c/d   440,000                _____ | bal c/d  11,000
          440,000 |       440,000               12,000 |        12,000
bal b/f   440,000 |                     bal b/f   11,000 |
```

382

This mechanism ensures:

- cash is available at Chessington to fund departments' salary costs at the end of the month; and

- the year end March salaries can be recorded in the Vote, as the cash has already moved from the department to CCC and was paid on 31 March. Thus when the Booking Minute arrives in April the March salaries can be recorded in the March Vote. The cash paid in April is merely to restore the deposit ready for the salary bill at the end of April.

Although this transaction is common in Government Departments it is less common in an examination question. However you should be aware of how interdepartmental advances operate and the payroll advances demonstrate the mechanism. A practice question is provided at the end of the chapter.

Parliamentary Grant Account

Year End

At the end of the year the expense accounts are closed and transferred to the Parliamentary Grant Account (PGA). The authorised Appropriations in Aid are also transferred to the PGA. This gives the surplus or deficit of grant over expenditure which the department gives back. Any surplus Appropriations in Aid (authorised receipts) above the amount allowed in the Appropriation Act is surrendered.

Any receipts which are not Appropriations in Aid must also be given back. Example of such receipts may be certain sales transactions, unexpected receipts such as compensation receipts, or revoked payable orders.

The Parliamentary Grant Account is then reported to the House of Commons and the Public Accounts Committee in the form of the Appropriation Account.

Appropriation Account

This is not part of the double entry. The account records ledger totals against estimates and notes variations by subhead. It is the account of how the grant was spent. It is extracted from the cash books of the department. the Appropriation Account is a statement for non financial readers e.g. MPs. A special feature of the Appropriation Account is that it compares outturn with the budget, i.e. the estimate.

Any variation greater than 10% or £500,000 (whichever is greater) must be explained in a note to the Appropriation Account.

Conclusion

The key points to note are:

1. Funds are advanced to the PGO who acts as the banker for the Department

2. Accounting entries in the PGO account are exactly the same as cash book entries.

3. Advances from the Consolidated Fund will be made up to the net supply estimate sum.

4. A department may use only the amount of A in A authorised. Any extra A in A must be surrendered separately.

5. A Parliamentary Grant Account records the net amount of grant available. At year end cash expenditure accounts are transferred to this account to determine the surplus to surrender or the excess vote required. Cash receipts (A in A) realised up to the <u>authorised</u> amount, or the <u>realised</u> amount if lower, are also transferred to the Parliamentary Grant Account.

6. The Appropriation Account is not part of the double entry. It compares actual outturn with the estimate.

7. Virements can be carried out. Overspends reduce next year's grant amount. Underspends are surrendered the following financial year.

Finally remember that in the following examples we see only one or two expense transactions. In real life there will be hundreds going on every month.

Fully Worked Example 1

This question asks you to prepare the journals, ledgers and Appropriation Account for a small Government Department.

The following transactions relate to the supply grant of a small government department for the year ending 31 March 1992.

1. The supply grant vote for the year amounted to £20,000,000 gross. Authorised Appropriations in Aid amount to £1,000,000.

2. Of the net figure for the supply grant vote the following was received:

	£
Votes on account	10,000,000
Balance of grant	9,000,000

    The planned expenditure gross was made up as follows:

	£
Salaries	14,000,000
General expenses	1,500,000
Supplies	2,500,000
Transport	1,200,000
Miscellaneous	800,000

3. The total sum drawn by the Paymaster General amounted to £18,900,000.

4. Receipts collected during the year as Appropriations in Aid were £1,200,000.

5. Orders drawn on the Paymaster General for the year were as follows:

	£
Salaries	13,200,000
General expenses	1,600,000
Supplies	2,600,000
Transport	1,300,000
Miscellaneous	1,000,000

Required - Prepare

(a)   Ledger Accounts.

(b)   An Appropriation Account for the year ending 31 March 1992.

(c)   Define the matching concept and examine its application in the accounting system of government departments.

Tutorial Answer

1. This tells us the amount due from the fund is £20,000,000 less authorised A. in A. of £1,000,000 = £19,000,000

2.

	Dr. £	Cr. £.
Journal (1)		
Consolidated Fund	10,000,000	
Parliamentary Grant Account		10,000,000

being receipt of Vote on Account recording sum due from the Con Fund and receivable as Grant

	Dr. £	Cr. £.
Journal (2)		
Consolidated Fund	9,000,000	
Parliamentary Grant Account		9,000,000

being the balance of grant due on approval of the Appropriation Act

The information on planned expenditure goes into the Appropriation Account for comparative purposes.

3.

	Dr. £	Cr. £.
Journal (3)		
Paymaster General	18,900,000	
Consolidated Fund		18,900,000

being the cash drawn from the Con Fund into the Paymaster General (bank) to defray expenses

4.

	Dr. £	Cr. £.
Journal (4)		
Paymaster General	1,200,000	
Appropriations in Aid		1,200,000

    being record of receipts of
    Authorised A. in A. and cash
    banked by PGO

	Dr. £	Cr. £.
Journal (5)		
Appropriations in Aid (A in A)	200,000	
Consolidated Fund Extra Receipts (CFER)		200,000

    being the transfer of surplus
    A. in A. to CFER for
    surrender

5. All cash payments appear to have been cleared. You do not have to use orders payable but I have here.

	Dr. £	Cr. £.
Journal (6)		
Salaries	13,200,000	
Orders Payable		13,200,000
General Expenses	1,600,000	
Orders Payable		1,600,000
Supplies	2,600,000	
Orders Payable		2,600,000
Transport	1,300,000	
Orders Payable		1,300,000
Miscellaneous	1,000,000	
Orders Payable		1,000,000

    being record of expenditure
    and payable orders issued

	Dr. £	Cr. £.
Journal (7)		
Orders Payable	19,700,000	
PGO		19,700,000

    being payment of all payable
    orders, issue of cash by PGO
    and clearance of orders payable

Ledger accounts are as follows:

Parliamentary Grant Account

£,000		£,000	
		(1)C Fund	10,000
(9)All expense accounts	19,700	(2)C Fund	9,000
bal c/d	300	(8)A in A	1,000
	20,000		20,000
		b/f	300

Consolidated Fund Account

£,000		£,000	
(1) PGA	10,000	(3)PGO	18,900
(2) PGA	9,000		
		c/d	100
	19,000		19,000
b/f	100		

Paymaster General Office (PGO)

£,000		£,000	
(3)C Fund	18,900	(7)Ord Pay	19,700
(4)A in A	1,200		
		c/d	400
	20,100		20,100
b/f	400		

Appropriations in Aid (A. in A.)

£,000		£,000	
(5)CFER	200	(4)PGO	1,200
(8)PGA	1,000		
	1,200		1,200

Orders Payable

£,000		£,000	
(7)PGO	19,700	(6)Sal	13,200
		(6)GenExp	1,600
		(6)Supplies	2,600
		(6)Transp't	1,300
		(6)Misc	1,000
	19,700		19,700

Consolidated Fund Extra Receipts (CFER)

£,000		£,000	
		(5)A in A	200

Salaries

£,000		£,000	
(6)Orders Pay	13,200	(9)PGA	13,200

General Expenses

£,000		£,000	
(6)Orders Pay	1,600	(9)PGA	1,600

Supplies

£,000		£,000	
(6)Orders Pay	2,600	(9)PGA	2,600

Transport

£,000		£,000	
(6)Orders Pay	1,300	(9)PGA	1,300

Miscellaneous

£,000		£,000	
(6)Orders Pay	1,000	(9)PGA	1,000

At this stage the balances on the <u>authorised</u> Appropriations in Aid can be transferred to the Parliamentary Grant Account (PGA). Remenber that Appropriations in Aid up to the authorised amount can be transferred to the PGA. Any excess Appropriations in Aid are to be surrendered and must be transferred to a surplus A. in A. account. If the department realises less than the authorised amount of Appropriations in Aid then the realised amount is transferred to the PGA.

All cash expenditure whether capital in nature or running cost is also transferred to the PGA. The transfer of capital cash expenditure to the Parliamentary Grant Account is an unusual feature but is necessary in order to be able to account for how the cash grant was spent. Thus the Parliamentary Grant Account is not like an income and expenditure account which deals with operating costs alone. The Parliamentary Grant Account records **all** cash expenditure whether running cost or capital.

	Dr. £	Cr. £.
Journal (8)		
Appropriations in Aid (A in A)	1,000,000	
Parliamentary Grant Account (PGA)		1,000,000

    being transfer of authorised
    Appropriations in Aid

	Dr. £	Cr. £.
Journal (9)		
Parliamentary Grant Account	19,700,000	
Salaries		13,200,000
General Expenses		1,600,000
Supplies		2,600,000
Transport		300,000
Miscellaneous		1,000,000

    being transfer of expenses to
    the Parliamentary Grant Account

<u>Appropriation Account</u>

Small Government Department for the year ending 31/3/92

Subhead	Grant £000	Expenditure £000	Underspend £000	Overspend £000
Salaries	14,000	13,200	800	
General Expenses	1,500	1,600		100
Supplies	2,500	2,600		100
Transport	1,200	1,300		100
Miscellaneous	800	1,000		200
	20,000	19,700	800	500

Less:

	Estimated	Applied	
Appropriations in Aid	1,000	1,000	surplus to be surrendered
	19,000	18,700	300,000

Receipts
Receipts payable to Consolidated Fund

	Estimated	Realised
Receipts authorised to be used as Appropriations in Aid	1,000,000	1,200,000
Other Receipts		------
Gross Total		1,200,000
Appropriations in Aid		1,000,000
Actual sum of receipts payable separately to Con Fund		200,000

You should be able to see how the Appropriation Account statements tie in with the ledgers.

The Appropriation Account is not part of the double entry but it should agree with the ledgers. The Appropriation Account effectively compares outurn with the budget, i.e. the estimate.

The ledgers show assets and liabilities as follows.

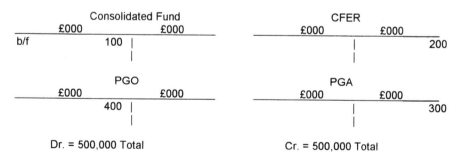

389

The Appropriation Account plus receipts statement tells us we have a total of £500,000 to surrender.

	£
Surplus to surrender from Appropriation Account	300,000
plus	
Surplus Appropriations in Aid we could not apply	200,000
	500,000

One final point. Where there is a subhead variation of £500,000 or 10%, whichever is the greater a note to the account is required explaining the variation.

A note is required for the variation in the salaries subhead. However as no explanation was given in the example do not make one up but be prepared to add a note if a reason is given in a question. Put the note at the bottom of the Appropriation Account after the receipts statement.

Fully Worked Example 2

This example requires you to eliminate internal transactions from the ledgers before preparing the Appropriation Account.

A small government department is split into four operational units and the following payments and receipts record has been extracted as at 31 March 1993.

	Units			
	1	2	3	4
Receipts	£	£	£	£
Appropriation in Aid	80,000	20,000	45,000	150,000
Section 4	15,000	5,000	5,000	
Payments				
Salaries	200,000	70,000	90,000	100,000
General Expenses	25,000	10,000	5,000	45,000
Supplies	5,000	3,000	2,000	42,000
Miscellaneous	17,000	20,000	60,000	50,000

The following information is also available.

1. Authorised Appropriations in Aid amounted to £200,000.

2. Inter unit payments by unit 4 to the remaining 3 units are included in unit 4's General Expenses and Supplies in the ratio 40% to 60% respectively.

3. Cash payments by sub-accountants amounted to £16,000 and were chargeable as follows:

	£
General Expenses	5,000
Supplies	3,000
Miscellaneous	8,000

4. The supply grant gross was £680,000 and made up as follows:

	£
Salaries	400,000
General Expenses	60,000
Supplies	65,000
Miscellaneous	155,000

Required:

Prepare an Appropriation Account for the year ended 31 March 1993 and comment on the department's outturn.

Answer

Appropriation Account for year ending 31 March 1993

	Grant	Actual Payments	Underspending Less than granted	Overspendings More than granted
	£	£	£	£
Salaries	400,000	460,000	---	60,000
General Expenses	60,000	80,000	---	20,000
Supplies	65,000	40,000	25,000	---
Miscellaneous	155,000	155,000	---	---
Total Gross Grant	680,000	735,000	25,000	80,000
Appropriations in Aid	200,000	200,000		
Net Total	480,000	535,000	excess	55,000.00

Receipts		
Receipts payable to Consolidated Fund	Estimated	Realised
Receipts authorised to be used as Appropriations in Aid	200,000	295,000
Other Receipts		------
Gross Total		295,000
Appropriations in Aid		200,000
Actual sum of receipts payable separately to Con Fund		95,000

Workings for Actual Payments

1. We must remove the internal transactions which are not part of the Supply Grant arrangement, but purely internal services. Also the income is not recorded in the Appropriation Account from internal sources.

    Therefore remove as follows:

    Deduct

		£	
General Expenses		10,000	(40% of £25,000 section 4 receipts)
Supplies		15,000	(60% of £25,000 section 4 receipts)
		25,000	

2. Add in the cash spent by sub-accountants. This is a form of imprest arrangement but once the cash is issued by the sub-accountant it is a real cash movement.

    Add

	£
General Expenses	5,000
Supplies	3,000
Miscellaneous	8,000
	16,000

Interpretation of Financial Position

Overspends have occured on Salaries and General Expenses slightly offset by an underspend on supplies with miscellaneous expenditure matching the estimate. This means that next year's Grant will be reduced by this year's overspend of £55,000. An Excess Vote is required.

Appropriations in Aid of £295,000 have been received which is £95,000 above estimated and this sum will be surrendered to the Consolidated Fund and cannot be retained by the department.

Expenditure in the next financial period will now need to be restricted severely. This seems a difficult proposition bearing in mind the level of salary overspend.

The Department should modify future estimates to allow use of the surplus Appropriations in Aid if it is under net running cost control. If the department is under gross running cost control this may not be possible, it could try to tackle the problem by tight control over recruitment, promotions and any performance related payments.

Fully Worked Example 3

This example deals with some of the prior year transactions and surrender of the previous years grant surplus. This is a typical vote account question.

(a)   Compare and contrast the accounting conventions and practices of a central government non-trading activity with those followed in respect of such activities in local authorities.

(b)   The following is a summary of the transactions of a supply grant for a small central government department for the year ended 31 March 1992.

(I)   Supply grant vote £1,780,000 gross and £1,700,000 net.

(II)   Vote on account £1,000,000
         Balance of grant   £700,000

(III)   Total sum drawn during the year per Paymaster General's monthly statements
         was £1,596,000

(IV)   Payable orders drawn on the Paymaster General total £1,614,800 for the year.
         £10,000 of these orders was for imprests to Sub-accountants and £1,604,800
         for final payments which are chargeable to:

Subhead	£
Salaries etc	1,468,400
General admin expenses	126,900
Miscellaneous expenses	9,500
	1,604,800

         The Paymaster' General's statements show that of the total of the payable
         orders, £7,800 remained uncashed up to 31 March 1992.

(V)   During the financial year the department has collected receipts amounting to
         £98,000 (to be used as Appropriations in Aid).

(VI)   Periodical accounts rendered by sub-accountants show final payments for the
         year of £8,000 chargeable to :

Subhead	£
Salaries etc	2,800
Miscellaneous expenses	5,200

(VII)   The ledgers for the previous year 1990/91 show that as at March 1991 the
         balance of the supply grant for that year to be surrendered was £68,400, of
         which £49,300 remained undrawn from the Consolidated Fund, £18,300 was
         with the Paymaster General, and £800 with Sub-accountants. The Treasury has
         informed the department that £49,300 undrawn from the Consolidated Fund is
         cancelled, and that the remaining balances are to be treated as though they had
         been taken out of the Supply Grant for the current year.

(VIII)   Orders drawn in 1991/92 but unpaid on 30 June 1992 amount to £2,200. These
         orders are to be cancelled and are in respect of General Administrative
         Expenses.

(IX)   The Paymaster General's monthly statements for April and May 1992 show that
         Payable Orders drawn in 1991/92 but presented for encashment after 31 March
         1992 amounted to £5,600.

(X)   The amount of receipts authorised to be used as Appropriations in Aid of
         expenditure is limited by the Appropriations Act to £80,000, and any surplus
         receipts are therefore payable to the Consolidated Fund.

As the Accounting Officer responsible to Parliament you are required to produce:

(a)   Ledger accounts to record the above transactions for 1991/92

(b)   An Appropriation Account for 1991/92.

Answer

(I)

	£
Vote	1,780,000
Net	1,700,000
AZ	80,000

(II) Vote on Account

	Dr.	Cr.
	£	£.
Consolidated Fund	1,000,000	
Parliamentary Grant A/c		1,000,000

Balance of Grant

	Dr.	Cr.
	£	£.
Consolidated Fund	700,000	
Parliamentary Grant A/c		700,000

(III) Sum drawn

	Dr.	Cr.
	£	£.
PGO (Bank)	1,596,000	
Consolidated Fund		1,596,000

(IV)

	Dr.	Cr.
	£	£.
Salaries	1,468,400	
General Admin Expenses	126,900	
Miscellaneous Expenses	9,500	
Orders Payable		1,604,800

being payable orders issued
for expenses

	Dr.	Cr.
	£	£.
Sub Accountants	10,000	
Orders Payable		10,000

being cash advances for sub
accountants

Calculation

	£
Amount undrawn at 31/3/92	7,800
Total orders payable issued	1,614,800
Total cleared by bank	1,607,000

	Dr.	Cr.
	£	£.
Orders Payable	1,607,000	
PGO (Bank)		1,607,000

being clearance of payable
orders issued

See notes (VIII) and (IX) which deal with the £7,800 uncleared payable orders.

(V)

	£
Authorised Appropriations in Aid	80,000
Realised Appropriations in Aid	98,000
Surplus Appropriations in Aid	18,000

	Dr.	Cr.
	£	£.
PGO (Bank)	98,000	
Appropriations in Aid		98,000

being receipt of Appropriations
in Aid

	Dr.	Cr.
	£	£.
Appropriations in Aid	18,000	
Consolidated Fund Extra		18,000
Receipts		

being transfer of surplus
Appropriations in Aid to Extra
Receipts payable to
Consolidated Fund

(VI) £8,000 charged to vote from accounts rendered by sub accountants

	Dr.	Cr.
	£	£.
Sub accountants advance		2,800
Salaries	2,800	
Sub accountants advance		5,200
Miscellaneous	5,200	

being transfer to the vote of
expenses incurred by sub
accountants

(VII) Trial Balance at 31/3/91

	Dr. £	Cr. £.
Consolidated Fund	49,300	
PGO (Bank)	18,300	
Sub Accountants	800	
90/91 Parliamentary Grant		
Surplus		68,400
	68,400	68,400

Use these balances in the opening ledgers for 1991/92.

This instruction means clear the 90/91 Parliamentary Grant Account surplus which is £68,400 Cr. balance and reduce the equivalent sum owed by the Consolidated Fund.

	Dr. £	Cr. £.
1990/91 PGA	68,400	
Consolidated Fund		68,400

> being the surrender of the 90/91
> Grant surplus and removal of the
> liability by reducing the sum
> owed by the Consolidated Fund

(If all the grant was already drawn from the fund, the department could pay the sum from the bank or do the surrender the following year according to instructions from the Treasury.)

(VIII) The period allowed to clear payments ends on 31 May when the department must close its books.

The sum of expired payable orders not cleared must be removed from the vote.

	Dr. £	Cr. £.
General Admin Expenses		2,200
Orders Payable	2,200	

> being removal of uncleared
> payable orders from the vote

(IX) This tells you the sum of the payable orders issued by 31/3/92 and cleared before close of books on 31/5/92. Clear orders payable and show the cash payment.

	Dr. £	Cr. £.
Orders Payable	5,600	
Paymaster General's Office		5,600

(X) This tells you that the department can use £80,000 of Appropriations in Aid. Any additional Appropriations in Aid over £80,000 must be surrendered as Consolidated Fund Extra Receipts (CFER). See note (V).

In the Appropriation Account layout use the word Applied for the A. in A. applied to offset expenditure. If the department had received below the authorised £80,000 A. in A. the word used is "Realised".

(a) Accounting in central government is on a cash basis. Local authorities produce accruals accounts thereby following the matching concept of SSAP 2.

Surpluses of grant are surrendered by central government departments the following year whereas in local authorities a surplus may be brought forward and applied to subsequent years.

In central government under gross running cost control the level of authorised receipts is set and any extra receipts must be surrendered. In local government additional revenues can be used to finance further expenditure.

CENTRAL GOVERNMENT DEPARTMENT LEDGERS

Consolidated Fund						90/91 Parliamentary Grant A/c (PGA)				
b/f	49,300					C Fund	68,400	b/f (Net)	68,400
91/2 PGA	1,000,000	PGO	1,596,000				=====		=====
91/2 PGA	700,000	90/1 PGA	68,400						
		c/d	84,900						
	1,749,300		1,749,300						
b/f	84,900								

Paymaster General's Office (PGO)						Orders Payable			
b/f	18,300						Salaries	1,468,400
C Fund	1,596,000	Orders Pay	1,607,000				GAE	126,900
A in A	98,000	Orders Pay	5,600				Misc	9,500
		c/d	99,700		PGO	1,607,000	Sub A/c	10,000
	1,712,300		1,712,300		GAE	2,200		
b/f	99,700				PGO	5,600		
						1,614,800		1,614,800

91/92 Parliamentary Grant A/c (PGA)						Sub Accountants			
Salaries	1,471,200	C Fund	1,000,000		b/f	800	Salaries	2,800
GAE	124,700	C Fund	700,000		Orders Pay	10,000	Misc	5,200
Misc	14,700	A in A	80,000					
c/d	169,400						c/d	2,800
	1,780,000		1,780,000			10,800		10,800
		b/f	169,400		b/f	2,800		

Appropriations In Aid						CFER		
CFER	18,000	PGO	98,000				A in A	18,000
PGA	80,000							
	98,000		98,000					

Salaries						General Admin Expenses		
Orders P.	1,468,400	PGA	1,471,200		Orders P.	126,900	Orders P.	2,200
Sub A/c	2,800						PGA	124,700
	1,471,200		1,471,200			126,900		126,900

	Miscellaneous		
Orders P.	9,500	PGA	14,700
Sub A/c	5,200		
	14,700		14,700

Appropriation Account

Small Government Department for the year ending 31/3/92

Subhead	Grant £	Expenditure £	Underspend £	Overspend £
Running Costs	1,780,000	1,610,600	169,400	------
Gross Expenditure	1,780,000	1,610,600	169,400	------

Less:

	Estimated	Applied	
			_____
Appropriations in Aid	80,000	80,000	surplus to be surrendered
Net Expenditure	1,700,000	1,530,600	169,400

Receipts

Receipts payable to Consolidated Fund	Estimated	Realised
Receipts authorised to be used as Appropriations in Aid	80,000	98,000
Other Receipts		------
Gross Total Receipts		98,000
Appropriations in Aid		80,000
Actual sum of receipts payable separately to Con Fund		18,000

In the examination, if you are not asked to show the journals you can save time posting transactions direct to the ledgers. Do show the journals if you are asked.

Try the questions on vote accounts at the end of the chapter. Once you have learnt the names of the accounts you will see that the entries are quite straightforward.

Trading Funds : Off Vote Agency Accounts

Off vote agencies are usually trading funds for example Companies House or the Royal Mint.

Although agencies are part of the "Next Steps" initiative some government bodies were already trading funds before the initiative started, for example Her Majesty's Stationery Office (HMSO). These organisations which are referred to as trading fund agencies have been joined by new agencies set up as a result of the Next Steps Initiative. There are currently eight agencies operating as trading funds: HMSO; Royal Mint; Vehicle Inspectorate; Central Office of Information; Companies House; The Patent Office; The Buying Agency; and The Fire Service College.

These trading fund agencies operate more like a commercial company, for example by making a return on capital according to Treasury requirements.

The accounting requirements for these agencies are set out in the Government Trading Funds Act 1973 which requires the matching concept to be applied and a balance sheet to be prepared at year end. Trading fund agencies are financed by public dividend capital and loans from the National Loans Fund.

Her Majesty's Stationery Office - Trading Fund

HMSO was established in 1786, and supplied stationery to a small number of public offices, levying charges for stationery supplied.

In 1824 The Government designated HMSO an "allied service" and supplies were provided free to Government departments, with HMSO receiving funding from the Parliamentary vote. The reasoning behind this move was to simplify the accounting procedures and strengthen HMSO's role in laying down standards of quality, and to curb extravagance.

During the nineteenth century HMSO became the publisher for Parliament and Government, printing works and bookshops were established.

By 1980 the arrangement had turned full circle. On 1 April 1980 HMSO was established as a trading fund under the provisions of the Government trading Funds Act 1973 and the 1980 HMSO Trading Fund Order (SI 1980/456). This required HMSO to prepare commercial accounts, and charge customers to attain economy, efficiency and effectiveness.

HMSO was required by a Treasury Minute to make a 5% return on a current cost basis for the period 1 April 1985 to 31 March 1990. A Treasury minute on 28 January 1988 restated the 5% return target. However on the 14th December 1988 HMSO was given Executive Agency status. A Treasury minute of the same date required HMSO to "substantially increase its annual profit after interest in current cost terms over the next five years". A further Treasury minute dated 30th January 1992 set a target for the 1992 financial year of a profit after interest, in current cost terms, of £6,000,000. Like other trading fund Agencies HMSO staff are civil servants.

When you tackle a Trading Fund agency question you will be dealing with account formats with which you are already familiar: the balance sheet; operating account or profit and loss account; and a cash flow reconciliation statement.

Fully Worked Example 4

The following information relates to the Government's Stationery Office (GSO) for the year ending 31 March 1992.

Balances as at 31 March	1991 £000	1992 £000
Fixed Assets	44,100	?
Accumulated Depreciation	12,400	?
National Loans Fund	20,840	?
Current Cost Reserve	26,260	?
Stocks	46,840	61,050
Debtors	31,200	32,240
Creditors	62,400	58,100
Provision for Insurance	4,100	?
Retained Surplus	2,400	?
Cash in hand	6,260	?
Cash overdrawn	---	3,700

Transactions During 1991/92	Supply Division £000	Print Procurement Division £000	Publication Division £000	Total £000
Turnover				
Fees and charges	149,000	110,000	21,000	280,000
Other income	---	10	590	600
Operating expenditure				
Staff costs	24,000	26,000	2,010	52,010
Cost of materials	105,000	70,000	5,200	180,200
Other charges	12,400	12,100	1,900	26,400

Other information	£000
Additions to Fixed Assets	17,200
Interest payable	2,900
Loans raised	11,200
Loans repaid	7,800
Proceeds from sale of assets	450

Notes

1. To avoid discouraging sales, reports of Parliamentary debates are priced at cost, in accordance with Goverment policy. This year's payment to the Goverment Stationery Office (GSO) has not been accounted for in the revenue account, and the cash was transferred from the Treasury on 31 March 1992 in the sum of £3,850,000, and is included in the final cash figure.

2. Depreciation calculations have been made and the total charge for historic cost depreciation is as follows:

	£000
Supply Division	1,800
Print Division	1,100

Publications   200
                                     ─────
                                     3,100

3.   The following current cost adjustments need to be included :

     Adjustments   £000

     Cost of Sales   400
     Monetary Working Capital   270
     Stock Uplift   20
     Current Cost Depreciation   4,500

4.   Revaluation of fixed assets produced a surplus of £1,800,000.

5.   The Supply Division assets sold had a current replacement cost of £3,100,000 as at 1 April 1991, and depreciation to this date had been £2,810,000. Any profit or loss should not be treated as an extraordinary item.

6.   An extra contribution to the insurance reserve should be made as part of operating expenditure of £500,000, chargeable to each operation in proportion to fees and charges.

7.   A contribution for the pension payments of staff is outstanding for the year. The GSO owes the Treasury £6,200,000 in this respect.

You are required to

(a) Prepare a summary current cost profit and loss account and a balance sheet as at 31 March 1992 and 31 March 1991.

(b) Prepare a cash flow reconciliation statement for year ending 31 March 1992.

(c) Prepare a statement of historic profit before interest which reveals the profit or loss as far as is possible split between the different operations of the GSO for the year ending 31 March 1992.

(d) Prepare a statement which reveals the current cost operating profit as a percentage of averaged net current cost assets. A Treasury Minute has been issued placing a requirement of a 5% return on the GSO.

Tutorial answer to GSO

Treatment of notes

Note 1

	Dr. £	Cr. £.
Cash Account (already done)		
Income : Publication Grant		3,850,000
being Treasury contribution to allow sale of publications at cost		

Note 2

	Dr. £	Cr. £.
Supply Division	1,800,000	
Paint Division	1,100,000	
Publications	200,000	
Depreciation Reserve		3,100,000

being historic depreciation charges

Note 3

	Dr. £	Cr. £.
Cost of Sales Adjustment - P&L	400,000	
Current Cost Reserve		400,000
Monetary Working Capital - P&L	270,000	
Current Cost Reserve		270,000
Stock Account	20,000	
Current Cost Reserve		20,000

being current cost adjustment

	Dr. £	Cr. £.
Current Cost Depreciation Adj	4,500,000	
Depreciation Reserve		4,500,000

being current cost depreciation adjustment

Note 4

	Dr. £	Cr. £.
Fixed Assets	1,800,000	
Current Cost Reserve		1,800,000

being revaluation of fixed assets

Note 5

The "Other information" section tells you the proceeds from sale of assets were £450,000.

	Dr. £	Cr. £.
Fixed Assets		3,100,000
Disposal Account	3,100,000	
Depreciation Reserve	2,810,000	
Disposal Account		2,810,000

being journals to remove assets sold and the related depreciation to the disposal account

Assume cash receipt for asset sale proceeds

	Dr. £	Cr. £.
Cash A/c (already done)		
Disposal Account		450,000

Disposal Account			
Fixed Assets	3,100,000	Depreciation	2,810,000
P&L A/c	160,000	Cash	450,000
	3,260,000		3,260,000

Note 6

Charge extra insurance contribution of £500,000 in proportion to fees and charges for each Division (for historic operating account).

Division	Fees £000	%	Insurance Contribution
Supply	149,000	53	265,000
Print Procurement	110,000	39	195,000
Publication	21,000	8	40,000
	280,000	100	500,000

	Dr. £	Cr. £.
P&L Supply Division	265,000	
P&L Print Procurement Division	195,000	
P&L Publication Division	40,000	
Insurance Reserve		500,000

being the extra contribution to the insurance reserve

Note 7

Pension costs form part of the staffing costs to GSO. They should be apportioned according to the staff costs for each division.

Division	Staff Costs	%	Allocated Pension Costs £000
Supply	24,000	46	2,852
Print Procurement	26,000	50	3,100
Publication	2,010	4	248
Total	52,010	100	6,200

	Dr. £	Cr. £.
P&L Account Pensions	6,200,000	
HM Treasury Creditor		6,200,000

Answer to part (a)

Government Stationery Office Balance Sheet as at 31/3/91

	£000	£000	£000
Fixed Assets			44,100
Depreciation			12,400
			31,700
Current Assets:			
Stocks	46,840		
Debtors	31,200		
Bank	6,260		
		84,300	
Current liabilities:			
Creditors		62,400	
Net Current Assets			21,900
Net Assets			53,600
Financed by :			
National Loans Fund			20,840
Current Cost Reserve		26,260	
Insurance Provision		4,100	
			30,360
Retained Surplus			2,400
			53,600

Government Stationery Office Operating Account for year ending 31/3/92
(Profit and Loss Account)

	£000	£000
Turnover		
Fees and Charges		280,000
Other Income		600
Treasury Publication Contribution		3,850
Profit on Sale of Assets		160
		284,610
LESS :		
Operating Expenses		
Staff Costs	52,010	
Staff Pensions	6,200	
Cost of Materials	180,200	
Other Charges	26,400	
Historic Depreciation	3,100	
Insurance Provision	500	268,410
Historic Operating Profit		16,200
LESS :		
Current Cost Adjustments :		
COSA	400	
MWCA	270	
CC Dep Adjustment	4,500	
		5170
Current Cost Operating Profit		11,030
Interest Charges		2,900
Current Cost Surplus for year		8,130
Surplus b/f		2,400
Surplus c/d		10,530

405

GSO Ledgers

Fixed Assets

	£,000		£,000
b/f	44,100	Disposal	3,100
Reval CCR	1,800		
Additions	17,200		
		c/d	60,000
	63,100		63,100
b/f	60,000		

Depreciation

	£,000		£,000
Disposal	2,810	b/f	12,400
		Historic	3,100
		Current	4,500
c/d	17,190		
	20,000		20,000
		b/f	17,190

Current Cost Reserve

	£,000		£,000
		b/f	26,260
		COSA	400
		MWCA	270
		Stock Reval	20
		FA Reval	1,800
c/d	28,750		
	28,750		28,750
		b/f	28,750

Insurance Provision

	£,000		£,000
		b/f	4,100
		P&L	500
c/d	4,600		
	4,600		4,600
		b/f	400

National Loans Fund

	£,000		£,000
Cash Repaid	7,800	b/f	20,840
		Cash Raised	11,200
c/d	24,240		
	32,040		32,040
		b/f	24,240

Stock

	£,000		£,000
b/f 31/3/92	61,050		
Reval	20		
		c/d	61,070
	61,070		61,070
b/f	61,070		

Government Stationery Office Balance Sheet as at 31/3/92

	£000	£000	£000
Fixed Assets			60,000
Depreciation			17,190
			42,810
Current Assets:			
Stocks	61,070		
Debtors	32,240		
Bank cash in hand	----------		
		93,310	
Current liabilities:			
HM Treasury	6,200		
Creditors	58,100		
Cash Overdrawn	3,700		
		68,000	
Net Current Assets			25,310
Net Assets			68,120
Financed by :			
National Loans Fund			24,240
Current Cost Reserve		28,750	
Insurance Provision		4,600	
			33,350
Retained Surplus			10,530
			68,120

Answer to part (b)

Government Stationery Office Cash Flow Reconciliation Statement for Year Ending 31/3/92

	£000	£000
1. Net cash inflow from operating activities		6,290
2. Returns on investment and servicing of finance		
Interest Received	------	
Interest Paid	2,900	
Net cash outflow from returns on investments and servicing of finance		(2,900)
3. Tax Paid		-------
4. Investing Activities		
Payments to acquire fixed assets	(17,200)	
Receipts from sale of fixed assets	450	
Payments/receipts to acquire /dispose investments	--------	
Net cash outflow from investing activities		(16,750)
5. Financing		
Loans Raised	11,200	
Loans Repaid	(7,800)	
Net cash outflow from financing		3,400
		9,960
Decrease in cash and cash equivalents		

Notes to the cash flow statement

1. Reconciliation of Operating Surplus to net cash inflow

	£000
Operating Profit (Current Cost)	11,030
Add back:	
Current Cost Adjustments:	
COSA	400
MWCA	270
CC Depreciation Adjustment	4,500
Historic Adjustment:	
Depreciation	3,100
Insurance Provision increase	500
Other Adjustments:	
Profit on sale of fixed assets	(160)
Increase in stocks (exclude revaluation, which is not cash flow)	(14,210)
Increase in debtors	(1,040)
Increase in creditors (including HM Treasury)	1,900
	6,290

2. Analysis of changes in cash and cash equivalents during the year

	£000
Balance at 31/3/91	6,260 Dr
Net cash outflow	9,960 Cr
Balance at 31/3/92	3,700 Cr

3. Analysis of balances of cash and cash equivalents as shown in the balance sheet

	1991	1992	Change in year
	£000	£000	£000
Cash at bank and in hand	6,260	---	(6,260)
Short term investments	---	---	---
Bank overdrawn	---	3,700	(3,700)
	6,260	(3,700)	(9,960)

4. Analysis of changes in financing during the year

	Public Dividend Capital
	£000
Opening balance	NA
Cash inflow/outflow	NA
Balance	NA

5. Major non cash transactions

On 31/3/92 stocks were revalued by £20,000.
On 31/3/92 fixed assets were revalued by £1,800,000.

Answer to part (c)

Government Stationery Office Historic Profit Statement Analysed by Division

	Supply Division £000	Print Division £000	Publication Division £000	TOTAL £000
Turnover				
Fees and charges	149,000	110,000	21,000	280,000
Other Income	----	10	590	600
Publication Contrib			3850	3850
Profit on Sale	160			160
Total	149,160	110,010	25,440	284,610
Operating Expenditure				
Staff costs	24,000	26,000	2,010	52,010
Pensions	2,852	3,100	248	6,200
Materials	105,000	70,000	5,200	180,200
Other Charges	12,400	12,100	1,900	26,400
Insurance Contributions	265	195	40	500
Depreciation	1,800	1,100	200	3,100
Total Expenditure	146,317	112,405	9,598	268,410
Historic Profit (loss)	2,843	(2,485)	15,842	16,200

Answer to part (d)

Government Stationery Office Required Rate of Return Statement for year ending 31/3/92

	£000
1. Current cost operating surplus.	11,030
2. Averaged net assets	60,860
3. Rate of return achieved	18%
4. Rate required by Treasury	5%

Calculation of Average Net Assets

	31/3/91 £000	31/3/92 £000	Total £000
From opening and closing balance sheets part (a)	53,600	68,120	121,170

Open and close total = 121,170,000/2 = 60,860,000

This was a long question to attempt. However you should be familiar with the format and be able to attempt an agency trading fund question without too much difficulty. Try practising the questions at the end of the chapter. The data available on asset sale and interest payable did not include any opening or closing debtor/creditor analysis. I assumed the interest payable was paid in full and that the revenue from asset sales was received in cash within the financial year.

You may get a question which gives you an analysis of opening and closing debtors/ creditors balances. You can use this to work out the actual cash paid on interest or cash received on interest receivable or assets sold.

Example:

Opening Debtors Balance	100,000
Element relating to interest due prior year	8,000
Remaining opening Debtors	92,000
Closing Debtors Balance	90,000
Element relating to interest due at year end	15,000
Remaining closing Debtors	75,000
Sum given as interest due in the year to P&L	29,000

Workings to calculate cash received for interest due:

```
              Debtors Interest Due
          £,000                £,000
b/f           8,000 |
                    | Cash Rec'd  22,000
                    |
Interest in yr. 29,000 | c/d      15,000
              37,000 |            37,000
```

The actual cash received relating to the interest element can then be deduced as shown above. The next thing to do is to calculate the movement in debtors sum to be adjusted in the note 1 to the cash flow statement. This is the cash inflow or outflow from operating activities. This is done by excluding the interest debtors amounts from the opening and closing figures:

	Opening Debtors £000	Closing Debtors £000	Difference £000
Other debtors	92,000	75,000	17,000
Interest rec. debtors	8,000	15,000	-7,000
Total	100,000	90,000	10,000

Using the example figures above, the net cash inflow in note one on the cash flow statement is £17,000 not the total movement of £10,000. The other debtors movement is in the adjustment for the cash interest received figure which goes in the note 2 on cash flows from investments and servicing of finance. Have a go at question seven at the end of the chapter if you are not sure. Try questions five and six first because they are easier.

On Vote Agency Accounts

On Vote Agencies are usually small government departments or parts of a department, that have been identified as candidates for agency status. They may not generate much income and therefore continue to need a vote to finance their activities. The autonomy of agency status and the requirement to produce accruals based accounts should lead to better management of resources and more effective monitoring of costs.

There are some key features you should note about On Vote Agency accruals accounts:

- the accounting systems are likely to be set up on an accruals basis. Expenditure and income is transacted via creditors and debtors first and bank second. The traditional way of logging expenditure and income as payments and receipts is not possible once the switch to accruals is made;

- the "vote" reports are likely to be extracted from an analysis of the bank transactions ie. creditors paid and debtors' payments received and banked; and

- because of the variety of On Vote Agencies and their funding arrangements, Agencies are likely to establish different mechanisms for achieving vote and accruals based reporting.

The format of these accounts will vary because of the diverse nature of the agencies and the functions they provide. Examples of on vote agencies are the Veterinary Medicines Directorate, Welsh Historic Monuments and the Planning Inspectorate. Some agencies such as the Planning Inspectorate can be jointly owned or funded by two departments.

Each On Vote Agency will specify the format of accruals accounts when seeking an Accounts Direction from the Treasury. An Accounts Direction specifies the format of accounts to be used in the annual report. Until more on vote agencies produce accruals accounts, an exam question in this area is less likely. However for completeness the example below shows an on vote agency with limited revenues from its activities. The cash flow statement is a suggestion but Treasury require a reconciliation between the vote and the accruals in the annual report. Not all the possible complications are included but the principles involved in producing vote and accruals accounts are shown.

Fully worked example 5

First examine the vote account preceeding the year of accruals.

On Vote Agency
Vote Account Year End 31/3/91

	Estimate £	Outturn £	Difference £
Capital	2,000,000	1,000,000	-1,000,000
Pay	15,500,000	14,000,000	-1,500,000
Running Costs	4,500,000	4,000,000	-500,000
	22,000,000	19,000,000	-3,000,000
Approp. in Aid	2,000,000	2,000,000	
	20,000,000	17,000,000	-3,000,000

Next examine the cash based trial balance as at 31/3/91 and the opening accruals adjustments.

On Vote Agency

Opening Trial Balance 31/3/91

Cash Trial Balance	Dr £	Cr £
Fixed Assets	1,000,000	
Pay Costs	14,000,000	
Running Costs	4,000,000	
PGA 90/91		20,000,000
Appropriations in Aid		2,000,000
Consolidated Fund	2,500,000	
Paymaster General's Office	500,000	
	22,000,000	22,000,000
Accrual Adjustments		
Debtors (A in A)	250,000	
Appropriations in Aid (Accruals)		250,000
Creditors (running costs)		40,000
Running Costs (Accruals)	40,000	
Fixed Assets	5,000,000	
General Reserve		5,000,000
	27,290,000	27,290,000

The accruals adjustments are for receipts (£250,000) and expenses (£40,000). The remaining adjustment is to post all the fixed assets from the previous years Parliamentary Grant Accounts. Since no depreciation was ever posted on these assets they are included at a written down value or net book value to reflect their age and obsolescence. The credit entry is to a General Reserve account.

From this accruals trial balance an Income and Expenditure account can be drawn up. The account will show the net cost of output. However once the net cost of output is shown in the I&E account the vote based expenditure ie cash expenditure is reversed out to the Parliamentary Grant Account in the usual way for a vote account.

413

On Vote Agency

Opening Income & Expenditure Account 31/3/91

	£000	£000	
Expenditure:			
Pay		14,000	Dr.
Running Costs		4,040	Dr.
Total expenditure		18,040	Dr.
Receipts:			
Appropriations in Aid		2,250	Cr.
Net Cost of output		**15,790**	Dr.
Transfers to 90/91 PGA (Vote expenditure ie cash)			
Vote : Pay Costs	14,000		
Running Costs	4,000	18,000	Cr.
		2,210	Cr.
Vote: Appropriations in Aid		2,000	Dr.
Income and Expenditure c/d		210	Cr.

The retained surplus in the Income and Expenditure is in the debtors figure £250,000 and the creditors figure £40,000 the net being £210,000.

The journals required to achieve the transfers from the Income and Expenditure to the Parliamentary Grant Account as shown above are summarised below.

	Dr £000	Cr £000
1. Pay (I&E) cash spend only		14,000
90/91 PGA	14,000	
being the transfer of vote pay expenditure to the 90/91 PGA		
2. Running Costs (I&E) cash spend only		4,000
90/91 PGA	4,000	
being the transfer of vote running costs to the 90/91 PGA		
3. Receipts (I&E) cash receipts only	2,000	
90/91 PGA		2,000
being transfer of A in A to the 90/91 PGA		

In addition to transferring the cash running costs to the Parliamentary Grant Account the cash spend on fixed assets must be transferred to the PGA. The assets should still be in the balance sheet and so must be written back but are financed by the General Reserve.

	Dr £000	Cr £000
4.Fixed Assets Bal. Sheet cash spend only		1,000
90/91 PGA	1,000	
being the transfer of vote capital expenditure to the 90/91 PGA		
5. Fixed Assets Bal. Sheet cash spend only	1,000	
General Reserve		1,000
being the restatement of vote capital in the Balance Sheet financed by the Gen. Reserve		

Journals 4 and 5 transfer the cash spend on fixed assets to the PGA and restate the assets in the balance sheet financed by a General Reserve.

The balance on the 1990/91 Parliamentary grant Account will be as follows.

1990/91 Parliamentary Grant Account

	£000		£000
Fixed Assets	1,000	Con Fund	20,000
I&E Pay	14,000	I&E A in A	2,000
I&E Run Costs	4,000		
c/d	3,000		
	22,000		22,000
		b/f	3,000

The balance on the General Reserve Account will now be as follows:

General Reserve

	£000		£000
		Fixed Assets b/f	5,000
		Fixed Assets	1,000
c/d	6,000		
	6,000		6,000
		b/f	6,000

Now we can draw up the opening balance sheet on an accruals basis.

On Vote Agency
Opening Balance Sheet
As At 31/3/91

	£000	£000	
Fixed Assets (£1m + £5m)		6,000	
Current Assets			
Stock	----		
Debtors	250		
Consolidated Fund	2,500		
Bank	500		
	3,250		
Current Liabilities			
Ceditors	40		
Net Current Assets		3,210	
NET ASSETS		9,210	Dr.
Finance			
General Reserve (£5m + £1m)		6,000	Cr.
P&L to Year End 31/3/91		210	Cr.
PGA To Year End 31/3/91		3,000	Cr.
		9,210	Cr.

During the year the surplus on the 1990/91 Parliamentary Grant Account must be surrendered as follows.

On Vote Agency Example
Surrender of 1990/91 Grant Surplus During 1991/92

	Dr. £000	Cr. £000
6. PGA 1990/91	3,000	
Consolidated Fund		3,000

Next consider the following Vote Account for 1991/92.

On Vote Agency
Vote Account Year End 31/3/92

	Estimate £	Outturn £	Difference £
Capital	2,000,000	1,800,000	-200,000
Pay	15,00,000	14,300,000	-700,000
Running Costs	5,000,000	4,700,000	-300,000
	22,000,000	20,800,000	-1,200,000
Approp. in Aid	2,000,000	2,100,000	+100,000
	20,000,000	18,700,000	surrender 1,300,000

		£
PGA Grant Surplus	:	1,200,000
Surplus A in A	:	100,000
Total Surplus		1,300,000

The vote account is based on the following journals and ledgers and in particular the analysis of the bank account.

		Dr. £000	Cr. £000
7.	Fixed Assets	1,800	
	PGO		1,800
	being the cash paid for fixed assets		
8.	Pay costs	14,300	
	PGO		14,300
	being cash paid on salaries		
9.	Running costs	4,685	
	PGO		4,685
	being invoices logged in respect of running costs		
10.	Creditors	4,700	
	PGO		4,700
	being cash paid to creditors in respect of running costs in the year		

		Dr. £000	Cr. £000
11.	Debtors	1,880	
	Appropriations in Aid		1,880

being income invoiced in 91/92

		Dr. £000	Cr. £000
12.	PGO	2,100	
	Debtors		2,100

being cash received from debtors for A. in A. in 91/2

		Dr. £000	Cr. £000
13.	PGO	18,500	
	Consolidated Fund		18,500

being draw down of cash from the Consolidated Fund for payments

		Dr. £000	Cr. £000
14.	Depreciation	800	
	Depreciation Reserve		800

being the depreciation charge for 91/2 & credit to reserve

The trial balance at this stage would be as follows:

Trial Balance as at 31/3/92
before transfer to PGA

	Dr £000	Cr £000
Fixed Assets	7,800	
Pay Costs	14,300	
Running Costs	4,685	
PGA 91/92		20,000
Appropriations in Aid (AZ)		1,880
Consolidated Fund	1,000	
PGO	300	
Debtors (AZ)	30	
Creditors (Running Costs)		25
Depreciation P&L	800	
P&L		210
General reserve		6,000
Depreciation Reserve		800
	28,915	28,915

Next the Income and Expenditure account can be drawn up and the vote expenditure transferred to the Parliamentary Grant Account.

		Dr £000	Cr £000
15.	PGA 1991/92 I & E Pay	14,300	
			14,300
	being transfer of cash payments of pay to 1991/92 PGA		
16.	PGA 91/2 I & E Running Costs	4,700	
			4,700
	being transfer of cash payments on running costs to 91/2 PGA		
17.	I & E Appropriations in Aid PGA 91/2	2,000	
			2,000
	being transfer of Authorised A. in A. to 91/2 PGA		
18.*	I & E Surplus A. in A. Surplus A. in A.	100	
			100
	being transfer of surplus authorised A. in A. from I & E to surplus A. in A. account		
19.	PGA 91/2 Fixed Assets	1,800	
			1,800
	being transfer of cash vote expenditure on fixed assets to 91/2 PGA		
20.	Fixed Assets General Reserve	1,800	
			1,800
	being restatement of fixed assets to the balance sheet financed by the general reserve		

* Note

This journal may not be necessary. The Agency could leave the £100,000 balance lying in the P&L account and surrender the sum from the P&L during 1992/93. A note would be needed to indicate the liability, but since the P&L balance rolls forward this would be an acceptable alternative treatment. See the notes in the cash flow statement for a further explanation.

On Vote Agency
Profit and Loss Account 31/3/92

	£000		£000	
Expenditure				
Pay Costs			14,300	Dr.
Running Costs			4,685	Dr.
Depreciation (14)			800	Dr.
Total expenditure			19,785	Dr.
Receipts				
Appropriations in Aid			1,880	Cr.
Net Cost of output			17,905	Dr.
Transfers to 91/92 PGA:				
(Vote expenditure ie cash)				
Vote : Pay Costs (15)	14,300	Cr.		
Running Costs (16)	4,700	Cr.	19,000	Cr.
			1,095	Cr.
Vote: Appropriations in Aid (17)			2,000	Dr.
			905	Dr.
Other transfers to Surplus AZ (18)			100	Dr.
Net loss to I & E			1,005	Dr.
P&L b/f			210	Cr.
P&L c/d			**795**	**Dr.**

Note:

The balance in the income and expenditure account is the depreciation charged plus creditors excluding Excess A. in A. less debtors excluding the Consolidated Fund.

	£	
Depreciation	800,000	Cr.
Creditors excluding A. in A.	25,000	Cr.
Debtors excluding Consolidated Fund	30,000	Dr.
	795,000	Cr.

On Vote Agency
Balance Sheet Year End 31/3/92

	£000	£000	
Fixed Assets		7,800	
Depreciation		800	
		7,000	
Current Assets:			
Stock	----		
Debtors	30		
Consolidated Fund	1,000		
Bank	300		
	1,330		
Current Liabilities:			
Ceditors	25		
Surplus AZ	100		
Net Current Assets		1,205	Dr.
NET ASSETS		8,205	Dr.
Finance			
General Reserve		7,800	Cr.
P&L b/f		795	Dr.
PGA 91/92		1,200	Cr.
		8,205	Cr.

On Vote Agency
Cash Flow Reconciliation for Year Ended 31/3/92

		£000	£000
1.	Cash inflows/Outflows from operating activities		15,400
2.	Returns on investments/servicing of finance		
	Cash inflows from servicing of finance	-----	
3.	Tax paid/surrenders		
	Surrender of 1990/91 PGA surplus	3,000	3,000
			18,400
4.	Investing activities		
	Payments to acquire fixed assets	1,800	1,800
	Net cash outflow before financing		20,200
5.	Financing		
	Source of finance from 1991/92 PGA	20,000	20,000
	Net cash outflow		200

Notes to the cash flow statement.

1. Reconciliation of operating profit to net cash inflow from operating activities.

	£000
Net cost of output	-17,905
Less Depreciation	+800
Decrease in Debtors	+220
Decrease in Creditors	-15
Decrease in Consolidated Fund	+1,500
	-15,400

Note:

The increase in creditors (AZ) is excluded from the note 1 adjustment because this does not reflect a cash inflow. This is merely an adjustment from the I & E account to reflect the excess of cash A. in A. over the Estimate figure which must be surrendered and is therefore a liability.

It would be possible to not transfer the £100,000 from the P&L and let it roll forward into 1992/93. The surrender of surplus A. in A. would be debited to the P&L in 1992/93. If this method is used, the closing P&L figure in 1991/92 would be £695,000 and the closing creditors figure would be just £25,000. The balance sheet closing figure would be struck as £8,305,000 instead of £8,205,000 as shown overleaf.

2. Analysis of changes in cash and cash equivalents.

	£000
Balance as at 31/3/91	500
Net cash outflow	200
Balance at 31/3/92	300

On Vote Agency Ledgers
1991/92

Consolidated Fund

	£000		£000
b/f	2,500	90/1 PGA	3,000
91/92 PGA	20,000	PGO	18,500
		c/d	1,000
	22,500		22,500
b/f	1,000		

PGO

	£000		£000
b/f	500		
Debt's AZ	2,100	Capital	1,800
C. Fund	18,500	Pay	14,300
		Credit'rs	4,700
		c/d	300
	21,100		21,100
b/f	300		

Debtors (AZ)

	£000		£000
b/f	250		
AZ	1,880	PGO	2,100
		c/d	30
	2,130		2,130
b/f	30		

Creditors

	£000		£000
		b/f	40
PGO	4,700	RC	4,685
c/d	25		
	4,725		4,725
		b/f	25

AZ

	£000		£000
P&L	1,880	Debtors	1,880
	====		====

Running Costs

	£000		£000
Creditors	4,685	P&L	4,685
	====		====

Pay

	£000		£000
PGO	14,300	P&L	14,300
	=====		=====

PGA 1990/91

	£000		£000
C Fund	3,000	b/f	3,000
	====		====

Fixed Assets

	£000		£000
b/f	6,000	PGA	1,800
PGO	1,800		
Gen Res	1,800		
		c/d	7,800
	9,600		9,600
b/f	7,800		

PGA

	£000		£000
FA	1,800	ConFund	20,000
P&L(Pay)	14,300	P&LCash	
P&LRun		AZ	2,000
Cost	4,700		
c/d	1,200		
	22,000		22,000
		b/f	1,200

Dep Reserve

£000	£000
	800

Gen Reserve

£000		£000
	b/f	6,000
	FA	1,800

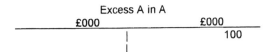

Excess A in A

£000	£000
	100

Profit & Loss

	£000		£000
Running Costs	4,685	b/f	210
Pay	14,300	AZ	1,880
Depreciation	800	PGA Cash Pay	14,300
PGA Cash AZ	2,000	PGA Cash Run Costs	4,700
Excess A in A	100	c/d	795
	21,885		21,885
b/f	795		

Conclusion

On Vote Agencies are still relatively new. As yet few have produced accruals accounts, therefore an examination question in this area is less likely. However in the future as the format of accounts becomes established and more common, examination question will be more likely.

Should you be required to prepare a set of On Vote agency accounts the key is to examine cash paid by analysis of debtors and creditors. This will reconcile the difference between vote figures and accruals.

Examination Question 1

The following transactions relate to the supply of a small government department for the year ended 31 March 1992.

(1) The supply grant vote for the year amounted to £20,000,000 gross. Authorised Appropriations in Aid amount to £1,000,000.

(2) Of the net figure for the supply grant vote the grant was as follows:

	£
Vote on account	10,000,000
Balance of grant	9,000,000

(3) The planned gross expenditure was as follows:

	£
Salaries	12,000,000
General Admin Expenditure	4,500,000
Capital	3,500,000

(4) Receipts collected during the year to be used as Appropriations in Aid were £1,250,000

(5) The total sum drawn by the Paymaster General was £18,000,000

(6) Orders payable drawn on the Paymaster General for the year were as follows

	£
Salaries	11,900,000
General Admin Expenditure	4,000,000
Capital	3,000,000
Imprests	100,000

(7) Accounts rendered re imprest payments have been analysed and give the following totals :

	£
General Admin Expenditure	80,000

REQUIRED

(a) Ledger accounts to record the above transactions.
(12 Marks)

(b) Appropriation Account and the receipts statements for the year ended 31 March 1992.
(8 Marks)

(c) Define the matching concept and examine its application in the accounting system found in Central Government Accounting.
(5 Marks)

Examination Question 2

A small department of Central Government is split into three sections each of which maintains its accounts on a receipts and payments basis.

The returns for the year ended 31st March 1986 are shown below

Section:	A £	B £	C £
Receipts:			
Appropriations in Aid	80,000	60,000	100,000
Section C Receipts	20,000	25,000	
Payments:			
Salaries	205,000	245,000	230,000
General Administration	45,000	45,000	50,000
Miscellaneous	17,000	20,000	64,000

The following information is also of relevance:

(1) The supply grant vote for the department as a whole amounted to £895,000 gross and was made up as follows:

Salaries	£685,000
General Administration	£155,000
Miscellaneous	£ 55,000

(2) Authorised Appropriations in Aid amounted to £230,000.

(3) The intersection payments made by Section C are included in the Miscellaneous figure.

(4) Accounts rendered by the sub-accountant show final payments for the year of £2,000. This was wholly chargeable to General Administration.

REQUIRED:

(a) Prepare an Appropriation Account for the year ended 31 March 1986 and comment briefly on the performance of the department.

(11 Marks)

(b) Explain the role of the Appropriation Account in Central Government.

(4 Marks)

426

(c) Draw up a revised Appropriation Account based on the following revised receipts figures.

	A	B	C
Receipts	£	£	£
Appropriations in Aid	80,000	60,000	80,000
	20,000	25,000	

- All expenditure figures including the sub-accountants return remain the same.

- Authorised Appropriations in Aid remain as £230,000.

(7 Marks)

(d) Outline the special circumstances that lead to the adoption of "fund accounting" in public sector organisations.

(8 Marks)

Examination Question 3

(a)   Compare and contrast the accounting conventions and practices of a central government non-trading activity with those followed in respect of such activities in local authorities.   (5 Marks)

(b)   The following is a summary of the transactions of a supply grant for a small central government department for the year ended 31 March 1992.

   (I)   Supply grant vote £680,000 gross and £640,000 net.

   (II)   Vote on account £280,000
           Balance of grant £360,000

   (III)   Total sum drawn during the year per Paymaster General's monthly statements £596,000

   (IV)   Payable orders drawn on the Paymaster General total £614,800 for the year. £10,000 of these orders was for imprests to Sub-accountants and £604,800 for final payments which are chargeable to:

Subhead	£
Salaries etc	568,400
General admin expenses	26,900
Miscellaneous expenses	9,500
	604,800

           The Paymaster' General's statements show that of the total of the payable orders, £7,800 remained uncashed up to 31 March 1992.

   (V)   During the financial year the department has collected receipts amounting to £48,200 (to be used as Appropriations in Aid).

   (VI)   Periodical accounts rendered by sub-accountants show final payments for the year of £8,000 chargeable to :

Subhead	£
Salaries etc	2,800
Miscellaneous expenses	5,200

   (VII)   The ledgers for the previous year 1990/91 show that as at March 1991 the balance of the supply grant for that year to be surrendered was £68,400, of which £49,300 remained undrawn from the Consolidated Fund, £18,300 was with the Paymaster General, and £800 with Sub-accountants. The Treasury has informed the department that £49,300 undrawn from the Consolidated Fund is cancelled, and that the remaining balances are to be treated as though they had been taken out of the Supply Grant for the current year.

   (VIII) Orders drawn in 1991/92 but unpaid on 30 June 1992 amount to £2,200. These orders are to be cancelled and are in respect of General Administrative Expenses.

(IX)   The Paymaster General's monthly statements for April and May 1992 show that Payable Orders drawn in 1991/92 but presented for encashment after 31 March 1992 amounted to £5,600.

(X)   The amount of receipts authorised to be used as Appropriations in Aid of expenditure is limited by the Appropriations Act to £40,000, and any surplus receipts are therefore payable to the Consolidated Fund.

As the Accounting Officer responsible to Parliament you are required to produce:

(a)   Ledger accounts to record the above transactions

(14 Marks)

(b)   An Appropriation Account.

(11 Marks)

Examination Question 4

You are given the following information relating to the Department of Government Records for 1992/93.

a) The Supply Grant Vote is made up as follows:

Sub Head	£
Salaries	14,000,000
Accommodation	4,000,000
Other G.A.E.	2,000,000
Capital	5,000,000
	25,000,000
Appropriations in Aid	1,200,000

b) The surplus grant from 1991/92 was £430,000 of which

£300,000	was in the Consolidated Fund.
£100,000	was with the Paymaster General.
£30,000	was with the subaccountants.

c) Of the net Supply Grant, funds were released as follows:

	£
Vote On Account	10,800,000
Balance of Grant	13,000,000
	23,800,000

d) The following payable orders were issued by the department:

	£
Accommodation	3,750,000
Other G.A.E.	1,800,000
Advances to sub a/c	50,000
Capital	4,700,000
Payments to Government Salaries Agency (GSA) see note (e)	13,885,250

All payable orders issued were cashed during the year.

e) In 1992/93 the Department set up a standing deposit with the Government Salaries Agency (GSA), transferring salary payment duties to the Agency. Of the total payments to the GSA, the following information is given:

1st payment

1st April 1992	£3,500,000

being an advance to GSA to establish a deposit a/c

2nd payment

GSA Booking Minute for Dept.   Date 6/7/92
Govt Records 1st quarter.
April-June 1992/93

	Dr £	Cr £
Salaries Vote	3,450,000	
Staff Advances	12,000	
Staff Recoveries		2,000
Balance due to GSA		3,460,000
	3,462,000	3,462,000

3rd payment

GSA Booking Minute for Dept.   Date 6/10/92
Govt Records 2nd quarter.
July-Sept 1992/93

	Dr £	Cr £
Salaries Vote	3,450,000	
Staff Advances	---	
Staff Recoveries		3,000
Balance due to GSA		3,447,000
	3,450,000	3,450,000

4th payment

GSA Booking Minute for Dept.   Date 6/1/93
Govt Records 3rd quarter.
Oct-Dec 1992/93

	Dr £	Cr £
Salaries Vote	3,470,000	
Staff Advances	15,000	
Staff Recoveries		6,750
Balance due to GSA		3,478,250
	3,485,000	3,485,000

<u>5th payment</u>

	GSA Booking Minute for Dept. Govt Records 4th quarter. Dec March 1992/93	Date 6/4/93

	Dr £	Cr £
Salaries Vote	3,460,000	
Staff Advances	30,000	
Staff Recoveries		14,250
Balance due to GSA		3,475,750
	3,490,000	3,490,000

Note: This is the April booking minute. The cash replenishment should not be processed in the ledgers for 1992/93.

f) Payments by sub accountants were as follows:

	£
G.A.E.	40,000
Accommodation	25,000
	65,000

g) During the year Treasury informed the department that the £430,000 to be surrendered from the previous year will be cleared as follows:

£300,000   in the Consolidated Fund is cancelled; and
£130,000   is to be taken out of the Supply Grant for the current year.

h) The sums drawn by the Paymaster General's Office from the Consolidated Fund were £23,000,000

i) Receipts banked during the year were as follows:

	£
Appropriations in Aid	1,580,000
CFER	12,000

REQUIRED

As the Accounting Officer responsible to Parliament you are required to produce:

(a) Ledger accounts to record the above transactions

(12 marks)

(b) An Appropriation Account for the year ended 31/3/93

(8 marks)

(c) Define the matching concept and comment on its application found in Central Government Vote Accounting

(5 marks)

Examination Question 5

Part (a)

From the following information prepare an Historic Cost Profit and Loss Account for the Crown Supplies Trading Fund for the year ending 31 March 1989 and a Balance Sheet as at 31 March 1989.

(20 Marks)

Balances as at 1 April 1988	Dr £000	Cr £000
Fixed Assets	74,200	
Depreciation		36,800
Asset Revaluation Reserve		16,100
Provision for Liabilities(insurance)		2,400
National Loans Fund		17,500
General Reserve		26,200

Transactions during the year

Discounts allowed	3,180	
Turnover	283,240	
Cost of Sales:		
-Product Supply	152,600	
-Fuel Supply	16,900	
-Operational Services	83,100	
Salaries and wages	8,210	
NAO fees	135	
Depreciation	4,230	
Rent, rates, and service charges	6,180	
Other Expenditure	7,250	

Balances as at 31 March 1989

Investments (long term)	9,200	
Current Assets	28,210	
Current Liabilities	7,065	

Notes

1.   All balances remaining on the Profit and Loss Account are transferred to the General Reserve Account.

2.   Interest charges amount to £2,530,000 of which £2,490,000 has been paid and the remainder was due during 1988/89, but has not been accounted for, and is not included in the Balance for Current Liabilities.

3.   Net Loans raised amounted to £3,200,000, the cash included in Current Assets includes this sum.

4.   Other expenditure includes a further £200,000 contribution to the Insurance Reserve Account.

Part (b)

With the assistance of the following information prepare a Statement which is based on the concepts of Current Cost Accounting, considering whether the 5% Current Cost Return required in the Treasury Minute, has been achieved for 1988/89.

1.   Averaged Current Cost Net Assets   £85,200,000

            Current Cost Adjustments

2.   COSA   £120,000
        MWCA   £ 60,000

        Depreciation   £4,260,000

(5 marks)

Total: 25 Marks

Examination Question 6

You are given the following information on the new Vehicle Inspection Agency which is required to produce accruals accounts with effect from 31/3/92.

Balances as at:	31/3/92 £000	31/3/93 £000
Land Buildings	30,089	?
Equipment	6,218	?
Debtors	---	589
Cash at bank & in hand	---	2,815
Creditors	2,961	5,130
Public Dividend Capital	19.100	?
Long Term Loans	14,246	?
Revaluation Reserve	---	?
Income & Expenditure A/c	---	?

Transactions during the year:	£000
Income from Vehicle Inspections	42,062
Other Operating Activities	1,903
Staff Costs	26,369
Depreciation Land Buildings	663
Depreciation Equipment	1,435
Provision for Insurance	250
Other Expenditure	12,356
Interest paid on Loans	1,491
Payments to acquire Equipment	135
Interest Received	547
Payments to acquire Land/Buildings	2,863
Provision for Early Retirement	171

Notes

(I)   The payments to acquire fixed assets were cash payments and the closing cash balance is already adjusted.

(II)   Payments from the insurance provision were £6,000. the closing bank balance has been adjusted.

(III)   The total pensions liability provision under early retirement is to be charged to the income and expenditure account. Payments from the provision fund during the year amounted to £57,000. The closing cash balance has been adjusted.

(IV)   Fixed asset revaluation were as follows:
        Equipment :   £281,000 increased
        Land & Buildings :   £2,417,000 decreased

435

Surplus deficits arising on revaluation are taken to the revaluation reserve. Permanent reductions in the value of fixed assets are charged to the I & E A/c. The view of the directing board is that the diminution in the fixed assets is not permanent and revaluation should not be charged to the Income and Expenditure account.

(V)   Interest receipts and payments were in cash. The closing cash balance has been adjusted.

REQUIRED:

Prepare   - a Balance Sheet as at 1/4/92   (2 marks)
             - an Income & Expenditure A/c to year end 31/3/93   (4 marks)
             - a Balance Sheet as at 1/4/93   (6 marks)
             - a cash flow statement to year end 31/3/93   (4 marks)

Identify the main source of funding for trading fund agencies and explain the circumstances under which each source of funding is appropriate.

                                                        (4 marks)

Identify the key features of the accounting and finance regimes that apply to

        Government Departments financed by a vote

        On Vote Agencies

        Trading Fund Agencies   (5 marks)

                                        Total :   25 marks

Examination Question 7

The following information is given to you on the Government Mint Office

Balances as at:	31/3/91 £000	31/3/92 £000
Fixed Assets	29,110	?
Stocks	52,061	65,585
Depreciation Reserve	11,233	?
Debtors	8,384	10,898
Creditors	45,541	62,505
Investments	3,000	-
Cash at Bank & in Hand	4,737	9,300
Public Dividend Capital	7,000	?
Retained Profit & Loss	32,459	?
Provisions for liabilities & charges	1,059	

Transactions during the year:

	£000
Turnover	82,962
Other Income	7,165

Expenditure	
Materials and Consumables	29,816
Staff Costs	16,883
Pensions	3,274
Operating Charges	14,954
External Charges	11,627
Notional Insurance Charge	441

Other Information;

Additions to Fixed Assets	3,266
Proceeds from sale of Fixed Assets	4
Interest Receivable	769
Interest Payable	439
Dividend Payable to the Consolidated Fund	10,000

Notes:

1.   The depreciation charge for the year is £2,040,000 and it has not been included in the above figures.

2.   An adjustment is required in respect of Audit Fees. The fee is £58,000 and this sum has not been included in the closing creditors figure shown above.

3. The Fixed Assets that were sold were in the ledgers at a £133,000 and the depreciation accumulated against these assets was £133,000.

The cash receipt from the sale of the Fixed Assets has not been included in the closing cash balance.

4. Included in the opening debtors balance is the sum £87,000 for interest receivable in the 1990/91 financial year.

Included in the closing debtors figure is the sum £10,000 for interest receivable in 1991/92.

5. The opening and closing creditors balances for interest payable and dividends payable are as follows:

	Dividends Payable: £000	Interest Payable: £000
Balance as at 31/3/91	14,000	17
Balance as at 31/3/92	10,000	2

These balances are included in the global opening and closing creditor balance figures.

6. Fixed Asset additions have not been accounted for in the asset ledgers. In order to establish the cash paid for Fixed Assets during the financial year the following information is provided

Creditors - Fixed Assets	£000
Balance 31/3/91	0
Balance 31/3/92	438,000

These balances are included in the global opening and closing creditor balance figures.

7. The provision for insurance has not been adjusted for in the operating account or the provision reserve.

Required:

From the above information prepare:

An opening balance sheet as at 31/3/91

(3 marks)

An operating account for the year ending 31/3/92

A closing Balance Sheet as at 31/3/92

(10 marks)

A cash flow statement for year ended 31/3/92

(7 marks)

(10 marks)
(Total 30 marks)

CHAPTER 16   INTRODUCTION TO THE NATIONAL HEALTH SERVICE

16.1 <u>Introduction</u>

Chapters 16, 17 and 18 look at the NHS, it's organisation and accounting requirements.

The NHS is huge - the largest employer in Western Europe - and by it's nature complex in the sense of both the services and activities it undertakes and it's financial structure. It would be impossible in this book to cover <u>all</u> of the financial information used and produced by the NHS, and therefore we concentrate on the major reports required by the Department of Health (DoH). Students are advised to study the DoH manual of accounts for a more complete picture of the financial requirements of the NHS. All students should acquire a set of Annual Accounts and Financial Returns for a Health Authority or NHS Trust, in order to appreciate the full complexity of the role of the Treasurer or Director of Finance in his statutory duty to produce these documents.

The organisation of the NHS has changed over the years since 1948, in response to social and environmental changes, and political re-organisations. Chapter 17 looks at the evolution of the NHS to the structure and financial regime present today. The emphasis is on the new internal market and contracting environment, with a brief look at the previous cash limited environment. Students should study the former organisation structure of the NHS in other texts in order to fully appreciate the cultural change the NHS is currently going through.

Chapter 18 looks at the financial requirements for the NHS. The introduction of capital accounting into the NHS and the creation of Trusts are two of the new and challenging accounting tasks studied in this chapter. Examples are fully worked through, and at the end of this chapter students will find a number of examination style questions for further practice.

CHAPTER 17   THE ORGANISATION OF THE NHS

17.1 The Evolution of the NHS

The NHS was established in 1948 and up until 1989
remained much the same in organisational terms. The
Whitley Council regulations introduced in 1948 still
exist even today. However, the 1989 White Paper
brought about radical change in the NHS and the
structure we see today is not only very different from
that in the earlier years, but is one that is still
changing and forming at a rapid pace. Authorities are
still adjusting to the new NHS environment and the
future holds major changes such as more NHS Trusts,
more external funding and service provision and the
introduction of new pay terms and conditions - yes the
Whitley Council regulations may be abandoned after over
45 years in existence!

Below is a summary of the evolution of the NHS in
England and Wales (the organisation in Scotland and
Northern Ireland is different):

1948   NHS ESTABLISHED
                WHITLEY COUNCIL ESTABLISHED

1968   DHSS CREATED FROM THE MINISTRIES OF HEALTH &
                SOCIAL SECURITY

1974   REORGANISATION   14 RHA's
                                    90 AREA HA's
                                       FPC's

1976   RESOURCE ALLOCATION WORKING PARTY (RAWP) -
                Allocation of funds based on needs and
                population served - Cash Limit System

1982   RESTRUCTURE   14 RHA's
                                    192 DHA's
                                     90 FPC's
                                      8 SHA's

1983   GRIFFITHS REPORT - GENERAL MANAGEMENT
                                  - PRP FOR GENERAL MANAGERS
                                  - BOARD OF DIRECTORS

1988   DHSS SPLIT INTO DoH AND DSS
1989   WHITE PAPER: WORKING FOR PATIENTS
                   - Business Environment
                   - Purchasers and Providers
                   - NHS Trusts
1989   WHITE PAPER: CARING FOR PEOPLE
                   - Local Authority role as Purchaser
                   - Care in the Community

17.2 The Structure of the NHS

The current structure of the NHS is shown in diagram 17.2.1. The roles of each tier are briefly explained below.

Diagram 17.2.1

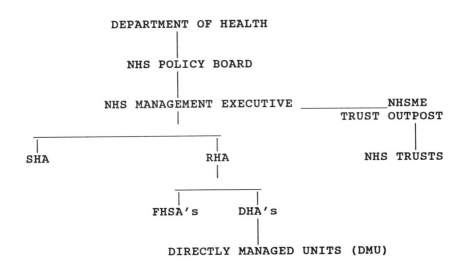

The Department of Health's role is to "continue the promotion of a comprehensive Health Service in the UK" e.g. they bid for funds for the NHS at the annual Public Expenditure Survey Committee (PESC).

The NHS Policy Board (chaired by the Secretary of State for Health) take the strategic decisions for the NHS. e.g. they will allocate the funds to particular projects and determine the basis of allocation of funds to the NHS bodies.

The NHS Management Executive (NHSME) are responsible for the day to day operational control of the NHS. e.g. they allocate the funds to the RHA's and SHA's. Regional NHSME outposts were set up to deal solely and directly with NHS Trusts due to their different operational and financial requirements.

The Regional Health Authorities (RHA) are responsible for Health Care Programmes and regional services such as the Blood Transfusion Service. The RHA's are also responsible for allocating funds to the DHA's and FHSA's, who are the "purchasers" in the new NHS financial regime. RHA members are appointed by the

Secretary of State.

The District Health Authorities (DHA) purchase health care for the their local population from providers within and outside the area. Prior to the 1989 re-organisation the DHA would allocate the cash limit to the hospitals and providers within their district. The revised method is to negotiate contracts with providers - see below. Two thirds of DHA members are appointed by the Secretary of State and the remainder are elected members from Local Authorities.

The Special Health Authorities (SHA) are providers of specialist health care with an emphasis on Research, Development and Teaching and Training in conjunction with the University Postgraduate Colleges - e.g. The Hospitals for Sick Children SHA in association with the Institute of Child Health, provides specialist health care for children at it's Great Ormond Street and Queen Elizabeth Hospitals in London. SHA's are currently funded directly by the DoH, however, they will be entering the NHS internal market in 1994 with direct funding for their research and development costs - this funding will be in the form of a "grant" and is called the SIFTR (Service Increment for Teaching and Research).

DMU's are the hospitals and other health care providers, such as Community Services units, managed by DHA's. The DMU usually has a unit General Manager and Finance Director, who are accountable to the DHA Board. DMU's provide health care services to their owning DHA, other DHA and RHA's and other purchasers within and outside the NHS. All surpluses/losses incurred by the DMU are retained by the owning DHA.

FHSA's are responsible to the RHA for the payment of general medical, dental, opthalmic and other practitioners, for the payment to pharmacists and others for certain services and drugs dispensed, for the collection of prescription income (including DHA's for hospital prescriptions), for setting and monitoring indicative drug prescribing amounts, the monitoring of GPFH budgets (on behalf of the RHA), providing advice and support to GPFHs and making payments to providers on behalf of GPFHs.

NHS Trusts are those health care providers who have "opted out" from their DHA and have been granted Trust status by the DoH. The Trusts receive their funds from the purchasers within and outside the NHS - see later.

GPFHs (General Practitioner Fund Holders) represent a purchaser in the new NHS. Subject to a maximum

practice list size and subject to ability to manage
funds, practices may seek fundholding status. The
doctors within such practices are empowered to contract
with providers of their choice and decide where money
allocated to the practice is spent (i.e. on drugs,
hospital services or other forms of care). The GPFHs
are allowed to carry forward surpluses and doctors may
personally benefit financially from being fundholders.

The white paper intends to create a NHS that provides a
better service to patients, promotes value for money
and makes the NHS more "business like". Hospitals are
encouraged to seek self governing status (NHS Trusts)
with incentives such as control over assets, investment
policies and employment terms and conditions - just as
Schools were encouraged to become self governing in
recent years. The changes have certainly led to much
financial activity in the NHS, costing and pricing
patient treatments, negotiation of contracts and the
production of many many invoices! Whether this has
achieved the intended objectives is yet to be proven.

17.3 The Financing of the NHS

Around 86% of the cost of the NHS is funded from the
national taxation pool. The remaining funds are from
the National Insurance contributions levied by the
Government. However, Hospitals and other providers
often generate their own funds, such as from Private
Patient activity, which increases the spending on the
NHS.

The estimated Government expenditure on the NHS for the
1993/4 financial year is £29bn. Table 17.3.1 shown
below details this.

Table 17.3.1   1993/4 NHS EXPENDITURE:

		£m
HOSPITAL AND COMMUNITY HEALTH		
SERVICES	- REVENUE	20,079
	- CAPITAL	1,908
FAMILY HEALTH SERVICES		6,088
DEPARTMENTAL ADMINISTRATION COSTS		290
CENTRALLY FINANCED SERVICES		705
NHS TRUSTS		-674

(Source: Autumn Statement 1992)

444

These funds are allocated by the Public Expenditure Survey Committee (PESC) to the DoH at the beginning of each financial year. The DoH then allocates these funds to the RHA's, SHA's and NHS Trusts and since 1976 this has been in the form of Revenue and Capital Cash Limits. Up to 1981 planning and resource allocation was done on a "volume" basis (i.e. the level of resources required to support a given volume of services). From 1982/83 cash planning was introduced in order to control the actual cash spent by the DoH - that is pay and price increase assumptions were built in to the original cash limits set and any variations to these assumptions had to be funded by the NHS. In the past the RHA's would then allocate the funds to DHA's and FHSA's. The DHA's would then allocate funds to the DMU's. From 1977, such allocations were based on the "RAWP" formula, developed by the Resource Allocation Working Party, which took into account population, age, sex, beds and caseloads. This form of funding (known as the cash limit system) changed from 1990 to a resident / capitation funding basis - the purchaser / provider split. Some of the deficiencies of RAWP that led to its demise were that it did not review the total resources allocated to the NHS, it was restricted to geographical disparities which were in themselves narrowly defined (e.g. Local Authority and FPC expenditures were excluded), and it used SMR's as a measure of morbidity and it is argued that mortality statistics do not reflect health care needs.

There is also an activity that is termed "top slicing" of funds - which is where allocations are reduced or "top sliced" to fund activities such as Supra Regional services, Training, etc. These are services used by all of the members receiving the initial allocation and is therefore in effect funded by them.

Prior to 1990, Health Authorities could carry forward underspendings on cash limit, transfer between capital and revenue cash limits (up to stated limits) and also use "brokerage" to meet cash limit in any one year. (Brokerage is where health authorities borrow each others cash limits in order to meet their own cash limit). This flexibility has now been replaced with Trusts being able to borrow from the DoH or externally (within external financing limits), and DMU's relying on the DHA to meet deficits or broker surpluses. Purchasers are still cash limited, and can presumably use these flexibilities, however the providers can only use the contracting system to meet the financial needs of the Authority. In 1991/92 Trusts were allowed to broker EFL between themselves with reversing entries in 1992/3.

17.4 The Purchaser / Provider System

The "Purchasers" are the RHA's, the DHA's, the FHSA's and the GP Fund Holders (GPFH). These organisations will be allocated funds based on a weighted capitation formula. Each regions' population has been weighted for demands on health services by different age groups then adjusted by the SMR and geographical supplements to derive their "weighted capitation" base. The funds are then allocated based upon these. The purchasers then purchase health care for their population from providers of health care. Providers include the DMU's, NHS Trusts, SHA's, Ambulance services and private health care providers. RHA's and DHA's are also providers of some services - e.g. blood donor and transfusion service. It is the duty of providers to set their prices for health care based upon the cost of that health care without cross subsidising services - this is not allowed under the DoH regulations.

It should be noted that the Weighted Capitation formula, like it's predecessors, is being phased in to reduce the impact upon local services in the short term.

17.5 Capital Charges in the NHS

Another change brought in under the 1990 Act is the introduction of capital accounting to the NHS. In the past the NHS received a separate cash limit allocation for capital expenditure. This cash limit would then be used to purchase capital assets. The definition of capital assets at that time was:

a   acquisition of land & premises
b   work schemes > £15,000
c   equipment > £7,500
d   salaries of staff on capital projects

Authorities would bid for capital allocations each year and plan spending on capital assets in accordance with the amount allocated by the DoH.

The requirement now is for assets to be depreciated based upon their replacement value and DoH estimated lives. In addition to the depreciation there is a "capital charge" made on all assets of 6%, which is a charge made by the DoH for the cost of the capital it has provided.

From 1/04/93 any good (or group of items, such as a
network of PC's) with a cost over £5,000 and a life of
more than one year is to be classified as a **capital
asset** in the NHS. As an asset it will therefore attract
capital charges.

Capital Charges are a revenue charge payable by
Purchasers to Providers and are included in the
provider prices for health care services. The DHA's
collect capital charges from the DMU's on behalf of the
RHA - they act as a collecting agent. The RHA and DHA
also pay capital charges on administrative use of
assets. Trusts pay capital charges directly to the RHA.
Any capital funds required will be from the capital
charges fund - however, the RHA must first approve the
scheme and determine the allocation to all providers
within it's area. In essence, therefore, providers
still need to bid for capital funds and compete for the
limited resources available - there is no guarantee
that the amount paid in will be returned at the time it
is required to replace or upgrade the asset.

The objectives of capital charging are to:

* increase awareness of NHS management of the cost of
  capital

* provide an incentive for the efficient use of capital
  assets

* ensure that capital charges are fully reflected in
  the pricing of hospital services which will promote
  fair competition within the NHS and with private
  health care providers.

There are 2 elements to the capital charge - the
DEPRECIATION charge and the INTEREST charge. There are
also a number of terms which students must be familiar
with if they are to understand the capital accounting
requirements of the NHS. These are discussed below.

Depreciation:

Depreciation is based on the average value of an asset
during the year. The value is currently indexed
quarterly by the DoH. Upon acquisition depreciation is
due in the quarter following the quarter of
acquisition. If an asset is disposed of the
depreciation is adjusted in the quarter of disposal.
This is intended to encourage managers to acquire and
dispose of assets quickly and at the most appropriate
and economic time. A recent review group has

recommended that capital charges are calculated
annually rather than quarterly, which will be far
easier and less time consuming for the NHS Finance
departments.

Straight line depreciation is used but there are two
formulae - one for assets with a variable value and
life (e.g. buildings have their replacement values and
lives revalued), and the other for assets with a
standard life (e.g. IT equipment). The formulae are
shown in the following section (the formulae shown are
those currently provided for quarterly repayments - if
this is changed to annual charges, then the student
only needs to remove the quarter figures and use the
same formulae).

Backlog depreciation is calculated in order to show the
net book value (NBV) of the current cost of the asset
BUT it is NOT charged to the revenue account as part of
the capital charges.

Interest:

Interest charges are made on the value of assets as a
charge for the cost of capital. The current rate
charged by the DoH is 6%. The charge is currently
levied on a quarterly basis on the opening net book
value for assets with variable lives and on the
previous quarters net book value for assets with
standard lives. (Again this could change to annual
charges in the near future).

Disposal Adjustment:

The disposal adjustment is the loss / profit made on
the sale of an asset. i.e. the NBV at the date of sale
(including the quarters depreciation) - sale proceeds.

Asset Register:

This is the register in which all capital assets
belonging to the HA and the Trust Funds of the
Authority, are recorded. The register will show the
date of purchase, the life, the original cost, the
current value and the depreciation charges for each
asset. The asset register needs to be maintained and
regularly checked if HA's are to be sure of incurring
the correct level of capital charges for the assets
they are using. It is vital that registers are promptly
updated for any additions or disposals during the year.

Donated Assets:

These are assets which have been donated or bought with

donated funds. Whilst they appear in the asset
register, they are not subject to capital charges. HA's
are expected to record and value such assets and
calculate the depreciation. This is important for good
accounting practice and arriving at the full cost of
health care services. Donated resources, in the pricing
mechanism, should be treated in accordance with the
donor's wishes. i.e. the authority must use the asset
to subsidise the cost of the specific area receiving
the donation.

The 1992/93 allocations were based on capital charges
being due on the assets recorded in the accounts. In
future they will be based on a WCF (weighted capitation
formula). Therefore it is only book entries in the
1992/93 accounts and not CASH.

The accounting entries for capital charges are shown in
the next section.

17.6 <u>Trust Funds:</u>

Trust Funds are all property received, held and
administered by NHS organisations. These are often
referred to as "non exchequer" items in the NHS.
Students must be careful to distinguish clearly between
NHS Trust Funds and NHS Trusts. Section 2.7 examines
the NHS Trusts recently created following the 1989
White Paper. Trust Funds have been in existence in the
NHS for a very long time and represent all donations
made to the NHS organisation owning the funds.

There are two types of Trust Fund:

a) GENERAL FUNDS
    General funds originate from donations and legacies
    given to NHS organisations which are not earmarked
    for a specific use. The use of these funds is
    determined by the Trustees of the organisation
    concerned.

b) SPECIFIC FUNDS
    Specific funds are donations and legacies granted to
    NHS organisations for specific uses, and can only be
    spent on those defined activities. For example a
    donation may be made for the purpose of purchasing a
    Scanner for a hospital, in this case the monies
    donated can only be used to fund the purchase of a
    Scanner.

The health authorities are able to invest the trust
funds received in stocks and shares (unlike NHS
exchequer funds) - in compliance with the Trustees
Investment Act 1961.

17.7 <u>NHS Trusts</u>

a) <u>Introduction:</u>

NHS Trusts are hospitals and other units which are run by their own Boards of Directors and are independent of district and regional management. Trusts have wide ranging freedoms not previously available to them or to DMU's or other units under HA control. The key difference is that Trusts are <u>operationally independent</u> from the NHS whilst remaining within the NHS. The benefits of independence for Trusts are briefly that they can;

* acquire, own & dispose of assets
* make their own case for capital developments
* borrow money within annually agreed limits (EFL)
* create their own management structures
* employ their own staff and determine terms and conditions of employment
* advertise their services (within professional guidelines).

To achieve Trust status a unit must demonstrate:

1   the benefits and improved quality of service to patients,

2   that management has the skills and capacity to run the unit effectively,

3   the involvement of their senior professional staff, especially medical consultants, in the management of the organisation

4   the financial viability of the unit.

The accounting requirements for NHS Trusts differ from the rest of the NHS and will be examined later in this chapter.

b) <u>Structure:</u>

A Trust is run by a Board of Directors consisting of a non-executive chairman appointed by the Secretary of State, up to 5 non-executive directors (2 appointed by RHA from local community and 3 by Secretary of State) and an equal number of executive directors up to a maximum of 5, including the Chief Executive and the Director of Finance.

Each Trust is accountable to the NHSME. There are three

main accountability tools:

1   An Annual Business Plan

2   An Annual Report

3   Annual Accounts

Trusts are also required to provide in-year financial
monitoring information, some statistical information
and AIP's (Approval in Principle) for capital schemes.

c) <u>Financial Requirements:</u>

The Financial requirements for Trusts are:

1) **Financial Target**
   The Trust must make a real pre-interest return on
   assets of a minimum of 6%.

2) **Break Even**
   The Trust is required to break even on the income
   and expenditure account, allowing for the repayment
   of interest and PDC (Public Dividend Capital)
   dividends over two years.

3) **External Financing Limit (EFL)**
   This is the approved borrowing limit for the Trust.
   The Trust is able to purchase assets etc from
   borrowing. The EFL is in effect a cash limit on net
   external financing. External Finance is defined as
   the difference between agreed capital spending by a
   Trust and internally generated resources, such as
   Depreciation and surpluses. The EFL includes leases
   (with the exception of operational leases). A
   national EFL is set for the NHS during the PESC. The
   NHSME set individual EFL's for each Trust based upon
   their business plans. A Trust may receive a positive
   or negative or zero EFL. A negative EFL is where the
   Trusts resources are greater than it's spending
   requirements and therefore the Trust is required to
   use those resources to repay debt. The Trust must
   stay within it's EFL, although there is some
   flexibility allowed in that a Trust can apply for
   additional EFL of up to 1% of total turnover + fixed
   asset expenditure.

d) <u>Capital Base:</u>

Each Trust owns land, buildings, equipment and other
assets. The value of the net assets (i.e. total assets
less total liabilities) transferred to a Trust when it
is set up are represented by an **originating capital**

debt which is owed by the Trust to the Consolidated Fund. The originating capital debt is made up of two elements:

a) **Interest Bearing Debt (IBD),** and

b) **Public Dividend Capital (PDC).**

IBD has defined interest (currently 9%) and repayment terms (related to the life of the asset). Trusts can apply to repay IBD early, including any originating debt. PDC is a form of long term Government finance on which the Trust pays dividends to the Government (currently at 3%). Trusts are only required to pay interest on this when they have made a surplus after repayment of other interest. The split between IBD and PDC is determined by the Secretary of State, with the consent of the Treasury.

e) Borrowing:

Trusts are able to borrow from the Secretary of State or the commercial sector as long as they can demonstrate value for money and take the best terms available (normally the Government), and have the Secretary of States consent. The borrowing becomes IBD and counts against the EFL. In some instances PDC may be considered - such as for the construction/purchase of assets that do not become operational immediately and therefore cannot generate revenues for the Trust.

There is some flexibility for Trusts in borrowing - they can borrow in the last quarter of the year, with DoH approval, up to 1% of the Turnover + Capital expenditure. This will be deducted from the following year's EFL.

As with most public sector organisations Trusts cannot speculate with their resources (e.g. no swaps deals!) and cannot mortgage their assets - because they are still public assets and funds.

f) Surpluses:

A Trust can use surpluses to:

1) Fund Capital expenditure
2) Repay Loans
3) Invest in Government securities or other approved public or private investments.

17.8 Contracting in the NHS

On 1/04/92 an "internal market" in the NHS became operational. As stated above the essential principle of the market is the split between Purchasers and Providers of health care. Provider units have lost their direct funding link with their host district and, to obtain funds to operate, are required to enter into contracts to meet the demands of health care purchasers within and outside their host district. A contract will contain details of the volume of activity, the price for that activity and the quality of service required. The majority of contracts are for a one year period and commence on 1st April. Negotiations take into account historic trends, money available, price comparisons and results of any health needs assessments. A contract could be one of the following types:

a) **Block Contract or Subscription Contract**
    This is a contract for a defined range of activities and patients usually described in terms of health care specialties and number of patients treated. Purchasers pay in equal monthly instalments throughout the year. "True" Block Contracts give Purchasers unlimited access to a range of services. More sophisticated contracts contain tolerance levels for upper and lower activity thresholds. Purchasers will then either:

    1   re-negotiate the contract, requiring the Provider to repay funds in cases of under performance, provide additional funds or insist the provider lives within those available - usually by constraining activity

    2   negotiate an additional contract

    3   rely on either Cost and Volume or ECR contractual activity.

b) **Cost and Volume Contract**
    A cost and volume contract is similar to the block contract except minimum and maximum limits ar set. Up to the threshold the purchaser is charged as for block contracts. Once the threshold has been reached, a previously agreed price per case is paid, up to a volume ceiling.

c) **Cost per Case Contracts**
    In a cost per case contract the provider and purchaser agree a specific price for each case treated. Because of the range of variability of

resource input on each case, cost per case contracts often refer to individual patients or very specific procedures. A typical use of cost per case contracts is in the care of chronically ill patients who have definable treatment needs over a period of time. Cost per case contracting is very time consuming and demanding of good cost and activity information about treatment provided to patients.

d) Extra Contractual Referrals

An Extra Contractual Referral (ECR) is where a patient is referred where there is no contract with the purchaser referring them. Alternatively the contract under which they would be treated may be exhausted. Purchasers set an ECR budget each year to fund this activity. ECR authorisation from the Purchaser is required prior to treatment except in emergency cases or tertiary referrals i.e. referrals from Consultant to Consultant . Some treatments are treated extra contractually by providers because of the high costs involved or infrequency of the case (e.g. Kidney transplantation) or the high level of risk in changing referral patterns or if purchasers wish to influence referrals as every ECR is assessed.

In summary the implications of this contracting environment for Health Authorities and Providers are:

- Costing methods and systems are required

- Pricing techniques and systems are required

- Financial Monitoring needs are changed

- Cash flow monitoring requirements

- Increased invoicing and debt collection requirements

- Capital accounting techniques are required

- Borrowing strategies and procedures are required

The future for the NHS Finance world is exciting with many challenging tasks required of accountants to help the NHS in providing an efficient and effective service to the public whilst improving accountability and

financial information available to the DoH and the
public. The growing role of the Local Authorities in
health care is also a feature in this new world, which
may be an accounting minefield at present but will no
doubt improve the service delivered as well as the
financial information produced.

CHAPTER 18   ACCOUNTING REQUIREMENTS IN THE NHS

18.1 Introduction

The Director of Finance of each NHS organisation is
required to prepare and submit by 30th June each year,
the annual accounts for the year ended 31st March.
These accounts are used as the basis for the
Appropriation Accounts and Summarised Accounts which
the DoH is required to prepare and submit to the C & AG
(see the chapter on Central Government Accounting) for
certification and submission to Parliament.

The annual accounts of HA's comprise three statements,
the Income & Expenditure Account, a Balance Sheet, and
a Source and Application of Funds Statement, supported
by five subsidiary sections as follows:

        1   Accounting Policies
        2   Notes to the Income and Expenditure Account
        3   Accounts of Directly Managed Units
        4   Accounts of Common Services
        5   Notes to the Balance Sheet

The purpose of the annual accounts is to satisfy the
primary requirements of public accountability for the
use of NHS resources. The accountable body remains the
Health Authority (RHA, DHA, FHSA, NHS TRUST and SHA's).

The standard format of accounts is laid out in the NHS
Manual of Accounts and the NHS Trusts Manual of
Accounts, which all HA's and Trusts are required to
comply to. There is also a section in the manual
covering the accounts for Trust Funds. The manual also
defines where expenses are to be coded in the annual
accounts - to aid consistency and uniformity in the
NHS. The summary accounts show the consolidated
financial performance of the accountable body - i.e.
the DHA or RHA or SHA. The notes detail the Purchaser
and Provider financial performance.

The Accounts are audited in the same way that other
private and public sector organisation accounts are
audited. The NHS external Auditor is the Audit
Commission. Students should examine the certificates
required to be included in the Accounts by the Auditor
and the Authority in a set of Health Authority
Accounts.

18.2 Accounting for Capital Charges

As discussed in section 1 the NHS is now required to account for capital items in the accounts. This involves the inclusion of fixed assets in the Balance Sheet and the calculation of both depreciation and interest charges. The capital charges are charged to the revenue account with corresponding entries in the Balance Sheet. In 1993/4 they will become cash transactions and the cash equivalent will actually transfer to RHA's and the DoH. The accounting entries for capital charges are shown on the following pages.

ACCOUNTING ENTRIES FOR CAPITAL CHARGES:

1) DEPRECIATION:

	DR	CR
CAPITAL ACCOUNT	Deprec.	
DEPRECIATION A/C		Deprec.

being the depreciation of the asset in the Balance Sheet.

	DR	CR
REVENUE A/C - CAPITAL CHARGES	Deprec.	
NON CASH SETTLEMENT A/C		Deprec.

being the charge to the Revenue a/c and the relevant DHA or RHA a/c.

2) INTEREST:

	DR	CR
REVENUE A/C - CAPITAL CHARGES	Interest	
NON CASH SETTLEMENT A/C		Interest

being the interest charged to the revenue a/c and the DHA/RHA a/c.

3) DISPOSAL:

	DR	CR
CURRENT A/C - RHA	Profit on disposal	
(or DHA non cash)		
CAPITAL CHARGES		Profit

being the offset of profits from disposal on the capital charges. These are reversed for a loss on disposal.

4) REVALUATION:

```
TANGIBLE ASSETS          Reval adjustment
  CAPITAL A/C                        Reval adj
```

being the increase of fixed asset values and the
credit to the capital a/c.
(Revaluation adjustment = old depreciated value -
new value)

5) INDEXATION:

a) Of the asset:

```
ASSETS                   Indexation adj
  CAPITAL A/C                        Index. adj
```

b) Of the depreciation:

```
CAPITAL A/C              indexation of dep.
  DEPRECIATION A/C                   Index. Dep
```

6) DONATED ASSETS:

a) CAPITALISE:
```
        FIXED ASSETS             DR
          DEFERRED DONATION              CR
```

b) INDEXATION:
```
        FIXED ASSETS             DR
          DEFERRED DONATION              CR
```

c) DEPRECIATION:
```
        REVENUE A/C - DEP        DR
          DEPRECIATION A/C               CR
```

d) BACKLOG DEPRECIATION:
```
        DEFERRED DONATION        DR
          DEPRECIATION A/C               CR
```

7) NHS TRUSTS:

Depreciation is the same but not paid over to RHA's.
The depreciation is retained by the NHS Trust for
the future replacement of capital assets. No
interest is charged on the assets, however, the
Trust is required to make a target rate of return on
assets (currently 6%) - as discussed in the previous
section.

The calculation of depreciation is carried out quarterly using the two formulae set by the DoH in the Capital Charges Manual. These formulae are shown below.

<u>DEPRECIATION FORMULAE:</u>

<u>Formula For Assets with Variable Life and Value.</u>

i)   The opening value (OV) of the new quarter equals the closing value (CV) of the quarter just ended.

ii)   The opening value is depreciated over the asset's remaining life expressed in quarters:

$$\text{Depreciation Charge for quarter (D)} = \frac{OV}{RL}$$

where RL = remaining life in quarters

iii)   The opening value less Depreciation (D) for the quarter is indexed:

$$\text{Indexation (I)} = (OV - D) \times \frac{CI - OI}{OI}$$

where CI = Closing Index
and   OI = Opening Index

iv)   The closing value for each quarter is:

$$\text{Closing Value (CV)} = OV - D + I$$

v)   When an asset is revalued the valuation becomes the new closing value. The adjusting entry in the accounts would be:

$$\text{Revaluation Adjustment} = \text{new valuation} - \text{previous closing value}$$

Formula For Assets with a Standard Life.

i)   The OV of the new quarter equals the CV of the previous quarter.

ii)   The opening replacement cost (ORC) has an index applied to it to give the closing replacement cost (CRC):

Indexation (I) = ORC x $\dfrac{CI - OI}{OI}$

CRC = ORC + I

iii)   The opening replacement value is depreciated over the asset's standard life expressed in quarters:

Depreciation
Charge for quarter = $\dfrac{ORC}{SL}$

where SL = Standard Life in quarters

iv)   The opening accumulated depreciation (OAD) equals the closing accumulated depreciation (CAD) of the previous quarter.

v)   The accumulated depreciation at the end of the quarter is indexed in the same way as the opening replacement cost:

Indexation I(d) = OAD + D x $\dfrac{CI - OI}{OI}$

This is the backlog depreciation which is calculated to ensure that the net book value (NBV) is at current cost. Backlog depreciation is <u>not</u> charged as part of capital charges in the revenue account.

vi)   CAD = OAD + D + I(d)

vii)   The Net Book Value can now be calculated

NBV = CRC - CAD

18.2 continued:

Exercise 18.1 below uses the above formulae to calculate capital charges for particular items of equipment. Students should be able to determine which formulae to use for assets.

Exercise 18.1

A District Health Authority purchased a building to be used for geriatric patients. The building cost £3,000,000 on 1/04/92 and has a standard life of 30 years.

A weighing and measuring machine was purchased for the new geriatric unit costing £20,000, also on 1/04/92 and has a life of 10 years.

On 1/05/92 the Authority sells a Cherrytree Laundry machine for £8,000. The machine has a replacement value of £10,400 and a life of 5 years at 1/04/92. The accumulated depreciation is £2,080.

The index at the start of each quarter are as follows:

Quarter:			
April	-	June	100
July	-	September	102
October	-	December	103
January	-	March	104

You are required to calculate the first quarters capital charges for the purchase of assets, and the disposal adjustment for the sale of the asset.

ANSWER TO EXERCISE 18.1

Geriatric JULY - SEPT (as due in quarter following
                      the quarter in which purchased)

		£
Opening value for quarter		3,000,000
Depreciation = $\dfrac{3,000,000}{120}$ no of quarters remaining		25,000

Net value		2,975,000
Indexation (2975000 x $\dfrac{103-102}{102}$)		29,167

Closing value for quarter		3,004,167

Capital Charge: 3000000 x 6% / 4		45,000

Total Capital Charges (45000+25000)		70,000

Weighing & Measuring Machine: JULY - SEPT (as above)

Opening Replacement Value		20,000
Indexation (20000 x $\dfrac{(103-102)}{102}$)		196

Closing replacement value		20,196
Depreciation Based on standard life of 10 years (20196/40)		500
Indexation on Depreciation		5

Accumulated indexed depreciation		505
Net Book Value (20196 - 505)		19,691
Capital Charges: opening NBV @ 6% (20000 x 6% / 4)		300

Total Capital Charge (500 + 300)		800

```
Washing Machine Disposal Adjustment:    APRIL - MAY
  (AS DUE IN QUARTER OF SALE)

Replacement cost @ 1/05/92                  10,400
Depreciation @ 1/04/92                       2,080
                                        ------------
Opening NBV                                  8,320
Depreciation for quarter (Life = 5yrs)         520
                                        ------------
                                             7,800
Less: Sale proceeds                          8,000
                                        ------------
Disposal Adjustment                           -200
                                        ------------


Capital Charges:
  Profit made on disposal                     -200
  Depreciation for qtr                         520
  Interest (8320 x 6% / 4)                     125
                                        ------------
Total Capital Charges for quarter
  of disposal                                  445
                                        ------------
```

18.3 The Revenue Income and Expenditure (I & E) Account

This is the first of the three summary statements and represents the accountable body's overall I & E performance for the year. In terms of RHA's this is a "headquarters" type account, for DHA's however, it is a summary of the Authority's purchasing activities and its management activities in relation to the provision of health care at DMU's. SHA's present provider type accounts for specific health care services. The accounts of NHS Trusts will be examined separately.

Each expenditure line of the I & E account is taken from a supporting note to the accounts, which detail the various components of the income or expenditure item. The I & E account is shown on the following page. Below is a description of each line of the account.

Allocations (subcode 100)
This is the total amount of cash received by the Authority (RHA, DHA or SHA) under the Cash Limit system.

Miscellaneous Income (subcode 110)
This is all other income received by the DHA or RHA, such as income from private patient activity, charitable contributions, income generation, etc. This does not include the income received by DMU's as this is shown separately in their accounts (see note 3.2).

Health care & related services purchased (subcode 150)
This is the total health care purchased from DMU's, SHA's, NHS Trusts and other providers within and outside the district. The figure is taken from subcode 150 on note 2.1.

Authority administration & purchasing expenses (subcode 160)
This is the total costs of administration, members costs etc and is shown in detail in note 2.2 to the accounts.

Other Services Expenditure (subcode 170)
This includes expenditure on the emergency bed service, registration and inspection of nursing homes and joint finance expenditure.

Community Health Councils (subcode 180)
This is the total spending on CHC's.

Net Revenue Operating Surplus or deficit of Directly Managed Units (subcode 210)
This is the figure shown at subcode 150 of note 3.1 to

the Accounts, and represents the performance in income and expenditure terms of the DMU's within the HA area.

Net Revenue Operating Surplus or deficit of Common Services (subcode 220)
This is the total net spend on common services as shown in note 4 to the accounts.

18.4 Notes to the Income & Expenditure Account

The notes to the I & E Account comprise of the following:

Note 2   Notes To The Income And Expenditure Account
Note 2.1   Purchase of Health Care
Note 2.2   Authority Administration, Purchasing, Other Services and Community Health Council's Expenditure.

Note 3   Accounts of Directly Managed Units
Note 3.1   Net Revenue Operating Surplus or Deficit of Directly Managed Units
Note 3.2   Income from Activities
Note 3.3   Other Operating Income (not involving patient care)
Note 3.4   Operating Expenses
Note 4   Common Services

The notes show the detail of the items in the I & E account and require completion prior to the completion of the I & E account.

18.5 A Worked Example of the I & E Account and Notes

Exercise 18.2 shown on the following pages works through the build up of the I & E account for a District Health Authority with 2 Directly Managed Units. The process is to complete the detailed notes to the accounts for both the purchasing authority (i.e. the DHA) and the DMU's, then use these figures to complete the summary I & E account for the year. The capital charges have been given in this example. Students may find in examination questions that capital charges have to be calculated in addition to the completion of the annual accounts. In examinations the standard forms would probably be provided, however, students must be familiar with the layout of NHS accounts and should work through the examples in this book by drawing up the accounts in the DoH manual of accounts format.

Exercise 18.2 NHS Income and Expenditure Account

The Cashless DHA has two DMU's, a General Hospital in the centre of town and a local cottage hospital at the north end of the District. The DHA also purchases health care from other provider units in the area and outside.

Below are the trial balance figures at 31/03/92.

	General Hospital £000	Local Hospital £000	DHA £000
Income from private patients	5,006	500	
Contrib'n from the Special Trustees		250	
Salaries & Wages	35,302	9,775	3,500
Supplies & Services			
- Clinical	7,983	1,081	400
- General	707	240	1,000
Premises costs	490	110	600
Energy Costs	100	101	200
Transport costs	50	15	500
Fixed Plant & Equipt	2,816	580	3,000
Other costs	550	48	400
Recharges from HA's	64	2	
Laundry Services		200	
Income from DHA	36,500	9,500	
Charges to GPFH	3,410	915	
Income - other HA's	3,100	1,492	
Cash Drawings			70,000
Miscellaneous income			5,700
Purchases - other DMU's			12,100
- NHS Trusts			6,800

The following transactions have not yet been accounted for:

1) Capital charges for the year have been calculated as follows:

	General Hospital £000	Local Hospital £000	DHA £000
Depreciation	1,000	500	900
Capital charges	200	50	180

2) The HA members received £200,000 during the year.

3) The electricity account for the final quarter for the General Hospital had not been agreed due to a discrepancy. The account was settled on 1/04/92 at £95,000.

4) The Local cottage hospital discovered an ECR for a local GPFH worth £95,000, which had not been sent at 31/03/92.

5) The Special Trustees of the General Hospital decided on 29/03/92 to contribute £2,000,000 toward the running of the hospital for the year 1991/92.

6) The Common Services (e.g. Financial Services, Patient transport, etc) net operating surplus for the year was £15,000.

7) The Local Hospital contracted out the Laundry Service during the year, and as a result sold the Laundry equipment on 1/12/91 £12,300 (£8,800 for a washing machine and £3,500 for a dryer). The accumulated depreciation at the date of sale was £1,800 in respect of the washer and £800 for the dryer. The equipment was valued at £10,000 for the washer and £6,000 for the dryer at the date of sale. The life of both was recorded as 10 years. The capital charges up to the sale has been included in the figures at note 1, however the disposal adjustment & capital charges for the December quarter have not been included.

8) The CHC have informed the DHA that the charge for the year 199 has been agreed at £90,000.

YOU ARE REQUIRED TO:

a) Prepare the accounts and notes to the accounts for the DMU's.

b) Prepare the accounts and notes for the DHA (Purchaser).

c) Prepare the Income and Expenditure account of the DHA for the year.

<u>Answer to Exercise 18.2</u>

	DR	£000	CR
Notes:			
1) Depreciation:			

General Hospital A/C:
Capital A/C   1,000
  Depreciation a/c   1,000

being the depreciation of the asset in the balance sheet

Revenue A/C - capital cha   1,000
Non cash settlement A/C - DHA   1,000

being the charge to the revenue a/c & the DHA a/c

Local Hospital A/C:
Capital A/C   500
  Depreciation a/c   500

being the depreciation of the asset in the balance sheet

Revenue A/C - capital cha   500
Non cash settlement A/C - DHA   500

being the charge to the revenue a/c & the DHA a/c

DHA A/C:
Capital A/C   900
  Depreciation a/c   900

being the depreciation of the asset in the balance sheet

Revenue A/C - capital cha   900
Non cash settlement A/C - DHA   900

being the charge to the revenue a/c & the DHA a/c

   Interest:
General Hospital A/C:
Revenue A/C - Capital Cha   200
Non cash settlement a/c   200

being the charge to the revenue a/c for capital charges

Local Hospital A/C:
Revenue A/C - Capital Cha   50
Non cash settlement a/c   50

being the charge to the revenue a/c for capital charges

DHA A/C:
Revenue A/C - Capital Cha   180
Non cash settlement a/c   180

being the charge to the revenue a/c for capital charges

2)   Revenue a/c - note 2.2   200
                Cash a/c   200

being the recording of remunerations in the revenue a/c

3)   Revenue a/c - General Hos   95
                Creditors - General Hospital B/S   95

being the creditor due for electric in the General Hospital's
accounts

4)   Revenue a/c - Income (Local)   95
                Debtor - Local Hosp B/S   95

being the recording of the ECR income due

5)   Revenue a/c - income donations   2,000
                debtors - Special Truste   2,000

being the recording of income due in the General Hospital's
accounts

6)   Revenue a/c - Note 4   15
                Cash   15

being the recording of the surplus on Common Services in the
revenue a/c

	£ washer	£ dryer
7) Replacement cost @ 1/12/91	10,000	6,000
Depreciation @ 1/12/92	1,800	800
	--------	-------
Opening NBV	8,200	5,200
Depreciation for quarter	250	150
	--------	-------
	7,950	5,050
Less:		
Sale proceeds	8,800	3,500
	--------	-------
Disposal Adjustment	(850)	1,550

Capital Charges for Dec qtr:

	£ washer	£ dryer
Profit / Loss made on disposal	(850)	1,550
Depreciation for quarter	250	150
Interest (6% x (8,200 + 5,200))	492	312
	--------	-------
Total Capital charges for qtr	(108)	2,012
Total 1,904		

Journals:

Local Hospital a/c:	DR	CR
Revenue a/c - capital charges Depre	0.40	
- Interest	0.80	
- Profit / Loss	0.70	
DHA non cash a/c		1.90

being the final quarters capital charges in the revenue a/c
and the recording of the profit/loss on sale.

8) Revenue a/c - Community Health Coun	90	
Debtors a/c		90

being the charge to the revenue a/c for CHC expenses

CASHLESS DHA

INCOME & EXPENDITURE ACCOUNT FOR THE YEAR ENDING 31/03/92

	£000
INCOME:	
Cash Drawings	70,000
Miscellaneous Income	5,700

TOTAL INCOME	75,700
EXPENDITURE:	
Health Care & Related Services (note 2.1)	64,900
Authority administration & Purchasing Service	10,880
Other Services	
Community Health Councils	90

SUBTOTAL (note 2.2)	10,970

TOTAL EXPENDITURE	75,870

AUTHORITY SURPLUS (DEFICIT)	(170)
Net operating surplus / (deficit) of Directly Managed Units (note 3.1)	707
Net operating surplus / (deficit) of Common Services (note 4)	15

Surplus / (Deficit) for year	722
Profit / (Loss) on disposal of fixed assets	0

Net Surplus / (Deficit) for year	552
	----------

2   Notes to the Income and Expenditure Account:

2.1 Purchase of Health Care	£000
This Authority's Directly Managed Units	46,000
Other Authorities Directly Managed Units	12,100
NHS Trusts	6,800
Other Providers of Health Care	0

TOTAL	64,900

<u>2.2 Authority Administration, Purchasing, Other Services and
    Community Health Councils' expenditure</u>

	£000
Authority memebers remuneration	200
Other Salaries & Wages	3,500
Supplies & Services - Clincial	400
- General	1,000
Establishment Expenses	800
Transport & Moveable Plant	500
Premises and Fixed Plant	3,000
Agency Services	0
Capital - Assets not used by DMU's	
- Depreciation	900
- Interest	180
Profit / (Loss) on sale of fixed Assets	0
Auditors' remuneration	0
Recharges from other units or HA's	0
Miscellaneous	400

TOTAL	10,880

3   Accounts of Directly Managed Units

<u>3.1   Net revenue operating surplus or deficit of Directly
       Managed Units</u>

Income from Activities (note 3.2)	60,518
Other Operating Income (note3.3)	2,250

Subtotal	62,768
Operating Expenses (note 3.4)	62,061

Net Surplus or (Deficit)	707

<u>3.1   Net revenue operating surplus or deficit of Directly
       Managed Units</u>

	TOTAL	GENERAL HOSPITAL	LOCAL HOSPITAL
	£000	£000	£000
Income from Activities (note 3.2)	60,518	48,016	12,502
Other Operating Income (note3.3)	2,250	2,000	250
	---------	---------	---------
Subtotal	62,768	50,016	12,752
Operating Expenses (note 3.4)	62,061	49,357	12,704
Capital charges end of year adjustment			
	---------	---------	---------
Net Surplus or (Deficit)	707	659	48
	---------	---------	---------

3.2 Income from activities (patient related)

	Total £000	General £000	Local £000
This Authority	46,000	36,500	9,500
GPFH	4,420	3,410	1,010
Other HA's	4,592	3,100	1,492
NHS Trusts	0		
Department of Health	0		
Non-NHS - Private Patients	5,506	5,006	500
- Other	0		
TOTAL	60,518	48,016	12,502

3.3 Other operating income (not involving patient care)

Other income from activities			
Charitable & Other contributions to expenditure	2,250	2,000	250
Transfers from the donation reserve re depreciation of donated assets	0		
TOTAL	2,250	2,000	250

SUMMARY OF DMU NOTES 3.2 AND 3.3

3.2 Income from activities (patient related)

	£000
This Authority	46,000
GPFH	4,420
Other HA's	4,592
NHS Trusts	0
Department of Health	0
Non-NHS - Private Patients	5,506
- Other	0
TOTAL	60,518

3.3 Other operating income (not involving patient care)

Other income from activities	0
Charitable & Other contributions to expenditu	2,250
Transfers from the donation reserve re depreciation of donated assets	0
	0
TOTAL	2,250

3.4 Operating Expenses

	Total £000	General £000	Local £000
Salaries & Wages	45,077	35,302	9,775
Supplies & Services - clincial	9,064	7,983	1,081
- general	947	707	240
Establishment Expenses	896	685	211
Transport & Moveable Plant	65	50	15
Premises and Fixed Plant	3,396	2,816	580
Agency Services	200	0	200
Capital			
- Depreciation	1,500	1,000	500
- Capital charges (Interest)	251	200	51
Profit / Loss on sale of fixed Asse	1	0	1
Miscellaneous	598	550	48
Subtotal	61,995	49,293	12,702
Recharge from other units/HA's	66	64	2
TOTAL	62,061	49,357	12,704

3.4 Operating Expenses - SUMMARY

	£000
Salaries & Wages	45,077
Supplies &- clincial	9,064
- general	947
Establishment Expenses	896
Transport & Moveable Plant	65
Premises and Fixed Plant	3,396
Agency Services	200
Capital	
- Depreciation	1,500
- Capital charges (Interest)	251
Profit / Loss on sale of fixed Assets	1
Miscellaneous	598
Subtotal	61,995
Recharge from other units/HA's	66
TOTAL	62,061

18.6 The Balance Sheet
    The balance sheet represents the assets and liabilities
    of the Authority (not the Trustees of the Authority).
    The DoH standard format requires two years (this year
    and last year) balances to be shown - the format is
    shown below.

BALANCE SHEET
AS AT 31st MARCH 1993

MAINCODE 07A 1992		SUB CODE	MAIN CODE 07
£			£
	TOTAL FIXED ASSETS Net Book Value	100	
	CURRENT ASSETS Stocks & work in progress	150	
	Debtors	160	
	Cash at bank & in hand	170	
	Subtotal	180	
	Creditors: amounts falling due within one year	190	
	NET CURRENT ASSETS/ LIABILITIES	200	
	Creditors: amounts falling due after one year	210	
	TOTAL NET ASSETS	220	
	FINANCED BY: Capital Account	230	
	Donation Reserve	240	
	Balance due to/(from) DoH	250	
	TOTAL	260	

Most of the headings in the balance sheet will be
familiar to accounting students. However, the headings
unique to the NHS require some explanation first:

a) Capital Account
   This represents the total value of NHS assets
   (excluding donated assets) and is shown in a note to
   the Balance sheet. It is calculated by taking the
   opening reserve adding on additions, such as new
   purchases, revaluations, indexation adjustment,etc
   and subtracting values for assets sold or disposed

of, depreciation and capital charges and any other adjustments.

b) Donation Reserve
This is the same as (a) above but in respect to donated assets.

c) Balance due to/(from) the Department
This shows the difference between total assets and total liabilities and the balance on the capital account, and represents the sum due to or from the DoH to equalise these totals. If liabilities > total assets then this is a negative figure - i.e. the DoH owes the HA cash.

18.7 Worked example of the Balance Sheet

Exercise 18.3 on the following pages works through an Income & Expenditure Account and Balance Sheet for a DHA.

Exercise 18.3 NHS Income and Expenditure Account and Balance Sheet

The following information relates to the Nice Town District Health
Authority for the year ended 31/03/93. The DHA purchases health care
for its community from providers within the DHA, from providers in
other DHA's, from NHS Trusts and from other health care providers.

	£
Balances at 1/04/92:	
NBV: Land	37,527,000
Buildings	38,456,538
Equipment	3,713,400
Assets under construction	9,195,000
Transactions during the year:	
Miscellaneous Income	8,547,911
Salaries & Wages	2,133,115
Members Remunerations	47,389
Premises costs	337,623
Energy Costs	50,429
Other Etablishment costs	43,761
Other costs	102,499
Cash Drawings	50,201,000
Purchases - providers within DHA	33,387,869
- other DMU's	10,200,150
- NHS Trusts	8,916,417
- other providers	821,539

The following transactions have not yet been accounted for:

1) Capital charges for the year have been calculated as follows:

	Indexation £	Depreciation £
Land	(12,383,910)	
Buildings	(2,836,958)	1,086,242
Equipment	335,930	1,346,649
Assets under construction	(678,319)	

2) The following additions to fixed assets were acquired during
   the year:

   a) Buildings were acquired - the net book value at 31/03/93 is:

      £   1,387,029

   b) Equipment purchased during the year has a NBV at 31/03/93 of:

      £   904,997

c) During the year further building work commenced on the
   construction of new accomodation for the DHA. This was
   valued at 31/03/93 by the surveyor at:

   £ 24,992,290

3) Equipment sold during the year had a NBV of: 47,083

4) An audit fee for VFM work carried out during the year was received
   on 25/03/93 and remained unpaid at 31/03/93   34,976

5) Charges from other Health Authorities outstanding have been agreed
   at   114,460

6) Electricity charges of £   19,500   were outstanding at 31/03/93

7) A local firm has not yet paid a bill for the hire of the DHA
   conference room. The charge totalled 2,500

8) The CHC have informed the DHA that the charge for the year 1991/2
   has been agreed at   90,000

9) The DHA's DMU's reported a net surplus of   £   25,600

10) The balances at 31/03/93 before the transaction listed
    in notes 1 - 8 above have been accounted for are:
                                                    £
       Creditors   6,375,944
       Debtors   8,911,882
       Stocks and WIP   1,316,805
       Cash and Bank   102,031
       Balances due to/from the Department   3,653,945

YOU ARE REQUIRED TO:
a) Prepare the Income and Expenditure account for the DHA
   with accompanying notes.

b) Prepare the Balance Sheet for the year.

Notes:

Notes 1, 2 and 3 allow us to record the journal entries for capital
charges in the I & E account and also calculate the fixed asset values
at the year end:

1) Depreciation:	DR	£	CR
Capital A/C	2,432,891		
Depreciation a/c			2,432,891

being the depreciation of the asset in the balance sheet

Revenue A/C - capital charges	2,432,891		
Non cash settlement A/C - DHA			2,432,891

being the charge to the revenue a/c & the DHA a/c

The Indexation is shown in the table below calculating the fixed
asset value at 31/03/93

2) The assets purchased during the year are shown in the table below.

3) The assets sold are in the table below - assume no profit or loss on
sale as none given.

ASSET	Bal @ 01/04/92	Index'n	Deprec'n	Additions	Disposals	Bal @ 31/03/93
LAND	37,527,000	(12,383,910)				25,143,090
BUILD	38,456,538	(2,836,958)	1,086,242	1,387,029		35,920,367
EQUIP	3,713,400	335,930	1,346,649	904,997	47,083	3,560,595
AUC	9,195,000	(678,319)		24,992,290		33,508,971
TOTAL	88,891,938	(15,563,257)	2,432,891	27,284,316	47,083	98,133,023

4) This represents a creditor in the accounts:

	DR	CR
I & E a/c		
- Authority admin exps - audit fees	34,976	
Creditors		34,976

5) This is a creditor in the accounts

	DR	CR
I & E a/c		
- Authority admin exps - recharges HA'	114,460	
Creditors		114,460

6) This is a creditor in the accounts:

I & E a/c
  - Authority admin exps - energy costs   19,500
  Creditors   19,500

7) This is a debtor in the accounts:

I & E a/c
  - Miscellaneous income   2,500
  Debtors   2,500

8)   I & E a/c - CHC's   90,000
      Creditors a/c   90,000

     being the charge to the revenue a/c for CHC expenses

9) The DMU surplus is recorded in the I & E a/c.

10) These figures are for the Balance Sheet - the above journmals
    must be included in these balances:

	£
a) Debtors - a31/03/93	8,911,882
Adjustments:	
Note 7	2,500

Revised Debtors	8,914,382

	£
b) Creditors - a 31/03/93	6,375,944
Adjustments:	
Note 4	34,976
Note 5	114,460
Note 6	19,500
Note 8	90,000

Revised Creditors	6,634,880

Before we can complete the I & E a/c it is necessary to prepare a
note detailing the Authority Administration & Purchasing costs due
to the above changes - it is also wise tio show the examiner
exactly how your figures are calculated (also this note is required
by the DoH manual of accounts).

Notes to the Income and Expenditure Account:

NOTE A:
AUTHORITY ADMINISTRATION & PURCHASING EXPENSES 1992/93

	£
Members Remunerations	47,389
Salaries & Wages	2,133,115
Establishment Expenses (30429+43761+1950	113,690
Premises	337,623
Depreciation	2,432,891
Auditors Remunerations	34,976
Recharges from other HA's	114,460
Miscellaneous	102,499

	5,316,643

NOTE B:
PURCHASE OF HEALTH CARE 1992/3

	£
This Authority's Directly Managed Units	33,387,869
Other Authorities Directly Managed Units	10,200,150
NHS Trusts	8,916,417
Other Providers of Health Care	821,539

TOTAL	53,325,975

INCOME & EXPENDITURE ACCOUNT FOR THE YEAR ENDING 31/03/93

£

INCOME:
Cash Drawings	50,201,000
Miscellaneous Income	8,550,411

TOTAL INCOME	58,751,411

EXPENDITURE:
Health Care & Related Services (note B)	53,325,975
Authority administration & Purchasing Services (Note A)	5,316,643
Other Services	
Community Health Councils	90,000

SUBTOTAL	5,406,643

TOTAL EXPENDITURE	58,732,618

AUTHORITY SURPLUS (DEFICIT)	18,793

Net operating surplus / (deficit) of Directly Managed Units (note 9)	25,600
Net operating surplus / (deficit) of Common Services	0

Surplus / (Deficit) for year	25,600
Profit / (Loss) on disposal of fixed assets	0

Net Surplus / (Deficit) for year	44,393

CASHLESS DHA
BALANCE SHEET AS AT 31/03/93

£

TOTAL FIXED ASSETS (see note 1)	98,133,023

CURRENT ASSETS:
Stocks & WIP	1,316,805
Debtors (note 10)	8,914,382
Cash	102,031
Subtotal	10,333,218

CREDITORS: amounts falling within one year (note 10)	6,634,880
NET CURRENT ASSETS/(LIABILITIES)	3,698,338

TOTAL NET ASSETS	101,831,361

FINANCED BY:
Capital account	98,133,023
Balance due to/from the DoH (3653945 + 44393)	3,698,338

	101,831,361

482

18.8 NHS Performance Measurement

The measurement of the performance of the NHS is very
difficult and in most instances subjective. A number of
unit cost measures and indicators have been developed
in Financial Returns and other such forms required by
the DoH. These measures are mainly based upon the cost
of the service in relation to the activity, the quality
of service has then to be considered. The Financial
Returns analyse the Authority's expenditure in a
variety of ways, such as a subjective analysis,
Specialty analysis and an analysis of stocks. These are
useful in the consideration of the performance of the
Authority in comparison to, for example, previous
years, to other similar Authorities or to targets set
either locally or nationally. Students should examine
these returns, as whilst they are fairly straight
forward in their compilation (as they just re-analyse
expenditure) they require rules to be established (for
example, what constitutes a "Specialty", such as
"Urology") and interpretation of resulting figures.
This is the more subjective part of accounting and
requires the student to look beyond the simple figures
- a task for the P3 year.

We shall look at the calculation of some general
performance indicators for a provider seeking Trust
status and examine the implications of the results.
This is shown in exercise 18.4 below.

EXERCISE 18.4   HEALTH AUTHORITY - UNIT COSTS

GETBETTER HOSPITAL IS APPLYING FOR TRUST STATUS. THE DIRECTOR
OF FINANCE IS REQUIRED TO PUT FORWARD A CASE TO THE DEPARTMENT
OF HEALTH STATING WHY THE HOSPITAL SHOULD BE GRANTED TRUST
STATUS. THE DIRECTOR HAS ASKED YOU TO DRAFT A REPORT FOR HIM
OUTLINING:

1) THE PERFORMANCE OF THE HOSPITAL OVER THE LAST TWO YEARS
   (USING RELEVANT PERFORMANCE INDICATORS)
2) THE ADVANTAGES TO BE GAINED FROM BEING A TRUST HOSPITAL
3) THE EFFECTS OF THE INTRODUCTION OF CAPITAL ACCOUNTING

THE FOLLOWING INFORMATION IS AVAILABLE:

INCOME & EXPENDITURE	1991/92 £000	I/P % OF COST	1992/93 £000	I/P % OF COST
ADMINISTRATION	250	95%	270	95%
CATERING	500	90%	530	90%
CLEANING	800	85%	850	85%
FINANCE	300	90%	305	91%
PERSONNEL	270	95%	250	95%
NURSING	5,600	95%	6,200	95%
WARDS	2,500	100%	2,600	100%
PHYSIOTHERAPY	950	75%	1,020	75%
SURGERY	2,000	98%	2,100	95%
PHARMACY	500	70%	550	68%
PSYCHIATRY	200	85%	150	90%
UROLOGY	65	100%	80	100%

BALANCES AT 31st March
=======================

CREDITORS	600	385
DEBTORS	550	350
CASH IN HAND	-15	12

OTHER INFORMATION:

	1991/92	1992/93
NO OF BEDS AVAILABLE	600	600
NO OF IN-PATIENT DAYS	150,000	175,000
NO OF OUT-PATIENT ATTENDANCES	16,500	18,250
AVERAGE INFLATION RATE	7.55%	7.59%
DoH RECOMMENDED CREDITOR % OF SPEND	4%	
DoH RECOMMENDED DEBTOR % OF SPEND	3%	

484

ANSWER: GETBETTER HOSPITAL
          ===================

	1991/92 £000	COST PER I/P DAY £	COST PER O/P DAY £	1992/93 £000	COST PER I/P DAY £	COST PER O/P DAY £
INCOME & EXPENDITURE						
NON-CLINICAL:						
ADMINISTRATION	250	1.58	0.76	270	1.47	0.74
CATERING	500	3.00	3.03	530	2.73	2.90
CLEANING	800	4.53	7.27	850	4.13	6.99
FINANCE	300	1.80	1.82	305	1.59	1.50
PERSONNEL	270	1.71	0.82	250	1.36	0.68
TOTAL NON-CLINICAL	2,120	12.63	13.70	2,205	11.26	12.82
CLINICAL:						
NURSING	5,600	35.47	16.97	6,200	33.66	16.99
WARDS	2,500	16.67	0.00	2,600	14.86	0.00
PHYSIOTHERAPY	950	4.75	14.39	1,020	4.37	13.97
SURGERY	2,000	13.07	2.42	2,100	11.40	5.75
PHARMACY	500	2.33	9.09	550	2.14	9.64
PSYCHIATRY	200	1.13	1.82	150	0.77	0.82
UROLOGY	65	0.43	0.00	80	0.46	0.00
TOTAL CLINICAL	11,815	73.85	44.70	12,700	67.65	47.18
TOTAL COSTS	13,935	86.48	58.39	14,905	78.91	60.00
% INCREASE				6.96%	-8.74%	2.75%

BALANCE SHEET ITEMS:
====================

	£	£	INC/(RED) %
CREDITORS	600	385	(35.83%)
DEBTORS	550	350	(36.36%)
CASH IN HAND	-15	12	(180.00%)
CREDITORS AS A % OF SPEND	4.31%	2.58%	
DEBTORS AS A % OF SPEND	3.95%	2.35%	

OTHER PERFORMANCE INDICATORS:
==============================

	1991/92	INCREASE %	1992/93
NO OF BED DAYS AVAILABLE:	219,000		219,000
NO OF I/P DAYS	150,000		175,000
BED OCCUPANCY %	68.49%	11.42%	79.91%
COST PER BED:	21,619.17	6.46%	23,016.75
INCREASED O/P ATTENDANCES(%)		10.61%	

POINTS TO NOTE IN REPORT:
==========================

INCREASED COSTS ARE BELOW THE RATE OF INFLATION - INDICATES BETTER EFFICIENCY

COST PER BED DAY IS FALLING - DUE TO GREATER EFFICIENCY & INREASED PATIENTS

BED OCCUPANCY INCREASED BY ALMOST 12%

OUTPATIENT ATTENDANCES ARE INCREASING BY OVER 10% WHILST COSTS UP BY ONLY 2.75%

HOSPITAL HAS REDUCED IT'S CREDITOR BALANCES AND DEBTORS - INDICATING GREATER
CONTROL AND IMPROVED CASH FLOW PROCEDURES

THE HOSPITAL HAS REDUCED THE CREDITOR AND DEBTOR BALANCES TO BELOW THE DoH
RECOMMENDED LEVELS

THE OVERDRAUGHT HAS BEEN ELIMINATED AND THE HOSPITAL IS KEEPING A LOW CASH
BALANCE AS RECOMMENDED BY THE DoH

THE ADVANTAGES OF BECOMING A TRUST:
            - GREATER CONTROL OF OWN FINANCES
            - FLEXIBILITY WITH PAY SCALES AND TERMS & CONDITIONS
            - FLEXIBILITY WITH SELLING SERVICES
            - ABILITY TO BORROW WITHIN EFL
            - CONTROL OVER ASSET PURCHASE

THE EFFECTS OF CAPITAL ACCOUNTING:
            - NEED TO COMPILE ASSET REGISTER
            - NEED TO CALCULATE DEPRECIATION ETC
            - CHANGE TO BALANCE SHEET
            - NEED TO MAINTAIN ASSET REGISTER
            - SYSTEMS REQUIRED FOR MONITORING & CONTROL OF ASSETS
            - NEED TO INCLUDE CAPITAL CHARGES IN PRICES
            - CONSIDER EFFECT ON RETURNS REQUIRED

18.9 <u>NHS Trading Accounts</u>

Within the NHS there are also services which operate in a "trading capacity". These services are required by the DoH to complete memorandum trading accounts. These actually form a Financial Return. An example is the private patients service offered by many NHS organisations, and also services which have been subject to competition, such as Laundry and Catering services. Exercise 18.5 below shows how such accounts must be presented.

The Quickside NHS Trust has a Catering unit which provides all the Catering services for the Authority, including the Patient and Staff catering. The unit operates as a separate trading unit and produces a trading account each year in the format required by the DoH. The following information is available for the year ended 31/03/93.

	£
Income - Patients	23,870
- Staff	331,619
- Other	27,485
Provisions	483,223
A & C Salaries	137,347
Ancillary staff	535,578
Equipment	54,660
Staff Clothing	11,670
Travelling expenses	2,849
Energy	30,892
Maintenance of equipt	18,153

Other information available:

1 Notional rent charges for the unit has been calculated at
        £64,880
2 Depreciation has been calculated for the year at:
        £50,000
3 The total number of meals provided during the year were:

Staff	450,000
Patient days	80,000
Other Functions	35,000

4 The expenditure is apportioned to Staff, Patients and Other Customers as follows:

	%
Patients	20.00%
Staff	75.00%
Other	5.00%

REQUIRED:

a) Prepare the Memorandum Trading Account for the Authority.

b) Prepare some performance statistics useful to management and users of the Accounts.

c) Comment upon the performance of the unit.

ANSWER TO EXERCISE 18.5

Notes:

NOTE 1:	DR	CR
Revenue a/c - rent	64,880	
Notional rent		64,880

As this is notional it is not a real entry in the books
of the Authority, however is shown in the MTA of the
Catering Unit.

NOTE 2:		
Revenue a/c - Depreciation	50,000	
Capital charges a/c		50,000

Being the charge for capital charges in the revenue a/c

NOTE 3:

This will be used to calculate statistics

NOTE 4:

These will be used to split the expenditure figures
up in the MTA

GENERAL NOTE:

The resulting MTA shows a loss for this particular trading unit.
The significance of this is that the Trust is either not
charging enough, is costing more than planned, has activity
lower than planned or some other reason. It will be important to
identify the reason(s) and remedy the situation as this loss
will reduce the Trusts overall performance and could result in
it not meeting it's required rate of return.

QUICKSIDE NHS TRUST   CATERING UNIT

MEMORANDUM TRADING ACCOUNT FOR THE YEAR ENDED 31/03/93

STATISTICS:

NO OF PATIENT DAYS 80,000   NO OF STAFF
                                   RESTARAUNTS   1

		PATIENTS £	STAFF £	OTHER £	TOTAL £
A	INCOME:				
	SALES	23,870	1,065,286	27,485	1,116,641
	SUB TOTAL (A)	23,870	1,065,286	27,485	1,116,641
B	EXPENDITURE:				
	Provisions	96,645	362,417	24,161	483,223
	A & C Salaries	27,469	103,010	6,867	137,347
	Ancillary staff	107,116	401,684	26,779	535,578
	Equipment	10,932	40,995	2,733	54,660
	Staff Clothing	2,334	8,753	584	11,670
	Travelling expenses	570	2,137	142	2,849
	Energy	6,178	23,169	1,545	30,892
	Maintenance of equip	3,631	13,615	908	18,153
	Notional Rent	12,976	48,660	3,244	64,880
	Capital Depreciation	10,000	37,500	2,500	50,000
	SUB TOTAL (B)	277,850	1,041,939	69,463	1,389,252
C	NET COST (B-A)	253,980	(23,347)	41,978	272,611

MANAGEMENT INFORMATION:

	PER PATIENT DAY £	STAFF PER MEAL £	OTHER PER MEAL £
NO OF MEALS	80,000	450,000	35,000
GROSS COST OF MEALS	3.47	2.32	1.98
COST OF PROVISIONS	1.21	0.81	0.69
INCOME PER MEAL	0.30	2.37	0.79
NET COST/(PROFIT)	3.17	(0.05)	1.20

18.10   Trust Fund Accounts

The Trust Funds and Special Trustees of NHS
organisations are required to produce annual accounts
at 31st March each year in accordance with the NHS
Manual of Accounts. This also applies to NHS Trust
Trust Funds. The examples shown in this section are
compliant with the manual of accounts.

Separate ledgers and bank accounts are maintained by
the Trust Funds and a separate set of accounts are
required.

In exams and at work students must be careful to
identify clearly between Trust Fund Accounts and NHS
Trust accounts - the format and requirements for each
are very different. NHS Trust Accounts are examined in
the next section.

Exercise 18.6 on the following pages is a worked
example of Trust Fund accounts for an NHS Trust
Authority - the requirement is the same for all NHS
Trust Funds regardless of the owning organisations
status (i.e. Trust vs DMU).

Exercise 18.6   NHS Trust Fund Accounts

The following figures have been extracted from the Trust
Fund Cash Book of the Drift NHS Trust for the year ended
31/03/93:

	£
Welfare & Amenities:	
Staff	12,570
Patients	17,400
Other expenditure	4,120
Research	7,000
Contribution to Drift NHST for Capital Exp	3,000
Fund raising expenses	600
Legacies	5,000
Subscriptions, Donations & Grants	23,500
Net income from Property	5,760
Dividends & Interest	15,340
Fund Raising Income	2,600
Other Income	3,330

The following transactions have not yet been accounted for:

1   Balances at 1/04/92 are:

		£
Fund A/c		170,900
Property		20,000
Investments:	a) Narrower Range	139,700
	b) Wider Range	8,800
Stocks		3,800
Cash overdrawn		1,400

2   Dividends outstanding at 31/03/93 are   £   1,200

3   Income Tax of £   3,350 may be reclaimed from the
    Inland Revenue in respect of interest paid net.

4   Investments held in the wider range with a book value of
    £7,800   at 1/04/92 were sold for   £6,800
    on 24/03/93. The amount due has not yet been received.
    During the year additional investments totalling
    £5,600 were made in the Narrower Range.

5   Administrative expenses of   £350   are to be charged to
    the fund and the cash balance adjusted accordingly.

6   The property held by the Trust Fund was professionally
    revalued during the year ended 31/03/93. The revised
    valuation of the property is   £   25,000
    and this is to be reflected in the accounts.

7   Fund Raising expenses of £   200   have been
    incorrectly charged to Exchequer funds. A cash transfer
    will be made in 1993/94.

8   Stocks at 31/03/93 are £   2,400

REQUIRED:

a) The Trust Fund Income and Expenditure account for the
   year ended 31/03/93.

                                           11 marks
b) The Trust Fund Balance Sheet as at 31/03/93.
                                           10 marks

c) The NHS is currently introducing Capital Accounting,
   including the charging for depreciation of assets.
   Outline the problems that need to be overcome for any
   organisation moving to such an accounting system for
   the first time.

                                            9 marks

                      TOTAL   30 marks

Exercise 18.6 Answer to the NHS Trust Fund Accounts

Notes:

		DR	CR
2	DEBTORS	1,200	
	INCOME - DIVIDENDS		1,200
3	DEBTORS	3,350	
	INCOME - INTEREST		3,350
4	DEBTORS	6,800	
	I & E OTHER EXPS (LOSS)	1,000	
	INVESTMENT A/C -WIDER RANGE		7,800
5	I & E A/C ADMIN EXPS	350	
	CASH		350
6	PROPERTY REVALUATION	5,000	
	REVALUATION RESERVE		5,000

```
                        CASH ACCOUNT
----------------------------------------------------------
CASH IN        55,530   | B/FWD         1,400
                        | CASH SPEND   50,640
                        | C/DOWN        3,490
               ----------                ----------
               55,530                    55,530
```

DRIFT NHS TRUST

INCOME AND EXPENDITURE ACCOUNT FOR THE YEAR ENDED 31/03/93

INCOME: £

Subscriptions & Donations   23,500
Legacies   5,000
Dividends & Interest   19,890
Net income from freehold & leasehold property   5,760
Income from Fund Raising   2,600
Other Income   3,330
(Net expenditure transferred to capital
 reserves:-other funds)

TOTAL INCOME   60,080

EXPENDITURE:

Administration Expenses   350
Patients Welfare and Amenities   17,400
Staff Welfare and Amenities   12,570
Research   7,000
Contributions to hospital capital exp.   3,000
Fund Raising Expenses   800
Other Expenditure   6,520
(Net income transferred to capital
 reserves:-other funds)   12,440

TOTAL EXPENDITURE   60,080

                            494

```
                       DRIFT NHS TRUST

             BALANCE SHEET AS AT 31/03/93


       ASSETS:                                              £

       Property                                          25,000

       Investments:
        a) Narrower Range                               145,300
        b) Wider Range                                    1,000

       Stocks                                             2,400
       Debtors                                           11,350
       Cash/Bank                                          3,490
                                                       ----------
       TOTAL ASSETS                                     188,540
                                                       ----------


       RESERVES:

       Capital Reserves: funds held in perpetuity
        a) General Purpose
        b) Special Purposes

       Capital Reserves: other funds
        a) General Purpose                              183,340
        b) Special Purposes (Revaluation Reserve)         5,000

       LIABILITIES

       Creditors                                            200
       Overdrawn at Bank
                                                       ----------
       TOTAL RESERVES AND LIABILITIES                   188,540
                                                       ----------
```

18.11   NHS Trusts

The annual accounts of the NHS Trusts are very similar to the other NHS organisations in their compilation. The format is slightly different, however, and is shown on the following pages. The accounts comprise of three main documents:

1) Income & Expenditure Account
2) Balance Sheet
3) Cash flow statement

STANDARD FORMAT OF NHS TRUST ACCOUNTS:

NHS TRUST

INCOME & EXPENDITURE ACCOUNT FOR THE YEAR ENDED 31 MARCH 19XX

	NOTE	£000	Previous Year £000
Income from activities	2	6000	5000
Other operating income	3	200	300
Operating Expenses	4	5250	4300
		------	------
OPERATING SURPLUS (DEFICIT)		950	1000
Interest Receivable	6	20	10
Interest Payable	7	30	25
		------	------
SURPLUS (DEFICIT) ON ORDINARY ACTIVITIES		940	985
Extraordinary Items	8		
		------	------
SURPLUS (DEFICIT) FOR THE YEAR		940	985
PDC Dividends payable		800	750
RETAINED SURPLUS (DEFICIT) FOR YEAR		140	235
Surplus (Deficit) brought forward		235	0
Surplus (Deficit) carried forward		375	235

FINANCIAL TARGET PERFORMANCE: 6%

NHS TRUST

BALANCE SHEET AS AT 31 MARCH 19XX

	NOTE	£000	Previous Year £000
FIXED ASSETS			
Intangible Assets	10	100	100
Tangible Assets	11	13400	13100
		13500	13200
CURRENT ASSETS			
Stocks & Work In Progress	12	1500	2000
Debtors	13	2200	2500
Short term Investments	14		
Cash at bank & in hand		800	1000
		4500	5500
CREDITORS: Amounts falling due within one year	15	3125	4865
NET CURRENT ASSETS (LIABILITIES)		1375	1635
TOTAL ASSETS LESS CURRENT LIABILITIES		14875	13835
CREDITORS: Amounts falling due after more than one year	16	0	0
		14875	13835
FINANCED BY:			
CAPITAL & RESERVES			
Public Dividend Capital	17	6500	6500
Long term loans	18	6500	6500
Revaluation Reserve	19	0	0
Donation Reserve	19	500	200
Other Reserves	19	1000	400
Income & Expenditure Account		375	235
		14875	13835

As a general rule NHS Trusts are expected to follow accounting standards issued by the ASB (formerly the ASC) and SORPs and ED's where applicable.

Exercise 18.7 on the following pages works through the compilation of a NHS Trust Income and Expenditure account, Balance Sheet and Cash Flow Statement.

EXERCISE 18.7
NHS TRUST: I & E A/C, BALANCE SHEET AND CASH FLOW STATEMENT

The Brightside NHS Trust has just completed it's first
years operations. The Trust is keen to meet all of it's
objectives and has tried to keep within budget. The
following information is available:

		£000
Balances @ 1/04/92		
	Cash	500
	Debtors	10,000
	Stocks	2,500
	Tangible Assets	200,000
	Creditors	12,500
Transactions during the year:		
	Salaries & Wages	85,000
	All other expenditure	8,000
	Depreciation	18,000
	Income from GPFH	8,700
	Income from DHA	117,200
	Income from DoH	3,500
	Private Patient Income	5,600
	Donations	5,000
	Stocks purchased	15,000

The following information is also available:

1   The Closing stock at 31/03/93   £2,800,000

2   The Originating Capital Debt was split evenly between
    IBD and PDC.

3   The DHA debtors at the end of the year amounted to
                                              £12,000,000
4   An asset was sold on 31/03/93 for   £500,000
    The asset had a NBV at 1/04/92 of   £400,000
    Depreciation for the year amounted to   £55,000

5   The Creditors outstanding at 31/03/93 were £11,000,000

6   The indexation figures provided by DoH are:
            100   01/04/92
            104   31/03/93

YOU ARE REQUIRED TO:

a) Prepare the Trust's Income & Expenditure account for
   the year.
b) Prepare the Balance Sheet at 31/03/93

c) Prepare a Cash Flow Statement for the year.

d) Comment upon the financial performance of the Trust in
   it's first year of operation.

498

The first task is to prepare the notes to the accounts. This involves organising all of the above data. Students should note the difference in format of a Trust I & E a/c and also that Profit/Loss on sale of assets is charged to operational expenses.

NOTES TO THE ACCOUNTS:

1 INCOME FROM ACTIVITIES   £000
   Income from GPFH   8,700
   Income from DHA+closing DBRS-opening DBRS   119,200
   Income from DoH   3,500
   PP Income   5,600

   Total   137,000

2 OTHER OPERATING INCOME
   Donations   5,000

3 OPERATING EXPENSES
   Salaries & Wages   85,000
   Stocks purchased   (opening+purch-closing)   14,700
   All other exp + closing creds-opening creds   6,500
   Depreciation   18,000
   (Profit)/Loss on Sale of asset (see below)   -155

                                                          124,045

4 PROFIT/LOSS ON ASSET SALE   £
   NBV @ 1/04/92   400,000
   Depreciation for year   55,000

                                                          345,000

   less sale proceeds   500,000

   Disposal Adjustment   155,000

5 TANGIBLE ASSETS   Asset
                                        Depreciation   Value
   NBV @ 1/04/92   0   200,000
   Additions   0
   Indexation(200000*((104-100)/100)   8,000
   Disposals   -55   -400
   Depreciation   18,000

   NBV @ 31/03/93   17,945   207,600

499

6   Interest payable on IBD

    Calculation of Original Capital Debt (OCD):

                    Cash   500
                    Debtors   10,000
                    Stocks   2,500
                    Tangible Assets   200,000
                    Creditors   -12,500

                    Total OCD   200,500

                    ORIGINAL CAPITAL DEBT:
                    IBD @ 50%   100,250,000
                    PDC @ 50%   100,250,000

                                         200,500,000

                    IBD Interest
                          @ 9%   9,022,500

7   PDC   100,250,000

                DIVIDEND @ 3 %   3,007,500

8 CASH ACCOUNT

   opening cash   500

   cash in   Income from GPFH   8,700
             Income from DHA   117,200
             Income from DoH   3,500
             Private Patient Inco   5,600
             Donations   5,000
             Sale of asset   500

             Total Income   140,500

   cash out Salaries & Wages   85,000
             All other expenditur   8,000
             Stocks purchased   15,000

             Total cash payments   108,000

             Cash @ 31/03/93   33,000

                         500

```
9 CREDITORS
          CLOSING                    11,000
          IBD INTEREST                9,023
          PDC INTEREST                3,008
                                 -------------
                                     23,030

10 NET CASH INFLOW FROM OPERATING ACTIVITIES

     CASH IN FROM CASH A/C           140,500
     LESS CASH FROM ASSET SALE          -500
     LESS EXPENDITURE FROM CASH A/C  -108,000
                                 -------------
                                      32,000

11 ANALYSIS OF CHANGE IN CASH & CASH EQUIVALENTS
                           1992      1993      Change
     Cash at bank           500     33,000     32,500
     Short term investm's     0          0          0
     Bank overdraft           0          0          0
                        ------------------------------------
                           500     33,000     32,500
```

INCOME & EXPENDITURE ACOUNT FOR THE YEAR ENDED 31/03/93

```
NOTE                                        £000

  1 INCOME FROM ACTIVITIES                 137,000

  2 OTHER OPERATING INCOME                   5,000

  3 OPERATING EXPENSES                    -124,045
                                       ------------
    OPERAING SURPLUS(DEFICIT)              17,955

  6 INTEREST PAYABLE                         9,023
                                       ------------
    SURPLUS(DEFICIT) ON ORDINARY ACTIVITIES  8,933

    EXTRAORDINARY ITEMS                          0
    SURPLUS(DEFICIT) FOR FINANCIAL YEAR      8,933

  7 PDC DIVIDENDS PAYABLE                    3,008
                                       ------------
    RETAINED SURPLUS FOR YEAR               5,925

    FINANCIAL TARGET PERFORMANCE            8.96%
```

BRIGHTSIDE NHS TRUST

BALANCE SHEET AS AT 31/03/93

		£000
	FIXED ASSETS:	
	INTANGIBLE ASSETS	0
5	TANGIBLE ASSETS	189,655
	CURRENT ASSETS:	
	STOCKS & WIP	2,800
	DEBTORS	12,000
8	CASH	33,000

		47,800
9	CREDITORS: Amounts falling due within one year	23,030

	NET CURRENT ASSETS/(LIAILITIES)	24,770

	TOTAL ASSETS	214,425

	FINANCED BY:	
	PDC	100,250
	IBD	100,250
	I & E A/C	5,925
	INDEXATION RESERVE	8,000

		214,425

CASH FLOW STATEMENT FOR THE YEAR ENDED 31ST MARCH 1993

		£000
	Operating Activities:	
	Cash received from customers	140,000
	Cash Payments to Suppliers	-23,000
	Cash to & on behalf of employees	-85,000
	Other cash payments	0
10	Net Cash inflow from operating activities:	32,000
	Returns on investments & servicing of finance	
	Interest Received	0
	Interest Paid	0
	Interest on lease/rentals	0
	Dividends paid	0
	Net cash outflow from returns on investments & servicing of finance	0
	Investing Activities:	
	Payments to acquire fixed assets	0
	Receipts from sale of fixed assets	500
	Net cash outflow from investing activities	-500
	Net cash outflow before financing	-32,500
	Financing:	
	New PDC	0
	New long term loans	0
	New short term loans	0
	Repayments of amounts borrowed	0
	Capital element of lease/rentals	0
	Net cash inflow from financing	0
11	Increase in cash and cash equivalents	32,500

Each year as well as producing the normal annual accounts and financial returns a Trust has to calculate it's performance against it's targets. Below is a worked example (exercise 18.8) of the calculation of a Trust's performance against it's financial target.

EXERCISE 18.8   NHS TRUST - MEETING THE FINANCIAL OBJECTIVES

OBJECTIVE 1   THE FINANCIAL TARGET
The financial target is a 6% return on the assets employed.

OBJECTIVE 2   TO BREAKEVEN
The Trust must break even after deducitng the interest due on all debt - external and IBD from the Government (incl orginal IBD). The rate charged is 9%.

OBJECTIVE 3   PAY DIVIDENDS ON THE PDC
The surplus (if any) must then be used to pay dividends on PDC - the rate is currently 3%

A Trust owns the following assets:

	£
HOSPITAL SITE	37,000,000
OFFICES	4,300,000
EQUIPMENT ETC	6,700,000
CURRENT ASSETS	6,500,000
	54,500,000

A 6% RETURN IS =	3,270,000 TARGET

THEREFORE IF BUDGETED EXPENDITURE IS £	68,500,000
ADD TARGET RETURN	3,270,000
TOTAL INCOME REQUIRED	71,770,000

Therefore when setting prices, the Trust must ensure that this income requirement is met - that is costs of services must include an element for recovering the 6% return (£3.6m).

The Trust has the following debt structure:

ORIGINAL CAPITAL DEBT:	
IBD @ 50%	27,250,000
PDC @ 50%	27,250,000
	54,500,000

INTEREST AT 9% IS	2,452,500

If the Trust performed according to budget then the following
I & E account would be found:

	£
INCOME	71,770,000
EXPENDITURE	68,500,000
SURPLUS *	3,270,000
INTEREST PAYABLE	2,452,500
SURPLUS AFTER INTEREST	817,500

* NOTE THAT SURPLUS = FINANCIAL TARGET

THEREFORE FINANCIAL TARGET AND BREAK EVEN TARGET HAVE BEEN MET.

THE DIVIDEND PAYABLE IS:

PDC	27,250,000
DIVIDEND @ 3 %	817,500

THEREFORE THIS TRUST HAS MET ALL TARGETS - PERFECT!

18.12   <u>EXAMINATION QUESTIONS:</u>

    On the following pages there are a number of
    examination questions similar to those worked through
    in chapter 18. Students should attempt these questions
    without the use of books or notes in order to become
    familiar with the layout of, and the process of
    building up NHS accounts.

Examination Question 1:   NHS Trust Fund Accounts

The following figures have been extracted from the Trust Fund Cash
Book of the Health Care NHS Trust (HCT) for the year ended 31/03/93:

	£
Welfare & Amenities:	
Staff	3,900
Patients	10,333
Other expenditure	0
Research	4,000
Contribution to HCT for Capital Exp	3,520
Grants received	2,407
Fund raising expenses	348
Sale of Investments	15,600
Subscriptions, Donations & Grants	13,200
Net income from Property	4,580
Dividends & Interest	7,890
Fund Raising Income	907
Other Income	140

The following transactions have not yet been accounted for:

1 Balances at 1/04/92 are: £

Fund A/c	208,660
Property	44,000
Investments: a) Narrower Range	163,200
b) Wider Range	0
Stocks - Welfare & Amenities (patients)	1,120
Cash	780
Debtors	800
Creditors	1,240

2 Investment income outstanding at 31/03/93 is £   506

3 Income Tax of £   485 may be reclaimed from the Inland Revenue
   in respect of interest paid net.

4 Investments held in the wider range with a book value of £12,100
   at 1/04/92 were sold for   £16,950 on 24/03/93.
   During the year additional investments totalling   £9,680
   were made in the Narrower Range.

5 The opening detors relate to investment income
   The opening creditors relate to Welfare & Amenities (Patients)

6 A company in which shares were purchased some years ago has been
   liquidated. The shares had cost £   12,500 and had been
   recorded at that valuation at 1/04/92.

7 Fund Raising creditors at 31/03/93 are £   34
   Fund Raising debtors at 31/03/93 are £   51

8 Stocks (Welfare & Amenities (Patients) at 31/03/93 are £ 1,670
   Creditors (Welfare & Amenities (Patients) @ 31/03/93 are   £1,253

REQUIRED:

a) The Trust Fund Income and Expenditure account for the year ended
   31/03/93.

                                                    11 marks

b) The Trust Fund Balance Sheet as at 31/03/93.

                                                    10 marks

c) Explain the impact that charitable funding can have on Health
   Authorities and Trusts, with particular reference to the new
   financial regime in the NHS.

                                                     9 marks

                           TOTAL   30 marks

EXAMINATION QUESTION 2   CAPITAL CHARGES

The Well Side NHS Trust has the following fixed assets at 01/04/92.

	Opening Replacement Cost £000	Accumulated Depreciation £000
LAND	53,000	
BUILDINGS	28,030	30
EQUIPMENT	19,010	10

The estimated life of assets is set at 25 years for buildings and 10 years for equipment. The existing assets have remaining lives of 20 and 8 years respectively.

The following information is also available:

1   Equipment sold during the year:

	£000
Opening replacement cost	20
Accumulated Depreciation	4
Life Remaining	8 years
Sale Price	14

2   Buildings were purchased on 1/10/93 for £250,000

3   The index figures for the year are:

01/04/92	100
31/03/93	106

4   On 31/03/93 a hospital building was revalued at £6,500,000. The Opening Replacement Cost was £5,800,000.

REQUIRED:
a) Calculate the capital charges for the year, showing the journal entries for each asset category.
(9 marks)

b) Summarise the answer to (a) above in the standard format for inclusion in the notes to the accounts of the NHS Trust. (6 marks)

c) Show the Balance Sheet entries for the above in the standard format. (5 marks)

d) Explain the purpose of capital charges and the expected benefits of their implementation in the NHS.
(5 marks)

TOTAL   25 MARKS

EXAM QUESTION 3

NHS TRUST - I & E A/C, BALANCE SHEET AND CASH FLOW STATEMEN

The following information is available for the Waterside
NHS Trust for the year ended 31/03/93.

Balances @ 1/04/92	£000
Cash	25
Debtors	2,500
Stocks	800
Tangible Assets	175,000
Creditors	6,200

Transactions during the year:	
Salaries & Wages	62,500
All other expenditure	7,500
Depreciation	12,500
Income from GPFH	7,800
Income from DHA	82,000
Income from DoH	8,000
Private Patient Income	1,500
Donations	2,000
Stocks purchased	11,500

The following information is also available:

1 The Closing stock at 31/03/93   £950,000

2 The Originating Capital Debt was split evenly between
   IBD and PDC.

3 The DHA debtors at the end of the year amounted to
                                              £3,000,000

4 An asset was sold on 31/03/93 for   £150,000
   The asset had a NBV at 1/04/92 of   £200,000
   Depreciation for the year amounted to   £5,000

5 The Creditors outstanding at 31/03/93 were
                                              £4,500,000

6 The indexation figures provided by DoH are:
                    100   01/04/92
                    103   31/03/93

YOU ARE REQUIRED TO:
a) Prepare the Trust's Income & Expenditure account for
   the year.

b) Prepare the Balance Sheet at 31/03/93

c) Prepare a Cash Flow Statement for the year.

d) Comment upon the financial performance of the Trust in
   it's first year of operation.

71

EXAMINATION QUESTION 4

The Waterside Hospital operates a Private Patient Service
in a large ward within the Hospital. The ward has 25 beds
with a combination of shared and single rooms. The
expenditure directly charged to the Private Patient Unit
(PPU) comprises of the staff costs and Medical and
Surgical Supplies to the ward. At the 31/03/93 the PPU
Manager had the following expenditure statement:

	£
Income - In-Patients	2,920,000
- Out-Patients	550,000
Total Income	3,470,000
Nursing staff	450,000
A & C Salaries	45,000
Equipment	25,000
M & S Supplies	800,000
Drugs	150,000
Out-Patient Rooms	115,000
Total Spend	1,585,000
Net Income for Year	1,885,000

Other information available:
1 Notional rent charges for the unit has been calculated
   at   £520,000

2 Depreciation has been calculated for the year at:
             £95,000

3 The following statistics are available :

             No of beddays   7,300
             No of O/P attendance 3,667

4 The Chief Accountant has calculated central service
   costs (e.g. Finance, Admin, Cleaning etc) for the year:

   In-Patients   (£per bedday)   150
   Out-Patients   (£ per attendance)   35

   These costs are to be apportioned to every ward.

REQUIRED:
a) Prepare the Memorandum Trading Account for the PPU

b) Prepare some performance statistics useful to the
   PPU manager.

c) Comment upon the performance of the unit, giving
   suggestions as to how the PPU manager could improve
   the performance of the unit.

511

EXAMINATION QUESTION 5

The Health Care Trust has two small hospitals providing
Paediatric Services to the local community. The Trust has
recently hit financial problems and is considering the
rationalisation of its services. The Accountant is preparing
a comparison of the two small childrens hospitals with a
view to closing one of the units. The closure will be based
on the relative costs of the hospitals as well as the
ability of each to provide the required level of service.

You are REQUIRED to prepare the report for the Accountant
identifying the following:

* The financial performance of each hospital
* Relevant statisitics to show overall performance of each
* The consequences of closure of either hospital
* Your recommendation for closure.

THE FOLLOWING INFORMATION IS AVAILABLE:

INCOME & EXPENDITURE	HOSPITAL A £000	HOSPITAL B £000
ADMINISTRATION	250	270
CATERING	500	480
CLEANING	900	850
FINANCE	400	305
PERSONNEL	270	350
NURSING	5,600	6,200
WARDS	3,200	3,000
PHYSIOTHERAPY	950	1,020
SURGERY	2,000	2,100
PHARMACY	500	550
PSYCHIATRY	200	150
UROLOGY	65	80

BALANCES AT 31st March
=======================

CREDITORS	600	385
DEBTORS	550	350
CASH IN HAND	-15	12

OTHER INFORMATION:

NO OF BEDS AVAILABLE	250	180
NO OF IN-PATIENT DAYS	56,575	55,845
NO OF OUT-PATIENT ATTENDANCES	5,000	10,000
DoH RECOMMENDED CREDITOR % OF SPEND	4%	
DoH RECOMMENDED DEBTOR % OF SPEND	3%	
IN-PATIENT % OF COSTS	95%	91%

INDEX